Students

iCheck Express

Microsoft Excel 2007 Real World Applications

Log on to the Online Learning Center through

glencoe.com!

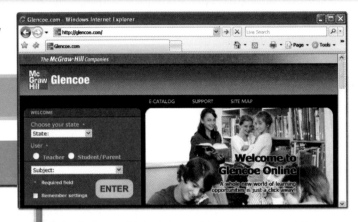

Integrated Academics

- Academic Skills: English Language Arts and Math
- Writing Matters
- Math Matters
- Academic Vocabulary
- Academic Connections

New Student Edition Features

- Quick Write Activities
- Study Skills
- 21st Century Workplace Skills
- Ethics in Action
- Careers and Technology
- Go Online: Real World Connections
- What's New in Office 2007

Reading Skills and Assessments

- Reading Guides
- Graphic Organizers
- Reading Strategies
- Reading Skills Handbook
- After You Read Activities
- Lesson Review and Activities
- Unit Portfolio Projects

Online Learning Center

- Self-Check Quizzes and Reviews
- Rubrics
- Data Files
- Technology Handbook
- Math Skills Handbook
- Additional Projects
- Microsoft Outlook and Windows Vista Exercises
- *Presentation Plus!™* PowerPoint Presentations
- Study-to-Go

GLENCOE

i Check Express

Microsoft® Excel® 2007

Real World Applications

Supports NCLB Requirements

Microsoft CERTIFIED Application Specialist | Approved Courseware

Lead Consultants

C. Jacqueline Schultz, Ph.D.
Career and Business Education Instructor
Warrensville Heights High School
Warrensville Heights, Ohio

Linda Wooldridge, M.B.A.
School of Information Technology Instructor
Santa Susana High School
Simi Valley, California

 glencoe.com

McGraw Hill Glencoe

 **Glencoe**

The *McGraw·Hill* Companies

Printed in the United States of America

Send all inquiries to:

Glencoe/McGraw-Hill
21600 Oxnard Street, Suite 500
Woodland Hills, CA 91367

MHID: 0-07-880265-2 (Student Edition)
ISBN: 978-0-07-880265-2 (Student Edition)

1 2 3 4 5 6 7 8 9 043/027 11 10 09 08

PHOTO CREDITS

iv Esbin Anderson/Age Fotostock America, Inc., **v** Jose L. Pelaez/CORBIS, **vii** Dynamic Graphic Group/Alamy Images, **ix** Royalty-free/Alamay **1** Royalty-free/Alamay, **3** Walter Hodges/Getty Images, **26** Rob Glodmen/Getty Images, **27** Robert E. Daemmrich/Getty Images, **41** Doug Menuez/Getty Images, **49** Alexander Walter/Getty Images, **50** Klaus Lahnstein/Getty Images, **74** Royalty-free from File, **82** Ron Fehling/Masterfile, **83** Esbin Anderson/Age Fotostock America, Inc., **113** Bob Daemmrich/PhotoEdit, **114** Jeff Maloney/Getty Images, **142** Jose Luis Pelaez Inc./Corbis, **143** Mug Shots/Corbis, **145** David Young-Wolff/Getty Images, **146** David Young-Wolff/PhotoEdit, **147** Jeff Greenberg/Age Fotostock America, Inc.,

149 Manchan/Getty Images, **151** Royalty-free/Photodisc/Getty Images, **167** Gabe Palmer/CORBIS, **175** Stone/Getty Images, **176** Stone/Getty Images, **202** David Young-Wolff/PhotoEdit, **203** Jose Luis Pelaez, Inc./CORBIS, **219** Stephen Marks, Inc./Getty Images, **227** image100/Age Fotostock, **228** David Young-Wolff/PhotoEdit, **244** Getty Images, **252** Bill Aron/PhotoEdit, **253** Dynamic Graphic Group/Alamy Images, **276** Anton Vengo/SuperStock, **277** Novastock/PhotoEdit, **279** John Neubauer/PhotoEdit, **280** Jose L. Pelaez/CORBIS, **281** Bonnie Kamin/PhotoEdit

SCREEN CAPTURE CREDITS

Abbreviation Key: MS = Screen shots used by permission from Microsoft Corporation.
©2007 MS Excel **5-18, 20-24, 29-40, 43-46, 52-73, 76-80, 85-104, 107-111, 116-134, 136-140, 153-166, 169-173, 178-193, 196-200, 205-218, 221-225, 230-243, 246-250, 255-267, 270-274.**

Table of Contents

Table of Contents

Index

Table of Contents

Table of Contents

Table of Contents

Table of Contents

Index

Table of Contents

FEATURE CONTENTS

21st Century WORKPLACE

MATH MATTERS

Writing MATTERS

Sizing handle/Manija de tamaño Señala en un pequeño cuadro un objeto seleccionado que puede ser arrastrado para cambiar su tamaño. (pp. 96, 211)

SmartArt/SmartArt Galería que contiene seis tipos de diagramas adaptables. (p. 72)

Sort/Ordenar Hacer una lista de datos en orden ascendente o descendente. (pp. 86, 148)

Source/Fuente Origen. (p. 243)

Split/Dividir Dividir una ventana en dos paneles para poder desplazarte independientemente. (pp. 120, 166)

Spreadsheet/Hoja de cálculos Tabla de datos numéricos que están organizados en columnas y filas. (pp. 5, 8, 116)

Start Menu/Menú de inicio En Windows es un menú que proporciona herramientas para localizar documentos, encontrar ayuda, modificar parámetros del sistema y correr programas. (p. xliii)

Subset/Subconjunto Cantidad menor de datos que han sido filtrados desde un grupo mayor de datos en un rango de celdas o una columna de la tabla. (p. 153)

SUBSTITUTE/SUSTITUIR Función que sustituye una palabra por otra. (p. 181)

Subtotal/Subtotal Total de un grupo de objectos dentro de un conjunto más grande de objectos. (p. 156)

Sum/Suma Total. (p. 156)

Summary worksheet/Hoja de trabajo de resumen Hoja de trabajo que contiene todos los datos esenciales de varias hojas de trabajo en una sola ubicación. (p. 267)

Tab/Pestaña Pequeña solapa en la barra que muestra un botón (o instrucción). (p. 7)

Table Style/Estilo de Tabla Conjunto predefinido de formatos que pueden aplicarse a un rango de datos. (p. 56)

Task pane/El Cristal de Tarea Un crystal que se puede utilizar para simplificar last areas. Por ejemplo, el crystal de tarea ClipArt se utiliza para reducir los terminus de búsqueda cuando se busca en la Galería de ClipArt. (p. 18)

Template/Plantilla Guía que contiene el formato de un documento, presentación o libro de trabajo específico. (pp. 116, 259)

Text/El Texto Las palabras en una página o en un documento. (p. 53)

Theme/Tema Colección de elementos de diseño, gráficas y colores que dan a los documentos, presentaciones y páginas Web una imagen consistente. (pp. 56, 216)

Title bar/Barra de título Barra de la parte superior de la pantalla que muestra el nombre de la ventana actual. (p. 6)

Track Changes/Control de Cambios Característica que muestra las revisions tales como adiciones, borrados y comentarios con formatos diferentes. (p. 235)

Trend/Tendencia Patrón. (p. 207)

U

UPPER/MAYUSC Función que cambia el texto a mayúsculas. (p. 180)

User-defined template/Plantilla definida por el usuario Plantilla creada por uno mismo que puede usarse como base para nuevos libros de trabajo. (p. 259)

Utilize/Utilizar Usar. (p. 206)

V

Version/Versión Forma o variante de un tipo u original. (p. 101)

Vertical alignment/Alineación vertical Colocación vertical de los contenidos de una celda. (p. 67)

W

Web query/Consulta Web Función que abre una página Web e importa una o más tablas de datos desde la página Web hacia el libro de trabajo. (p. 256)

What-If Analysis/Análisis "Qué pasa si" Prueba en que se comparan escenarios alternativos. (p. 182)

Window/Ventana Área en la pantalla de la computadora donde puede verse y usarse una aplicación. (p. 6)

Workbook/Libro de trabajo Archivo de Excel que contiene una o más hojas de trabajo. (pp. 8, 11)

Worksheet/Hoja de trabajo Hoja de celdas organizada en filas y columnas. (pp. 8, 25)

Zoom/La Ampliación Un instrumento que aumenta o reduce el tamaño de los objetos dentro de la ventana. (p. 13)

Why Study Computer Applications?

When you master the computer skills used in Microsoft Office 2007, you will benefit in both your business and academic careers. There is no business today that is untouched by computers. Whether you plan to become a mechanic, an architect, a photographer, or the CEO of a corporation, you will be expected to have some basic computer skills. In any business, time is money. People who can use the computer to save time give themselves a competitive advantage in the job market.

Book reports that are free of misspelled words and research papers that include accurate citations and footnotes will result in better grades. The student who knows how to import tables or graphics into a report will be able to make a stronger case for a particular point of view.

The architectural firm described below illustrates how Microsoft Office is used in every aspect of a typical business.

- **Microsoft Word** is used to generate detailed drawing notes that are inserted into computer-aided-drafting. Large projects require specification books that are thousands of pages long. These books make sure that builders meet critical safety codes. Careful documentation is required in memo form to communicate with every member of a design team.

- **Microsoft Excel** is used to calculate costs for code requirements. Excel files are inserted into computer-drafted drawings for door schedules, window schedules, and finish schedules. Area calculations for large buildings use Excel spreadsheets to make sure that the required space is provided to exit a building in the case of an emergency.

PMT/PAGO Función que calcula los pagos de un préstamo basándose en la tasa de interés, número de abonos y cantidad total del préstamo. (p. 101)

Pointer/Apuntador (Puntero) Flecha que se usa para seleccionar objetos en pantalla como menús y botones. En Excel, al apuntador cambia a una flecha doble para cambiar el tamaño de columnas. Cambia a un cuadro y signo de menos sobre las celdas de la hoja de trabajo y cambia a un signo de más negro sobre la manija de llenar de una celda. (p. 6)

Portrait/Orientación vertical Orientación de la página, la hoja de trabajo o la presentación que se muestra más alta que ancha. (p. 124)

Print area/Área de impresión Parte de una hoja de trabajo que puede imprimirse. (p. 125, 130)

Print Preview/Preestreno Impreso Un preestreno de los documentos, las hojas de ejercicio, o de las diapositivas para imprimir. (p. 17)

Process Diagram/Diagrama de Proceso Diagrama que muestra cómo cambia la información en un proceso. (p. 72)

Productivity/La Productividad Una medida de la capacidad de un individuo o de un equipo a conseguir los resultados. (pp. 3, 25)

Proofread/La Corrección de Pruebas Leer para encontrar y corregir los errores. (pp. 46, 145)

PROPER/NOMPROPIO Función que hace que sólo la primera letra sea mayúscula. (p. 180)

Property/Propiedad Detalle acerca de un objeto, por ejemplo tamaño o valor predeterminado. (p. 258)

Protect/Proteger Evitar que otras personan hagan cambios en un documento. (p. 230)

Q

Quick Access Toolbar (QAT)/Barra de Herramientas de Acceso Rápido Barra de herramientas que permite a los usuarios localizar instrucciones rápidamente. (pp. xxxvi, 6, 13)

Quick Styles/Estilos Rápidos Característica que permite aplicar fácilmente nuevos estilos al texto. (p. xlvii, 61)

R

Range/Rango Un conjunto de celdas. (pp. 85, 153, 165)

Reject/Rechazar Rehusar. (p. 236)

Relative reference/Referencia relativa Una referencia de celda que cambia cuando se copia la fórmula en una nueva ubicación. (p. 92)

Replace/Reemplazar Herramienta que sa usa para reemplazar datos localizados. (p. 33)

Responsibility/La Responsabilidad La obligación. Cuando le dé a uno una responsabilidad, éste se encarga de ser alguien de confianza y de llevarla hasta el fin. (p. 27)

Reveal/Revelar Divulgar. (p. 257)

Ribbon/Cinta Panel en Microsoft Office que organiza instrucciones en pestañas. La Cinta cambia dependiendo de los programas y herramientas que estén activos. (pp. 7, 13)

Rotate/Girar Girar un objeto en dirección en el sentido de las manecillas del reloj o en el sentido opuesto. (p. 214)

S

Save As dialog box/Una Cajita de Diálogo Marcada Guardar Como Una cajita que se presenta cuando uno hace clic en el botón Guardar o en el botón Guardar Como. En la cajita Guardar Como, se cambia el nombre del archivo, el tipo de archivo, o la situación del archivo. (pp. xlvi, 10)

Scale/Escala Cambiar el tamaño de una imagen en una proporcion determinada de su tamaño original. (p. 213)

Scenario/Escenario Versión de una hoja de trabajo designada para probar uno de un número de resultados posibles. (p. 182)

ScreenTip/ScreenTip Descripción de un botón que aparece cuando apuntas hacia ese botón. (p. 7)

Scroll bar/Barra de desplazamiento Barra que se encuentra a la derecha o en la parte inferior de la pantalla y que te permite moverte hacia arriba o hacia abajo o a la izquierda o derecha de un documento o hoja de trabajo. (pp. 6, 9)

Share/Compartir Configurar un libro de trabajo para que pueda editarlo más de un usuario a la vez. (p. 234)

Sheet tab/Pestaña de hoja Pequeña parte en la parte inferior de una hoja de trabajo que despliega el nombre de la hoja de trabajo y te permite moverte de una hoja de trabajo a otra en el mismo libro de trabajo. (pp. 9, 78)

Why Study Computer Applications? (Continued)

- **Microsoft Access** databases are used to track the use of building materials on a project. Databases are also used to track documentation and to manage the contact information of the many members of design and construction teams.

- **Microsoft PowerPoint** is used by the initial architect to communicate his or her ideas to clients and to the community. PowerPoint is the tool used to create presentations in many industries and professions.

- **Microsoft Outlook** extends beyond sending and receiving e-mail. It is an organizational tool that allows team members to schedule meetings with design team members, check their schedules, and organize communication to groups within the team.

- **Windows Vista** is an operating system used on personal computers, including home and business desktops, notebooks, and tablet PCs. More than just an operating system, Vista contains graphical interfaces not seen in other operating systems. It also has a higher level of security not seen in its predecessors.

The managers in an architecture firm require all staff members, from architects to accountants to administrative personnel, to know these software applications well. In today's competitive job market, the person with the greatest computer abilities is often placed at the top of the hiring list.

Throughout the book, you will notice this logo. This logo indicates that the exercise or activity meets one of the **Microsoft Certified Application Specialist** standards. These standards cover topics from the Microsoft Certified Application Specialist certification exam.

The Microsoft Certified Application Specialist logo means that this book has been approved by the Microsoft Certified Application Specialist Program to help you master Microsoft Office desktop applications. This book can also help you prepare for the Microsoft Certified Application Specialist certification exam. For more information about Microsoft Certified Application Specialist certification, see page 314.

Locate/Localizar Determinar o indicar el lugar, sitio o límites de algo. (p. 132)

Lock/Proteger Proteger una celda para que no pueda cambiarse su contenido. (p. 230)

LOWER/MINUSC Función que cambia el texto a minúsculas. (p. 180)

M

Macro/Macro Acción que hace automática una tarea con múltiples pasos. (p. 263)

Margin/Margen Espacio en blanco que aparece entre el texto y la orilla de la página. (p. 128)

Mark as Final/Indicar como Final Una orden que hace su documento sólo-leer, impidiendo algún cambio. (p. 242)

MAX/Máximo Función que se usa para identificar el valor más grande de un grupo de celdas. (p. 30)

Maximize/Aumentar Aumentar una ventana para que llene la pantalla. (p. 121)

Merge/Intercalar Combinar. Por ejemplo, se puede intercalar dos documentos o se puede intercalar dos celdas en una tabla. (p. 241)

MIN/Mínimo Función que se usa para identificar el valor más pequeño de un grupo de celdas. (p. 30)

Minimize/Reducir Quitar una ventana del escritorio (o fondo de la pantalla) sin cerrarla. (p. 22)

Mini Toolbar/Mini Barra de Herramientas Cuando se elige un texto, una barra de herramientas de formateo en miniatura desde la cual se puede cambiar el estilo de letras, el color del estilo de letras, y más. La mini Barra de Herramientas es semitransparente hasta que se mueva el cursor por encima. Cuando el cursor se quede en la barra de herramientas, se hace opaco. (p. xxxviii)

Mixed reference/Referencia mixta Referencia de celda que contiene una parte relativa y una parte absoluta. (p. 94)

Monitor/Controlar Vigilar y confirmar. Se refiere también a la parte de la computadora que expone la pantalla. (p. xlviii)

N

Name/Nombre Palabra o palabras que representa una celda o un rango de celdas. (p. 163)

Name Manager/Administrador de Nombres Herramienta que permite modificar o borrar los nombres definidos que se usan en una hoja de trabajo. (p. 165)

NOW/AHORA Función que despliega la fecha y la hora en que se abre o usa una hoja de trabajo. (p. 101)

O

Office Button/Un Botón de Despacho Un botón situado en el rincón de arriba a la izquierda de Microsoft Word, Excel, Access, y PowerPoint. Haga clic en este botón para abrir, guardar, e imprimir los archivos. (pp. 6, 8)

Operating system/El Sistema de Operación El programa total que controla todos los otros programas de software en una máquina y que permite a funcionar correctamente los mecanismos de hardware. Windows XP y Windows Vista son los sistemas de operación en los cuales funciona Office 2007. (p. xliii)

Operator/Operario Un símbolo que representa una función matemática. (p. 87)

Organizational chart/Organigrama Tabla gráfica que muestra el arreglo jerárquico de una organización. (p. 72)

P

Page break/Salto de página Lugar donde termina una página impresa y empieza la otra. Un salto de página automático se produce cuando Word automáticamente mueve el texto a una nueva página. Un salto de página manual o forzado se produce cuando el usuario inserta manualmente el texto en una nueva página. (p. 127)

Page orientation/Orientación de la página Se refiere a la orientación vertical o horizontal de la página. (p. 124)

Password/Contraseña Serie de caracteres usados para encriptar una documento. (p. 232)

Paste/Pegar Insertar texto previamente cortado o copiado en otro documento. (pp. 35, 107)

Perform/Efectuar Llevar a cabo. (p. 263)

Pivot Chart/Gráfico pivote Gráfico automáticamente generade que resume información. (p. 178)

PivotTable/Tabla Pivote Tabla que puede mostrar información y presentarla de varias maneras diferentes. (pp. 178, 195, 200)

Plagiarism/El Plagio El acto de tomar las palabras y las ideas de otra persona como si fueran las suyas de usted. (p. 144)

Take the iCheck Office 2007 Cyberhunt!

Did you know that your text contains many features that can **make learning easier for you**? Explore how to get the most out of your textbook by following the clues on pages xiii-xiv to discover useful features, activities, tips, and tools that are integrated into the lessons in this text. Then use these elements to help reach your computer applications learning goals.

Get Started

The scavenger hunt on these pages highlights features that will help you get the most out of your textbook. Collect points as you complete each step.

1 It is easier to learn a new skill if you understand how this knowledge will help you get ahead and stay ahead. How could learning Excel help you reach personal goals? *(8 points. Hint: see* **Why It Matters** *on page 1.)*

2 You will move through projects more quickly if you know the basics before you begin. What will the projects on page 252 teach you about collaboration? *(4 points. Hint: See* **Before You Begin**.*)*

3 Improving interpersonal ("soft") skills, such as communication and goal setting, will help you succeed in school, in work, and in daily life. What **21st Century Workplace** skill is featured on page 27? *(4 points. Hint: Creating budgets is a very important skill to learn in today's world.)*

4 Learning new skills is made easier by breaking them into small steps, so any one task or exercise does not seem too hard or time consuming. In the Insert and Delete Cells exercise, how many **Step-By-Steps** are included to complete the activity? *(9 points. Hint: See page 38.)*

5 All people learn and progress at different rates. How does the **iCheck icon** help you know if you are completing an exercise correctly or not? *(4 points. Hint: See Exercise 3-1 on page 52.)*

6 You need to repeat a skill or action many times to become proficient. Practicing the skills you have learned earlier will help you become proficient with Office. How many opportunities do you have to complete the **Practice It Activities** in a single lesson? *(3 points. Hint: see pages 169-171.)*

7 What additional program resources are highlighted in the **Beyond the Book** section, in the Unit Closers? *(5 points. Hint: See page 148.)*

8 Reading, writing, and arithmetic are fundamental skills for lifelong learning. In any career you choose, you will need to be able to read and to perform basic calculations. What is Allen calculating in the Math Matters feature on page 244? *(6 points. Hint: Starting a business can be expensive!)*

Error/Error Equivocación. (p. 160)

Evaluate Formula/Evaluar Fórmula Herramienta que revisa fórmulas y proporciona detalles acerca de un error mostrando la manera en que Excel intentó calcular la fórmula. (p. 162)

F

File format/El Formato de Archivos El tipo de fichero, como tal .docx o .rtf. Se puede cambiar el formato de archivo de un documento para que los usuarios que no usen Microsoft Office pueden leer sus datos. (p. 133)

Fill handle/Manija de llenado Herramienta que te permite llenar múltiples celdas con el mismo contenido usando una celda como ejemplo. (p. 39)

Filter/Filtrar Elemento que te permite ver sólo la información que necesitas. (pp. 85, 155)

Find/Buscar Herramienta que se usa para encontrar datos específicos en una tabla o documento. (p. 33)

Folder/Carpeta Objeto que le ayuda al usuario a organizar archivos. (pp. 10, 15, 32)

Font/Fuente Diseño general de un conjunto de caracteres. (También llamado tipo de letra.) (p. 52)

Font style/Estilo de fuente Efecto que puede aplicarse a una fuente, tal como negritas, cursivas y subrayado. (p. 52)

Formula/Fórmula Ecuación que contiene valores, referencias de celda o ambas. (p. 16, 41, 87)

Formula Bar/Barra de Fórmulas Barra que despliega el contenido de una celda. (pp. 12, 16, 87, 204)

Freeze/Congelar Mantener los encabezados en su lugar mientras te desplazas por la hoja de trabajo. (p. 120)

Function/Función Lista de fórmulas previamente configuradas que se usan para resolver ecuaciones. (pp. 30, 89)

G

Generate/Generar Crear. (p. 178)

Graphical list/Lista gráfica Gráficos que pueden usarse en una lista con viñetas o numerada. (p. 72)

Group/Grupo Conjunto organizado de instrucciones que se relaciona con una actividad específica. (pp. 7, 157)

H

Header/Encabezado Texto que aparece en la parte superior de cada página o presentación. (pp. 126, 137, 239)

Help Menu/Menú de ayuda Menú que ofrece instrucciones y sugerencias sobre varios temas relacionados con las aplicaciones. (pp. 18, 25)

Horizontal alignment/Alineación horizontal Colocación paralela del contenido de una celda. (p. 65)

Hyperlink/Hiperenlace (Hipervínculo) Enlace en un documento que lleva a una página Web o a otro documento. (p. 40)

I

Icon set/Conjunto de iconos Opción de formato condicional que aplica iconos a las celdas basándose en criterios específicos. (p. 207)

IF/SI Función que verifica que si se cumple una condición, se obtiene un resultado si es falsa y otro si es verdadera. (p. 103)

Illustrate/Ilustrar Mostrar claramente. (p. 17)

Import/Importar Traer datos de otras fuentes y formatos de archivo. (p. 255)

Insert/Insertar Añadir un texto a un documento; añadir artículos como tallas filas o las columnas a un documento, a una diapositiva, a una hoja de cálculo o a un archivo de base de datos. (pp. 20, 37, 128)

Interpret/Interpretar Explicar. (p. 164)

K

Keyboard shortcut/El Atajo de Teclado Una manera alternativa de realizar una tarea oprimiendo las teclas en el teclado en vez de hacer clic en una opción o en un icono. Por ejemplo, oprim [CTRL] + [B] para hacer en negrita el texto. (p. 266)

L

Landscape/Orientación horizontal Orientación en que la página, hoja de trabajo o diapositiva es más ancha que alta. (p. 124)

Learn/Aprender Familiarizarse con algo. (p. 6)

Legend/Leyenda Parte de una gráfica que indica lo que representa cada color o dibujo. (p. 215)

9 Before an assessment, it can be helpful to know whether you have really learned the lessons. What activities can be found on the Online Learning Center to help you reinforce the skills you have learned? *(6 points. Hint: the quizzes are not in the text. See page 81.)*

10 The real importance of learning new skills is to be able to apply this knowledge to create something of your own. What original Portfolio Projects do you create after completing Unit 2? *(10 points. Hint: See pages 279–282.)*

11 When beginning a new lesson, it is very important to know what topics you will be reading about. It is also necessary to know what vocabulary words and ideas you will need to think about while reading. All this information can be found in the Reading Guide. What section of the Reading Guide can give you tips on reading before you start a lesson? *(4 points. Hint: See page 229.)*

12 What new feature is highlighted in the Microsoft Office 2007 minifeature on page 65? *(5 points)*

13 Summarizing reference material is a very useful tool for reviewing and reinforcing what you have learned. Which material does the Quick Reference Summary give to you in Appendix B? *(5 points. Hint: See page 298.)*

14 What section of the Reading Skills Handbook might you review to learn how to understand and remember text that you just read? *(4 points. Hint: See page xxvii.)*

15 What activities on the After You Read page help you review the Key Terms and Academic Vocabulary taught in a lesson? *(4 points. Hint: See page 42.)*

16 In Appendix A, Integrated Applications, what Microsoft Office suites are included in the exercises? *(5 points. Hint: See page 283.)*

17 The Data File icon appears in the top right corner of some exercises. What is the purpose of the Data File icon? *(4 points. Hint: See page 136.)*

18 If you read and come across a key term and you are not certain of its meaning, what section of the book can you use to find the word and its definition? *(5 points. Hint: See page 314.)*

19 The Academic Skills minifeature shows you how learning computer skills can also help you learn academic skills. In Unit 1 Excel, Lesson 4, how many Academic Skills minifeatures are present? *(4 points. Hint: See pages 83–104.)*

20 The Microsoft Certified Application Specialist (MCAS) standards were created to help you take the Microsoft Certified Application Specialist exams for each Office 2007 application. The exams can certify you as a Specialist for each application area. Where in the lesson opener can you find a listing of the MCAS standards hit in that particular lesson? *(5 points. Hint: See page 3.)*

Conditional Formatting Rules Manager/ Administrador de Reglas de Formato Condicionales Herramienta que permite a los usuarios crear, editar, borrar y ver todas las reglas de formato condicionales en una hoja o libro de trabajo. (p. 209)

Conditional logic/Lógica condicional Función que verifica si las declaraciones son verdaderas o falsas y hace comparaciones lógicas entre resultados. (p. 190)

Conflict/Conflicto No estar de acuerdo. (p. 209)

Consolidate/Consolidar Combinar datos de múltiples libros de trabajo. (p. 267)

Constraint/Límite Límite que se fija. (p. 185)

Contextual tab/Cinta contextual Pestaña que aparece en la Cinta y que contiene instrucciones que pueden usarse solamente en un orden elegido. (pp. xxxix)

Contrast/Contraste Nitidez visual de una imagen; La diferencia entre las áreas claras y oscuras de un gráfico. (p. 211)

Convert/Convertir Cambiar el formato de un documento o de un archivo. (pp. 122, 133, 153)

Convey/Transmitir Comunicar visualmente. (p. 76)

Copy/Copiar Seleccionar y reproducir texto en alguna otra parte del documento o aplicación. (pp. 90, 107)

COUNT/Contar Función que cuenta el número de celdas en el rango que contiene números. (p. 99)

COUNTA/CONTARA Función que se usa para encontrar el número de celdas en un rango que contiene datos (tanto números como texto). (p. 99)

Criteria/Criterios Condiciones que deben cumplirse. (pp. 155, 180)

Custom number format/Formato de número personalizado Formato de número diseñado por el usuario. (p. 205)

Cut/Cortar Seleccionar y borrar texto, normalmente con el propósito de pegarlo en alguna otra parte de un documento o aplicación. (p. 35)

D

Data/Datos Información factual usada como base para razonar, discutir o calcular. (pp. 5, 150)

Data bar/Barra de datos Opción de formato condicional que aplica barras de diferentes longitudes a las celdas basándose en criterios específicos. (p. 207)

Data validation/Validación de datos Función que le permite al usuario controlar el tipo de datos ingresados en las celdas. (p. 158)

Database function/Función de base de datos Fórmula que sirve sólo para aquellos objectos que cumplen ciertas especificaciones. (p. 180)

Delete/Suprimir Tachar o borrar (pp. 32, 36, 38, 165)

Delimited/Delimitados Datos que son sparados por el tabular, como o por otro carácter. (p. 255)

Delimiter/Delimitador Divisores que separan texto. (p. 55)

Determine/Determinar Resolver o decidir, eligiendo de entre alternativas o posibilidades. (p. 30)

Dialog box/Cuadro de diálogo Cuadro abierto por algunos comandos del menú que permite seleccionar opciones o especificar información para efectuar el comando. (pp. 7, 8)

Dialog Box Launcher/El Lanzamiento del Cuadro de Diálogo Un botón en donde se puede hacer clic que aparece en el rincón abajo a la derecha de un grupo en la Cinta (Ribbon). El lanzamiento del Cuadro de Diálogo indicado Párrafo en Word abre la ventana Párrafo Cuadro de Diálogo. (p. xxxv, 7)

Digital signature/La Firma Digital Una característica de seguridad que autentifica la información digital que Ud. crea. Insertando una firma digital significa que no se ha cambiado el contenido desde que se ha firmado el documento. (p. 243)

Distinct/Distinto Que se puede distinguir visual o mentalmente de manera discreta; separado. (p. 60)

Distribute/Distribuir Repartir. (p. 238)

Document/Documento Archivo en el cual se teclea texto. Los documentos pueden contener texto, imágenes, gráficas y otros objetos. (p. 241)

Document Information Panel/Panel de Información del Documento Panel que permite a los usuarios ver, agregar y editar las propiedades del documento de manera fácil mientras se trabaja en el mismo. (p. 258)

Document Inspector/Inspector de Documentos Herramienta que examina en los documentos datos ocultos o información personal que se almacena en el documento o en las propiedades del mismo. (p. 257)

Duplicate value/Valor duplicado Situación en donde todos los datos de una fila son una copia exacta de los datos en otra fila. (p. 161)

E

Edit/Editar Hacer cambios en un documento, en el contenido de una celda o en una presentación. (pp. 31, 88, 96)

What Is Your Cyberhunt Skill Rating?

POINTS	CYBERHUNT RATING
90 to 100	You really know how to let your textbook work for you!
70 to 89	You know how to find your way around a textbook!
Less than 70	Consider working with your teacher or classmates to learn how to use your textbook more effectively—you will gain skills you can use your whole life.

1. If you are a skilled Excel user, you will be a good candidate for a variety of jobs. Excel can also help you now. You could use Excel to create a budget for yourself or to keep track of friends' addresses.

2. The projects on page 252 will teach you how to set passwords, track changes, and merge workbooks.

3. Managing money responsibly.

4. Eleven

5. When you you see the iCheck icon, compare your screen to the figure shown on the exercise page. If your screen looks like the figure, then you are completing the steps correctly. you can verify your screen with the figures located on the exercise page. Your screen should look like the called out figure.

6. Three

7. Beyond the Book highlights the additional exercises, projects, and resources available on the Online Learning Center.

8. A business loan.

9. Self Check quizzes and Interactive Reviews.

10. Portfolio Project—Stock Market Expert: Part 1: Create a Template, Part 2: Make Your First Report, Part 3: Create a Chart, Part 4: Protect the Work

11. Before You Read

12. The Microsoft Office 2007 minifeature gives information about using the Mini Toolbar to change alignment.

13. The Quick Reference Summary shows you how to use buttons, menus, and keyboard shortcuts to perform specific tasks.

14. Techniques to Understand and Remember What You Read

15. Review Vocabulary and Vocabulary Activity

16. Word, Excel, Access, and PowerPoint

17. The Data File icon lets you know that you will need to access a data file to complete an exercise.

18. Glossary

19. Eight

20. In the Standards Box

A

Absolute reference/Referencia absoluta Referencia de celda que no cambia cuando se copia una fórmula en otro lugar. (p. 93)

Adjust/Ajustar Adaptar o conformar. (p. 90)

Advanced filter/Filtro avanzado Función que despliega solo aquellos objetos que cumplen ciertas especificaciones. (p. 155)

Alignment/Alineación Manera en que el texto se alinea con respecto a los márgenes o tabuladores. (p. 65)

Alteration/Modificación Cambio. (p. 233)

Argument/Argumento Valor en una fórmula. (p. 180)

Arrange/Organizar Organizar al mismo tiempo más de una ventana en la pantalla. (p. 119)

Author/Autor Fuente. (p. 258)

AutoSum/Autosuma Función que se usa para agregar valores en filas o columnas. (pp. 16, 30, 45)

AVERAGE/Promedio Función que se usa para determinar el promedio numérico de un grupo de celdas. (pp. 30, 45)

B

Background/Fondo (Segundo plano) Gráfico que aparece detrás de la información en una hoja de trabajo; Colores, estampados o figuras que llenan toda la diapositiva y aparecen detrás del contenido de la diapositiva. (p. 70)

Border/Borde Línea o cuadro que enmarca a un texto o una celda. (p. 53)

Brightness/Brillo La oscuridad o claridad de un gráfico. (p. 211)

Browser/Navegador Programa de software que se usa para navegar en Internet e interactuar con sitios Web. (p. 122)

Budget/Presupuesto Cálculo aproximado de ingresos y egresos durante cierto período de tiempo. (p. 29, 48)

Button/Botón Icono gráfico en el que se hace clic para efectuar una tarea específica. (p. 7)

C

Case sensitive/Distinguir entre miniscúla y mayascúla Informacion de entrada (así como una contraseña) que debe tener mayascúlas, miniscúlas o una combinación de las dos para ser proceda correctemente. (p. 232)

Cell/Celda Intersección de una fila y una columna en una tabla o hoja de trabajo. (pp. 12, 32, 45)

Cell content/Contenido de celda Letras, números y símbolos que aparecen dentro de una celda. (p. 12)

Cell reference/Referencia de celda La letra de la columna y el número de la fila de una celda. (pp. 12, 92, 93, 94)

Cell style/Formato de celda Grupo de rasgos de formato al que se ha dado un nombre específico. (p. 61)

Chart/Gráfica (Gráfico) Presentación gráfica que organiza visualmente los datos. Las gráficas comunes incluyen las gráficas circulares, las de barras y las de líneas. (pp. 95, 109)

Clear/Borrar Quitar todos los contenidos de una celda. (p. 32)

Clipboard/Portapapeles Lugar donde se almacena el texto cortado o copiado para usarse después. (p. 35)

Color scale/Escala de color Opción de formato condicional que aplica sombras de colores para indicar diferencias en los datos basadas en criterios específicos. (p. 207)

Column/Columna Celdas arregladas verticalmente bajo un encabezado de letras. (pp. 12, 36, 37)

Command/Comando Controles que señalan que la computadora realice una tarea específica. (p. 7)

Comment/Comentario Notas que pueden agregarse a un documento sin que aparezcan como cambios reales. (p. 236)

Common/Común Compartido por dos o más partes. (p. 116)

Compatibility Checker/Control de Compatabilidad Un instrumento de Office 2007 que identifica características en un documento de Word, Excel, Access, o PowerPoint que no funcionará correctamente si se abre con una versión previa del software, como tal Office 2003 o Office 2000. (p. 261)

Computer/Computadora (Computador) Dispositivo electrónico que procesa los datos y los convierte en información que se puede usar. (p. 2)

Condition/Condición Regla. (p. 103)

Conditional formatting/El Formateo Condicional Un formato que está fijado para aparecer de una cierta manera si ciertas condiciones o reglas están cumplidas. (p. 206)

Online Learning Center

Follow these steps to access the textbook resources on the Student Online Learning Center.

Step 1
Go to glencoe.com.

Step 2
Select your state from the pull-down menu.

Step 3
Select Student/Parent.

Step 4
Select Computer Education.

Step 5
Click ENTER.

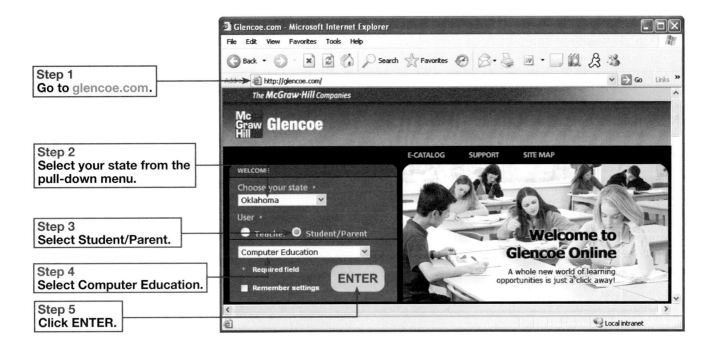

Step 6
Select your book.

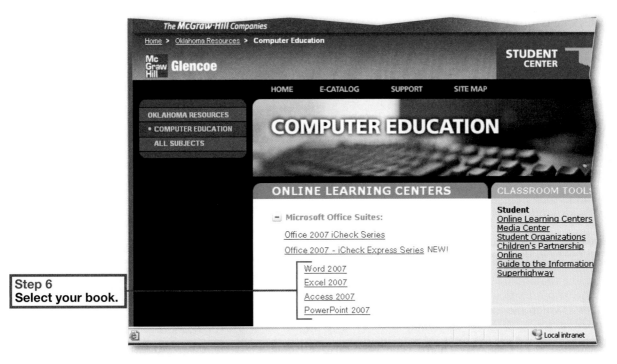

ScreenTip A description that appears when you point to a button. (p. 7)

Scroll bar A bar at the right side or bottom of the screen that allows you to move up and down or left and right in a document or a worksheet. (pp. 6, 9)

Share To set up a workbook so that more than one user can edit it at a time. (p. 234)

Sheet tab A small flap at the bottom of a worksheet that displays the name of the worksheet, and allows you to move from one worksheet to another within the same workbook. (pp. 9, 78)

Sizing handle Points on a small square around a selected object that can be dragged to change the object's size. (p. 211)

SmartArt A gallery that contains six types of customizable diagrams. (p. 72)

Sort To put a list of data in ascending or descending order. (pp. 86, 148)

Source Origin. (p. 243)

Split To divide a window into two panes that you can scroll independently. (pp. 120, 166)

Spreadsheet A table of numerical data organized into columns and rows. (pp. 5, 8, 116)

Start Menu A Windows menu that provides tools to locate documents, find help, change system settings, and run programs. (p. xliii)

Subset A smaller amount of data filtered from a larger group of data in a range of cells or table column. (p.153)

SUBSTITUTE A function that substitutes one word for another. (p. 181)

Subtotal A total of items within a larger group of items. (p. 156)

Sum Total. (p. 156)

Summary worksheet A worksheet that contains all essential data from several worksheets in one location. (p. 267)

Tab A clickable area of the Ribbon that displays menu options. (p. 7)

Table Style A pre-defined set of formats that can be applied to a range of data. (p. 56)

Task pane A pane that can be used to simplify tasks. For example, the Clip Art task pane is used to narrow down search terms when the Clip Art Gallery is searched. (p. 18)

Template A guide that contains the formatting of a particular type of document, workbook, or presentation. (pp. 116, 259)

Text Words on a page or in a document. (p. 53)

Theme A collection of design elements, graphics, and colors that help items such as documents, presentations, and Web pages maintain a consistent image. (p. 56)

Title bar The bar at the top of the screen that displays the name of the current window. (p. 6)

Track Changes A feature that keeps track of the changes you make to a document, including inserts and deletions. (p. 235)

Trend a pattern. (p. 207)

UPPER A function to make the text uppercase. (p. 180)

User-defined template A self-created template that can be used as a basis for new workbooks. (p. 259)

Utilize to use. (p. 206)

Version A form or variant of a type or original. (p. 101)

Vertical alignment The top-to-bottom placement of the contents of a cell. (p. 67)

Web query A function that opens a Web page and then imports one or more tables of data from the Web page into your workbook. (p. 256)

What-If Analysis A function to test alternative scenarios. (p. 182)

Window An area on the computer screen where an application can be viewed and accessed. (p. 6)

Workbook An Excel file that contains one or more worksheets. (pp. 8, 11, 15, 47, 252)

Worksheet A sheet of cells organized into rows and columns. (pp. 8, 25, 118, 119)

Zoom A tool that increases or decreases the size of objects within the window (pp. xxxvii, 13)

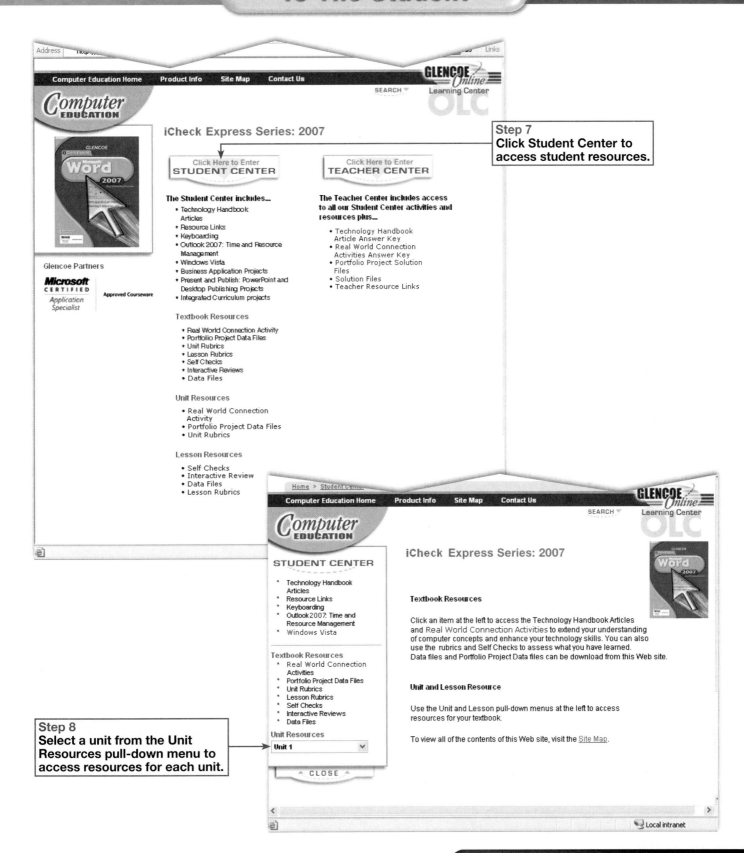

Step 7
Click Student Center to access student resources.

Step 8
Select a unit from the Unit Resources pull-down menu to access resources for each unit.

O

Office Button A button located in the upper-left corner of Microsoft Word, Excel, Access, and PowerPoint. Click this button to open, save, and print files. (pp. 6, 8)

Operating system The overall program that controls all the other software programs on a machine and allows hardware devices to work properly. Windows XP and Windows Vista are the operating systems on which Office 2007 runs. (p. xliii)

Operator A symbol that represents a mathematical function. (p. 87)

Organizational chart A chart that demonstrates an organizational arrangement. (p. 72)

P

Page break The place where one printed page ends and the next begins. A soft page break automatically moves text to a new page. A hard page break can be inserted to force text to a new page. (p. 127)

Page orientation Refers to whether a page is laid out vertically (Portrait) or horizontally (Landscape). (p. 124)

Password A combination of letters, numbers, or symbols that someone must know in order to open or make changes to a file. (p. 232)

Paste To place previously cut or copied text into a document. (pp. 35, 107)

Perform To carry out. (p. 263)

PivotChart An automatically generated chart summarizing data. (p. 178)

PivotTable A table that can display information and present it in several different ways. (pp. 178)

Plagiarism The act of taking another person's words and ideas as one's own. (p. 144)

PMT A function that calculates payments for a loan based on interest rate, number of payments and the amount of the loan. (p. 101)

Pointer The arrow used to select on-screen items, such as menus and buttons. In Excel, the pointer changes to a two-headed arrow to resize columns. It changes to a block plus sign over the worksheet cells and it changes to a black plus sign over the fill handle of a cell. (p. 6)

Portrait The orientation of a page, worksheet, or presentation that is taller than it is wide. (p. 124)

Print area The part of a worksheet that prints. (p. 125)

Print Preview A preview of documents, worksheets, or slides to be printed. (p. 17)

Process Diagram A diagram that shows how information changes in a process. (p. 72)

Productivity A measure of a person or team's ability to achieve results. (pp. 3, 25)

Proofread To read for the purpose of finding and correcting errors. (pp. 46, 145)

PROPER A function to make only the first letter uppercase. (p. 180)

Property A detail about an object, such as the size or default value. (p. 258)

Protect To prevent changes to cells, worksheets, or workbooks. (p. 230)

Q

Quick Access Toolbar (QAT) A toolbar that allows users to quickly find commands. (pp. xxxvi, 6, 13)

Quick Styles A feature that lets you easily apply new styles to text. (p. xlvii, 61)

R

Range A group of cells. (pp. 85, 153, 165)

Reject To refuse. (p. 236)

Relative reference A cell reference that changes when a formula is copied to a new location. (p. 92)

Replace A tool used to substitute data (p. 33)

Responsibility An obligation. When a person is given a responsibility, he or she has a duty to be reliable and to follow through. (p. 27)

Reveal To disclose. (p. 257)

Ribbon A panel in Microsoft Office that organizes commands into tabs. The Ribbon changes depending on which applications and tools are activated. (pp. 7, 13)

Rotate To turn an object clockwise or counterclockwise. (p. 214)

S

Save As dialog box A dialog box that appears when you click the Save or the Save As button. In the Save As dialog box, you change the filename, file type, or location of the file. (pp. xlvi, 10)

Scale The size of a graphic relative to a percentage of its original size. (p. 213)

Scenario A version of a worksheet designed to test one of a number of possible outcomes. (p. 182)

Prepare for 21st Century Success!

ISTE and NETS

The International Society for Technology in Education (ISTE) has developed National Educational Technology Standards to define educational technology standards for students (NETS•S). The activities in this book are designed to meet ISTE standards. The Standards box on each lesson opening page indicates which standards and performance indicators are covered in the lesson.

NETS•S Standards

To live, learn, and work successfully in an increasingly complex and information-rich society, students must be able to use technology effectively. Although the ISTE standards identify skills that students can practice and master in school, the skills are also used outside of school, at home, and at work. For more information about ISTE and the NETS, please visit www.iste.org.

Glossary

Formula Bar The bar that displays the contents of a cell. (pp. 12, 16, 87, 204)

Freeze To keep headings in place while you scroll through a worksheet. (p. 120)

Function A list of preset formulas that are used to solve equations. (pp. 30, 89)

G

Generate To create. (p. 178)

Graphical list A graphic that may be used in a list, such as a bulleted or numbered list. (p. 72)

Group An organized set of commands that relates to a specific activity. (pp. xxxiii, 7, 157)

H

Header Text that appears at the top of every page or presentation. (pp. 126, 137, 239)

Help feature A feature that offers instructions and tips about many application-related topics. (pp. 18, 25)

Horizontal alignment The side-to-side placement of the contents of a cell. (p. 65)

Hyperlink A link in a document to a Web page or to another document. (p. 40)

I

Icon set A conditional formatting option that applies icons to cells based on specific criteria. (p. 207)

IF A function that checks to see if a condition is met and then has one result if it is true and another if it is false. (p. 103)

Illustrate To show clearly. (p. 17)

Import To bring data from other sources and file formats. (p. 255)

Insert To add text to a document; to add items such as rows or columns to a document, slide, spreadsheet, or database file. (pp. 20, 37, 118)

Interpret To explain. (p. 164)

K

Keyboard shortcut An alternate manner of performing a task by pressing keys on the keyboard instead of clicking an option or icon. For example, press CTRL+B to make text boldface. (p. 266)

L

Landscape The orientation of a page, worksheet, or a slide that is wider than it is tall. (p. 124)

Learn To become familiar with. (p. 6)

Legend The legend is the part of a chart that indicates what each color or pattern represents. (p. 215)

Locate To determine or indicate the place, site, or limits of. (p. 132)

Lock To secure a cell so the information cannot be altered. (p. 230)

LOWER A function to change text to lowercase. (p. 180)

M

Macro An action that automates a task with multiple steps. (p. 263)

Margin The amount of space between the text and the edge of the page. (p. 128)

Mark as Final A command that makes your document read-only, preventing any changes from being made to it. (p. 242)

MAX A function used to identify the largest value in a group of cells. (p. 30)

Maximize To make a window fill up the screen. (p. 121)

Merge To combine. For example, you can merge two documents or you can merge two cells in a table. (p. 241)

MIN A function used to identify the smallest value in a group of cells. (p. 30)

Minimize To take a window off the desktop without closing it. (p. 22)

Mini Toolbar When text is selected, a miniature formatting toolbar from which you can change font styling. The Mini Toolbar is semitransparent until the mouse pointer is moved over it. When the pointer rests on the toolbar, it becomes opaque. (pp. xxxviii, 12)

Mixed reference A cell reference that is part relative and part absolute. (p. 94)

Monitor To watch and confirm. Also refers to the part of a computer that displays the screen. (p. xlviii)

N

Name A word or words that represent one cell or range of cells. (p. 163)

Name Manager A tool that allows modification or deletion of the defined names used in a workbook. (p. 165)

NOW A function that displays the date and time that a worksheet is opened or used. (p. 101)

National Educational Technology Standards and Performance Indicators for Students

The NETS are divided into the six broad categories that are listed below. Activities in the book meet the standards within each category.

❶ Creativity and Innovation

Students demonstrate creative thinking, construct knowledge, and develop innovative products and processes using technology. Students:

    a. apply existing knowledge to generate new ideas, products, or processes.
    b. create original works as a means of personal or group expression.
    c. use models and simulations to explore complex systems and issues.
    d. identify trends and forecast possibilities.

❷ Communication and Collaboration

Students use digital media and environments to communicate and work collaboratively, including at a distance, to support individual learning and contribute to the learning of others. Students:

    a. interact, collaborate, and publish with peers, experts or others employing a variety of digital environments and media.
    b. communicate information and ideas effectively to multiple audiences using a variety of media and formats.
    c. develop cultural understanding and global awareness by engaging with learners of other cultures.
    d. contribute to project teams to produce original works or solve problems.

❸ Research and Information Fluency

Students apply digital tools to gather, evaluate, and use information. Students:

    a. plan strategies to guide inquiry.
    b. locate, organize, analyze, evaluate, synthesize, and ethically use information from a variety of sources and media.
    c. evaluate and select information sources and digital tools based on the appropriateness to specific tasks.
    d. process data and report results.

Convert To change the format of a document or file. (pp. 122, 133, 153)

Convey To visually communicate. (p. 76)

Copy To select and reproduce text somewhere else in a document or application. (pp. 35, 90, 107)

COUNT A function that counts the number of cells in the range that contain numbers. (p. 99)

COUNTA A function used to find the number of cells in a range that contain data (both numbers and text). (p. 99)

Criteria Specifications or conditions that must be met to be satisfied. (p. 155, 180)

Custom number format A number format designed by the user. (p. 205)

Cut To select and remove text, usually for the purpose of pasting somewhere else in a document or application. (p. 35)

D

Data Factual information used as a basis for reasoning, discussion, or calculation. (pp. 5, 150)

Data bar A conditional formatting option that applies bars of differing length to cells based on specific criteria. (p. 207)

Data validation The process of ensuring that data is correct based on specific criteria. (p. 158)

Database function A formula that acts on only those items that meet certain specifications. (p. 180)

Delete To remove or erase (pp. 32, 36)

Delimited Data that are separated by a tab, comma, or other character (p. 255)

Delimiter A divider that separates text. (p. 55)

Determine To identify or decide by weighing alternatives or possibilities. (p. 30)

Dialog box A box opened by a menu command that allows you to select options or specify information to perform the command. (pp. 7, 8)

Dialog Box Launcher A clickable button that appears in the lower-right corner of a group on the Ribbon. For example, the Paragraph Dialog Box Launcher in Word opens the Paragraph dialog box. (p. xxxv, 7)

Digital signature A security feature that authenticates the digital information you create. Inserting a digital signature signifies that the content has not been changed since the document was signed. (p. 243)

Distinct Distinguishable to the eye or mind as discrete; separate. (p. 60)

Distribute To give out. (p. 238)

Document A file into which text is keyed. Documents can contain text, pictures, charts, and other objects. (p. 6)

Document Information Panel A panel that allows users to view, add, and edit the document properties easily while you work on the document. (p. 258)

Document Inspector A tool that reviews documents for hidden data or personal information that is stored in the document or document properties. (p. 257)

Duplicate value A situation where all data in a row is an exact match of the data in another row. (p. 161)

E

Edit To make changes to a document, contents of a cell, or presentation. (pp. 31, 88, 96)

Error Mistake. (p. 160)

Evaluate Formula A tool that checks formulas and gives detail about an error value by showing how Excel attempted to calculate the formula. (p. 162)

F

File format The file type, such as .docx or .rtf. You can change the file format of a document so that users who do not use Microsoft Office can read your data. (p. 133)

Fill handle A tool that lets you fill multiple cells with the same content by using one cell as an example. (p. 39)

Filter A feature that allows you to look at only the data that you need. (pp. 85, 155)

Find A tool used to find specific data in a table or document. (p. 33)

Folder An item that helps the user organize files. (pp. 10, 15, 32)

Font The overall design of a full set of characters. Also known as typeface. (p. 52)

Font style An effect that can be applied to a font, such as bold, italic, or underline. (p. 52)

Formula An equation containing values, cell references, or both. (pp. 16, 41, 87, 187)

④ Critical Thinking, Problem-Solving, and Decision-Making

Students use critical thinking skills to plan and conduct research, manage projects, solve problems and make informed decisions using appropriate digital tools and resources. Students:

   a. identify and define authentic problems and significant questions for investigation.
   b. plan and manage activities to develop a solution or complete a project.
   c. collect and analyze data to identify solutions and/or make informed decisions.
   d. use multiple processes and diverse perspectives to explore alternative solutions.

⑤ Digital Citizenship

Students understand human, cultural, and societal issues related to technology and practice legal and ethical behavior. Students:

   a. advocate and practice safe, legal, and responsible use of information and technology.
   b. exhibit a positive attitude toward using technology that supports collaboration, learning, and productivity.
   c. demonstrate personal responsibility for lifelong learning.
   d. exhibit leadership for digital citizenship.

⑥ Technology Operations and Concepts

Students demonstrate a sound understanding of technology concepts, systems and operations. Students:

   a. understand and use technology systems.
   b. select and use applications effectively and productively.
   c. troubleshoot systems and applications.
   d. transfer current knowledge to learning of new technologies.

Glossary

A

Absolute reference A cell reference that does not change when a formula is copied to a new location. (p. 93)

Adjust To adapt or conform. (p. 90)

Advanced filter A filtering feature that allows users to specify criteria within a set in a range of cells or table that meet the criteria will be displayed. (p. 155)

Alignment The way text lines up with respect to margins or tabs; the position of text and graphics in relation to a text box's margins and to other text and graphics on a slide. (p. 65)

Alteration A change. (p. 233)

Argument A value in a formula. (p. 180)

Arrange To organize more than one window on the screen at the same time. (p. 119)

Author Source. (p. 258)

AutoSum A function used to add values in rows or columns. (pp. 16, 30, 45)

AVERAGE A function used to find the numeric average of a group of cells. (pp. 30, 45)

B

Background A graphic that appears behind the information in a worksheet; solid colors, patterns, or pictures that fill the entire slide and appear behind the slide's content. (p. 70)

Border A line or box that frames text or a cell. (p. 53)

Brightness The lightness or darkness of a graphic. (p. 211)

Browser A software program that can surf the Web and interact with Web sites. (p. 122)

Budget A detailed estimate of income and expenses over a period of time. (pp. 29, 48)

Button A graphic icon that can be clicked to perform a specific task. (p. 7)

C

Case sensitive A setting that requires that letters must be keyed as uppercase, lowercase, or a combination of uppercase and lowercase letters every time. (p. 232)

Cell The intersection of a row and a column in a table or worksheet. (pp. 12, 32, 45)

Cell content The words, numbers, and symbols that appear inside a cell. (pp. 12, 29, 32)

Cell reference The column letter and row number of a cell. (pp. 12, 92, 93, 94)

Cell style A set of formatting traits that has been given a name. (p. 61)

Chart A graphic that organizes data visually. Common charts are pie charts, bar charts, and line charts. (pp. 95, 109)

Clear To remove all of the contents. You can clear the contents of a cell or of a text box. (p. 32)

Clipboard A place where cut or copied text is stored so that it can be copied into a document in the future. (p. 35)

Color scale A conditional formatting option that applies shades of colors to indicate differences in data based on specific criteria. (p. 207)

Column All of the cells arranged vertically under a lettered column heading. (pp. 12, 36, 37)

Command Controls that tell the computer to perform a particular task. (p. 7)

Comment A note added to a document without making any changes to the text itself. (p. 236)

Common Shared by two or more parties. (p. 116)

Compatibility Checker An Office 2007 tool that identifies features in a Word, Excel, Access, or PowerPoint document that will not operate correctly if opened with a previous version of the software, such as Office 2003 or Office 2000. (p. 261)

Computer An electronic device that processes data and converts it into information that people can use. (p. 2)

Condition A rule. (p. 103)

Conditional formatting Formatting that is set to appear a certain way if certain conditions, or rules, are met. (p. 206)

Conditional Formatting Rules Manager A tool that allows users to create, edit, delete, and view all conditional formatting rules in a worksheet or workbook. (p. 209)

Conditional logic A function that tests whether statements are true or false and makes logical comparisons between outcomes. (p. 190)

Conflict Not in agreement. (p. 209)

Consolidate To combine data from multiple worksheets. (p. 267)

Constraint A limit that is set. (p. 185)

Contextual tab A tab that appears on the Ribbon that contains commands that can only be used with a selected object. (p. xxxix)

Contrast The difference between the lighter and darker areas of a graphic. (p. 211)

Microsoft Certified Application Specialist Standards

What is the Microsoft Business Certification Program?

The Microsoft Business Certification Program allows users to show that they have proven expertise in Microsoft Office programs. Users who prove this expertise achieve the Microsoft Certified Application Specialist certification. The Microsoft Business Certification Program is the only Microsoft-approved certification program of its kind, recognized by businesses and schools around the world.

How can I get Microsoft Certified Application Specialist (MCAS) certification?

In order to achieve MCAS certification, a user must pass an exam based on specific skill sets within a Microsoft® Office application. Users can take as many exams as they want and can achieve as many certifications as they want. The Application Specialist exams include:

- Using Microsoft® Office Word 2007
- Using Microsoft® Office Excel® 2007
- Using Microsoft® Office Access 2007
- Using Microsoft® Office PowerPoint® 2007
- Using Microsoft® Office Outlook® 2007
- Using Microsoft® Windows Vista™

How can Glencoe iCheck Series Microsoft Office 2007 help me achieve certification?

Glencoe *iCheck Microsoft Office 2007* has been written to cover all standards necessary to complete and pass the Application Specialist exams listed above. A correlation to the Microsoft Certified Application Specialist standards is provided on page 314. This correlation indicates where specific standards are covered in the Student Edition or on the Online Learning Center. The beginning of every lesson also contains a Standards box that shows you which MCAS standards are taught in that lesson.

Microsoft Excel 2007 Certified Application Specialist Standards		
Standard	**Skill Sets and Skills**	**Text Correlation**
4.5	Outline data	156, 157, 170
4.6	Sort and filter data	85, 86, 148, 155, 167, 277
5	**Collaborating and Securing Data**	
5.1	Manage changes to workbooks	235, 236, 237, 246, 247, 251, 252
5.2	Protect and share workbooks	230, 231, 232, 233, 234, 246, 249, 250, 252, 282
5.3	Prepare workbooks for distribution	242, 243, 250, 251, 257, 258, 271, 275
5.4	Save workbooks	122, 133, 136, 141, 259, 260, 261, 262, 263, 271, 272, 274, 276, 279
5.5	Set print options for printing data, worksheets, and workbooks	124, 125, 126, 127, 128, 130, 131, 137, 138, 140, 240

Prepare for Academic Success!

National Language Arts Standards

To help incorporate literacy skills (reading, writing, listening, and speaking) into Glencoe *iCheck Series Microsoft Office 2007*, each lesson contains a listing of the language arts skills covered. These skills have been developed into standards by the *National Council of Teachers of English and International Reading Association*.

- Read texts to acquire new information.
- Read literature to build an understanding of the human experience.
- Apply strategies to interpret texts.
- Use written language to communicate effectively.
- Use different writing process elements to communicate effectively.
- Apply knowledge of language structure and conventions to discuss texts.
- Conduct research and gather, evaluate, and synthesize data to communicate discoveries.
- Use information resources to gather information and create and communicate knowledge.
- Develop an understanding of diversity in language used across cultures.
- Use first language to develop competency in English language arts and develop an understanding of content across the curriculum.
- Participate as members of literacy communities.
- Use language to accomplish individual purposes.

National Math Standards

Glencoe's *iCheck Series* provides students with opportunities to practice the math skills indicated in the national math standards developed by the *National Council of Teachers of Mathematics*. The basic skills are:

- Number and Operations
- Algebra
- Geometry
- Measurement
- Data Analysis and Probability
- Problem Solving
- Communication
- Connections
- Representation

Microsoft
CERTIFIED
Application
Specialist

Approved Courseware

Microsoft Certified Application Specialist Standards

iCheck Express Microsoft Excel 2007 covers the Microsoft Certified Application Specialist (MCAS) standards for Excel. This chart provides an overview of the coverage of the MCAS standards in *iCheck Express Microsoft Excel2007*.

\multicolumn{3}{c}{**Microsoft Excel 2007 Certified Application Specialist Standards**}		
Standard	**Skill Sets and Skills**	**Text Correlation**
1	**Creating and Manipulating Data**	
1.1	Insert data using AutoFill	35, 39, 60
1.2	Ensure data integrity	158, 159, 161, 171, 174, 175
1.3	Modify cell contents and formats	52, 53
1.4	Change worksheet views	13, 20, 22, 23, 120, 121, 127,136
1.5	Manage worksheets	169, 171, 218, 219, 238, 239
2	**Formatting Data and Content**	
2.1	Format worksheets	68, 69, 70, 76, 78, 147, 217, 218
2.2	Insert and modify rows and columns	35, 36, 37, 38, 44, 49, 55, 62, 63, 64, 65, 66, 143, 145
2.3	Format cells and cell content	40, 48, 52, 53, 55, 60, 65, 66, 79, 80, 82, 101, 145, 147, 166, 206, 221, 226, 227
2.4	Format data as a table	55, 56, 58, 61, 77, 81, 143
3	**Creating and Modifying Formulas**	
3.1	Reference data in formulas	92, 93, 94, 108, 110, 112, 113, 146, 153, 154, 162, 163, 164, 165, 173, 174, 197, 277
3.2	Summarize data using a formula	16, 22, 24, 26, 30, 45, 47, 49, 82, 99, 107, 108, 110, 112, 113, 141, 142, 143
3.3	Summarize data using subtotals	153, 154, 156, 169, 170
3.4	Conditionally summarize data using a formula	187, 188, 189, 197, 200, 202
3.5	Look up data using a formula	192, 193
3.6	Use conditional logic in a formula	103, 113, 190
3.7	Format or modify text using formulas	180, 181, 201
3.8	Display and print formulas	191, 202
4	**Presenting Data Visually**	
4.1	Create and format charts	95, 109, 111, 112, 148, 215, 224, 227, 280, 281
4.2	Modify charts	96, 97, 98, 109, 111, 281
4.3	Apply conditional formatting	207, 208, 209, 210, 222, 226
4.4	Insert and modify illustrations	72, 82, 211, 212, 213, 214, 223, 225

Reading Skills Handbook

▶ Reading: What's in It for You?

What role does reading play in your life? The possibilities are countless. Are you on a sports team? Perhaps you like to read about the latest news and statistics in your sport or find out about new training techniques. Are you looking for a part-time job? You might be looking for advice about résumé writing, interview techniques, or information about a company. Are you enrolled in an English class, an algebra class, or a business class? Then your assignments require a lot of reading.

Improving or Fine-tuning Your Reading Skills Will:

◆ Improve your grades
◆ Allow you to read faster and more efficiently
◆ Improve your study skills
◆ Help you remember more information accurately
◆ Improve your writing

▶ The Reading Process

Good reading skills build on one another, overlap, and spiral around in much the same way that a winding staircase goes around and around while leading you to a higher place. This handbook is designed to help you find and use the tools you will need **before, during,** and **after** reading.

Strategies You Can Use

◆ Identify, understand, and learn new words
◆ Understand why you read
◆ Take a quick look at the whole text
◆ Try to predict what you are about to read
◆ Take breaks while you read and ask yourself questions about the text
◆ Take notes
◆ Keep thinking about what will come next
◆ Summarize

▶ Vocabulary Development

Word identification and vocabulary skills are the building blocks of the reading and the writing process. By learning to use a variety of strategies to build your word skills and vocabulary, you will become a stronger reader.

What is the Microsoft Business Certification Program?

The Microsoft Business Certification Program enables candidates to show that they have something exceptional to offer—proven expertise in Microsoft Office programs. The two certification tracks allow candidates to choose how they want to exhibit their skills, either through validating skills within a specific Microsoft product or taking their knowledge to the next level and combining Microsoft programs to show that they can apply multiple skills sets to complete more complex office tasks. Recognized by businesses and schools around the world, over 3 million certifications have been obtained in over 100 different countries. The Microsoft Business Certification Program is the only Microsoft-approved certification program of its kind.

What is the Microsoft Certification Application Specialist Certification?

 Approved Courseware

The Microsoft Certified Application Specialist Certification exams focus on validating specific skill sets within each of the Microsoft® Office system programs. The candidate can choose which exam(s) they want to take according to which skills they want to validate. The available Application Specialist exams include:

- Using Microsoft® Windows Vista™
- Using Microsoft® Office Word 2007
- Using Microsoft® Office Excel® 2007
- Using Microsoft® Office PowerPoint® 2007
- Using Microsoft® Office Access 2007
- Using Microsoft® Office Outlook® 2007

What does the Microsoft Business Certification Vendor of Approved Courseware logo represent?

 Approved Courseware

The logo validates that the courseware has been approved by the Microsoft® Business Certification Vendor program: these courses cover objectives that will be included in the relevant exam. It also means that after utilizing this courseware, you may be prepared to pass the exams required to become a Microsoft Certified Application Specialist.

For more information:

To learn more about the Microsoft Certified Application Specialist exam, visit microsoft.com/learning/msbc.

To learn about other Microsoft Certified Application Specialist approved courseware from Glencoe/McGraw-Hill, visit www.glencoe.com.

*The availability of Microsoft Certified Application exams varies by Microsoft Office program. program version and language. Visit www.microsoft.com/learning for exam availability.

Microsoft, the Office Logo, Outlook, and PowerPoint are either registered trademarks or trademarks of Microsoft Corporation in the United States and/or other countries. The Microsoft Certified Application Specialist Logo is used under license from Microsoft Corporation.

Use Context to Determine Meaning

The best way to expand and extend your vocabulary is to read widely, listen carefully, and participate in a rich variety of discussions. When reading on your own, though, you can often figure out the meanings of new words by looking at their **context,** the other words and sentences that surround them.

Tips for Using Context

Look for clues such as:

A synonym or an explanation of the unknown word in the sentence:
*Elise's shop specialized in **millinery**, or **hats for women**.*

A reference to what the word is or is not like:
*An **archaeologist**, like a **historian**, deals with the past.*

A general topic associated with the word:
*The **cooking** teacher discussed the best way to **braise** meat.*

A description or action associated with the word:
*He used the **shovel** to **dig up** the garden.*

Predict a Possible Meaning

Another way to determine the meaning of a word is to take the word apart. If you understand the meaning of the **base,** or **root,** part of a word, and also know the meanings of key syllables added either to the beginning or end of the base word, you can usually figure out what the word means.

Word Origins Since Latin, Greek, and Anglo-Saxon roots are the basis for much of our English vocabulary, having some background in languages can be a useful vocabulary tool. For example, *astronomy* comes from the Greek root *astro*, which means "relating to the stars." *Stellar* also has a meaning referring to stars, but its origin is Latin. Knowing root words in other languages can help you determine meanings, derivations, and spellings in English.

Prefixes and Suffixes A prefix is a word part that can be added to the beginning of a word. For example, the prefix *semi* means "half" or "partial," so *semicircle* means "half a circle." A suffix is a word part that can be added to the end of a word. Adding a suffix often changes a word from one part of speech to another.

Recognize Word Meanings Across Subjects
Have you learned a new word in one class and then noticed it in your reading for other subjects? The word might not mean exactly the same thing in each class, but you can use the meaning you already know to help you understand the word's meaning in another subject area.

Format for Envelopes

A standard large (No. 10) envelope is 9½ by 4⅛ inches. A standard small (No. 6¾) envelope is 6½ by 3⅝ inches. The format shown is recommended by the U.S. Postal Service for mail that will be sorted by an electronic scanning device.

Your Name
4112 Bay View Drive
San Jose, CA 95192

  Mrs. Maria Chavez
  1021 West Palm Blvd.
  San Jose, CA 95192

George Washington High School
6021 Brobeck Street
Flint, MI 48532

  Dr. John Harvey
  Environmental Science Department
  Central College
  1900 W. Innes Blvd.
  Salisbury, NC 28144

How to Fold Letters

To fold a letter for a small envelope:
1. Place the letter *face up* and fold up the bottom half to 0.5 inch from the top edge of the paper.
2. Fold the right third over to the left.
3. Fold the left third over to 0.5 inch from the right edge of the paper.
4. Insert the last crease into the envelope first, with the flap facing up.

To fold a letter for a large envelope:
1. Place the letter *face up* and fold up the bottom third.
2. Fold the top third down to 0.5 inch from the bottom edge of the paper.
3. Insert the last crease into the envelope first, with the flap facing up.

Dictionary Entry

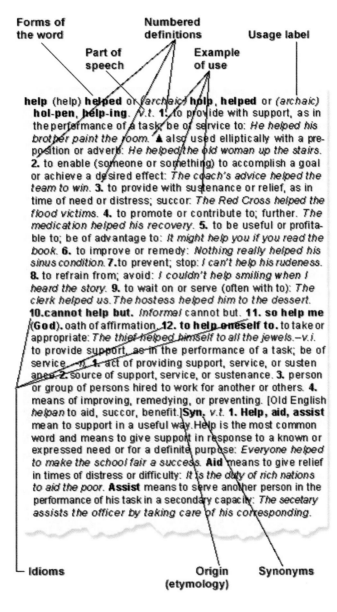

Forms of
the word

Part of
speech

Numbered
definitions

Example
of use

Usage label

help (help) helped or (archaic) holp, helped or (archaic)
hol-pen, help-ing. v.t. 1. to provide with support, as in
the performance of a task; be of service to: *He helped his
brother paint the room.* ▲ also used elliptically with a pre-
position or adverb: *He helped the old woman up the stairs.*
2. to enable (someone or something) to accomplish a goal
or achieve a desired effect: *The coach's advice helped the
team to win.* 3. to provide with sustenance or relief, as in
time of need or distress; succor: *The Red Cross helped the
flood victims.* 4. to promote or contribute to; further. *The
medication helped his recovery.* 5. to be useful or profitable to; be of advantage to: *It might help you if you read the
book.* 6. to improve or remedy: *Nothing really helped his
sinus condition.* 7.to prevent; stop: *I can't help his rudeness.*
8. to refrain from; avoid: *I couldn't help smiling when I
heard the story.* 9. to wait on or serve (often with to): *The
clerk helped us. The hostess helped him to the dessert.*
10.**cannot help but.** *Informal* cannot but. 11. **so help me
(God).** oath of affirmation. 12. **to help oneself to.** to take or
appropriate: *The thief helped himself to all the jewels.*—*v.i.*
to provide support, as in the performance of a task; be of
service.—*n.* 1. act of providing support, service, or susten
ance. 2. source of support, service, or sustenance. 3. person
or group of persons hired to work for another or others. 4.
means of improving, remedying, or preventing. [Old English
helpan to aid, succor, benefit.]**Syn.** *v.t.* 1. **Help, aid, assist**
mean to support in a useful way. Help is the most common
word and means to give support in response to a known or
expressed need or for a definite purpose: *Everyone helped
to make the school fair a success.* **Aid** means to give relief
in times of distress or difficulty: *It is the duty of rich nations
to aid the poor.* **Assist** means to serve another person in the
performance of his task in a secondary capacity: *The secetary
assists the officer by taking care of his corresponding.*

Idioms

Origin
(etymology)

Synonyms

Using Dictionaries A dictionary provides the meaning or meanings of a word. Look at the sample dictionary
entry above to see what other information it provides.

Thesauruses and Specialized Reference Books A thesaurus provides synonyms and often antonyms. Specialized dictionaries, such as *Barron's Dictionary of Business Terms* or *Black's Law Dictionary,* list terms and expressions
that are not commonly included in a general dictionary. You can also use online dictionaries.

Glossaries Many textbooks and technical works contain condensed dictionaries that provide an alphabetical listing of words used in the text and their specific definitions.

Boxed Table

Bills Passed for E-Waste or E-Cycling	
State	Bill
Arkansas	SB807, Enacted 6/20/10
California	SP1253, Introduced 2/20/09 SB1619, Introduced 6/13/09
Florida	SB1922, Introduced 7/23/10
Georgia	HB2, Passed the House, in the Senate, 7/9/09
Hawaii	HB1638, Carried over to the 2011 session
Idaho	S1416, Sent to Committee 9/22/09
Illinois	HB14464, Passed the House, in the Senate 4/24/09
Maryland	HB111, Unfavorable Environmental Committee Report

Contents

CONTENTS

Cover Letter

Julie Smith
2842 South Central Park
Burbank, CA 91365
(818) 555-1212
jsmith@jules.com
↓2x

March 12, 2009
↓4x

David C. Jones
Director of Personnel
Bank of the North
47108 Monterey Avenue
Burbank, CA 91365
(818) 555-1000
↓2x

Dear Mr. Jones:
↓2x

The accompanying résumé is in response to your listing in *The Los Angeles Times* for a full-time security officer. I believe that I have the skills and experience that will serve the Bank of the North.
↓2x

I am especially interested in this position because my experience as a senior security professional in the U.S. Army has prepared me for a disciplined, secure work environment. I am looking forward to using this experience for enhancing the security of a growing, community-conscious bank.
↓2x

I would appreciate an opportunity to meet with you to discuss how my experience will best meet your needs. My ideas on how to improve your bank's security posture may be of particular interest to you. Therefore, I will call your office on the morning of March 17 to inquire if a meeting can be scheduled at a convenient time.
↓2x

Sincerely yours,
↓3x

Julie Smith

Résumé

Julie Smith
2842 South Central Park Burbank, CA 91365
(818) 555-1212
jsmith@jules.com

OBJECTIVE Experienced and dependable security guard dedicated to ensuring the safety of employees and visitors while minimizing potential losses. Proficient in operating security systems, including two-way radios, CCTVs, and two-way/convex wall mirrors. Committed to enhancing knowledge of security techniques. Completed intensive security training program through ABC Retail Company. Possess clean California driver's license; drug free; physically fit; and available to work various shifts.

TARGET JOB
Desired Job Type: Employee, Temporary/Contract
Desired Status: Full-Time
Career Level: Mid Career (2+ years of experience)

EXPERIENCE
Security Guard
10/2007 to Present   ABC Retail Company   Burbank, CA
Provide a high profile presence in the 10,000-square foot retail store, monitoring the facility to prevent loss and ensure the full protection of occupants. Operate surveillance systems and patrol the grounds to protect against possible hazards. Write informative reports to update management on all emergency situations. Exercise sound judgment and maintain confidentiality at all times. Highlights:

- Offered a full-time position after two months of temporary employment based on exemplary performance
- Awarded "Certificate of Achievement" (5/2009) for identifying and reporting internal theft, potentially saving the company tens of thousands of dollars annually.
- Apprehended numerous shoplifters by recognizing suspicious behavior, using available surveillance systems, and taking action at the appropriate time.
- Completed two-week security training program.

EDUCATION
10/2007   ABC Retail Company   Burbank, CA
Certification
Professional Training: Crisis Intervention, Public Relations, Report Writing, Legal Authority and Limitations, Risk Analysis, First Aid, CPR, Fire Protection, Crime Prevention, Arrest Procedures, CCTV Surveillance
6/2005   ABC High School   Burbank, CA
Academic diploma

REFERENCES References are available on request.

▶ Understanding What You Read

Reading comprehension means understanding—deriving meaning from—what you have read. Using a variety of strategies can help you improve your comprehension and make reading more interesting and more fun.

Read for a Reason

To get the greatest benefit from what you read, you should **establish a purpose for reading**. In school, you have many reasons for reading. Some of them are:

- To learn and understand new information
- To find specific information
- To review before a test
- To complete an assignment
- To prepare (research) before you write

As your reading skills improve, you will notice that you apply different strategies to fit the different purposes for reading. For example, if you are reading for entertainment, you might read quickly, but if you read to gather information or follow directions, you might read more slowly, take notes, construct a graphic organizer, or reread sections of text.

Draw on Personal Background

Drawing on personal background may also be called activating prior knowledge. Before you start reading a text, ask yourself questions like these:

- What have I heard or read about this topic?
- Do I have any personal experience relating to this topic?

Using a KWL Chart A KWL chart is a good device for organizing information you gather before, during, and after reading. In the first column, list what you already **know**, then list what you **want** to know in the middle column. Use the third column when you review and you assess what you **learned**. You can also add more columns to record places where you found information and places where you can look for more information.

K (What I already know)	W (What I want to know)	L (What I have learned)

Adjust Your Reading Speed Your reading speed is a key factor in how well you understand what you are reading. You will need to adjust your speed depending on your reading purpose.

Scanning means running your eyes quickly over the material to look for words or phrases. Scan when you need a specific piece of information.

Skimming means reading a passage quickly to find its main idea or to get an overview. Skim a text when you preview to determine what the material is about.

Title Page

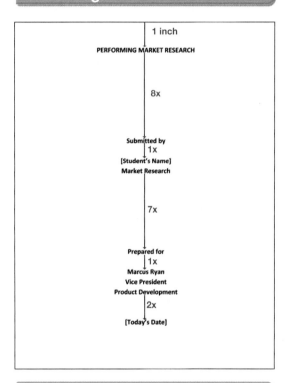

```
                          1 inch

              PERFORMING MARKET RESEARCH


                           8x




                       Submitted by
                          1x
                     [Student's Name]
                     Market Research


                           7x




                       Prepared for
                          1x
                       Marcus Ryan
                      Vice President
                   Product Development
                          2x

                      [Today's Date]
```

Simple Business Report

```
                                    1 inch        .5 inch
                                              Marketing Research 1
```

Market Research—Why?
Your new product is terrific. Your planned service support for the new product is outstanding. However, even if you have the greatest product and the best service support, your new venture can still fail if you do not have effective marketing.

People cannot purchase a product if they do not know that that product exists. It is up to you to let your potential customers know what you have to offer. Effective marketing begins with careful, systematic research. It is dangerous to assume that you are already familiar with your intended market. You must perform market research to make sure you are on track. Use the business planning process as your opportunity to uncover data and to question your marketing efforts. Your time will be well spent.

Market Research—How?
There are two kinds of market research: primary and secondary. Both types of research are necessary for an effective marketing campaign.

Primary Research
Primary research means gathering your own data. For example, performing your own traffic count at a proposed location is a form of primary research. Using the yellow pages to identify competitors, and doing surveys or focus-group interviews to learn about consumer preferences are also forms of primary research. Hiring professional market researchers can be very costly. If money is tight, you can look for a book that illustrates how small business owners can perform effective research themselves. Such books are plentiful, and will help you perform your own primary research.

1 inch ———————————————————————————————— 1 inch

Secondary Research
Secondary research means using published information to research your market. Published information can include industry profiles, trade journals, newspapers, magazines, census data, and demographic profiles.[1] This type of information is available at many locations, including public libraries, industry associations, and Chambers of Commerce. You can also get important information from vendors who sell to your industry, and from government agencies.

When performing secondary research, try starting with your local library. Most librarians are pleased to guide you through their business data collection. You will be amazed at what is there. In particular, ask the librarian to help you navigate the many online sources that inevitably exist for your industry. You will probably find that there are more online sources than you could ever possibly use!

Beside the library, search for information at your local Chamber of Commerce. The Chamber of Commerce usually has comprehensive information about the local area. Trade associations and trade publications often have excellent industry-specific data.

_____
[1] Keiko Kimura, "Sources for Secondary Market Research," *Marketing Research Essentials*, New York: All Biz Publishing, 2009, pp. 47-58.

Simple Business Report continued

```
                                              Marketing Research 2
```

Market Research—Get the Facts
When performing marketing research, you need to focus on identifying some important facts about your industry. These facts will help you better understand your market. This, in turn, will help you decide what marketing efforts you need to implement to promote your product.

Developing the Marketing Plan
Use your primary and secondary research to develop a marketing plan for your product. Be as specific as possible in your marketing plan. Provide statistics, numbers, and sources. It is important that you be as exact as possible, for your marketing plan will become the basis, later on, for your all-important sales projections.[1]

Define Your Market
1 inch — Market research will also help you narrow your focus. When researching your market, ask the — 1 inch following questions:
- What is the total size of your market?
- What percent share of the market will you have? (This is important only if you think you will be a major factor in the market.)
- What is the current demand in your target market?
- What are the current trends in your target market? Try to identify growth trends, trends in consumer preferences, and trends in product development.
- What is the growth potential and opportunity for a business of your size in this market?

Identify Barriers
When researching the market, you also need to try and identify potential barriers to success. What factors may prevent you from successfully entering the market with your new product? Some typical barriers to consider include:
- High capital costs
- High production costs
- High marketing costs
- Consumer acceptance and brand recognition

Conclusion
Introducing a new product to the market can be a scary experience. You and many others have invested time, money, and sweat into the new product, and you all want it to succeed. Careful market research can help you help your product to succeed.

_____
[1] Trey Smith, "Developing Sales Projections," *Sales Review Monthly*, October 2010, p. 67-73.

Bibliography

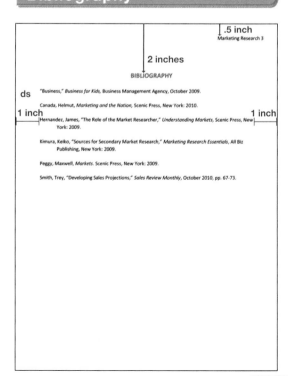

```
                                                .5 inch
                                           Marketing Research 3

                        2 inches
                      BIBLIOGRAPHY
```

ds "Business," *Business for Kids*, Business Management Agency, October 2009.

Canada, Helmut, *Marketing and the Nation*, Scenic Press, New York: 2010.

1 inch — Hernandez, James, "The Role of the Market Researcher," *Understanding Markets*, Scenic Press, New York: 2009. — 1 inch

Kimura, Keiko, "Sources for Secondary Market Research," *Marketing Research Essentials*, All Biz Publishing, New York: 2009.

Peggy, Maxwell, *Markets*. Scenic Press, New York: 2009.

Smith, Trey, "Developing Sales Projections," *Sales Review Monthly*, October 2010, pp. 67-73.

Reading for detail involves careful reading while paying attention to text structure and monitoring your understanding. Read for detail when you are learning concepts, following complicated directions, or preparing to analyze a text.

▶ Techniques to Understand and Remember What You Read

Preview

Before beginning a selection, it is helpful to **preview** what you are about to read.

> ### Previewing Strategies
>
> ◆ Read the title, headings, and subheadings of the selection.
> ◆ Look at the illustrations and notice how the text is organized.
> ◆ Skim the selection: Take a glance at the whole thing.
> ◆ Decide what the main idea might be.
> ◆ Predict what the selection will be about.

Predict

Have you ever read a mystery, decided who committed the crime, and then changed your mind as more clues were revealed? You were adjusting your predictions. Did you smile when you found out you guessed the murderer? You were verifying your predictions.

As you read, take educated guesses about story events and outcomes; that is, **make predictions** before and during reading. This will help you focus your attention on the text and it will improve your understanding.

Determine the Main Idea

When you look for the **main idea**, you are looking for the most important statement in a text. Depending on what kind of text you are reading, the main idea can be located at the very beginning (as in news stories in a newspaper or a magazine) or at the end (as in a scientific research document). Ask yourself:

• What is each sentence about?
• Is there one sentence that is more important than all the others?
• What idea do details support or point out?

Newsletter

The Hillside High Gazette

Band Tryouts on Tuesday
Show off your school spirit and your musical talent by joining the band! Band tryouts will be this Tuesday, from 3:30-5:30 in the North field. Please bring your own instrument.

The Hillside High Band is in need of all musicians, especially trumpet and flute players. Band rehearsals will be held every Monday, Wednesday, and Friday after school during football season. Off-season, rehearsals will be held every Monday and Wednesday after school.

The tryouts will be judged by our band leader Mr. Schaefer, as well as by two senior band members in each instrumental group.

Recycling Challenge
Hillside High is proud to announce the first annual Recycling Challenge. Each homeroom class will compete to see who can bring in the most paper, plastic bottles, cans, and boxes. The winning homeroom class will receive a free pizza party.

Bike Week Continues
The Bicycle Club would like to acknowledge the efforts of Janet McSimmons, Steve Yuan, Maggie Estevez, Jill Pierce, James Mazur, Jason Trevor, and Yolanda Washington, who organized our first annual Bike Week. The event wraps up this Friday with the competition finals.

We had great turnout for all the rides, from spectators and participants alike. Leaders in each category will compete for the grand prize—a free PedalCo bike, helmet, and safety pads. Good luck to all the competitors! Here is a list of events and times to beat.

Event	Type of Bike	Time to Beat
Hills Ride	Mountain Bike	1:05:24
Distance Ride	Road Bike	1:42:07
Obstacle Course	Hybrid	15:32
Beach Ride	Beach Cruiser	37:59
Speed Ride	Racing Bike	25:30

MLA Style Academic Report

MLA Style Academic Report cont.

Davy then married Elizabeth Patton in 1817. She was a widow and she had two children of her own, George and Margaret Ann (The Texas State Historical Association).

Davy was well known in Tennessee as a frontiersman. He was a sharpshooter, a famous Indian fighter, and a bear hunter. In 1821, he started his career in politics as a Tennessee legislator. People liked Davy because he had a good humor and they thought he was one of their own. He was re-elected to the Legislature in 1823, but he lost the election in 1825.

In 1827 Davy was elected to Congress. He fought for the land bill. The land bill allowed those who settled the land to buy it at a very low cost. He was re-elected to Congress in 1829 and again in 1833, but he lost in 1836 (Lofaro, 1148d).

Many Americans had gone to Texas to settle. In 1835, Davy left his kids, his wife, his brothers, and his sisters to go to Texas. He loved Texas. When the Texans were fighting for their independence from Mexico, Davy joined the fight. He was fighting with a group of Tennessee volunteers defending the Alamo in San Antonio on March 6, 1836 (The Texas State Historical Association). He was 49 years old.

Works Cited

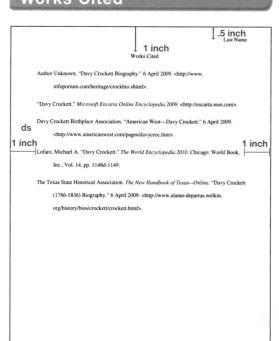

Taking Notes

Cornell Note-Taking System There are many methods for note taking. The **Cornell Note-Taking System** is a well-known method that can help you organize what you read. To the right is a diagram that shows how the Cornell Note-Taking System organizes information.

Graphic Organizers Using a graphic organizer to retell content in a visual representation will help you remember and retain content. You might make a **chart** or **diagram**, organizing what you have read. Here are some examples of graphic organizers:

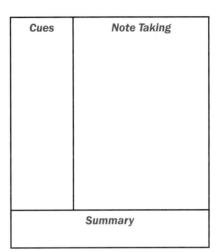

Venn diagrams When mapping out a compare-and-contrast text structure, you can use a Venn diagram. The outer portions of the circles will show how two characters, ideas, or items contrast, or are different, and the overlapping part will compare two things, or show how they are similar.

Flow charts To help you track the sequence of events, or cause and effect, use a flow chart. Arrange ideas or events in their logical, sequential order. Then draw arrows between your ideas to indicate how one idea or event flows into another.

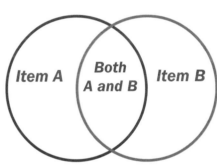

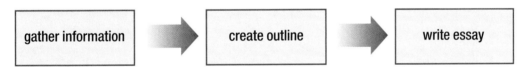

Visualize

Try to form a mental picture of scenes, characters, and events as you read. Use the details and descriptions the author gives you. If you can **visualize** what you read, it will be more interesting and you will remember it better.

Question

Ask yourself questions about the text as you read. Ask yourself about the importance of the sentences, how they relate to one another, if you understand what you just read, and what you think is going to come next.

Memo

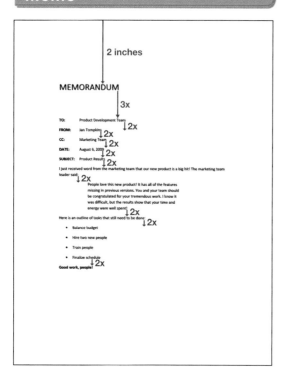

Business Letter

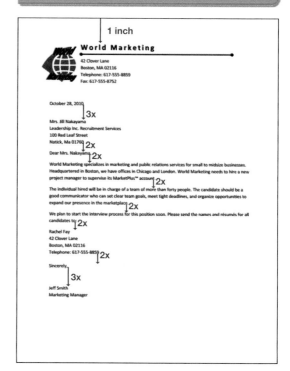

Personal Business Letter

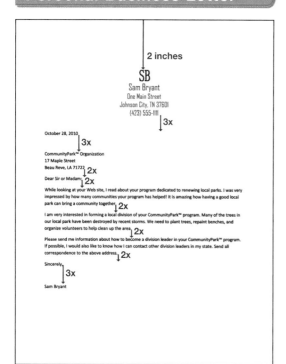

Outline

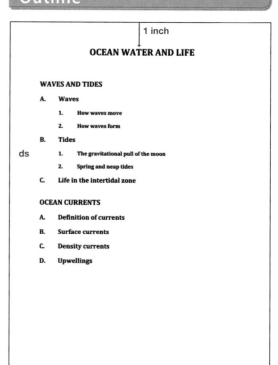

Clarify

If you feel you do not understand meaning (through questioning), try these techniques:

> **What to Do When You Do Not Understand**
>
> ◆ Reread confusing parts of the text.
> ◆ Diagram (chart) relationships between chunks of text, ideas, and sentences.
> ◆ Look up unfamiliar words.
> ◆ Talk out the text to yourself.
> ◆ Read the passage once more.

Review

Take time to stop and review what you have read. Use your note-taking tools (graphic organizers or Cornell notes charts). Also, review and consider your KWL chart.

Monitor Your Comprehension

Continue to check your understanding by using the following two strategies:

Summarize Pause and tell yourself the main ideas of the text and the key supporting details. Try to answer the following questions: Who? What? When? Where? Why? How?

Paraphrase Pause, close the book, and try to retell what you have just read in your own words. It might help to pretend you are explaining the text to someone who has not read it and does not know the material.

▶ Understanding Text Structure

Good writers do not just put together sentences and paragraphs. They organize their writing with a specific purpose in mind. That organization is called text structure. When you understand and follow the structure of a text, it is easier to remember the information you are reading. There are many ways text may be structured. Watch for **signal words**. They will help you follow the text's organization. Also, remember to use these techniques when you write.

Compare and Contrast

The compare and contrast structure shows similarities and differences between people, things, and ideas. This is often used to demonstrate that things that seem alike are really different, or vice versa.

> **Signal words:** similarly, more, less, on the one hand/on the other hand, in contrast, but, however

How To Use the Reference Guide

The information on the following pages will help you format various kinds of documents. Use the Contents below to quickly locate the type of document you are creating. Then use the examples shown as a guide to help you format your document properly. The arrows and numbers shown in red on each sample tell you how many times to press Enter on your keyboard to separate items in your document. Double space is indicated by 'ds'.

Remember that your work should reflect your own original research and content and that the information provided here is for reference purposes only. If you use other sources to create your documents, remember to cite your sources properly.

Contents

Cause and Effect

Writers use the cause and effect structure to explore the reasons for something happening and to examine the results, or consequences, of events.

Signal words: so, because, as a result, therefore, for the following reasons

Problem and Solution

When they organize text around the question "how?", writers state a problem and suggest solutions.

Signal words: how, help, problem, obstruction, overcome, difficulty, need, attempt, have to, must

Sequence

Sequencing tells you the order in which to consider thoughts or facts. Examples of sequencing are:

Chronological order refers to the order in which events take place.

Signal words: first, next, then, finally

Spatial order describes the organization of things in space (to describe a room, for example).

Signal words: above, below, behind, next to

Order of importance lists things or thoughts from the most important to the least important (or the other way around).

Signal words: principal, central, main, important, fundamental

▶ Reading for Meaning

It is important to think about what you are reading to get the most information out of a text, to understand the consequences of what the text says, to remember the content, and to form your own opinion about what the content means.

Interpret

Interpreting is asking yourself, "What is the writer really saying?" and then using what you already know to answer that question.

Infer

Writers do not always directly state everything they want you to understand. By providing clues and details, they sometimes imply certain information. An **inference** involves using your reason and experience to develop the idea on your own, based on what an author implies or suggests. When drawing inferences, be sure that you have accurately based your guesses on supporting details from the text. If you cannot point to a place in the selection to help back up your inference, you may need to rethink your guess.

Proofreader's Marks		Draft	Final Copy
∿ Boldface		Chapter Title	**Chapter Title**
ital Italics	_ital_	Business Week	_Business Week_
_u/l_ Underline	_u/l_	Business Week readers	<u>Business Week</u> readers
¶ New paragraph	¶	Once upon a time	Once upon a time
○ Spell out		There were ⑤.	There were five.
⌒ Close up; omit space		no thing	nothing
# Insert space	#	allright	all right
∨ or ∧ Insert		Dont go over there.	Don't go over there.
⊙ Insert period		She went home⊙	She went home.
∧ Insert comma		Alex said "Let's go."	Alex said, "Let's go."
⤶ Delete		the ~~very~~ last time	the last time
⋯ Don't delete; stet		a red ball	a red ball
≡ Capitalize		Third avenue	Third Avenue
/ Make lowercase		the Teacher	the teacher
when if Change word		Wear the ~~blue~~ orange hat.	Wear the orange hat.
∽ Transpose		is it cold	it is cold
⊐ Move right	⊐	$93.87	$93.87
⊏ Move left		‖ Shall we	Shall we dance
♂ Move as shown		Let's go dance	Let's go
SS Single-space	SS	I heard that you are leaving.	I heard that you are leaving.
ds Double-space	ds	When will it take place?	When will it take place?

Draw Conclusions

A conclusion is a general statement you can make and explain with reasoning, or with supporting details from a text. If you read a story describing a sport in which five players bounce a ball and throw it through a high hoop, you may conclude that the sport is basketball.

Analyze

To understand persuasive nonfiction (a text that discusses facts and opinions to arrive at a conclusion), you need to analyze statements and examples to see if they support the main idea. To understand an informational text (such as a textbook, which gives you information, not opinions), you need to keep track of how the ideas are organized to find the main points.

> **Hint:** Use your graphic organizers and notes charts.

Distinguish Facts and Opinions

Learning to determine the difference between facts and opinions is one of the most important reading skills you can learn. A fact is a statement that can be proven. An opinion is what the writer believes. A writer may support opinions with facts, but an opinion cannot be proven. For example:

> **Fact:** California produces fruit and other agricultural products.

> **Opinion:** California produces the best fruit and other agricultural products.

Evaluate

Would you seriously consider an article on nuclear fission if you knew it was written by a comedic actor? If you need to rely on accurate information, you need to find out who wrote what you are reading and why. Where did the writer get information? Is the information one-sided? Can you verify the information?

▶ Reading for Research

You will need to **read actively** in order to research a topic. You might also need to generate an interesting, relevant, and researchable **question** on your own and locate appropriate print and nonprint information from a wide variety of sources. Then you will need to **categorize** that information, evaluate it, and **organize** it in a new way in order to produce a research project for a specific audience. Finally, **draw conclusions** about your original research question. These conclusions may lead you to other areas for further inquiry.

Function	Button	Ribbon	Keyboard Shortcuts	Application
Top 10		Home>Styles>Conditional Formatting>Top/Bottom Rules>Top 10		Excel
Track Changes		Review>Changes>Track Changes		Excel
Underline		Home>Font>Underline		Excel
Undo		Quick Access Toolbar>Undo	CTRL + Z	Excel
Unfreeze panes		View>Window>Freeze Panes>Unfreeze Panes		Excel
View in Full Screen Mode		View>Workbook Views>Full Screen		Excel
What-If		Data>Data Tools>What If Analysis		Excel
WordArt		Insert>Text>WordArt		Excel
Worksheet Background		Page Layout>Page Setup>Background		Excel
Zoom In or Out		View>Zoom>Zoom		Excel

Locate Appropriate Print and Nonprint Information

In your research, try to use a variety of sources. Because different sources present information in different ways, your research project will be more interesting and balanced when you read a variety of sources.

Literature and Textbooks These texts include any book used as a basis for instruction or a source of information.

Book Indexes A book index, or a bibliography, is an alphabetical listing of books. Some book indexes list books on specific subjects. Others are more general. Some list a variety of topics or resources.

Periodicals Magazines and journals are issued at regular intervals, such as weekly or monthly. One way to locate information in magazines is to use the *Readers' Guide to Periodical Literature.* This guide is available in print form in most libraries.

Technical Manuals A manual is a guide, or handbook, intended to give instruction on how to perform a task or operation. A vehicle owner's manual might give information on how to operate and service a car.

Reference Books Reference books include encyclopedias and almanacs, and are used to locate specific pieces of information.

Electronic Encyclopedias, Databases, and the Internet There are many ways to locate extensive information using your computer. Infotrac, for instance, acts as an online readers guide. CD-ROM encyclopedias can provide easy access to all subjects.

Organize and Convert Information

As you gather information from different sources, taking careful notes, you will need to think about how to **synthesize** the information, or convert it into a unified whole, as well as how to change it into a form your audience will easily understand and that will meet your assignment guidelines.

1. First, ask yourself what you want your audience to know.
2. Then, think about a pattern of organization, a structure that will best show your main ideas. You might ask yourself the following questions:

- When comparing items or ideas, what graphic aids can I use?
- When showing the reasons something happened and the effects of certain actions, what text structure would be best?
- How can I briefly and clearly show important information to my audience?
- Would an illustration or even a cartoon help to make a certain point?

Function	Button	Ribbon	Keyboard Shortcuts	Application
Show or Hide Worksheet Headings		View>Show/Hide>Headings		Excel
SmartArt		Insert>Illustrations>SmartArt		Excel
Solver		Data>Analysis>Solver		Excel
Sort & Filter		Home>Editing>Sort & Filter		Excel
Sort Ascending Order		Data>Sort & Filter> Sort A to Z		Excel
Sort Descending Order		Data>Sort & Filter> Sort Z to A		Excel
Spelling		Review>Proofing>Spelling	F7	Excel
Split Window		View>Window>Split		Excel
Start Excel		Start>Programs>Microsoft Office>Microsoft Office Excel 2007		Excel
Stop Recording		Developer>Code>Stop Recording		Excel
Subtotal		Data>Outline>Subtotal		Excel
Switch Between Open Windows		View>Window>Switch Windows>[Name of Window]	SHIFT + F6	Excel
Symbol		Insert>Text>Symbol		Excel
Table		Insert>Tables>Table		Excel
Text Box		Insert>Text>Text Box		Excel
Themes		Page Layout>Themes> Themes		Excel
Theme Colors		Page Layout>Themes>Colors		Excel
Theme Fonts		Page Layout>Themes>Fonts		Excel
Thesaurus		Review>Proofing>Thesaurus	SHIFT + F7	Excel

New Features in Microsoft Office 2007

Microsoft Office 2007 is a collection of software applications, including Word, Excel, Access, and PowerPoint. Like previous versions of Office, Microsoft Office 2007 allows you to create, communicate, and work in a productive manner. Office 2007 contains new features that allow users to create and format documents with greater ease and with a more professional look.

Interface Tools

The Office Ribbon

The Microsoft Office 2007 interface is based around a new tool called the **Ribbon**. The Ribbon groups tools by their functions. The Ribbon is broken into three different portions:

- The **tabs** are divided among the different tasks you can do in an application.
- The **groups** within each tab break the tasks into subtasks. The groups replace the menus used in previous versions of Office.
- The **buttons** within each group carry out commands or display menus of subcommands.

The **Word Ribbon** provides you with related tasks for formatting text. For example, on the Home tab, the Font group contains tasks related to fonts. Next to the Font group is the Paragraph group, where you can format text. Other tabs, such as Page Layout and Review, contain tools for those areas.

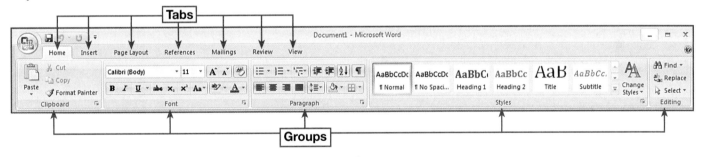

The **Excel Ribbon** allows you to find related tasks involving cell formatting. For example, on the Formulas tab, you can find all major commands involving functions in the Function Library group.

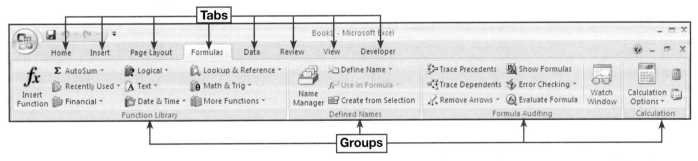

Function	Button	Ribbon	Keyboard Shortcuts	Application
Print Preview		Office>Print>Print Preview		Excel
Properties		Office>Prepare>Properties		Excel
Protect Sheet		Review>Changes>Protect Sheet		Excel
Protect Workbook		Review>Changes>Protect Workbook		Excel
Record Macro		View>Macros>Macros>Record Macro Developer>Code>Macros		Excel
Remove Duplicates		Data>Data Tools>Remove Duplicates		Excel
Remove Split in Window		View>Window>Split		Excel
Repeat		Quick Access Toolbar>Redo	CTRL + Y	Excel
Rotate		Picture Tools>Format>Arrange>Rotate Chart Tools>Format>Arrange>Rotate		Excel
Save		Office>Save	CTRL + S	Excel
Save As		Office>Save As	F12	Excel
Save Macro Enabled		Office>Save As>Excel Macro-Enabled Workbook		Excel
Share Workbook		Review>Changes>Share Workbook		Excel
Show Detail		Data>Outline>Show Detail		Excel
Show All Comments		Review>Comments>Show All Comments		Excel
Show Formula		Formulas>Formula Auditing>Show Formulas	CTRL + `	Excel
Show Markup		Review>Comments>Show Markup		Excel
Show or Hide Worksheet Gridlines		View>Show/Hide>Gridlines		Excel

The **Access Ribbon** makes it easy to create and use a database:
- You can insert records into a datasheet with the Records group on the Home tab.
- You can then use the Database Tools tab to examine the records more closely.
- The Show/Hide group, located in the Database Tools tab, allows you to see relationships between multiple records as well as multiple databases.

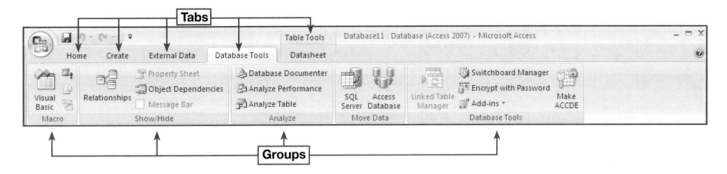

The **PowerPoint Ribbon** helps you to design and create presentations with ease:
- You can manage a presentation with the Slide Show tab, which includes the Set Up group and the Start Slide Show group.
- The other tabs separate the basic areas of presentations, such as design and animation, and enable you to create a visual and informative slide show.

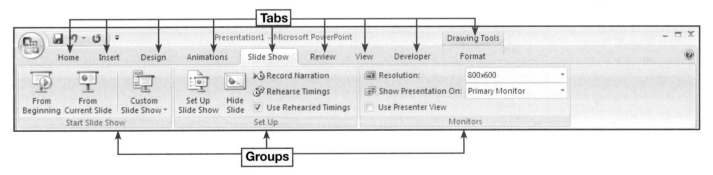

Function	Button	Ribbon	Keyboard Shortcuts	Application
Manage Rules		Home>Styles>Conditional Formatting		Excel
Margins		Page Layout>Page Setup> Margins		Excel
Mark As Final		Office>Prepare>Mark as Final		Excel
Merge Center		Home>Alignment>Merge & Center		Excel
Move Chart		Chart Tools>Design> Location>Move Chart		Excel
Move Chart to New Worksheet		Design>Location>Move Chart		Excel
Name Manager		Formulas>Defined Names>Name Manager	CTRL + F3	Excel
New Comment		Review>Comments> New Comment		Excel
Normal View		View>Workbook Views>Normal View		Excel
Open a File		Office>Open	CTRL + O	Excel
Open a Workbook		Office>Open	CTRL + O	Excel
Orientation		Page Layout>Page Setup>Orientation		Excel
Page Break Preview		View>Workbook Views> Page Break Preview		Excel
Paste		Home>Clipboard>Paste	CTRL + V	Excel
Paste Special		Home>Clipboard>Paste> Paste Special		Excel
Percent Style		Home>Number>Percent Style	CTRL + SHIFT + F9	Excel
PivotChart		Insert>Tables>Pivot Table drop-down Arrow>Pivot Chart		Excel
PivotTable		Insert>Tables>Pivot Table		Excel
Print		Office>Print	CTRL + P	Excel
Print Area		Page Layout>Page Setup> Print Area		Excel

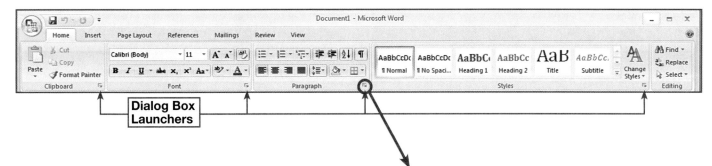

Dialog Box
Launchers

The Dialog Box Launcher

In Office 2007, the dialog boxes have been moved to the appropriate groups in the Ribbon. If a dialog box is available, the **Dialog Box Launcher** will be in the bottom right corner of the group and will open a dialog box with the same name as the group. For example, the Paragraph group's Dialog Box Launcher opens the Paragraph dialog box.

Paragraph Dialog Box

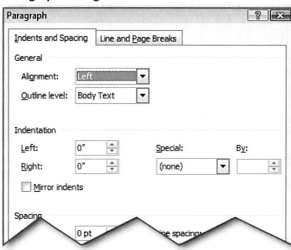

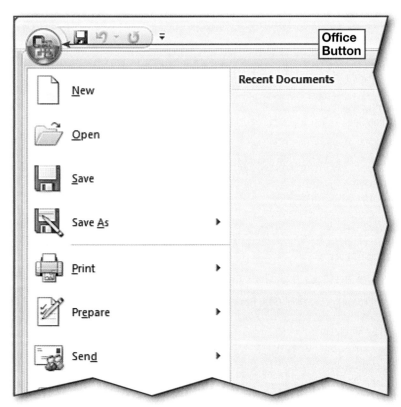

Office
Button

The Microsoft Office Button

The Microsoft Office Button, located in the upper-left corner of Microsoft Word, Excel, Access, and PowerPoint, replaces the File menu. You can use the Office Button to open, save, and print your files. The Publish command, new in Office 2007, also allows you to save your file to a server or to sign your document digitally.

Function	Button	Ribbon	Keyboard Shortcuts	Application
Format Painter		Home>Clipboard> Format Painter		Excel
Freeze Panes		View>Window>Freeze Panes		Excel
From Text		Data>Get External Data>From Text		Excel
From Web		Data>Get External Data>From Web		Excel
Function	fx	Formulas>Function Library> Insert Function	SHIFT + F3	Excel
Header		Insert>Text>Header & Footer		Excel
Help		Microsoft Office Word Help Microsoft Office Excel Help Microsoft Office Access Help Microsoft Office PowerPoint Help	F1	Excel
Hide Detail		Data>Outline>Hide Detail		Excel
Highlight Changes		Review>Changes>Track Changes>Highlight Changes		Excel
Hide Window		View>Window>Hide		Excel
Hyperlink		Insert>Links>Hyperlink	CTRL + K	Excel
Icon Sets		Home>Styles>Conditional Fomatting>Icon Sets		Excel
Increase Decimal		Home>Number>Increase Decimal		Excel
Insert Worksheet		Insert>Cells>Insert> Insert Sheet		Excel
Insert Worksheet Cells		Home>Cells>Insert> Insert Cells		Excel
Inspect Document		Office>Prepare>Inspect Document		Excel
Italic	I	Home>Font>Italic	CTRL + I	Excel
Legend		Chart Tools>Layout>Labels> Legend		Excel
Macros		View>Macros>Macros Developer>Code>Macros	ALT + F8	Excel

The Quick Access Toolbar

The Quick Access Toolbar (or QAT) contains frequently used commands. The default location of the QAT is in the upper-left corner of the screen, next to the Microsoft Office Button. To maximize the work area on your screen, keep the Quick Access Toolbar in its default location.

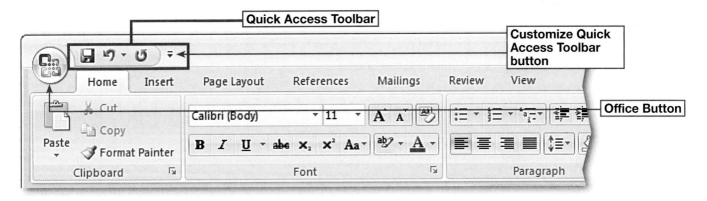

The **Quick Access Toolbar is customizable**, which means that you can add any command to it. To add a command to the Quick Access Toolbar:

- Click the appropriate tab
- Locate the command you want to add
- Right-click the command
- Select Add to Quick Access Toolbar from the shortcut menu

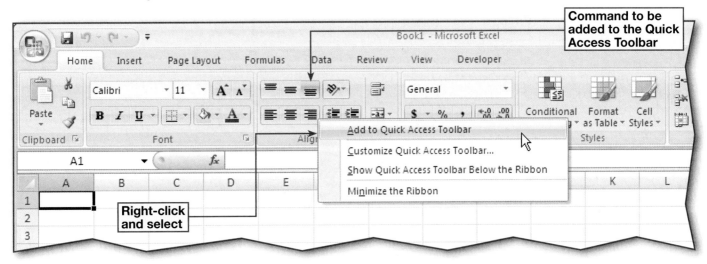

Function	Button	Ribbon	Keyboard Shortcuts	Application
Cut	✂	Home>Clipboard>Cut	`CTRL` + `X`	Excel
Data Bars	📊	Home>Styles>Conditional Formatting>Data Bars		Excel
Data Validation	📋	Data>Data Tools>Data Validation		Excel
Decrease Decimal	.00	Home>Number>Decrease Decimal		Excel
Define Name	📇	Formulas>Defined Names>Define Name		Excel
Delete Rule	✕			Excel
Delete Worksheet Cells	📇	Home>Cells>Delete>Delete Cells		Excel
Edit Comment	📝	Review>Comments>Edit Comment	`SHIFT` + `F2`	Excel
Evaluate Formula	🔍	Formulas>Formula Auditing>Evaluate Formula		Excel
Existing Connections	📄	Data>Get External Data>Existing Connections		Excel
Exit Excel	✕	Office>Exit Excel		Excel
Filter Select Cells	▼	Home>Editing>Sort & Filter>Filter	`CTRL` + `SHIFT` + `L`	Excel
Filter Selected Cells	▼	Data>Sort & Filter>Filter	`CTRL` + `SHIFT` + `L`	Excel
Find	🔍	Home>Editing>Find & Select	`CTRL` + `F`	Excel
Find a Synonym	📖	Review>Proofing>Thesaurus	`SHIFT` + `F7`	Excel
Font		Home>Font>Font		Excel
Font Color	A	Home>Font>Font Color		Excel
Font Size		Home>Font>Font Size		Excel
Format Cells	📋	Home>Cells>Format>Format Cells		Excel
Format Cells in Worksheet	📋	Home>Cells>Format		Excel

Zoom Settings

The zoom level of the screen increases or reduces the size of objects within the window. When proofreading a Word document, you might want a higher zoom level in order to see the text more clearly. When working in a large Excel worksheet, you might want a lower zoom level to see all of the data at once.

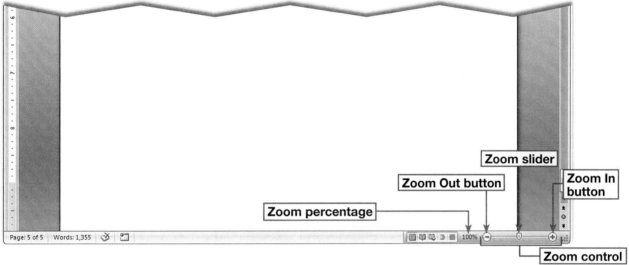

To adjust the zoom level of a program window, use the **Zoom control** at the lower-right corner of the window.

- Click the Zoom In or Zoom Out button to increase or decrease the size of the items on screen by 10 percent increments.

- You can also use the slider to select a specific zoom amount.

You can also adjust the zoom level in the **Zoom dialog box**. To access the Zoom dialog box:

- Click the View tab.
- In the Zoom group, select the Zoom button.

The Zoom dialog box allows you to select a preset zoom level or to enter a specific custom zoom level.

Zoom Dialog box

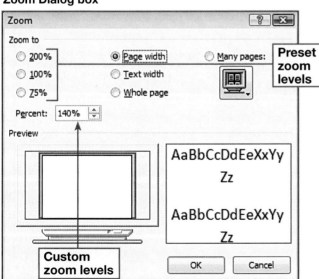

Function	Button	Ribbon	Keyboard Shortcuts	Application
Change Chart Type		Design>Type>Change Chart Type		Excel
Change Picture		Picture Tools>Format>Adjust>Change Picture		Excel
Chart		Insert>Charts>[Chart Type]		Excel
Chart Title		Layout>Labels>Chart Title		Excel
Chart Wall		Chart Tools>Layout>Background>Chart Wall		Excel
Clear		Data>Sort & Filter>Clear		Excel
Clip Art		Insert>Illustrations>Clip Art		Excel
Close a Window		Office>Close	CTRL + W or CTRL + F4	Excel
Close a Workbook		Office>Close	CTRL + W or CTRL + F4	Excel
Color Scales		Home>Styles>Conditional Formatting>Color Scales		Excel
Compare & Merge		Office>Excel Options>Customize>Compare and Merge Workbooks		Excel
Compatibility Checker		Office>Prepare>Run Compatibility Checker		Excel
Conditional Formatting		Home>Styles>Conditional Formatting		Excel
Contrast		Picture Tools>Format>Adjust>Contrast		Excel
Copy		Home>Clipboard>Copy	CTRL + C	Excel
Create a New File		Office>New	CTRL + N	Excel
Create a New Workbook		Office>New	CTRL + N	Excel
Create From Selection		Formulas>Defines Names>Create From Selection		Excel

The Mini Toolbar

The Mini Toolbar appears when you select text and enables you to format the text at the point of use in the document instead of with the Ribbon. The Mini Toolbar includes fonts, font styles, font size, alignment, indentation, bullets, and text color.

When text is selected, the Mini Toolbar is semitransparent until you roll your pointer over it. When the pointer rests on the toolbar, it becomes opaque.

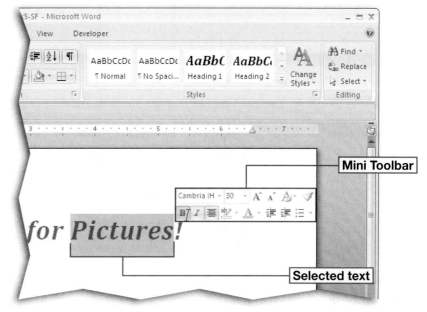

Mini Toolbar

for Pictures!

Selected text

Options Dialog box

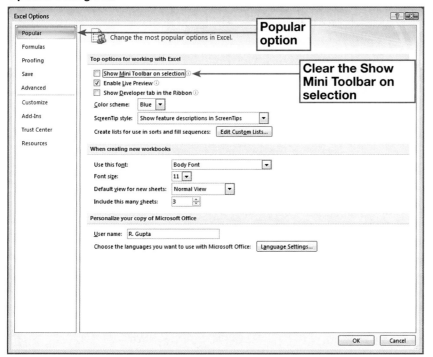

Popular option

Clear the Show Mini Toolbar on selection

To turn off the Mini Toolbar:
- Click the Microsoft Office Button
- Select the application's Options button in the lower-right corner
- Select Popular from the listing of options
- Clear the Show Mini Toolbar on selection check box.

To turn the Mini Toolbar back on:
- Click the Microsoft Office Button
- Select the application's Options button in the lower-right corner
- Select Popular from the listing of options
- Select the Show Mini Toolbar on selection check box

The following commands were covered in this book.

All of the commands have speech function accessibility, with the proper Office setup. See **Help>Speech Functions> Accessibility** in any Microsoft Office application for instructions.

Function	Button	Ribbon	Keyboard Shortcuts	Application
Accept/Reject Changes		Review>Changes>Track Changes>Accept/Reject Changes		Excel
Add Digital Signature		Office>Prepare>Add a Digital Signature		Excel
Advanced Filter		Data>Sort & Filter>Advanced Filter		Excel
Align Cell Contents in Worksheet		Home>Alignment> [Alignment Option]		Excel
Allow Users to Edit		Review>Changes>Allow Users to Edit Ranges		Excel
Arrange Windows		View>Window>Arrange All		Excel
AutoFilter		Data>Sort & Filter>Filter	CTRL + SHIFT + L	Excel
AutoSum	Σ	Formulas>Function Library>AutoSum	ALT + =	Excel
Axes		Chart Tools>Layout> Axes>Axes		Excel
Axis Titles of a Chart		Layout>Labels>Axis Titles		Excel
Bold	**B**	Home>Font>Bold	CTRL + B	Excel
Borders		Home>Font>Border		Excel
Bottom 10		Home>Styles>Conditional Formatting>Top/Bottom Rules>Bottom 10 Items		Excel
Brightness		Picture Tools>Format> Adjust>Brightness		Excel
Cell Styles		Home>Styles>Cell Styles		Excel

Contextual Tabs

Contextual tabs appear only when you work with certain objects. Contextual tabs are available with objects such as charts, tables, and pictures.

In Microsoft Word 2007 and Microsoft PowerPoint 2007, the Picture Tools contextual tab appears when you insert a picture into a document or slide. Included in the Picture Tools tab is the Format tab, which contains groups to help you adjust, place, and style the picture.

When you have finished working with the picture, select an area outside of the picture's boundaries. The Picture Tools tab disappears.

In Microsoft Excel 2007, the Chart Tools contextual tab appears when you want to insert a chart into a worksheet. Included in the Chart Tools tab are the Design, Layout, and Format tabs, which all contain groups to help you insert a chart.

When you have finished working on the chart and select an area outside of the chart's boundaries, the Chart Tools tab disappears.

Word Ribbon

Picture Tools contextual tab

PowerPoint Ribbon

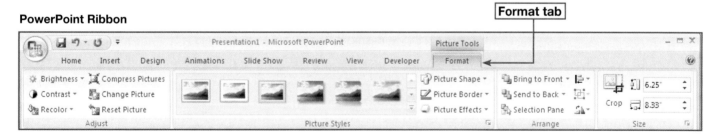

Format tab

Excel Ribbon

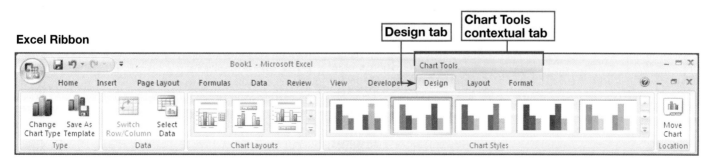

Design tab

Chart Tools contextual tab

Step-By-Step

1
In your **Historic** presentation, move to **Slide 2**.

2
Start **Word**. Locate and open the data file **Founder.docx**.

3
Select the bulleted list. Click **Home>Copy**. Save and close the document.

4
Switch to your **Historic** presentation. Click in the **Slide 2** text box. Press ←BACKSPACE once. Click **Home>Paste**.

5
Click the **Paste Options** drop-down arrow. Confirm that **Use Destination Theme** is selected (see Figure 1.27).

6
Select the text **First mayor of Greenhaven** and **Founder of Greenhaven University**. Click **Paragraph> Increase List Level**. Deselect the text box.

7
⒤CHECK Your screen should look like Figure 1.28.

8
Save and close your files.

APPENDIX A Integrated Applications

POWERPOINT INTEGRATION
Exercise 12: Copy and Paste Data between Applications

You can use the Cut, Copy, and Paste functions to insert information created in a Word document into a PowerPoint slide. If the slide has a bulleted format, each paragraph of the pasted material will become a bulleted item. Use Paste Options to specify if the pasted information will retain its original formatting.

FIGURE 1.27 Paste Options drop-down menu

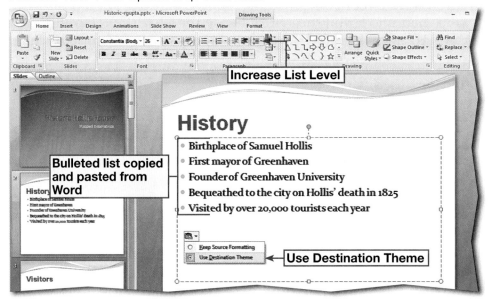

FIGURE 1.28 Text pasted in PowerPoint and formatted

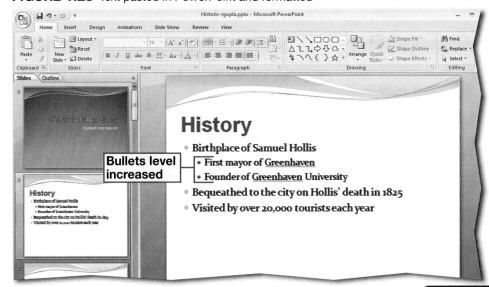

Design and Layout Tools

The enhanced design and layout functions in Microsoft Office 2007 allow you to produce professional-looking documents quickly and easily.

Themes

Themes can be applied with one click to provide consistent fonts, charts, shapes, tables, and so on throughout an entire document.

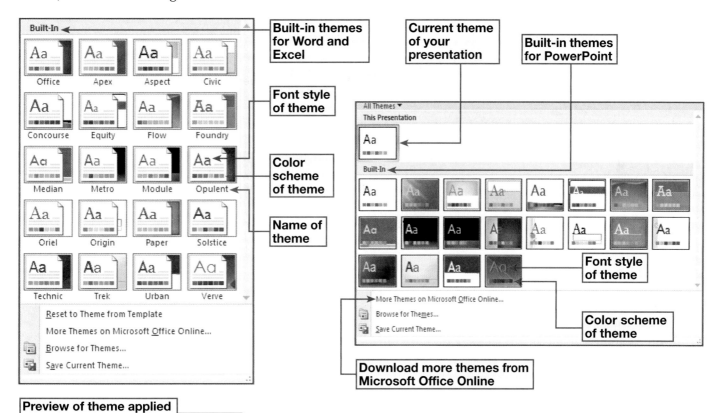

Built-in themes for Word and Excel

Current theme of your presentation

Built-in themes for PowerPoint

Font style of theme

Color scheme of theme

Name of theme

Font style of theme

Color scheme of theme

Download more themes from Microsoft Office Online

Preview of theme applied to document

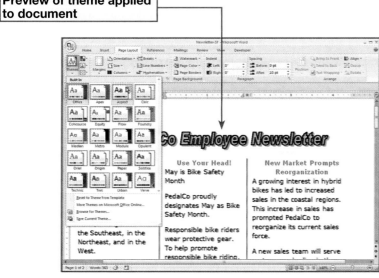

The entire document is linked to a theme. If the theme is changed, new colors, fonts, and effects are applied to the entire document.

Microsoft Office 2007 also allows you to see how a theme would look in a document without applying the theme. As the pointer is rolled over each theme, the document changes to show a Live Preview of what it would look like with each theme. Additional themes are available through Microsoft Office Online.

APPENDIX A Integrated Applications

Data File

1. Start **PowerPoint**.

2. Locate and open the data file **Historic.pptx**. Save as: Historic-[your first initial and last name].

3. Choose **Home>New Slide drop down menu>Slides from Outline**.

4. In the **Insert Outline** dialog box, browse to and select the data file **Needs.docx**. Click **Insert**.

5. Choose **Home>Slides> Layout**. Change the layout of the second slide to **Title and Content**.

6. **(i) CHECK** Your screen should look like Figure 1.25.

7. Choose **Design>Themes drop down arrow>More**. Select the **Flow** theme (use ScreenTips to find the correct theme).

8. Move to **Slide 4**.

9. **(i) CHECK** Your screen should look like Figure 1.26.

10. Save and close your files.

➥ *Continue to the next exercise.*

POWERPOINT INTEGRATION
Exercise 11: Insert Word Outlines into PowerPoint

You can use Word's Outline View to key the text of a presentation and then import the Word outline into PowerPoint. When you import an outline into PowerPoint, text that is formatted Level 1 becomes Title text, while Level 2 text is inserted into the body of the slides. Once you have imported your text, you can use the PowerPoint functions to design your presentation.

FIGURE 1.25 Word outline inserted into presentation

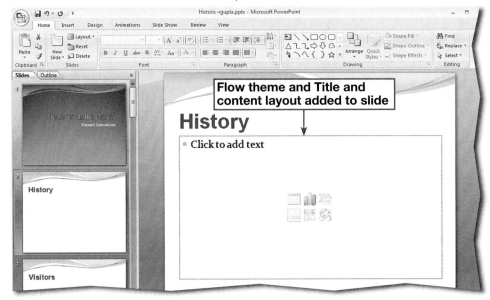

FIGURE 1.26 PowerPoint slide created from Word outline

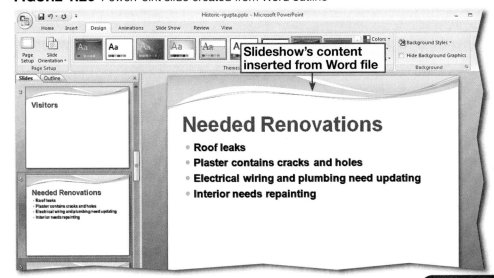

Quick Styles

While themes change the overall colors, fonts, and effects of a document, Quick Styles determine how those elements are combined and which color, font, and effect will be the dominant style. Roll your pointer over each Quick Style to get a Live Preview.

Word 2007 allows you to choose from specific styles for headings, quotations, and titles, or you can choose from a Style Set list to format your entire document. You can even choose a Style Set first and then apply Quick Styles to some elements.

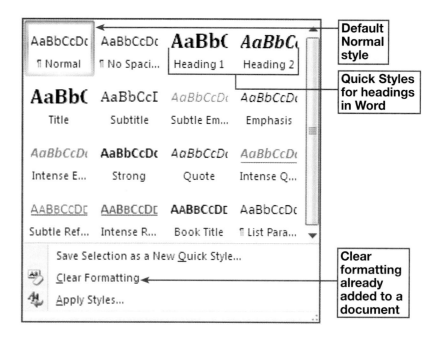

Default Normal style

Quick Styles for headings in Word

Clear formatting already added to a document

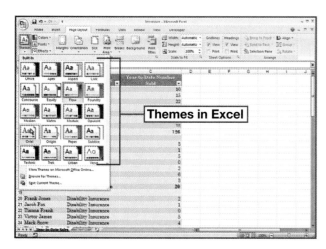

Themes in Excel

Background Styles

Excel 2007 offers cell styles that work like Quick Styles. In the Themes group, click the Themes drop-down arrow to choose a theme.

PowerPoint 2007 uses Quick Styles with the Background Styles function, located on the Design tab. The background styles can be used with any of the themes in PowerPoint.

1 In your **Estate** database, close the **Listings** table.

2 Choose **External Data> Import>Text File**.

3 In the **Get External Data– Text File** dialog box, click the **Browse** button.

4 In the **File Open** dialog box, locate and select the data file **Added.txt**. Click **Open**.

5 Select **Append a copy of the records to the Table:**, then click the drop-down arrow and choose **Listings**.

6 ⓘ**CHECK** Your dialog box should look like Figure 1.23.

7 Click **OK**. Click **Next**. Click the check box next to **First Row Contains Field Names**. Click **Finish**.

8 Click **Close**. Open the **Listings** table.

9 ⓘ**CHECK** Your screen should look like Figure 1.24.

10 Close the table.

➤ *Continue to the next exercise.*

ACCESS INTEGRATION
Exercise 10: Import Word Data

You can transfer data from Word to Access. To do so, you must first save the Word document in a Plain Text Format. Saving a Word document as a plain text file (.txt) removes the formatting from that document. Importing Word data, such as customer information, into an Access database is very similar to importing Excel data into a database.

FIGURE 1.23 Get External Data-Text File dialog box

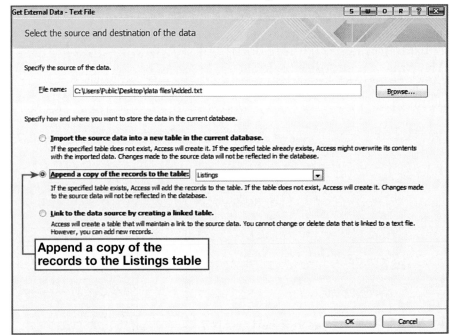

FIGURE 1.24 Text data imported into Access

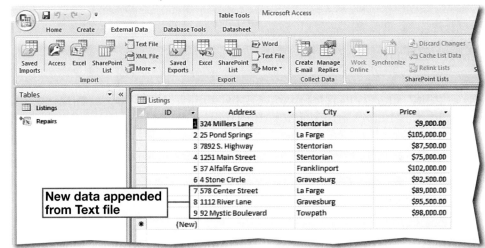

Security Tools

Microsoft Office 2007 includes new security features that protect your documents and computer from hacking and identity theft.

Mark as Final

After you have finished a document, you can use the Mark as Final command to make the document read-only, which prevents any changes from being made. This allows you to share the document with others without the fear of anything being lost or changed.

The Mark as Final command is located in the Microsoft Office Button menu, in the Prepare section.

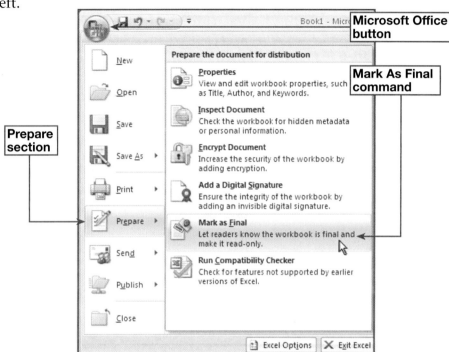

Digital Signatures

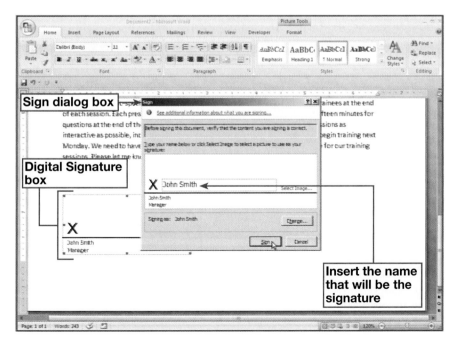

You can also digitally sign a document to authenticate any digital information that you create, such as documents, e-mails, macros, and databases. Cryptography assures that the content has not been changed since the document was signed.

1 In your **Estate** database, open the **Listings** table. Choose **External Data> Export>Word**.

2 In the **Export–RTF file** dialog box, click **Browse**. In the **File Save** dialog box, choose the correct location to save the file.

3 In the **File name** box, key: Realty-[your first initial and last name].

4 In the **Save as type** box, make sure **Rich Text Format** is selected.

5 ⓘ**CHECK** Your dialog box should look like Figure 1.21. Click **Save**. Click **OK**. Click **Close**.

6 Start Word. Open your **Realty.rtf** file.

7 ⓘ**CHECK** Your screen should look like Figure 1.22.

8 Save and close your files.

➡ *Continue to the next exercise.*

ACCESS INTEGRATION
Exercise 9: Export Access Data to Word

You might want to include data from an Access database in a Word document. For example, if you need the data for a business report, this is a quick and accurate option. You can export data from Access to Word while preserving the original formatting. If you are not sure what type of word processor you, or another person, will use later to read the data, you should export the data in Rich Text Format. Most word processors can read .rtf files.

FIGURE 1.21 Export as Rich Text Format

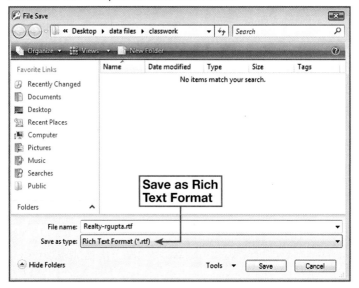

FIGURE 1.22 Access data exported to Word

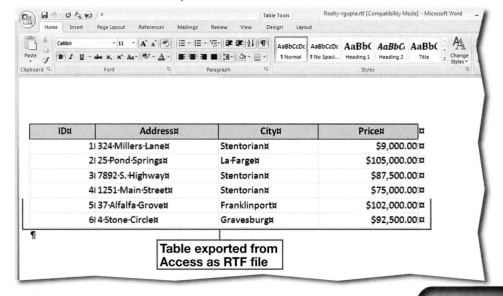

Operate Microsoft Office 2007 Using Windows XP

Glencoe *iCheck Series Microsoft Office 2007* has been created and written to show Microsoft Office 2007 on the new Windows Vista operating system. Microsoft Office 2007 can also be used with the Windows XP operating system.

Most tasks can be completed on either operating system with the instructions in this book. However, there are a few tasks that have slightly different instructions or may not look exactly the same as in the textbook. This section shows the steps needed to complete these tasks with Windows XP.

The following steps are shown using Microsoft Word 2007, but the steps apply to all Office 2007 applications. Depending on how hardware and software was installed on your computer, you may need to ask your teacher for further instruction.

Use Windows XP to Start a Program

1 In the Windows taskbar, click the Start button.

2 In the Start menu, select Programs.

3 In the Programs menu, select Microsoft Office.

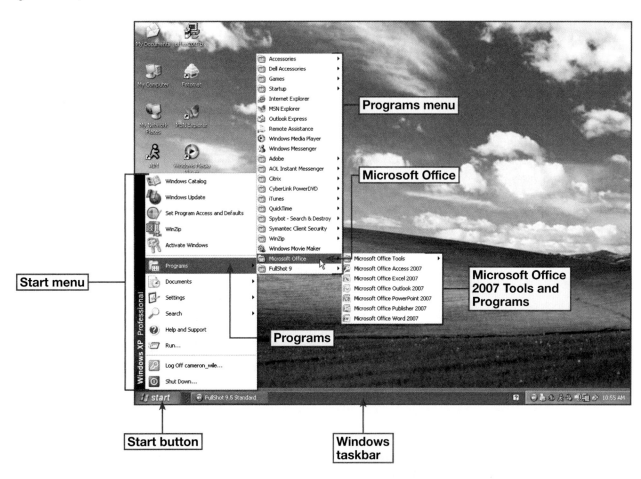

APPENDIX A Integrated Applications

ACCESS INTEGRATION
Exercise 8: Export Access Data to Excel

Sometimes people need to use data in Excel instead of Access. Exporting data from Access to Excel is as easy as importing data from Excel. For example, you can export the data from a table in an Access database and save it as an Excel worksheet.

1. Open your copy of the **Estate** file. Open the **Listings** table in **Datasheet** view. Select **External Data>Export> Excel**.

2. In the **Export-Excel Spreadsheet** dialog box, click **Browse**. In the **File Save** dialog box, choose the correct location to save your file. In the **File name** box, key: Current-[your first initial and last name]. Click **Save**.

3. Click the **File Format** drop-down arrow. Choose **Excel Workbook (*.xlsx)**.

4. Check the **Export Data with formatting and layout** box.

5. ⓘ**CHECK** Your dialog box should look like Figure 1.19. Click **OK**. Click **Close**.

6. Start Excel. Open your **Current.xlsx** file.

7. ⓘ**CHECK** Your screen should look like Figure 1.20.

8. Save and close your **Current** file.

➡ *Continue to the next exercise.*

FIGURE 1.19 Export-Excel Spreadsheet dialog box

FIGURE 1.20 Excel file with exported Access data

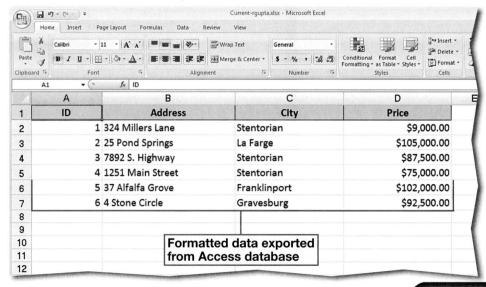

Operate Microsoft Office 2007 Using Windows XP (Continued)

Use Windows XP to Start a Program (Continued)

Document title

4 Select the program you would like to open.

5 Depending on your screen settings, your window may not be fully maximized. To maximize the window, select the Maximize button, located next to the Close button.

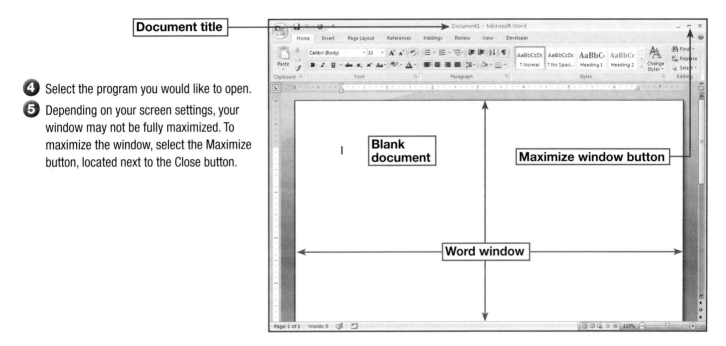

Blank document

Maximize window button

Word window

Use Windows XP to Open a Document

Office Button

Open

1 Start the desired Office program.

2 In the program window, select the Office Button to open the Office menu.

3 In the Office menu, select Open. The Open dialog box will appear.

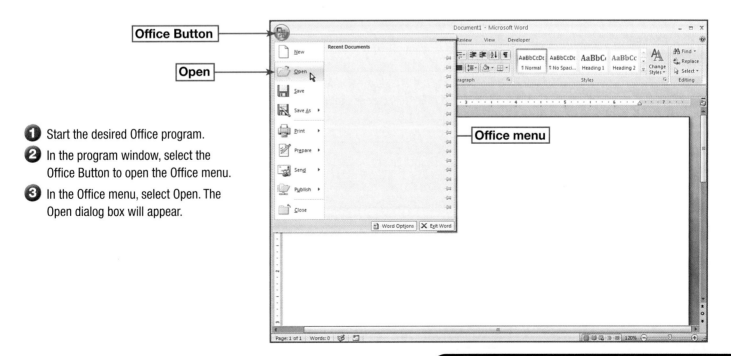

Office menu

APPENDIX **A** **Integrated Applications**

ACCESS INTEGRATION
Exercise 7: Link Excel Data to Access

You can link an Excel worksheet to a new Access table. When linking a table, you must create a new linked table in Access. You cannot link the Excel worksheet to an existing Access table. There are a few benefits to linking an Excel file to a database, as opposed to importing it. If you import an Excel file to a database and make changes to the original, you will have to reimport it. When a database is linked to an Excel file, the link is always to the most recent version of the Excel file.

FIGURE 1.17 Get External Data—Excel Spreadsheet dialog box

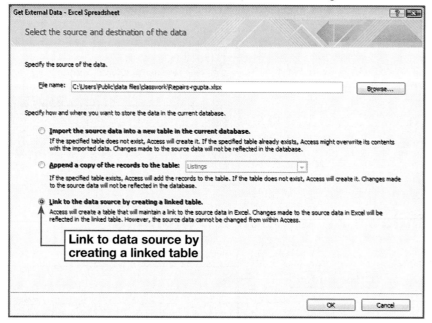

FIGURE 1.18 New Access table linked to Excel worksheet

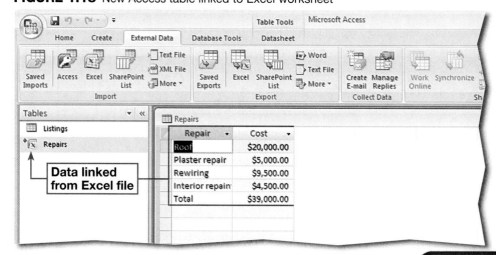

1. Open the data file **Repairs.xlsx**. Save as: Repairs-[your first initial and last name]. Exit Excel.

2. Open the data file **Estate.accdb**. Copy the file to your folder.

3. Choose **External Data> Import>Excel**. In the **Get External Data–Excel Spreadsheet** dialog box, in the **File name** box, navigate to your saved **Repairs.xlsx** file. Click **Open**.

4. Select **Link to the data source by creating a linked table** (see Figure 1.17). Click **OK**.

5. In the **Link Spreadsheet Wizard**, select **Show Worksheets** and click **Next**.

6. Check the **First Row Contains Column Headings** check box. Click **Next**.

7. In the **Linked Table Name** box, key: Repairs.

8. Click **Finish**. Click **OK**. Open the **Repairs** table.

9. **(i)CHECK)** Your screen should look like Figure 1.18. Save your Excel file.

➥ *Continue to the next exercise.*

Operate Microsoft Office 2007 Using Windows XP (Continued)

Use Windows XP to Open a Document (Continued)

④ In the Open dialog box, click the Look in drop-down arrow. Navigate to the location of the file to be opened. If necessary, ask your teacher for the file's location.

⑤ When you have navigated to the correct location, all files in that location will be displayed. Click the appropriate file.

⑥ In the lower-right corner of the dialog box, click Open.

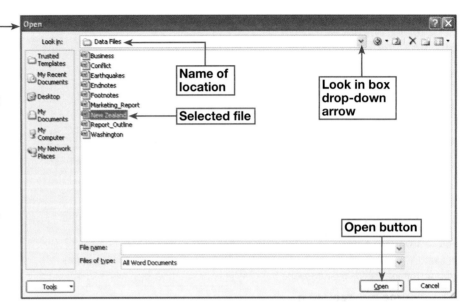

Use Windows XP to Save a Document

① When you are ready to save a file, click the Office Button to display the Office menu.

② In the Office menu, click Save. If the file has been saved before, it will be saved, with your changes, to the same location with the same file name. If the file has not been saved before, the Save As dialog box will open.

③ In the Save As dialog box, select the Save in box drop-down arrow. Ask your teacher where the file should be saved, and navigate to that location.

④ Double-click the name of the save location. The name should now be the only item located in the Save in box.

⑤ In the File name box, key the name under which you would like to save the file. Click the Save button in the lower-right corner.

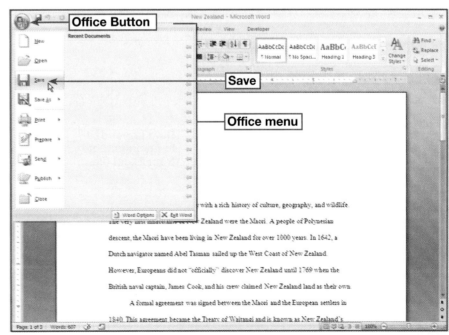

ACCESS INTEGRATION
Exercise 6: Import Excel Data (Continued)

8 Click **OK**.

9 Save and close the table. Click **Next**. The **Import Spreadsheet Wizard** dialog box appears (see Figure 1.15).

10 Click **Next**.

11 Click **Finish**. In the dialog box that opens, click **Save Import Steps**.

12 Click **Save Import**.

13 Open the **Listings** table from the **Tables** task pane.

14 (**CHECK**) Your screen should look like Figure 1.16.

15 Save and close your files.

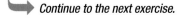 *Continue to the next exercise.*

FIGURE 1.15 Import Spreadsheet Wizard dialog box

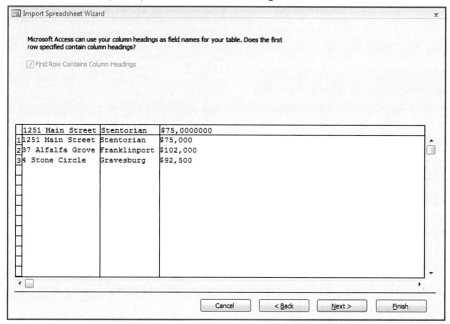

FIGURE 1.16 Excel data imported into Access

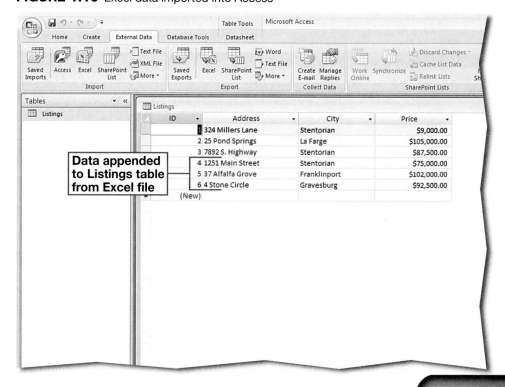

Operate Microsoft Office 2007 Using Windows XP (Continued)

Use Windows XP to Save a Document (Continued)

Sometimes you might want to use the Save As function instead of the Save function. The Save As and Save functions perform differently. The Save function will replace the original file with the new file. The Save As function will leave the original document as it was and will save the revised document as a separate file with a new name.

1 When you are ready to save a file, click the Office Button.

2 On the Office menu, select Save As. The Save As dialog box will open.

3 In the Save As dialog box, select the Save in box drop-down arrow. Ask your teacher where the file should be saved, and navigate to that location.

4 Double-click the name of the save location. The name should now be the only item located in the Save in box.

5 In the File name box, key the name under which you would like to save the file. Give the file a new name that distinguishes it from the original document. Click the Save button in the lower-right corner to save your file.

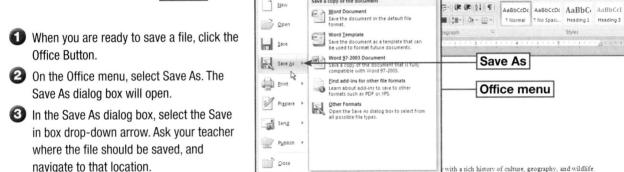

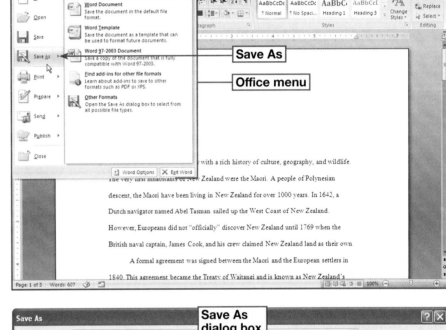

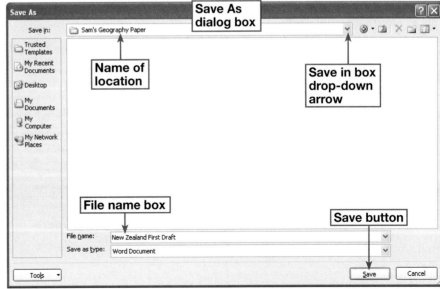

1. Start **Access**.

2. With your teacher's help, locate the data file **Estate.accdb**. Copy the database to your folder before working in it.

3. Open the **Listings** table in **Datasheet View**.

4. **①CHECK** Your screen should look like Figure 1.13.

5. Choose **External Data> Import>Excel**.

6. The **Get External Data– Excel Spreadsheet** dialog box opens. In the **File name** box, browse to and select the data file **Recent.xlsx**. Click **Open**. Click **Append a copy of the records to the table:** and select **Listings** from the drop-down menu.

7. **①CHECK** Your dialog box should look like Figure 1.14.

Continued on the next page.

ACCESS INTEGRATION
Exercise 6: Import Excel Data

Both Excel and Access allow you to organize and analyze related information. For example, you might use Excel to perform calculations on data. However, you might want to put that data into an Access database. For example, if you are creating a database that contains information about your customers, and some of that information already exists in an Excel file, you can import data from Excel to Access without having to rekey the data.

FIGURE 1.13 Listings table

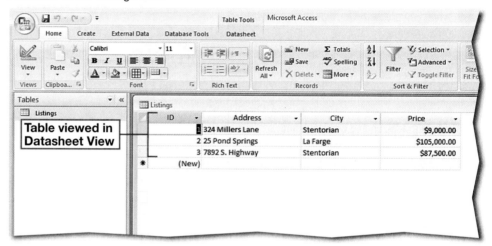

FIGURE 1.14 External Data—Excel Spreadsheet dialog box

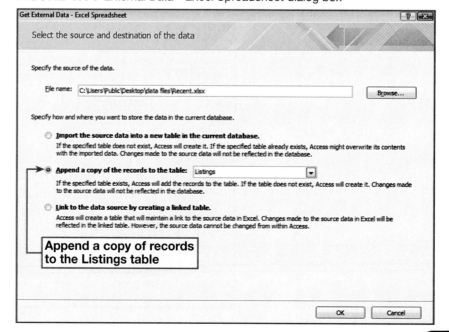

Operate Microsoft Office 2007 Using Windows XP (Continued)

Use Windows XP and Insert SmartArt

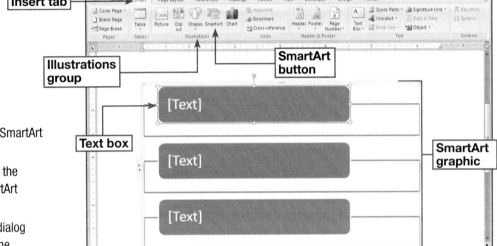

1. Click where you want to insert the SmartArt graphic.

2. On the Ribbon, on the Insert tab, in the Illustrations group, select the SmartArt button.

3. In the Choose a SmartArt Graphic dialog box, select the type and layout of the SmartArt graphic.

4. The graphic will appear in the area that you designated. On the left side of the SmartArt graphic is the Text Pane Launcher. Click the Launcher to enter text into the graphic.

5. The Text pane will open either on the left or right side of the graphic, depending on the space available. Key your text into the appropriate spots in the Text pane. The Live Preview function shows the text in the graphic as you key it in the Text pane.

6. To close the Text pane, select the Text pane close button in the top-right corner of the pane.

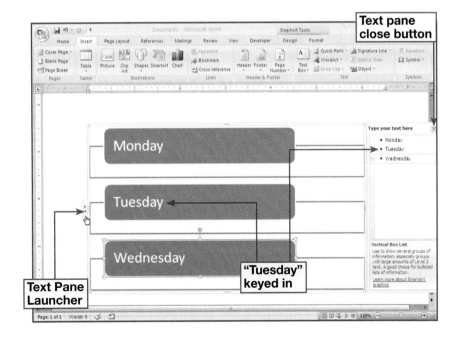

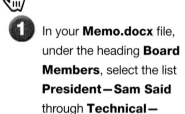

EXCEL INTEGRATION
Exercise 5: Create a Linked Object in Excel

A linked object is a file, table, worksheet, chart, or graphic that is inserted into an Excel workbook but is not located within the actual document. Instead, the content of a linked object is in a separate file known as the source file. In this exercise you will insert a Word document as a linked object in an Excel worksheet.

1. In your **Memo.docx** file, under the heading **Board Members**, select the list **President—Sam Said** through **Technical— Neville Jones**.

2. Click **Copy** .

3. In your **Budget.xlsx** file, select the **Board Members** tab. Click cell **A3**.

4. On the **Home** tab, select the **Paste** drop-down arrow. Select **Paste Special**.

5. In the **Paste Special** dialog box, select the button next to **Paste link**. Click **Text**.

6. ⓘ**CHECK** Your dialog box should look like Figure 1.11. Click **OK**.

7. In your **Memo** file, select the name **Neville**. Click **Cut** . Key: Faye. Press the **spacebar** once.

8. Click **Save** .

9. Go to your **Budget** workbook. Click in cell **A2**.

10. ⓘ**CHECK** Your screen should look like Figure 1.12.

11. Save and close your files.

➥ *Continue to the next exercise.*

FIGURE 1.11 Paste Special dialog box

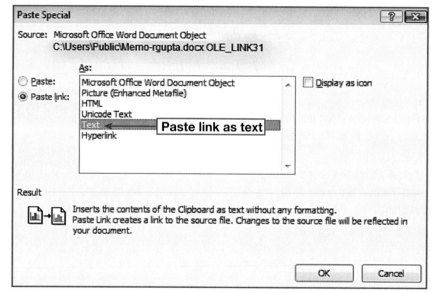

FIGURE 1.12 Linked object in Excel worksheet

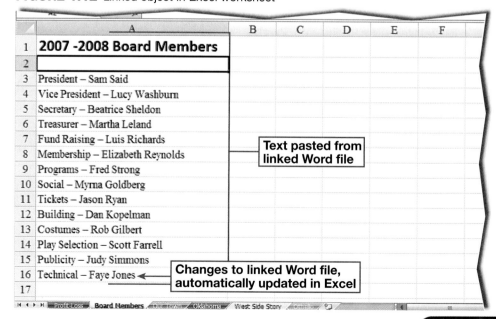

Operating Your Computer

The following tips should be used to operate your computer correctly. Your teacher may provide you with additional instructions.

Turning the computer on

✓ Make sure there are no disks in the computer's disk drives.

✓ Power on the computer and monitor.

✓ Wait for the start-up process to finish before starting any programs. You may be required to enter a network user ID and password at this time.

✓ Insert disks, DVDs, and CDs.

Turning the computer off

✓ Save data and files if necessary and close all windows.

✓ Remove any disks, DVDs, and CDs.

✓ Use the desktop shut-down procedure. Click Start on the taskbar, click Shut Down, choose the Shut down option, and click OK.

✓ Power off the computer and monitor (if necessary).

Disks and CD-ROMs

✓ Handle disks, DVDs, and CDs carefully, holding them by the edges.

✓ Protect disks, DVDs, and CDs from dirt, scratches, moisture, extremes in temperature, and magnetic fields.

✓ Insert and remove disks, DVDs, and CDs gently.

✓ Do not attempt to remove a disk, DVD, or CD when the drive indicator light is on.

Work area

✓ Keep the area around your computer neat and free from dust and dirt.

✓ Do not eat or drink near your computer, as spilled food and drinks can cause damage to the computer.

 Using Student Data Files

To complete some Exercises in this book, Data Files are required.

● When you see the Data File icon, locate the needed files before beginning the exercise.

● Data Files are available at the Student Online Learning Center at glencoe.com. Your teacher will tell you where to find these files.

● Some exercises require you to continue working on a file you created in an earlier exercise. If you were absent and could not complete the previous exercise, your teacher may choose to provide you with the Solution File for the missed exercise.

1. In your **Budget.xlsx** file, choose **Office>Excel Options**.

2. In the **Excel Options** dialog box, click **Advanced**.

3. Under **Cut, Copy, and Paste**, make sure the **Show Paste Options buttons** check box is selected. Click **OK**.

4. In your **Memo.docx** file, select all the text (through **$5,845.00**) in the table **Event Net**. Click **Copy**.

5. In your **Budget** file, select the **Othello** tab. Click cell **B27**. Click **Paste**.

6. Move your mouse over **Paste Options** so that the drop-down arrow appears.

7. Click the arrow. On the drop-down list, choose **Keep Source Formatting** (see Figure 1.9). Click cell **A31**.

8. **ⓘCHECK** Your screen should look like Figure 1.10.

9. Save your files.

Continue to the next exercise.

EXCEL INTEGRATION
Exercise 4: Use Paste Options

Use Paste Options to specify the format of the information you are pasting into Excel from another file or application. For example, you can use Paste Options to copy a long list of names from Word and paste them into a workbook. Paste Options allows you to choose whether pasted content should keep the formatting used in your source file, match the formatting used in your destination file, or apply no formatting at all.

FIGURE 1.9 Paste Options drop-down list

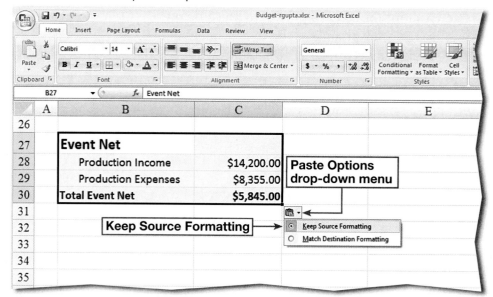

FIGURE 1.10 Document with pasted information

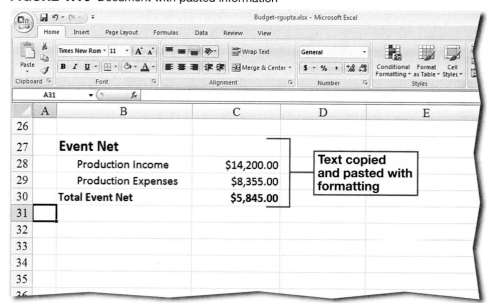

UNIT 1

Excel 2007: Business and Personal Finances

Unit Objectives:

After completing this Unit, you will be able to:

LESSON 1

Excel Basics

LESSON 2

Create Data and Content

LESSON 3

Format Data and Content

LESSON 4

Analyze Data

LESSON 5

Manage Workbooks

Why It Matters

Microsoft Excel is a powerful business tool. Using Excel, you can organize lists of data, calculate expenses for a project, create charts, and much more. A skilled Excel user is a good candidate for a variety of jobs. *What is one way that Excel might help you with your schoolwork?*

 Go Online   **REAL WORLD CONNECTION**

glencoe.com

Go to the **Online Learning Center** and select your book. Choose **Unit 1** to learn how businesses use spreadsheet applications in the real world.

1 In your **Memo.docx** file, select all the text (through **$14,200.00**) in the table **Production Income.** Click **Home>Clipboard> Copy** .

2 In your **Budget.xlsx** file, select the **Othello** tab. Click cell **B21**.

3 Choose **Home>Paste**. Click the **Paste Special** drop-down arrow.

4 In the **Paste Special** dialog box, under **As:**, choose **Text**.

5 ⓘ**CHECK** Your dialog box should look like Figure 1.7. Click **OK**.

6 ⓘ**CHECK** Your screen should look like Figure 1.8.

7 Insert dollar signs into the table. Save your files.

➡ *Continue to the next exercise.*

You Should Know

Use **Paste Special** to choose the file format of pasted data. Use **Paste Options** to format pasted text.

EXCEL INTEGRATION
Exercise 3: Use Paste Special

Use Paste Special to specify the file format of the information you are pasting into Excel from another file or application. Using Paste Special, you can paste information in a variety of formats, including rich text format (RTF) and HTML. You can also paste content as a hyperlink or as a picture.

FIGURE 1.7 Paste Special dialog box

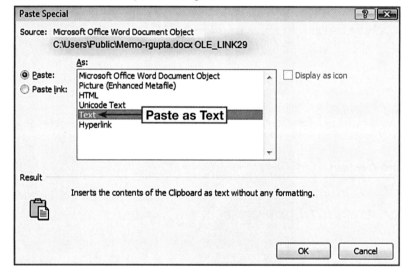

FIGURE 1.8 Document with pasted information

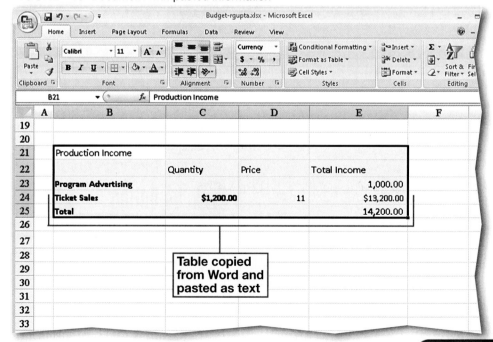

How Can Spreadsheet Skills Advance Your Career?

Career ✓ Checklist

To use spreadsheets effectively in the workplace, remember to:

✓ Use standard formats and fonts.

✓ Group related worksheets into a single file.

✓ Hide distracting rows, columns, or worksheets to focus on essential information.

✓ Use color to group and classify information.

✓ Format your spreadsheet for easy printing.

Spreadsheets are complex tools that are used to measure performance, plan a budget, and make other calculations. If you have spreadsheet skills, you can also learn to manage and manipulate information in the workplace. Spreadsheets are used to maintain schedules, track expenses, and manage large-scale projects in a variety of careers.

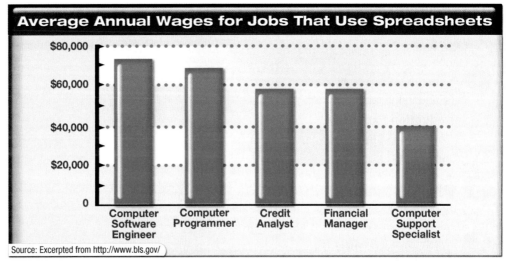

Average Annual Wages for Jobs That Use Spreadsheets

Source: Excerpted from http://www.bls.gov/

Business

Spreadsheet software is valuable in the world of business. Credit analysts and financial managers use a wide range of spreadsheet functions to input and assess credit histories, financial portfolios, and budgets.

Computer Occupations

There are a wide variety of high-salary jobs in the computer industry that use spreadsheets for their non-mathematical capabilities. Computer software engineers and computer programmers use spreadsheets to classify and manipulate the huge amount of complex information needed to analyze programming problems, write programs, and create software. Computer support specialists might use spreadsheets to log and track data from their support calls.

READING CHECK

1 **Evaluate** How could spreadsheet skills improve your chances of obtaining a higher salary?

2 **Math** Which of the careers listed in the chart has the highest annual wage potential?

1 Start **Excel**.

2 Locate and open the data file **Budget.xlsx**. Save as: Budget-[your first initial and last name] (for example, *Budget-rgupta*).

3 Start **Word**. Locate and open the data file **Memo.docx**. Save as: Memo-[your first initial and last name].

4 In the memo, select all the text in the table **Production Expenses**. Click **Home>Clipboard> Copy** 🗐.

5 **①CHECK** Your screen should look like Figure 1.5.

6 Switch to your **Budget** file. Select the **Othello** tab. Click cell **B1**.

7 Click **Home>Clipboard> Paste** 🗐. Click **A20**.

8 **①CHECK** Your screen should look like Figure 1.6.

9 Save your files.

➡ *Continue to the next exercise.*

EXCEL INTEGRATION
Exercise 2: Copy and Paste between Applications

If you have information in a Word document that you would like to import to an Excel spreadsheet, you can use the Copy and Paste functions on the Clipboard to copy text from Word and paste it into an Excel worksheet. When you copy and paste text instead of cutting and pasting, the text remains in both the original and the destination file.

FIGURE 1.5 Text copied in Word document

Production Expenses		Quantity	Price	Total Expense
Fees				
Rights and Rentals				$2,500.00
Theater Fees				$500.00
Posters		250	$3.00	$750.00
Programs		600	$1.50	$900.00
Copying				$40.00
Postal Fees				$50.00
Scene Shop Rental				$500.00
Daily Advertising				
Half Page Ad				$85.00
Full Page Ads		2	$165.00	$330.00
Technical Costs				
Costumes				$1,000.00
Props				$250.00
Set				$1,250.00
Lighting				$200.00
Total				$8,355.00

Table selected and copied

Section: 1 Page: 1 of 2 Words: 55/218 150%

FIGURE 1.6 Text pasted into Excel worksheet

	A	B	C	D	E	F	G
1		Production Expenses					
2			Quantity	Price	Total Expense		
3		Fees					
4		Rights and Rentals			$2,500.00		
5		Theater Fees			$500.00		
6		Posters	250	$3.00	$750.00		
7		Programs	600	$1.50	$900.00		
8		Copying			$40.00		
9		Postal Fees			$50.00		
10		Scene Shop Rental			$500.00		
11		Daily Advertising					
12		Half Page Ad			$85.00		
13		Full Page Ads	2	$165.00	$330.00		
14		Technical Costs					
15		Costumes			$1,000.00		
16		Props			$250.00		
17		Set			$1,250.00		
18		Lighting			$200.00		
19		Total			$8,355.00		

Table copied and pasted from Word

Othello tab

Prof. Cross Board Members Camelot Oklahoma West Side Story Othello

Ready   135%

Key Concepts

● Identify parts of the Excel screen

● Open and close workbooks

● Name and save a workbook

● Insert and edit cell contents

● Calculate a sum

● Print a worksheet

Standards

The following standards are covered in this lesson. Refer to pages xix and 314 for a description of the standards listed here.

ISTE Standards Correlation

NETS•S

2b, 3b, 3d, 4c, 6a, 6b

Microsoft Certified Applications Specialist

Excel

1.4, 3.2

In this lesson, you will learn basic Excel skills such as opening and closing a workbook, inserting and editing cell contents, and naming and saving a workbook. These basic skills will give you the foundation you need to learn more complex Excel skills.

21st CENTURY SKILLS

Be Productive Productivity is a measure of how well you use resources, such as time or money. If you think the results you are getting are worth the time and effort you put into a project, then you are probably being productive. Two people may spend the same amount of time on a project, but one person may be more productive if he or she has better tools or is more organized. Excel is a tool that can help you organize your work more productively. *What tools do you use to organize your work?*

8 If the table gridlines do not show, choose **Table Tools>Layout>Table> View Gridlines**. Select the table and click **Align Center**.

9 Switch to **Excel**. Close the **Properties.xlsx** data file. Click **No**. Open the **Cleaning.xlsx** data file. Save as: Cleaning-[your first initial and last name]. Select cells **A2** through **A6**. Click **Home>Clipboard>Copy**.

10 In your **Rental** file, click at the end of the sentence that ends **here are their names** and press ENTER twice.

11 On the **Home** tab, click the **Paste** drop-down arrow. Select **Paste Special**. In the **Paste Special** dialog box, under **As:**, choose **Unformatted Text** (see Figure 1.3). Click **OK**.

12 **ⓘCHECK** Your screen should look like Figure 1.4.

13 Close the Excel file. Save and close your **Rental** file.

➡ *Continue to the next exercise.*

WORD INTEGRATION
Exercise 1: Copy and Paste between Applications (Continued)

FIGURE 1.3 Paste Special dialog box

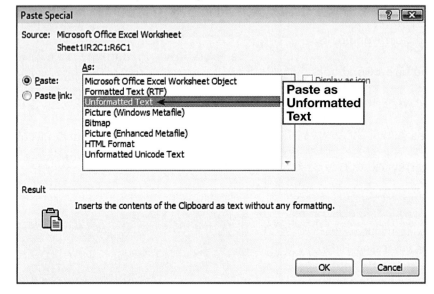

FIGURE 1.4 Document with pasted information

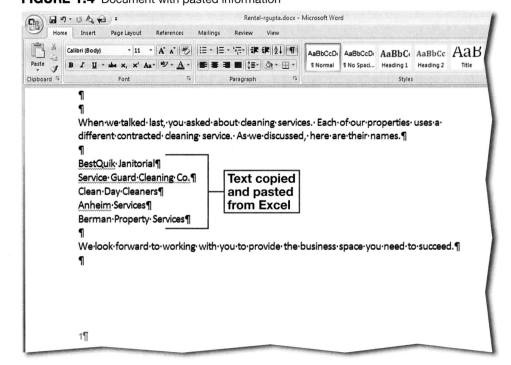

Before You Read

Prior Knowledge Look over the Key Concepts at the beginning of the lesson. Write down what you already know about each concept and what you want to find out by reading the lesson. As you read, find examples for both categories.

Read to Learn

- Explore the Excel application and how it works.
- Understand how to enter values and formulas into worksheet cells.
- Consider how Excel can help you organize important data, such as an inventory.

Main Idea

Excel is an important tool that allows you to create and edit spreadsheets.

Vocabulary

Key Terms

button	Quick Access Toolbar (QAT)
cell	Ribbon
cell reference	ScreenTip
command	sheet tab
dialog box	spreadsheet
folder	tab
formula	title bar
formula bar	workbook
group	worksheet

Academic Vocabulary

These words appear in your reading and on your tests. Make sure you know their meanings.

illustrate
learn

Quick Write Activity

Create a List Chances are that everyday you do simple calculations such as adding or subtracting numbers. Think about the tools you use on a daily basis to work with numbers (e.g., calculator, pencil and paper, etc.). On a separate piece of paper, make a list of these tools. In your list, describe how these tools help you make sense of numbers. How could these tools be improved to help you work better?

Study Skills

Avoid Distractions Is it sometimes hard for you to finish your homework? Talk to your family about establishing a set time every day for homework. Make sure both family and friends know that you are not available during this time.

Academic Standards

English Language Arts
  NCTE 3 Apply strategies to interpret texts.
  NCTE 4 Use written language to communicate effectively.

Math
  NCTM (Number and Operations) Understand numbers, ways of representing numbers, relationships among numbers, and number systems.
  NCTM (Number and Operations) Compute fluently and make reasonable estimates.

1 Start **Word**. Open the data file **Rental.docx**. Save as: Rental-[your first initial and last name] (for example, *Rental-rgupta*).

2 Start **Excel**. Open the data file **Properties.xlsx**. Save as: Properties-[your first initial and last name].

3 Select cells **A1** through **E6**. Click **Home>Clipboard> Copy** .

4 **⓵CHECK** Your screen should look like Figure 1.1.

5 Switch to your **Rental** file. Click at the end of the sentence that begins with **Below is**. Press ENTER twice.

6 Click **Home>Clipboard> Paste** . The Excel data is inserted in its original format.

7 **⓵CHECK** Your screen should look like Figure 1.2.

➡ Continued on the next page.

WORD INTEGRATION
Exercise 1: Copy and Paste between Applications

By now you are familiar with using Copy and Paste as functions in various Microsoft Office programs. You can use the Clipboard to paste data from one file to a file in another application, just like you do within a single application. Use Paste Special to specify the file format of the information you are pasting from another file or application. Use Paste Options to specify the format of the pasted information.

FIGURE 1.1 Data copied in Excel source file

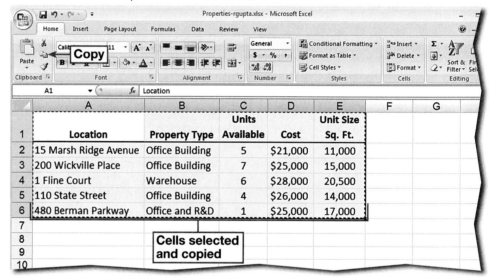

FIGURE 1.2 Excel data pasted into Word destination file

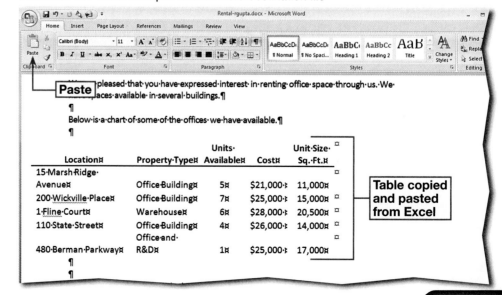

MATH MATTERS

Introduction to Excel

Excel is a type of spreadsheet software. Spreadsheet software allows users to organize and manipulate numbers and other data.

How Can I Use Excel?

Although Excel can be used to organize text, it is more commonly used to organize and process numbers in rows and columns. Businesses use Excel for many kinds of data, including budgets, sales figures, expense statements, and time cards.

You could use Excel to organize and process information about a variety of things, including:

- Your class schedule
- Your grades
- Your friends' addresses and phone numbers
- Your personal budget

When Should I Use Excel?

It is best to use Excel whenever you need to store and process data, especially numbers. There are many advantages to entering data in an Excel spreadsheet instead of a table in Word, including:

- A spreadsheet has ready-made columns and rows.
- Excel has built-in formulas that can automatically calculate sums, averages, maximum values, and minimum values.
- The formulas in Excel can be copied to other columns and rows to make quick and accurate calculations.

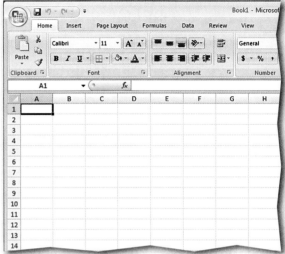

Excel is an excellent tool for tracking financial information.

SKILLBUILDER

1. **Identify** What are some additional ways that businesses might use Excel?

2. **Evaluate** Why do you think many people prefer using Excel's built-in formulas instead of calculators to process data?

3. **Analyze** Explain how Excel is different from Word.

4. **Describe** Use the Internet to find out more about Excel. Describe one new use for Excel that you learned.

Table of Contents

① To start **Excel**, click the **Start** button (see Figure 1.1). Choose **Programs>Microsoft Office®>Microsoft Office Excel 2007**.

② **ⓘCHECK** Your screen should look like Figure 1.1.

③ Find the **title bar** (see Figure 1.1). The name of your file should be **Book1**.

④ Find the **Quick Access Toolbar (QAT)**. Click the **drop-down arrow** for the **QAT**. Read the items listed in the menu.

⑤ Click the **Office Button** (⬢). Read the items listed in the menu. Click in a blank area to close the menu.

⑥ Locate the **scroll bars** at the right side and bottom of the screen. Scroll bars allow you to move up and down and left and right in a worksheet.

⑦ Locate the **status bar** at the bottom of the screen.

➡ *Continue to the next exercise.*

EXERCISE 1-1
Identify Parts of the Excel Screen

In this exercise, you will learn, or become familiar with, the different parts of the Excel window. You must know the parts of the Excel screen to use Excel productively. The **title bar** displays the Excel file name. The **Quick Access Toolbar** (or **QAT**) allows users to quickly find commands. You use scroll bars to scroll, or move up and down or left and right in the document. Use the pointer to select tabs and other tools.

FIGURE 1.1 The Excel screen

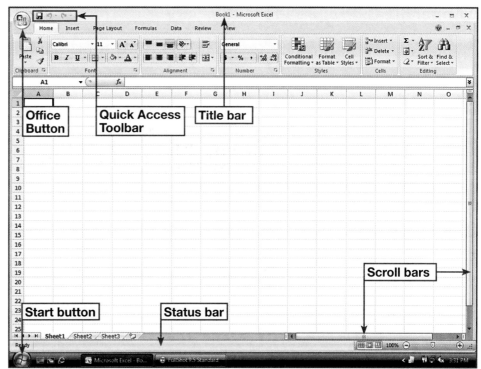

You Should Know

The location of Excel's functions may shift depending on the size of your viewing window.

Microsoft Office 2007

The Office Button is a new 2007 feature. You can use this button to perform important tasks such as creating, saving, and printing a document.

Contents of Appendixes

1. In Excel, on the **Ribbon**, click the **Home** tab (see Figure 1.2).

2. Roll your pointer arrow over the seven groups in the **Home** tab (see Figure 1.3).

3. Click the seven tabs across the Ribbon. Identify the groups displayed in the tab.

4. Click the **Home** tab. Read the **ScreenTip** for each button in the **Font** group.

5. In the **Font** group, click the arrow next to the **Font Color** A button to display the drop-down menu. Click outside the menu to close it.

6. In the **Font** group, click the **Dialog Box Launcher**.

7. **CHECK** Your screen should look like Figure 1.2. Click the **Close** X button on the dialog box.

Continue to the next exercise.

EXERCISE 1-2
Use Tabs, Groups, and Buttons

The **Ribbon** contains all of the buttons that you can use in Excel. Across the top of the Ribbon are **tabs**. The tabs display **buttons** (or **commands**) organized in logical **groups** that relate to a specific activity, such as keying text. When you point to a button, a **ScreenTip** appears to show you the button's name. More commands are available in **dialog boxes** that are located within the groups. Use the Dialog Box Launcher to open a group's dialog box. Not every group will have a Dialog Box Launcher.

FIGURE 1.2 The Excel Screen

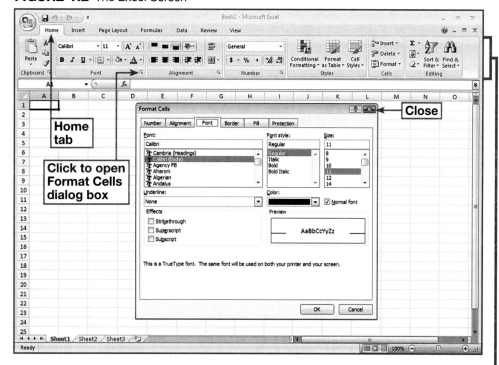

FIGURE 1.3 The Ribbon

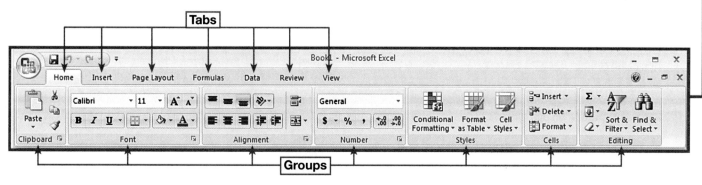

Part 4: Protect the Work

Goal The weekly report looks good. Your employer wants many people to see it. Unauthorized persons should not change the report by accident, however. In addition, your employer wants the report to be viewed only by clients to whom a password has been given.

Create Open the workbook you created in Part 3. Protect the workbook against unauthorized viewing or modification.

- Enable worksheet protection in your workbook.
- Set a password to open the workbook. Be sure to record your password so you do not forget what it is.
- Set a password to modify the workbook. Again, record your password so you do not forget it.
- Check to make sure both your passwords are active.
- With your teacher's permission, print your worksheet. Write both of your passwords on your printed worksheet.

Self Assess Use the Have You ...? checklist to review your report. Make sure your report matches the safety assessments on the checklist.

Follow your teacher's instructions for saving the workbook to your Portfolio Folder.

Have You...?

✓	Checked to make sure that data in the worksheet cannot be modified
✓	Checked that a password is required to open it
✓	Checked that a password is required to modify it
✓	Stored the passwords in a safe place
✓	Saved your work with the right name and in the right folder
✓	Printed out the worksheet if directed by your teacher
✓	Written your passwords on your printed worksheet

 Go Online   **BEYOND THE BOOK**

glencoe.com

Go to the Online Learning Center to learn additional skills and review what you have already learned.

Microsoft Excel
Extend your knowledge of Excel by visiting the Online Learning Center for more MCAS-based exercises. Select **Advanced Excel>Lessons**.

Microsoft Vista
Select **Windows Vista>Lessons** to explore Microsoft's operating system is fully.

Microsoft Outlook
Want to learn all about Outlook and how to use e-mail communication and scheduling? Select **Microsoft Outlook>Lessons** for all you need to know.

Additional Projects
Complete additional projects in the following areas:

- **Real-World Business Projects** reinforce Microsoft Office by focusing on real-world business applications.
- **Presentation and Publishing Projects** Use your Office skills to create exciting PowerPoint presentations and desktop publishing activities.
- **Academic Projects** Integrate academic skills while enriching your understanding of Microsoft Word.

More Online Resources
Access additional Web sites and online information relating to key topics covered in Glencoe's *iCheck Series*. Select **Resource Links**.

1 In your **Book1** file, click **Close Window** X (see Figure 1.4).

2 If prompted to save, click **No**. The current workbook closes.

3 Click the **Office Button** and select **New**.

4 In the **New Workbook** dialog box, under **Templates**, select **Blank and recent**.

5 In the middle pane, select **Blank Workbook**. Click **Create**.

6 (i)**CHECK** Your screen should look like Figure 1.5. Notice that the name of the workbook is now **Book2**.

➡ *Continue to the next exercise.*

Troubleshooter

When closing a workbook, be careful not to click the **Close** button on the title bar. The two **Close** buttons look the same. The **Close** button on the title bar will exit Excel and not just your workbook!

EXERCISE 1-3
Close and Create a Workbook

An Excel file is called a **workbook**. A workbook contains one or more sheets called **worksheets**, also known as **spreadsheets**. A worksheet contains data such as numbers and formulas. When you launch Excel, a new workbook appears automatically. In this exercise, you will learn how to close a workbook and how to create a new one.

FIGURE 1.4 Closing a workbook

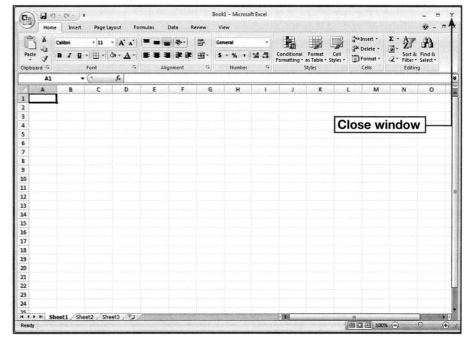

Close window

FIGURE 1.5 New workbook

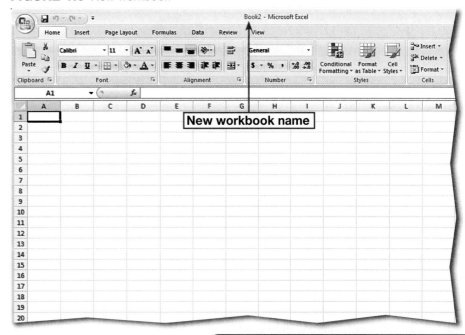

New workbook name

Part 3: Create a Chart

Rubric R

Goal Your employer is satisfied with your report so far. Now he wants you to add a chart that will summarize the table of stock quotations.

Create Open the Excel template you created in Part 1. In your template:

- Select the table of stock quotations. Use the **Chart Tools** to create and format a line chart for the three stocks.
- Place the chart on the same worksheet as the data.
- Move and resize the chart as needed so that it is clearly displayed on the page.
- Title the chart **Stock Summaries**.
- Make any changes that will make the chart easier to read or more attractive. For example, add data labels to the chart, or format different data as different colors to help users identify information quickly and easily.
- Set minimum and maximum values for the value axis.
- Set major and minor divisions for the value axis.

Self Assess Use the Have You ...? checklist to review your chart. Make sure you have done everything in the checklist.

Follow your teacher's instructions for saving the template. When finished, proceed to Part 4.

Have You...?

✓	Used the Chart Tools to create a line chart from the stock quotation table
✓	Placed the chart and sized it so that it can be seen clearly
✓	Added a title to the chart
✓	Changed the colors for the legend
✓	Chosen a color for the plot area
✓	Set the minimum and maximum values for the value axis
✓	Set the major and minor divisions for the value axis

EXERCISE 1-4
Scroll and Move Through Worksheets

Use the scroll bars to move left, right, up, or down through a worksheet. By default, when you create a new workbook, it always contains three worksheets. The **sheet tabs** allow you to move from one worksheet to another.

1 In your **Book2** file, click the **down arrow** ▼ on the vertical scroll bar (see Figure 1.6). The numbers along the worksheet's left edge increase as you scroll down.

2 Click the **up arrow** ▲ to return to the top of the worksheet.

3 Click the **right arrow** ▶ on the horizontal scroll bar. The letters along the top change as you scroll right.

4 Click the **left arrow** ◀.

5 ⓘ**CHECK** Your screen should look like Figure 1.6.

6 Locate the **sheet tabs**. Click the **Sheet2** tab.

7 ⓘ**CHECK** Your screen should look like Figure 1.7. The **Sheet2** tab turns white to show that you are currently using Sheet 2.

8 Click the **Sheet3** tab. Click the **Sheet1** tab to return to Sheet 1.

9 ⓘ**CHECK** Your screen should look like Figure 1.6.

➡ *Continue to the next exercise.*

Shortcuts

You can drag the scroll bar to scroll through a worksheet faster.

FIGURE 1.6 Scroll bars

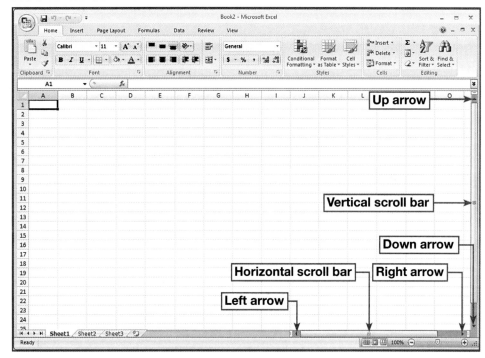

FIGURE 1.7 Identifying the sheet you are using

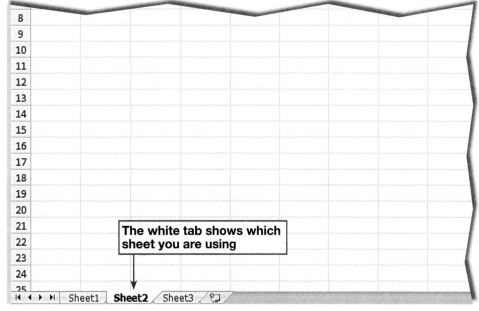

The white tab shows which sheet you are using

UNIT 2 Portfolio Project

Part 2: Make Your First Report

Goal Now it is time to produce the first of your weekly reports. If all goes well, you only need to add in the data file containing the names of the stocks of the week and their stock prices.

Create Create a new Excel workbook based on your template.

- In your stock table, click the first cell in the row containing the dates for the week.
- Choose **Data>Get External Data>From Text** and import the data from the data file **Quotes.txt** into your table.
- Review your table to make sure all of the data was imported correctly.
- Make any necessary text or formatting changes to your table.
- Make sure the chart based on the table contains correct information.

Self Assess Use the Have You ...? checklist to review your report. Make sure your report fills all of the requirements in the checklist.

Follow your teacher's instructions for naming the workbook and saving it to your Portfolio Folder.

When finished, proceed to Part 3.

Have You...?

✓	Imported the data from the data file **Quotes.txt** in the right place
✓	Made sure the five business days are formatted as dates
✓	Made sure the stock quotations are formatted as numbers with two decimal places
✓	Made sure the company names have the format you wanted
✓	Made sure the chart reflects the worksheet data

Step-By-Step

1. In your **Book2** file, choose **Office>Save As**. The **Save As** dialog box opens.
2. With your teacher's permission, click **New Folder** (see Figure 1.8).
3. In the **New Folder** text box, key: [your first initial and last name] (for example, *jking*). Press ENTER.
4. Click outside the text box. The new folder opens automatically.
5. Click **Back to Document** (see Figure 1.9).
6. **CHECK** Your dialog box should look like Figure 1.9. Notice the folder's name has changed.
7. Click **Close** to close the dialog box.

Continue to the next exercise.

Microsoft Office 2007

When the **>** symbol appears in a step, it means that you need to follow a path to complete a task. For example, **Home>Font>Bold** means go to the **Home** tab, then go to the **Font** group, then click the **Bold** button.

EXERCISE 1-5
Create a New Folder

You can store documents in folders. A **folder** helps you organize your files so you can find them quickly. One way to create a new folder is to use the Save As dialog box. The dialog box can be used to enter specific information to perform a task, such as naming and saving a workbook.

FIGURE 1.8 Save As dialog box

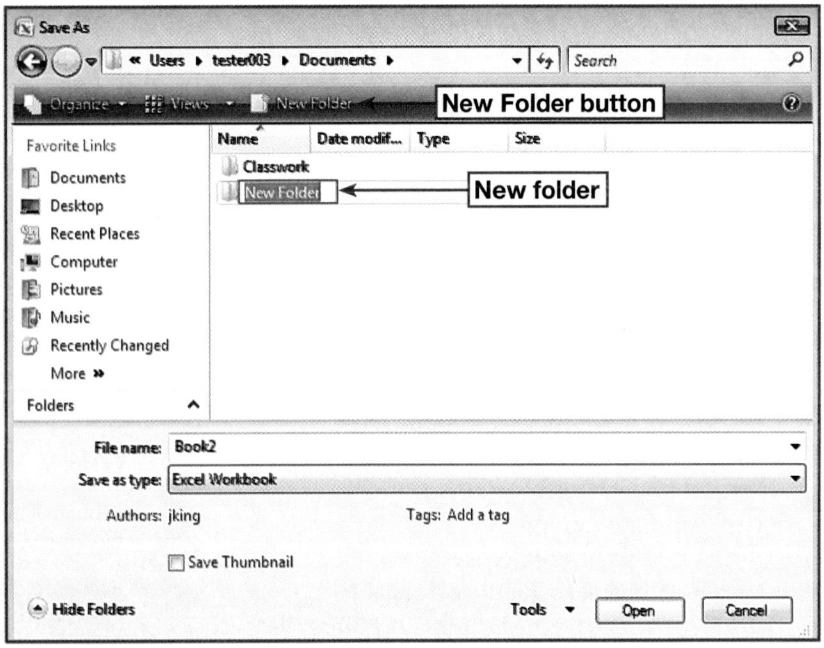

FIGURE 1.9 Naming a new folder

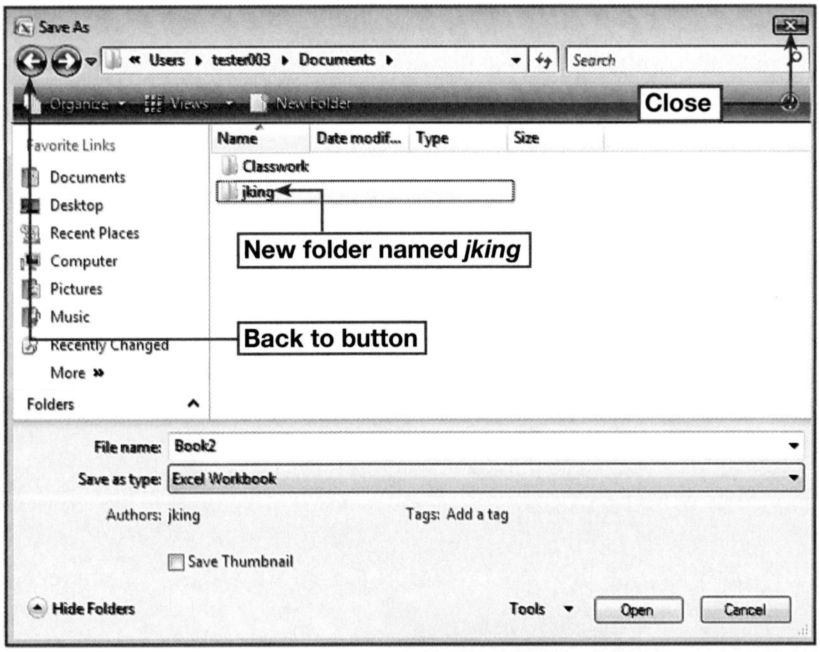

UNIT 2 Portfolio Project

Stock Market Expert

The business you work for advises clients on what stocks to buy. Your employer wants to put out a weekly newsletter. The newsletter will profile three stocks and how they performed during the week. You are asked to set up an Excel worksheet that can be used to display and summarize the information for each week.

Part 1: Create a Template

Rubric
R

Goal You need to create a template that will be reused every week. It should do as much as possible to make each week's task simpler. It should also look attractive and professional so it can be presented to customers.

Create Use Excel to create a template.

- Place your company's name, address, telephone number, and Internet address at the top of the template.
- Use Clip Art or another suitable graphic for the template's heading.
- Create a table of stock values. The table should have three rows to hold the names of stocks and five columns to hold the daily stock quotations. The column headers will be the dates of the five business days of the week in question. Format the stock quotations as a number with two decimal places.
- Format the column headers as dates. Boldface the column headers or use a larger type size to help them stand out.

Self Assess Use the Have You ...? checklist to review your template. Make sure your template contains all the necessary items and formatting. Follow your teacher's instructions for saving the template.

When finished, proceed to Part 2.

Have You...?

 Formatted the company name and address attractively in larger type

Rotated, cropped, and resized the graphic to fit the heading

Created a table with three rows and five columns

Formatted the stock quotations as a number with two decimal places

Formatted the column headers as dates

Formatted the column headers in boldface or a larger size

1. In your **Book2** file, choose **Office>Save As**. The **Save As** dialog box opens (see Figure 1.10).

2. In the **File name** box, key: e1-6-. Then key your first initial and your last name (for example, *e1-6-jking*).

3. Locate the folder you created in Exercise 1-5 or ask your teacher for the location you should select in the **Save in** box.

4. Click the folder twice to select that location.

5. Click **Save** in the **Save As** dialog box.

6. **⚡CHECK** Your screen should look like Figure 1.11. Notice that the workbook's new name appears on the title bar.

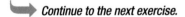 *Continue to the next exercise.*

Troubleshooter

If you are using Windows XP, go to page xliii to learn how to complete the steps in this exercise and in Exercise 1-5.

EXERCISE 1-6
Name and Save a Workbook

You must save a workbook if you want to use it again. Save your work every few minutes to keep it from being lost.

FIGURE 1.10 Save As dialog box with new file name

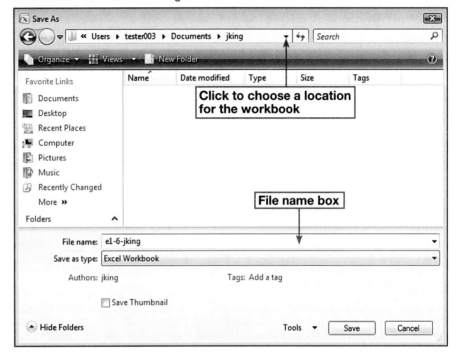

FIGURE 1.11 New file name in title bar

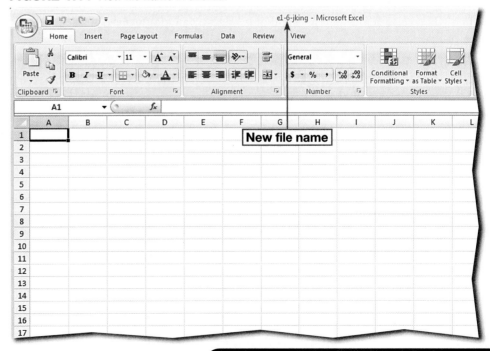

Honesty in the Workplace

There are many kinds of honesty. The most basic involves respecting the property of others. On a personal level, some people may hold back their real feelings about how a coworker or manager treats them. They may be afraid to speak the truth because they might hurt someone and are afraid of what might happen to them. Fearful of being blamed, people may fail to be honest about mistakes they may have made.

If people are not honest, difficult issues cannot be openly discussed. Many problems, bad feelings, mistakes, and failures may never be faced or resolved. An important issue for managers today is to understand how they can encourage people to become more honest in the workplace.

Is It Honest?

How do you know when something you say or do is not honest? Ask yourself these questions:

- Am I hiding something?
- Do I have the right to keep it hidden?
- What would happen if it were discovered?

Finally, you should act in ways that encourage honesty in others. Be accepting when you receive advice or criticism that is honestly and fairly given.

If you say what you mean, you never have to worry whether your words will be passed on. If you act honestly, you never have to worry whether your actions will be discovered.

CASE STUDY

You see your coworker, Fred, slipping a new notebook into his backpack. When you ask about it, Fred laughs and says, "I never go to the stationery store anymore. Everything is here in the supply cabinet. They have notebooks, boxes of pens, scissors, markers, rulers, you name it! I think of it as just a little bonus of the job. No one has noticed, so the company obviously does not care." Although you do not agree with Fred's actions, you do not want him angry with you, so you remain silent.

YOU DECIDE

1. **Restate in Your Own Words** Why does Fred think his conduct is acceptable?
2. **Explain** You have decided to talk with Fred. How will you answer the following arguments if he makes them?
   a. "I am entitled to these things as a little bonus."
   b. "The company will never miss it."
   c. "This is none of your business."
   d. "Do not say anything and no one will notice."

APPLICATION ACTIVITY

3. **Estimate** Create an Excel worksheet. In each row, list one of the items that Fred mentions. In the column to the right of each item, key a realistic price for that item. (Use the Internet, a newspaper, or other sources to research the cost of office supplies.) Use the Sum function to find the total. Multiply the total by 12 to see what Fred's stealing might cost his company if he continued taking supplies at that same rate for a year.

---

1 In your **e1-6** file, click cell **A1** (see Figure 1.12).

2 Key: First Quarter Sales. Press ENTER.

3 Click cell **A1**. Look in the formula bar to read the cell's content (see Figure 1.12).

4 Click cell **B1**. Notice the formula bar is empty. **B1** appears to contain text, but it does not.

5 Click cell **A1**.

6 In the column head row, move the pointer to the line between **A** and **B** until the pointer becomes a two-headed arrow (see Figure 1.13).

7 Click and drag to the right to make the column wider until *First Quarter Sales* fits in cell **A1**.

8 ⓘ**CHECK** Your screen should look like Figure 1.13.

9 Click **Save** 💾 on the **QAT** to save your work.

Continue to the next exercise.

EXERCISE 1-7
Insert and View Cell Contents

Worksheets are made up of boxes called **cells**. Cells are organized into horizontal rows and vertical columns. Rows are labeled with numbers, and columns are labeled with letters.

A cell is named by its **cell reference**, or its column letter and row number. For example, cell E14 is in column E, row 14. The **formula bar** shows a cell's contents. Sometimes cells must be resized to view all of the contents.

FIGURE 1.12 Cell content shown in formula bar

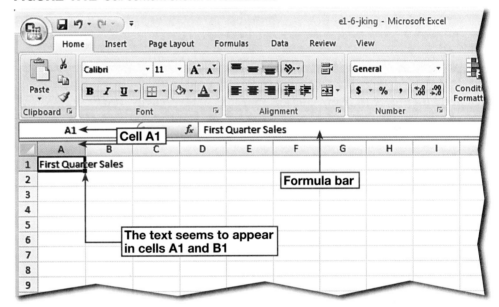

FIGURE 1.13 Making a column wider

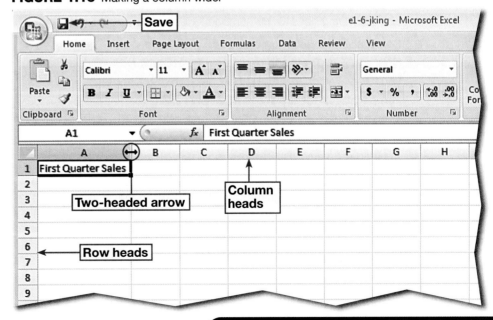

Rubric

In this activity, you will use your math skills to analyze weather data.

Create a Chart to Summarize Data

You may have noticed that weather reports on television often use charts and graphs to display information. The weather forecaster presents many kinds of statistics. In this activity, you will create a chart to display a week's worth of high and low temperatures. You will also find the average high and low temperatures for the week.

You can use Excel to create charts that track information such as weather statistics.

1. Obtain a week's worth of high and low temperatures for your city or region. You can get the information from the Internet, television, radio, or newspapers.

2. Create an Excel worksheet with the following column heads: **Day, Low, High**. Make the heads bold. (p. 155)

3. In the **Day** column, key the days of the week. (p. 155)

4. Enter the low and high temperatures you have collected in the **Low** and **High** columns for the corresponding days. Enter numbers only. (p. 205)

5. Select all of the cells containing text and numbers. Create a **PivotTable** and generate a **PivotChart** for your data. The chart's title should be **High and Low Temperatures for the Week of ...** The vertical axis should be labeled **Degrees Fahrenheit**. Make any other changes to the chart that you think will improve the readability and add interest. (p. 178)

6. In the **Day** column, under the last row, add a row for the average low and high temperatures value. In the **Low** column, enter a formula to compute the average low temperature for the week, using a name in the formula. Do the same for the high temperature. (p. 164)

7. Check and save your work.

1. In your **e1-6** file, Choose **View>Zoom>Zoom** 🔍. The **Zoom** dialog box opens. Click **75%**. Click **OK**.

2. Click **Zoom** 🔍. Click **Custom** and key: 200. Click **OK**.

3. **ⓘCHECK** Your screen should look like Figure 1.14.

4. Locate the **Zoom In** and **Zoom Out** buttons in the lower right corner of your screen. Click the **Zoom Out** button until the **Zoom** level is **100%**.

5. Click the **Customize Quick Access Toolbar** button ▽ on the **QAT** and choose **Minimize the Ribbon**. The Ribbon is now minimized.

6. Repeat **Step 5**. Save your file.

7. Choose **View>Workbook Views>Full Screen** 🗔.

8. **ⓘCHECK** Your screen should look like Figure 1.15.

9. Right-click the **Select All** button. Choose **Close Full Screen**. Your screen returns to **Normal View**.

➡ *Continue to the next exercise.*

EXERCISE 1-8
Change the View of a Screen

There are several ways to change the appearance of the Excel screen. One way is to use the zoom option. Increasing the zoom percentage makes everything appear larger, so it is easier to see a cell's content. Decreasing the zoom percentage makes everything appear smaller, which allows you to see more of the worksheet at once. Although items may appear larger or smaller on screen, depending on the zoom, the item itself will appear normal size when it prints. Another way is to minimize the Ribbon in order to see more of the screen.

FIGURE 1.14 Screen at 200% zoom

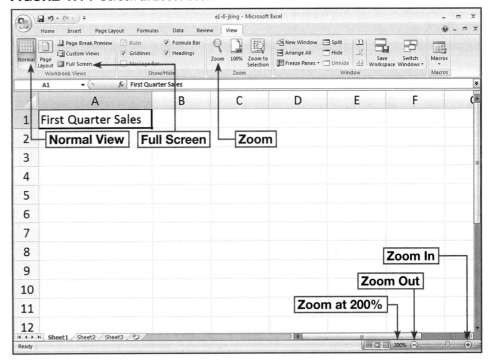

FIGURE 1.15 Full Screen Toggle View

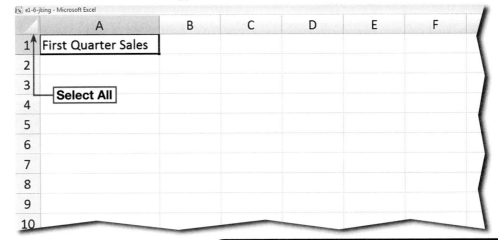

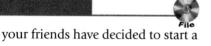

LESSON 5 — Challenge Yourself Projects

Before You Begin

Manage Data People often have to manage a lot of information. Data is hard to manage without special tools. These projects teach you how to use Excel's advanced tools to create a template, create a macro, and consolidate data from several worksheets.

Reflect Once you complete the projects, open a Word document and answer the following questions:

1. In what ways can you use Document Properties to control data that you have created?

2. Notice the actions you do repeatedly. How can you use a template or a macro in your day-to-day activities?

9. Set Up Your Supplies

 Math: Create a Template You and your friends have decided to start a small car-washing business for the summer. You decide to use Excel to keep track of the supplies you need each month.

- Open the data file **Carwash.xlsx**. Column A contains a list of supplies, such as soap and buckets.
- Fill in column B with zeros.
- Create a total for the month.
- Save the workbook as a template.
- Create a workbook based on the template and complete it for the first month.

Save your new template as: adv-e5rev-[your first initial and last name]9.

Save your original workbook as: Carwash-[your first initial and last name]9.

10. Create Shortcuts

Language Arts: Create a Macro Your supervisor is very impressed with your expertise in Excel. He asks you if you have any additional suggestions to help his employees work more efficiently. You decide to create some macros for employees to use. In a new worksheet, create a macro that will complete each of the following commands.

- Insert a worksheet.
- Change the Font Size to 12.
- Add a blank row or column.
- Create a keyboard shortcut and name the macro.
- Test the macro.

In a separate Word document, key a paragraph and reflect on how the shortcut makes it easier to complete the assigned task.

Save your file as: adv-e5rev-[your first initial and last name]10.

11. Find Total Sales

 Math: Consolidate Data It is the end of the summer. Now, you want to find out how much money your car-washing business made during the summer months.

- Open the data file **Summer.xlsx**.
- On the first three sheets, find the total sales for each month.
- On the fourth sheet, create a formula that finds the total sales for the summer.
- Use the **Currency** format for all the sales numbers.

Save your file as: Summer-[your first initial and last name]11.

1. In your **e1-6** file, click cell **A1**.

2. Key: Surplus Inventory. Press ENTER.

3. **(i)CHECK** Your screen should look like Figure 1.16.

4. On the **QAT**, click **Undo**. *First Quarter Sales* reappears.

5. **(i)CHECK** Your screen should look like Figure 1.17.

6. Click **Redo**. *Surplus Inventory* reappears.

7. Click **Undo**. *First Quarter Sales* reappears.

8. Click **Save**.

9. Choose **Office>Close** to close the workbook.

➡ *Continue to the next exercise.*

You Should Know

After you close and reopen a file, the **Undo** and **Redo** buttons will no longer be available.

EXERCISE 1-9
Use Undo and Redo

If you ever make a mistake or change your mind while working with Excel, choose Undo. Undo reverses your last action. You can choose Undo multiple times to undo multiple actions. If you choose Undo by accident, you can choose Redo.

FIGURE 1.16 Replacing text in a cell

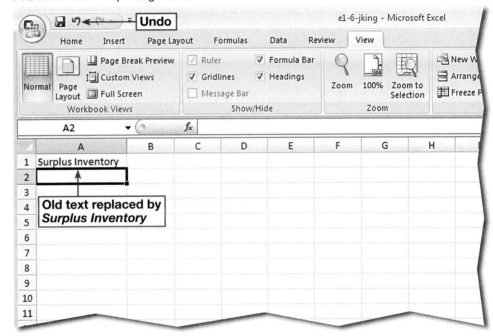

FIGURE 1.17 Using Undo

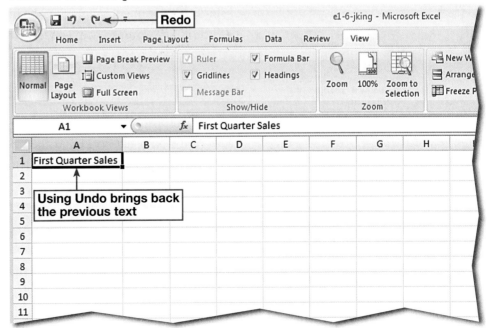

LESSON 5 Critical Thinking Activities

6. Beyond the Classroom Activity

 Language Arts: Link to a Web Page Your supervisor wants you to create a document that shows the current price of various stocks. You decide that the best option is a link to a regularly updated Web page.

- Open a new Excel workbook.
- Import data from the MSN MoneyCentral Investor Stock Quotes into your new workbook.

Think about other data available online. With your teacher's permission, use the Internet or your school library to gather information for at least one other Web page that offers up-to-date data. Add a hyperlink for the Web page to your workbook.

Save your file as: adv-e5rev-[your first initial and last name]6.

7. Standards at Work Activity

Microsoft Office Specialist Correlation
Excel 5.3 *Prepare workbooks for distribution*

Add Workbook Properties Your supervisor has asked employees to add file properties to all of their files so that everyone can see a short summary of each file before opening it.

- Open your **Deals** workbook that you used in Exercises 5-1 through 5-4.
- Fill in the subject and author properties.
- Include a comment stating that the file includes a link to a Web page.
- Include key words to help you identify the file.

Save the workbook as: adv-e5rev-[your first initial and last name]7.

8. 21st Century Skills Activity

Learn to Adapt One of your classmates created a tool for tracking quiz grades. You would like to extend the tracking for ten weeks. Adapt your classmate's quiz tracker and save it as a template.

- Open the data file **Quiz.xlsx**.
- In cell A5, key: Microsoft Office.
- Add new columns for the next six weeks.
- Save the worksheet as a template.
- Create a worksheet based on the template. Fill in quiz grades. Notice that the average is automatically calculated for you.

Save your worksheet as: Quiz-[your first initial and last name]8.

Go to the Online Learning Center to complete the following review activities

Online Self Check
To test your knowledge of the material, click **Unit 2> Lesson 5** and choose **Self Checks**.

Interactive Review
To review the main points of the lesson, click **Unit 2> Lesson 5** and choose **Interactive Review**.

Lesson 5: Critical Thinking Activities

EXERCISE 1-10
Open an Existing Workbook

① Click **Office>Open**. The **Open** dialog box opens.

② Click the up arrow on the **Folders** box.

③ Locate the folder where you save your work.

④ Select the name of the workbook that you saved and closed in Exercise 1-9 (the workbook named **e1-6**).

⑤ **ⓘCHECK** Your dialog box should look similar to Figure 1.18.

⑥ Click **Open**. The workbook that you saved in Exercise 1-9 will open.

⑦ **ⓘCHECK** Your screen should look like Figure 1.19.

⑧ Save your file.

➥ *Continue to the next exercise.*

To open an existing workbook, you need to know where (on what drive, in which folder, and so on) the workbook was saved and what the file was named.

FIGURE 1.18 Open dialog box

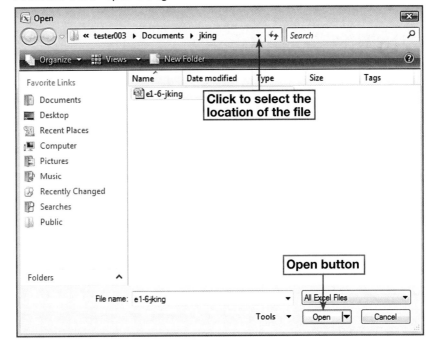

FIGURE 1.19 Open Excel workbook

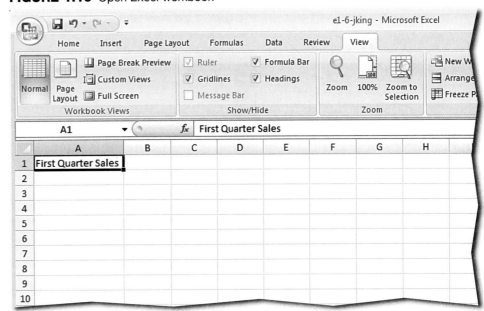

Academic Skills

When working with others, it is especially important to give your files memorable names. Your file names and folder structures should be logical to everyone who needs to access the files.

5. Save a Workbook as a PDF

Step-By-Step

Now that the data in your workbook has been consolidated into a summary sheet, your supervisor wants to e-mail the workbook containing the total number of homes sold to the team before the next meeting. She has asked you to create a PDF of the workbook. You must complete You Try It Activity 4 before doing this activity.

1 Open your **Downtown-4** file. Save as: Downtown-[your first initial and last name]5.

2 Select all three sheet tabs and choose **Office> Save As>PDF or XPS**.

3 Navigate to the folder holding the **Downtown** workbook file. In the **File name** box, key: Downtown-[your first initial and last name]5.

4 In the **Save as type** box, select **PDF**. Make sure the **Open file after publishing** box is checked.

5 ⓘ**CHECK** Your dialog box should look like Figure 5.35. Click **Publish**.

6 ⓘ**CHECK** Your screen should look similar to Figure 5.36.

7 Exit **Adobe Reader**.

8 Save and close your file. Exit Excel.

FIGURE 5.35 Publish as PDF or XPS dialog box

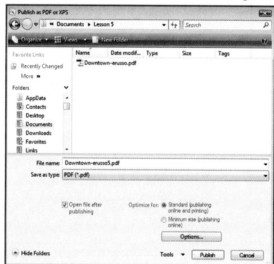

FIGURE 5.36 April Budget PDF

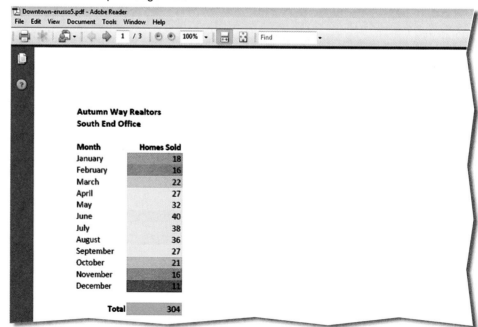

Autumn Way Realtors
South End Office

Month	Homes Sold
January	18
February	16
March	22
April	27
May	32
June	40
July	38
August	36
September	27
October	21
November	16
December	11
Total	304

1 In your **e1-6** file, click cell **A2** and key: January. Press TAB . In cell **B2** key: 1500.

2 Click cell **A3** and key: February. Press TAB . In cell **B3** key: 1350.

3 Click cell **A4** and key: March. Press TAB . In cell **B4** key: 2000.

4 Click cell **A6** and key: Total.

5 Click cell **B6** and then choose **Formulas> Function Library> AutoSum** Σ .

6 ⓘ**CHECK** Your screen should look like Figure 1.20. In cell B6 Excel displays **=SUM(B2:B5)**. This is also displayed in the formula bar. This indicates that Excel will add (sum) the numbers in cells B2, B3, B4, and B5 and display the answer in cell B6.

7 Click **AutoSum** Σ again.

8 ⓘ**CHECK** Your screen should look like Figure 1.21. Excel enters the sum of the First Quarter Sales in cell **B6**. Save your file.

→ *Continue to the next exercise.*

EXERCISE 1-11
Calculate a Sum

Excel has preprogrammed formulas that allow you to quickly add columns or rows of numbers. A **formula** is an equation that begins with an equal sign (=) and includes values or cell references. The formula bar displays the formulas and contents of selected cells. Different formulas allow you to perform different actions. For example, the formula used in this exercise allows you to add a column of numbers.

FIGURE 1.20 Sum button clicked once

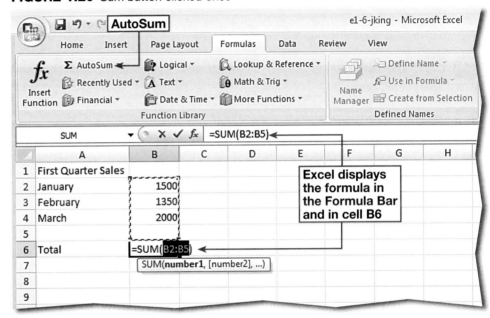

FIGURE 1.21 Sum of cells B2:B5

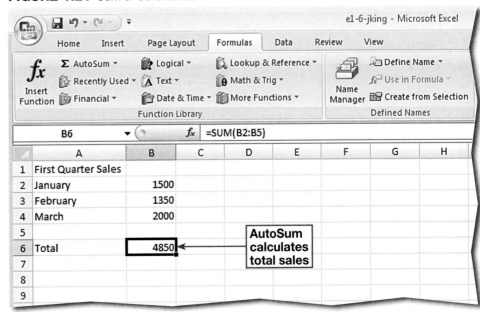

4. Consolidate Data

Over the past year, Autumn Way Realtors has been tracking the number of homes sold per month at its two Downtown offices. You have volunteered to consolidate the data for the two offices and announce the grand total to the team.

Step-By-Step

1. Open your **Downtown** workbook file. Save as: Downtown-[your first initial and last name]4.

2. Click the **Downtown Total** sheet tab.

3. **CHECK** Your screen should look like Figure 5.33.

4. Click cell **B4**. Key: =SUM.

5. Create a formula that finds the total number of homes sold by the South End office and the West End office.

6. Press ENTER. Click cell **B4**.

7. **CHECK** Your screen should look similar to Figure 5.34.

8. Save and close your file.

FIGURE 5.33 Downtown Total sheet

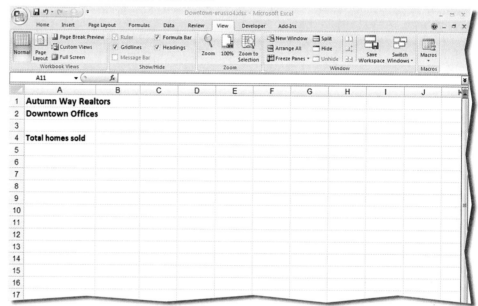

FIGURE 5.34 Creating a formula across multiple worksheets

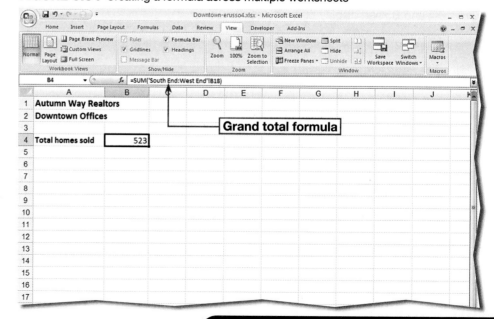

Grand total formula

1 In your **e1-6** file, choose **Office>Print>Print Preview**.

2 **ⓘCHECK** Your screen should look like Figure 1.22. Your worksheet is open in **Print Preview** view.

3 Click **Close Print Preview** to return to your file (see Figure 1.22).

4 Choose **Office>Print**. The **Print** dialog box opens.

5 Check with your teacher to make sure that the correct printer name is in the **Name** box.

6 Check that there is a **1** in the **Number of copies** box.

7 **ⓘCHECK** Your dialog box should look similar to Figure 1.23. With your teacher's permission, print the worksheet.

8 Save your file.

➡ *Continue to the next exercise.*

Shortcuts

You can zoom in on the worksheet by clicking the **Zoom** button in **Print Preview** view.

EXERCISE 1-12
Preview and Print a Worksheet

Print Preview view **illustrates**, or shows, what your worksheet will look like when you print it. The Print dialog box allows you to make choices such as the number of copies that will print, or where the document will print.

FIGURE 1.22 Worksheet in Print Preview view

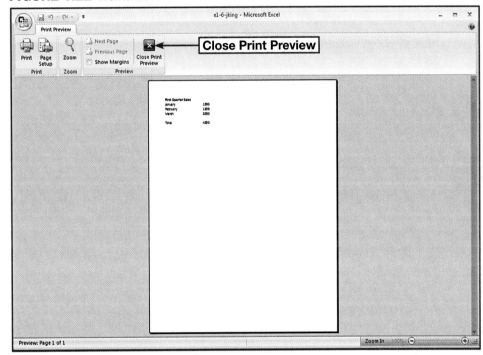

FIGURE 1.23 Print dialog box

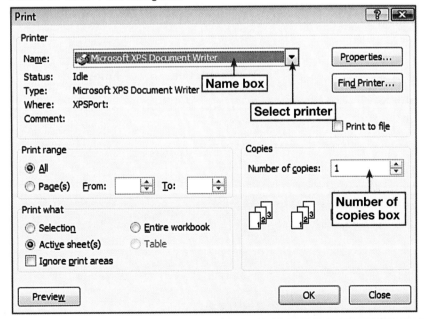

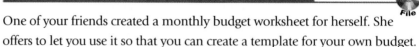

3. Create and Modify a Template

One of your friends created a monthly budget worksheet for herself. She offers to let you use it so that you can create a template for your own budget.

Step-By-Step

1. Open the data file: **Month .xlsx**. Save as: Month-[your first initial and last name]3.

2. Save your file as an **Excel Template (*.xltx)**.

3. Close your template.

4. Choose **Office** >**New**.

5. Click **My templates** to open the templates on your computer. Locate and open your **Month** template (see Figure 5.31).

6. Save as: April-[your first initial and last name]3.

7. Fill in the amounts for your April budget, according to Figure 5.32.

8. Select **A1:B1**. Change the Font Size to **14**. Click **B9**. Change the Font Size to **14**.

9. **CHECK** Your screen should look like Figure 5.32.

10. Save and close your file.

FIGURE 5.31 Month template

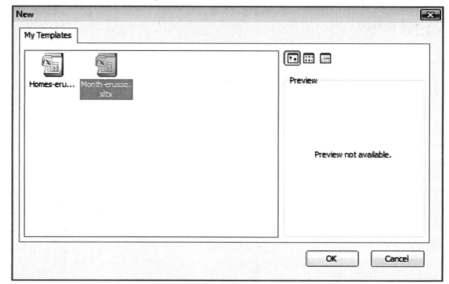

FIGURE 5.32 April budget

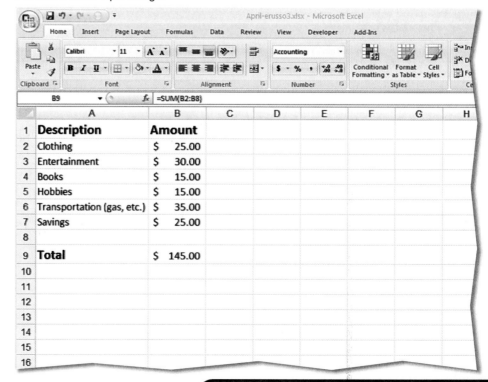

1. In your **e1-6** file, in the upper right corner, click **Microsoft Office Excel Help** 🔘. The Excel Help window opens.

2. In the **Search** box, key: cell contents.

3. Click **Search**.

4. **ⓘCHECK** Your screen should look similar to Figure 1.24.

5. Scroll down the **Results** list and click **Edit cell contents**. A **Help** window appears with information about editing cell contents.

6. **ⓘCHECK** Your screen should look like Figure 1.25.

7. Click **Close** ☒ in the **Excel Help** window.

8. Choose **Office>Close**. The workbook closes. If a warning box appears, click **Yes** to save your file.

9. To exit the **Excel** program, choose **Office>Exit Excel**.

EXERCISE 1-13
Use the Help Feature

You can work more productively if you know how to find help quickly. Use Microsoft Excel Help to find answers to questions about using Excel. Choosing Help brings up the Help window, allowing you to search for Help by keying the name of a topic.

FIGURE 1.24 Search Results in Excel Help window

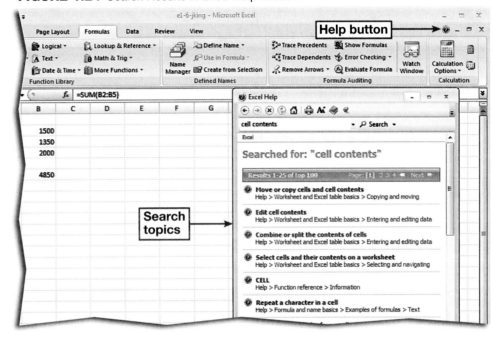

FIGURE 1.25 Help window

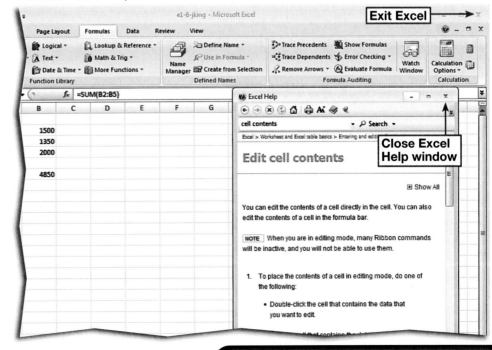

2. Modify Workbook Properties and Save as a Previous Version

Follow the steps to complete the activity. You must complete Practice It Activity 1 before doing this activity.

Step-By-Step

1 Open your **Trip-1** file. Save as: Trip-[your first initial and last name]2. Choose **Office > Prepare>Properties**.

2 **CHECK** Your screen should look like Figure 5.29.

3 In the **Document Information Panel**, click **Document Properties**. Click **Advanced Properties**. The Properties dialog box opens.

4 Click the **Summary** tab. In the **Subject** box, key: Student expenses for spring school band trip. Key your name as the author, if necessary.

5 **CHECK** Your screen should look like Figure 5.30.

6 Click **OK**. Save your file. Close the **Document Information Panel**.

7 Choose **Office >Save As**. Click the **Save as Type** drop-down arrow and select **Excel 97-2003 Workbook (*.xls)**. Click **Save**.

8 Close your file.

FIGURE 5.29 Document Information Panel

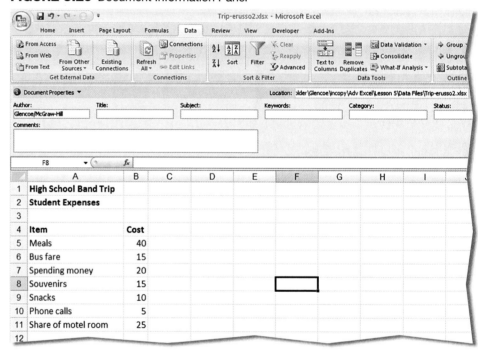

FIGURE 5.30 Subject added to Properties dialog box

Vocabulary

Key Terms

button

cell

cell reference

command

dialog box

folder

formula

formula bar

group

Quick Access Toolbar (QAT)

Ribbon

ScreenTip

sheet tab

spreadsheet

tab

title bar

workbook

worksheet

Academic Vocabulary

illustrate

learn

Review Vocabulary

Complete the following statements on a separate piece of paper. Choose from the Vocabulary list on the left to complete the statements.

1. To _____ is to become familiar with a new concept or idea. (p. 6)

2. Tabs on the _____ display commands and buttons organized in logical groups that relate to a specific activity. (p. 7)

3. The name of the workbook is shown in the _____ at the top of the screen. (p. 6)

4. You can view the contents of a cell in the _____. (p. 12)

5. You can click a(n) _____ to perform a specific task. (p. 7)

Vocabulary Activity

6. Make flash cards for each vocabulary word used in Lesson 1.
   A. On the front of the card, write the word.
   B. On the back of the card, write the definition.
   C. Team up with a classmate and take turns using the flash cards to quiz each other.
   D. When you know the definitions for all the terms, save the flash cards to review for the year-end or term-end assessment.

Review Key Concepts

Answer the following questions on a separate piece of paper.

7. Where can you find the Print and Print Preview commands? (p. 17)
   A. Home tab
   B. Quick Access Toolbar (QAT)
   C. Insert tab
   D. Office button

8. Which button allows you to quickly add columns or rows of numbers? (p. 16)
   A. AutoSum
   B. Equation
   C. Format
   D. Insert

9. Which feature makes everything in a workbook appear larger or smaller? (p. 13)
   A. Redo
   B. Zoom
   C. New
   D. Undo

10. Which button do you use to reverse your last action? (p. 14)
    A. Zoom
    B. Save
    C. Undo
    D. Close

11. Which bar displays the contents of a cell? (p. 12)
    A. Title bar
    B. Quick Access Toolbar (QAT)
    C. Scroll bar
    D. Formula bar

1. Import Data in Excel

Follow the steps to complete the activity.

Step-By-Step

FIGURE 5.27 Text Import Wizard

1 Open the data file **Trip .xlsx**. Save as: Trip-[your first initial and last name]1.

2 Click cell **A7**. Choose **Data>Get External Data>From Text**.

3 Locate and select the text data file **Band.txt**. Click **Import**. The **Text Import Wizard** opens.

4 Click **Next**. In the **Delimiters** box, make sure **Tab** is selected (see Figure 5.27).

5 Click **Next**. Click **Finish**. In the **Import Data** dialog box, click **OK**.

6 Click the **Select All** button.

7 Choose **Home>Cells Format** and click **AutoFit Column Width**. Deselect the range.

8 *i***CHECK** Your screen should look like Figure 5.28.

9 Save and close your file.

Text Import Wizard - Step 2 of 3

This screen lets you set the delimiters your data contains. You can see how your text is affected in the preview below.

Delimiters
☑ Tab
☐ Semicolon   ☐ Treat consecutive delimiters as one
☐ Comma
☐ Space   Text qualifier: "
☐ Other:

Data preview

```
Spending money   20
Souvenirs        15
Snacks           10
Phone calls      5
Share of motel room  25
```

Cancel   < Back   Next >   Finish

FIGURE 5.28 Worksheet with imported data

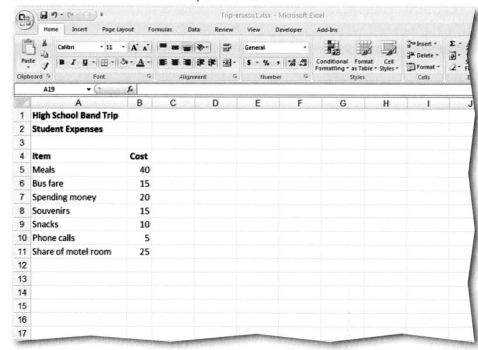

1. Insert Cell Contents and Change Zoom View

Follow the steps to complete the activity.

Step-By-Step

1. Open your **e1-6** file.

2. Choose **Office>Save As**. In the File name box, key: e1rev-[your first initial and last name]1.

3. Ask your teacher for the location you should select in the **Save in** box. Select that location. Click **Save**.

4. In cells **D1** through **E4**, key the new data shown in Figure 1.26.

5. Point to the line between the letters **D** and **E**. Drag the double arrow until all of the contents fit in column **D**.

6. Choose **View>Zoom**.

7. Click **Custom**. Key: 125. Click **OK**.

8. **ⓘCHECK** Your screen should look like Figure 1.27.

9. Choose **View>100%**.

10. Save and close your file.

FIGURE 1.26 New data added to worksheet

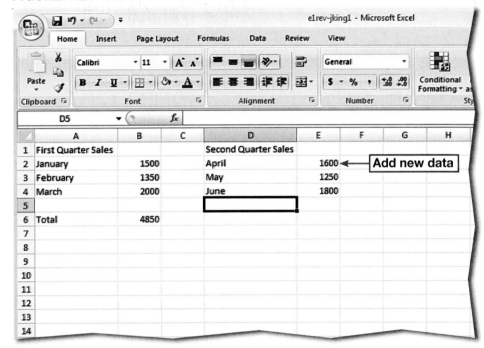

FIGURE 1.27 Screen at 125% zoom

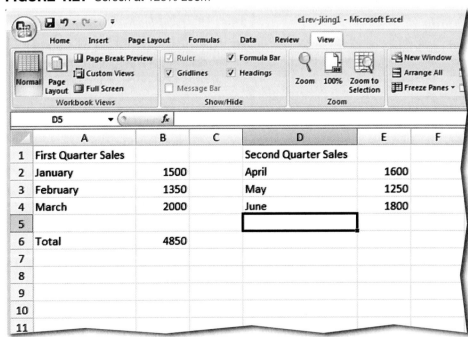

Vocabulary

Key Terms
Compatibility Checker
delimited
Document Information
  Panel
Document Inspector
import
keyboard shortcut
macro
property
summary worksheet
template
user-defined template
Web query

Academic Vocabulary
author
consolidate
perform
reveal

Review Vocabulary

Complete the following statements on a separate piece of paper. Choose from the Vocabulary list on the left to complete the statements.

1. The Document Inspector can help you remove sensitive information about a document that you would not want to ——————, or show to a reader. (p. 257)

2. To transfer data from Excel to another application, —————— the data. (p. 255)

3. A model worksheet ready to be filled in with new data is called a(n) ——————. (p. 259)

4. The author is one example of a workbook ——————. (p. 258)

5. —————— data are separated by a character such as a tab or comma. (p. 255)

Vocabulary Activity

6. Create a worksheet listing five of the vocabulary words that you learned in this lesson. Save the file as a PDF and print it out. Have a classmate fill in the definitions.
  A. Create a vocabulary list. Make sure there is a column for the definitions.
  B. Save the worksheet as a PDF in a location specified by your teacher.
  C. Have a classmate define the vocabulary words in your PDF file. Check his or her work.

Review Key Facts

Answer the following questions on a separate piece of paper.

7. How do you record the title, author, and subject of a workbook? (p. 258)
  A. Save the file as a template.   C. Import the data.
  B. Add workbook properties.   D. Save the file as a Web page.

8. How do you import data to Excel from a Web page? (p. 256)
  A. Save the file as a Web page.   C. Create a Web query.
  B. Consolidate the data.   D. Edit the template.

9. What do you create when you consolidate, or combine, data from multiple worksheets? (p. 267)
  A. Keyboard shortcut   C. User-defined template
  B. Summary Worksheet   D. Web query

10. What feature allows you to record a series of commands that can be played back using a single command? (p. 264)
  A. Web query   C. template
  B. Compatibility Checker   D. macro

2. Edit Cell Contents

Step-By-Step

Follow the steps to complete the activity. You must complete Practice It Activity 1 before doing this activity.

1 Open your **e1rev-1** file. Save as: e1rev-[your first initial and last name]2.

2 Click cell **B2**.

3 Key: 1550.

4 Press ENTER.

5 **CHECK** Your screen should look like Figure 1.28.

6 Click **Undo**.

7 **CHECK** Your screen should look like Figure 1.29.

8 Click **Redo**. The changes you made to cell B2 reappear, the total is recalculated.

9 **CHECK** Your screen should look like Figure 1.28.

10 Save and close your file.

FIGURE 1.28 Edited cell

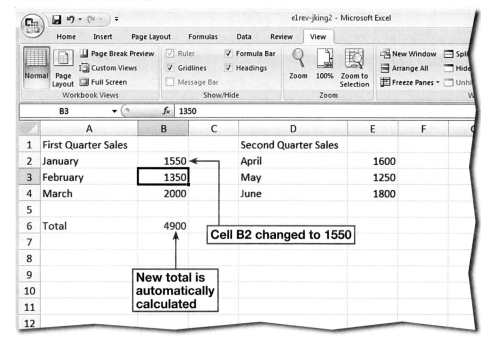

Cell B2 changed to 1550

New total is automatically calculated

FIGURE 1.29 Undo

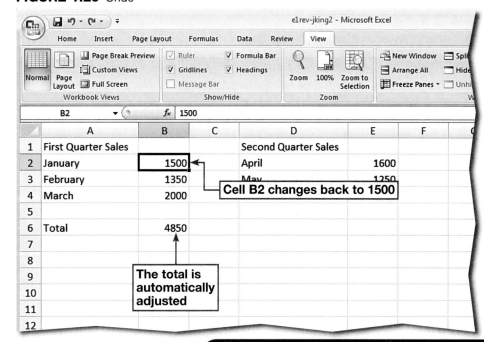

Cell B2 changes back to 1500

The total is automatically adjusted

MATH MATTERS

Payroll Sheet

C ongratulations! You just finished your first week at your first job. Because it is an entry-level position, you are working 35 hours a week, earning $7.50 an hour. On your first paycheck, you earned a total (gross pay) of $262.50. Deductions came to a total of $65.04, leaving you with a net pay of $197.46. What does all of this mean?

Federal Taxes, State Taxes, and Security

All workers need to pay taxes to the federal and state governments for many programs, including building roads and schools. The federal government also collects payments for Social Security, which provides income for retired and disabled persons.

Gross pay is the total amount that you earned before taxes are subtracted. Deductions are the amount of money that is subtracted from your earnings. Net pay, also called "take-home pay," is the amount after deductions are subtracted. Net pay is calculated as follows: Gross pay − Deductions = Net pay.

Payroll Records

Small to medium size employers may use Microsoft Excel to keep payroll records. The figure on the right shows a sample payroll record. Notice it contains each employee's gross pay, deductions, and net pay. Sometimes payroll sheets show other deductions, such as health insurance premiums or retirement payments. While larger employers often outsource payroll functions, Excel has the ability to calculate payroll checks.

Employee	Gross Pay	Deductions			Net Pay
		Federal Taxes	State Taxes	Social Security	
Adams, J.	297.50	26.78	14.88	18.45	237.39
Bart, L.	315.00	28.35	15.75	19.53	251.37
Moor, T.	314.50	28.31	15.73	19.50	250.96
Fisher, J.	400.00	36.00	20.00	24.80	319.20
Harris, B.	336.00	30.24	16.80	20.83	268.13

Payroll sheets show what employees have earned.

SKILLBUILDER

1. **Define** What is the net pay of a paycheck?
2. **Explain** Why is it important for businesses to keep payroll records?

3. **Calculate** Sandy works 17 hours a week at $9.50 an hour. Each pay period she has $29.13 in deductions. What is Sandy's net pay?

3. Calculate a Sum and Print a Worksheet

Follow the steps to complete the activity. You must complete Practice It Activity 2 before doing this activity.

Step-By-Step

1. Open your **e1rev-2** file. Save as: e1rev-[your first initial and last name]3.

2. Click cell **E6**.

3. Choose **Formulas> Function Library> AutoSum** Σ.

4. Select cells **E2** to **E4**. Press ENTER.

5. **①CHECK** Your screen should look like Figure 1.30.

6. Choose **Office>Print> Print Preview**.

7. **①CHECK** Your screen should look like Figure 1.31.

8. Click **Close Print Preview** to close Print Preview.

9. Choose **Office>Print**. With your teacher's permission, click **OK** to print the document.

10. Save and close your file.

FIGURE 1.30 AutoSum results

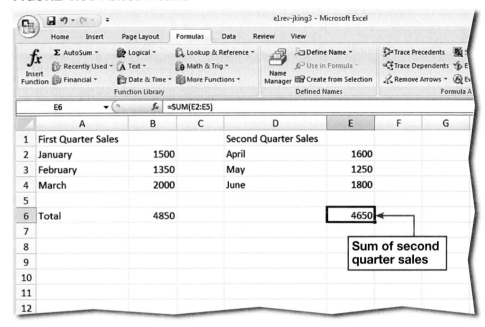

FIGURE 1.31 Print Preview

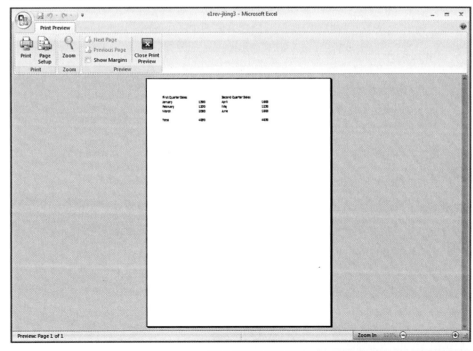

Step-By-Step

1. Open the data file **Paper. xlsx**. Save as: Paper-[your first initial and last name].

2. In cell **B9** on the **1stQuarter**, **2ndQuarter**, **3rdQuarter**, and **4thQuarter** sheets, use **AutoSum** to calculate a total for the three months.

3. In the **Summary** sheet, click cell **B3**. Key: =SUM((See Figure 5.25). Click the **1stQuarter** sheet tab. Click cell **B9**. Press ENTER.

4. In the **Summary** sheet, click cell **B4**. Key: =SUM(. Click the **2ndQuarter** sheet tab. Click cell **B9**. Press ENTER.

5. Repeat Steps 3 and 4 to enter the total sales for the **3rdQuarter** and **4thQuarter** in the **Summary** sheet.

6. In the **Summary** sheet, click cell **B8**. Key: =SUM(. Click the **1stQuarter** sheet tab. Click cell **B9**.

7. Press and hold SHIFT. Click the **4thQuarter** sheet tab. Press ENTER.

8. **i)CHECK** Your screen should look similar to Figure 5.26.

9. Save and close your file.

EXERCISE 5-11
Consolidate Data from Two or More Worksheets

You can create a **summary worksheet** to consolidate, or combine, data from multiple worksheets. Summary worksheets contain formulas that include references to cells on multiple sheets. They are useful because they contain all the essential data you need in a single location, each with its fully functioning formulas.

FIGURE 5.25 Creating a formula across multiple worksheets

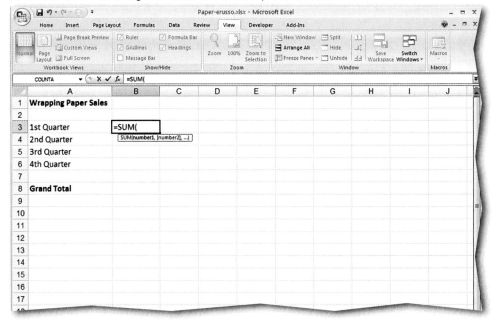

FIGURE 5.26 Summary worksheet

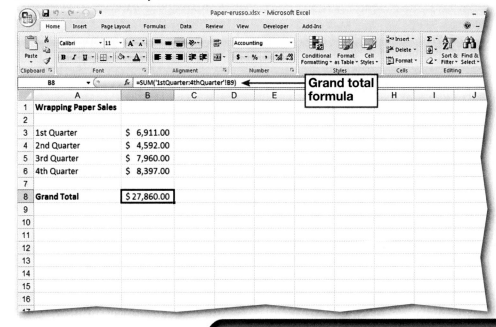

4. Make a Schedule

You have just started a new job. You have new responsibilities and a busy schedule. You decide to use Excel to create a schedule for each day of the work week.

Step-By-Step

1. Create a new workbook.

2. Save as: e1rev-[your first initial and last name]4.

3. In cell **A2**, key: Monday. In cell **A3**, key: Tuesday. Continue until Wednesday, Thursday, Friday, Saturday, and Sunday are keyed down the first column of the workbook.

4. Adjust the line between **A** and **B** until *Wednesday* fits in cell **A4**.

5. In cell **B1**, key: Week 1.

6. In cells **B2** to **B8**, key the number of hours shown in Figure 1.32.

7. Zoom in to **200%**.

8. **CHECK** Your screen should look like Figure 1.33.

9. Change the zoom back to **100%**.

10. Save and close your file.

FIGURE 1.32 Work schedule

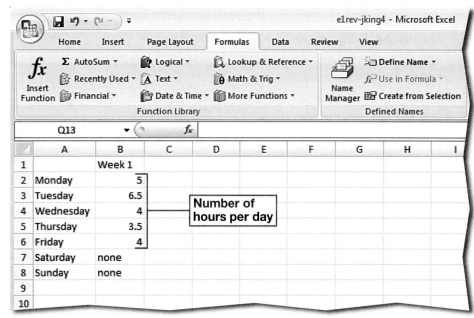

FIGURE 1.33 200% zoom

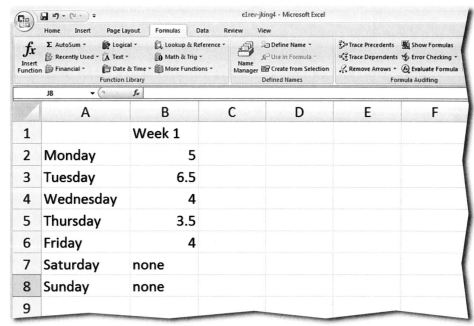

EXERCISE 5-10
Run a Macro

1 In your **Downtown** file, select the **West End** sheet tab. Choose **Developer> Code>Macros**.

2 In the **Macro** dialog box, in the **Macro Name** list, click **New_row**. Click **Run**.

3 ⓘ**CHECK** Your screen should look like Figure 5.23. Note that when new text is added, the macro will format it automatically.

4 In cell **A1**, key: Autumn Way Realtors. Press ENTER.

5 Select the **Downtown Total** sheet tab. Press CTRL + SHIFT + N. The macro runs again. Another formatted row is added to the top of the worksheet.

6 In the new cell **A1**, key: Autumn Way Realtors. Press ENTER.

7 ⓘ**CHECK** Your screen should look like Figure 5.24.

8 Save your file.

➡ *Continue to the next exercise.*

You Should Know

The shortcut key for your macro will override any default Excel shortcut keys while the workbook that contains the macro is open.

When you run a macro, you play back all of the actions that you recorded in one step. A macro is actually a small application that you created. You can run a macro from the Macro dialog box, but it is faster to use the **keyboard shortcut**, or set of keys that perform a task, that you specified when you created the macro.

FIGURE 5.23 New row inserted in worksheet.

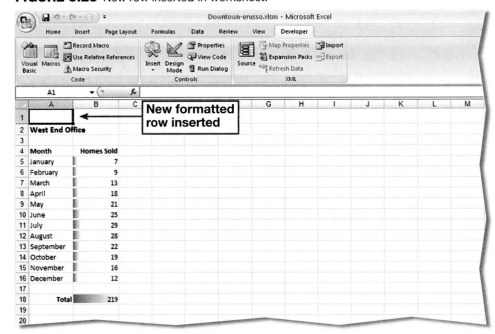

FIGURE 5.24 Macro run

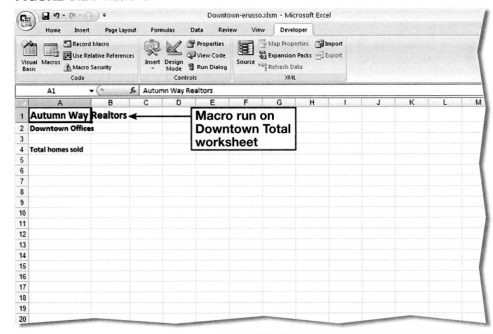

5. Calculate Weekly Hours

You decide to use AutoSum to compare how many hours you are working each week at your new job. You must complete You Try It Activity 4 before doing this activity.

Step-By-Step

1. Open your **e1rev-4** file.

2. Save as: e1rev-[your first initial and last name]5.

3. In cell **C1**, key: Week 2.

4. In cells **C2** to **C8**, key the number of hours shown in Figure 1.34.

5. In cell **C3**, change **5** to **6**.

6. In cell **A10**, key: Total Hours.

7. Click cell **B10**. Use **AutoSum** to calculate the total hours for Week 1.

8. Click cell **C10**. Use **AutoSum** to calculate the total hours for Week 2.

9. (i)**CHECK** Your screen should look like Figure 1.35.

10. Save and close your file.

FIGURE 1.34 Week 2 schedule

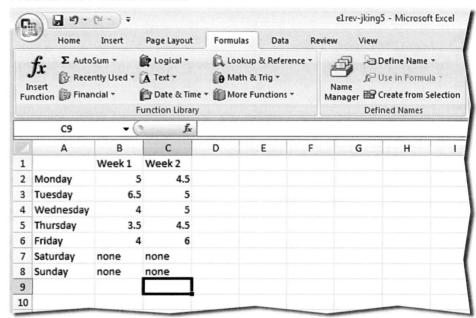

FIGURE 1.35 AutoSum results

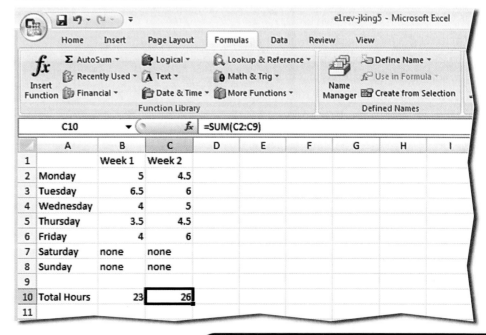

EXERCISE 5-9 (Continued)
Create a Macro

7 Choose **Home>Cells> Insert** to insert a new row. Click **Bold**.

8 Click the **Font Size** drop-down arrow. Choose **16**. Click **A1** to deselect the row.

9 Choose **Developer>Code> Stop Recording**.

10 **CHECK** Your screen should look like Figure 5.21.

11 In cell **A1**, key: Autumn Way Realtors. Press ENTER.

12 **CHECK** Your screen should look like Figure 5.22.

13 Save your file.

→ *Continue to the next exercise.*

Troubleshooter

If you make a mistake while recording a macro, you can delete the macro and start over. Choose **Developer> Code>Macros**. Click the name of the macro, and then click **Delete**.

FIGURE 5.21 New row added to worksheet

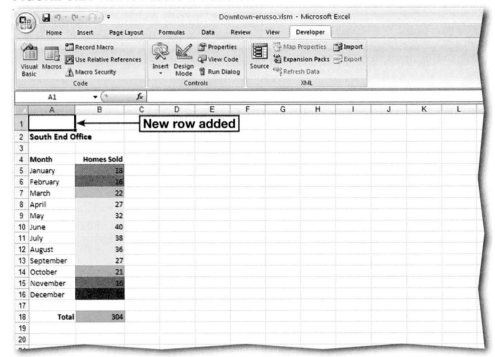

FIGURE 5.22 Macro controlled formatting

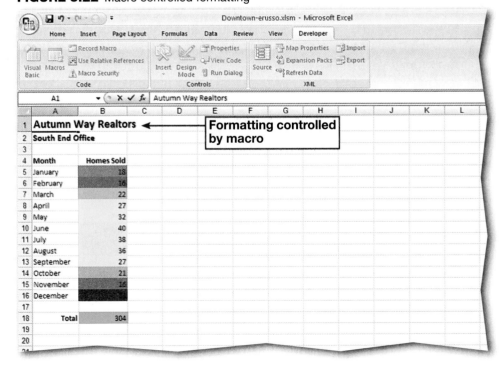

6. Beyond the Classroom Activity

 Language Arts: Describe Excel Excel can help you accomplish many tasks in your daily life. To learn more about how to use Excel, open the Excel Help feature. In the Excel Help window, search for Excel templates. Review the results of your search. You will see that Excel can be used to track anything from home repairs to sports results. Read any items that interest you. Then, key a paragraph in Word that describes how Excel could help you to track or complete a specific project you are currently working on.

Save your document as: e1rev-[your first initial and last name]6.

7. Standards at Work Activity

 Microsoft Certified Application Specialist Correlation
Excel 1.4 *Change Worksheet Views*

Organize Contact Information Your boss has asked you to create an Excel worksheet that will be used to store employees' contact information.

Create a new Excel worksheet. List the following titles in the first row: Name, Street Address, City, State, Zip Code. In the second row, fill in your contact data. Then add the contact information of three friends. Adjust column width so that all of the categories fit. Zoom in to 125%. Review your document and edit any cells with incorrect data. With your teacher's permission, print your worksheet. Key a paragraph explaining why you would want to change the zoom of a document.

Save your document as: e1rev-[your first initial and last name]7.

8. 21st Century Skills Activity

Increase Productivity One way to increase your productivity for a particular task is to practice. Practice will help you enter, edit, and calculate data quickly and efficiently. Another way to increase productivity is to ask others how they complete certain tasks efficiently.

Open your **e1rev-7** file. Add three more friends to your worksheet. Remember to adjust column width so that all of the categories fit. Share with your classmates any tips that help you enter and edit data more quickly in Excel. Add two relatives to your worksheet, using your classmates' productivity tips.

Save your document as: e1rev-[your first initial and last name]8.

Go Online e-REVIEW
glencoe.com

Go to the **Online Learning Center** to complete the following review activities.

Online Self Check
To test your knowledge of the material, click **Unit 1> Lesson 1** and choose **Self Checks.**

Interactive Review
To review the main points of the lesson, click **Unit 1> Lesson 1** and choose **Interactive Review.**

EXERCISE 5-9
Create a Macro

1 In your **Downtown.xlsm** file, choose **Office** > **Excel Options**. Under **Top Options for Working with Excel**, select **Show Developer Tab in the Ribbon**. Click **OK**.

2 Choose **Developer> Code>Record Macro**.

3 In the **Macro name** box, key: New_row (see Figure 5.19). Press TAB.

4 In the **Shortcut key** box, key: N. The keyboard shortcut will be CTRL + SHIFT + N.

5 **ⓘCHECK** Your dialog box should look like Figure 5.19. Click **OK**.

6 Click the row selector to the left of **row 1** to select the entire row (see Figure 5.20).

→ *Continued on the next page.*

Academic Skills

The term *macro* can also be used to describe something large. A computer macro is a single keystroke or set of keystrokes that substitutes for a larger group of commands. The antonym, or opposite, of macro is *micro*.

If you find that you regularly perform the same series of actions, you can create a macro to speed up your work. You must first save the workbook in a macro-enabled format. When you record a sequence of actions to be played back with a single command, the macro you create is actually a very simple and small application for use within Excel. Macros improve efficiency because they allow you to perform several commands in one step.

FIGURE 5.19 Record Macro dialog box

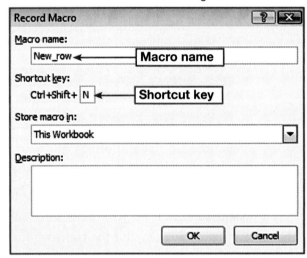

FIGURE 5.20 Macro Recording in worksheet

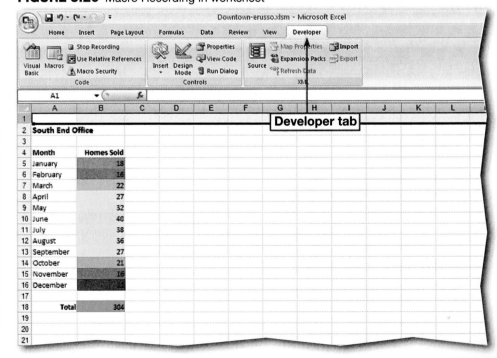

Before You Begin

Budget Expenses Whether you need to plan a party or buy school supplies, creating a budget can help you track costs and monitor your spending. These projects teach you how to use a spreadsheet to create a budget.

Reflect Once you complete the projects, open a Word document and answer the following questions:

1. What are some of the benefits of using Excel to create a budget?

2. How did Excel help you determine whether or not you were within your budget?

3. How might you use Excel to budget your time?

9. Create a Budget

Rubric
R

 Math: Track Expenses Your supervisor at your summer job has asked you to help organize an upcoming office party. She gives you a budget of $250. You decide to create an Excel worksheet that tracks the party's budget. List the following categories in the first column:

- Food
- Music
- Decorations
- Gift

Adjust column width so that all of the categories fit.

Save your worksheet as: e1rev-[your first initial and last name]9.

10. Calculate Total Costs

Rubric
R

 Math: Calculate Costs After looking into prices for your office party, you come up with estimates for each category. Enter the following costs in your party budget worksheet:

- Food = $85
- Music = $150
- Decorations = $25
- Gifts = $40

Use **AutoSum** to calculate the total cost of the party. Are the costs within your budget? Save your worksheet as: e1rev-[your first initial and last name]10.

11. Create an Alternative Budget

Rubric
R

 Math: Analyze Data Your supervisor looks at your budget and asks you to create a new budget that costs no more than $200.

- Create a new worksheet.
- In the third column of your worksheet, enter a different cost for each category.
- Use **AutoSum** to find the total cost of the alternative budget.
- If the budget is still over $200, reduce some of the costs and recalculate the total price of the party.

Save your workbook as: e1rev-[your first initial and last name]11.

Save a Workbook As Macro-Enabled

1 In your **Downtown** file, choose **Office** >
Save As>Excel Macro-Enabled Workbook .

2 ⓘ**CHECK** Your dialog box should look like Figure 5.17.

3 In the **Save As** dialog box, navigate to the folder holding the **Downtown** workbook file and click **Save**.

4 ⓘ**CHECK** Your screen should look like Figure 5.18.

5 Save your file.

➡ *Continue to the next exercise.*

A **macro** is a sequence of actions that you record and then play back with a single command. Macros improve efficiency because they allow you to **perform**, or carry out, several commands in one step. You can save a version of your workbook in the XML-based and macro-enabled file format. If you decide that you want to use macros in your documents, or to allow others to do so, you must save your workbook in a macro-enabled format first.

FIGURE 5.17 Save As dialog box

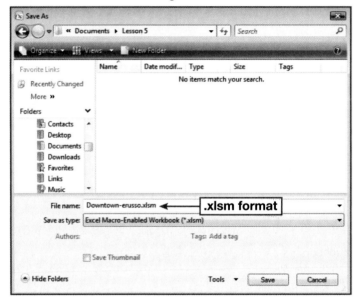

FIGURE 5.18 Macro-enabled file format

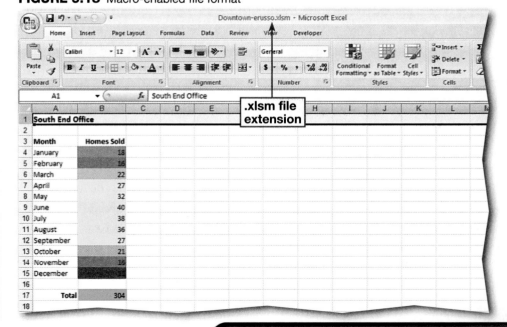

In this lesson, you will learn many new skills, including how AutoSum can add numerals and how to use Cut, Copy, and Paste commands. These skills will help you to use Excel to track budgets and inventory.

Key Concepts

- Enter, edit, clear, find, and replace cell contents

- Use AutoSum, AVERAGE, MIN, and MAX functions

- Use Cut, Copy, and Paste

- Use the Fill handle tool

- Insert, modify, and remove hyperlinks

Standards

The following standards are covered in this lesson. Refer to pages xix and 314 for a description of the standards listed here.

ISTE Standards Correlation

NETS•S

1a, 1d, 2b, 2d, 4a, 4c, 5c, 6a, 6b

Microsoft Certified Application Specialist

Excel

1.1, 2.2, 2.3, 3.2

21st CENTURY SKILLS

Manage Money Responsibly Have you ever bought two CDs on a Saturday afternoon and then found yourself without money the next week? Nearly everybody can improve their money management skills. The first step to managing your money is to create a budget, which is an estimate of income and expenses over a stated time. To create a monthly budget, write down the amount of money you have to spend each month. Then make a list of essential items that you buy each month, such as clothes or school supplies. Also list how much these items will cost over a month's time. Subtract this number from the amount you have to spend to find how much you have for things you would like but do not need.

Microsoft Excel is an excellent budgeting tool. In this lesson, you will learn the skills you need to create a budget. *Do you believe that a budget would help you better manage your money?*

Step-By-Step

1 Open the data file **Downtown.xlsx**. Follow your teacher's instructions to download and install the **Save As PDF** add-in.

2 Choose **Office** >**Save As**>**PDF or XPS**.

3 In the dialog box, navigate to the folder holding the **Downtown** workbook file. In the **File name** box, key: Downtown-[your first initial and last name].

4 In the **Save as type** box, select **PDF**. Make sure the **Open file after publishing** box is checked.

5 **CHECK** Your dialog box should look like Figure 5.15.

6 Click **Publish**.

7 **CHECK** Your screen should look similar to Figure 5.16.

8 Exit **Adobe Acrobat**.

➥ *Continue to the next exercise.*

Academic Skills

One way PDFs can be useful is in the classroom. For example, your chemistry teacher may provide a PDF version of the periodic table.

EXERCISE 5-7
Save a Workbook as a PDF

You can create a fixed-layout format of your file that is easy to share and print, but which cannot be modified. In order to do this, you must install the Save as PDF (Portable Document Format) or XPS (XML Paper Specification) add-in for the Microsoft Office 2007 system. After you install the add-in, you can export your file to PDF or XPS format to preserve document formatting when the file is viewed online or printed.

FIGURE 5.15 Publish as PDF or XPS dialog box

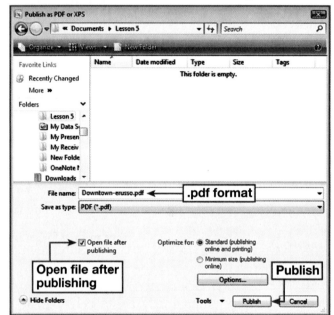

FIGURE 5.16 PDF file format in Adobe Reader

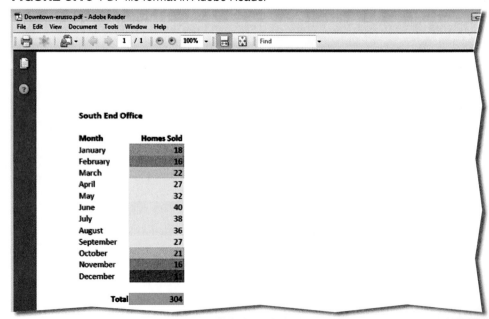

Before You Read

Prepare with a Partner Before you read, work with a partner. Read the exercise titles and ask each other questions about the topics that will be discussed. Write down the questions you both have about each section. As you read, answer the questions you have identified.

Read To Learn

- Perform tasks quickly and easily with Excel's automated tools and commands.
- Create and modify a budget to track expenses.
- Explore worksheet and workbook editing tools.
- Create and work with formulas and functions.

Main Idea

Excel has many functions that can help users create data and content for a spreadsheet.

Vocabulary

Key Terms

AutoSum	Clipboard	function
AVERAGE	copy	hyperlink
budget	cut	MAX
cell content	edit	MIN
clear	Fill handle	paste

Academic Vocabulary

These words appear in your reading and on your tests. Make sure you know their meanings.

determine

insert

Quick Write Activity

Explain On a separate sheet of paper, explore how you currently track how much you spend and how much money you save. Why is it important to track expenses? How might you use Excel to help you save money for an important purchase?

Study Skill

Make an Outline An outline is a good tool for organizing information. When you understand how information fits together, you will be more likely to remember what you have learned. On a separate sheet of paper, list the most important information from each exercise in the lesson.

Academic Standards

Math

NCTM (Number and Operations) Understand numbers, ways of representing numbers, relationships among numbers, and number systems.

NCTM (Number and Operations) Understand meanings of operations and how they relate to one another.

NCTM (Number and Operations) Compute fluently and make reasonable estimates.

NCTM (Algebra) Represent and analyze mathematical situations and structures using algebraic symbols.

1 In your **Bluehills** file, click **Office** and hold the pointer over the **Save As** option.

2 Under the **Save a copy of the document** header, select the **Excel 97-2003 Workbook** option.

3 In the **Save As** dialog box, navigate to the folder holding the **Bluehills** workbook file and click **Save**.

4 **CHECK** Your screen should look like Figure 5.13.

5 Navigate to and open the data file **Downtown**.

6 Choose **Office > Prepare>Run Compatibility Checker**.

7 **CHECK** Your screen should look like Figure 5.14. Click **OK**.

8 Choose **Save As> Excel 97-2003 Workbook**. In the **File name** box, key: Downtown-[your first initial and last name]. Click **Save**.

9 Click **Continue**.

10 Note the **.xls** file extension and the **Compatibility Mode** indicator in the title bar. Close your file.

→ *Continue to the next exercise.*

EXERCISE 5-6
Save Workbooks As Previous Versions

Office Excel 2007 works with previous versions of Excel. However, you cannot use all of the new and enhanced features and functionality without some conversion. If you decide to convert a workbook to or from an earlier version of an Excel workbook (with the document extension .xls), you can use a tool called the **Compatibility Checker**. The Compatibility Checker ensures that a workbook is compatible with earlier versions of Excel so that you can avoid the loss of data.

FIGURE 5.13 Excel 97-2003 file format

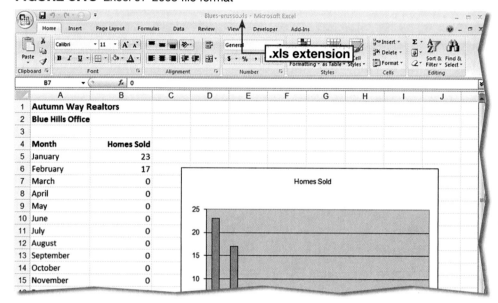

FIGURE 5.14 Microsoft Office Excel—Compatibility Checker box

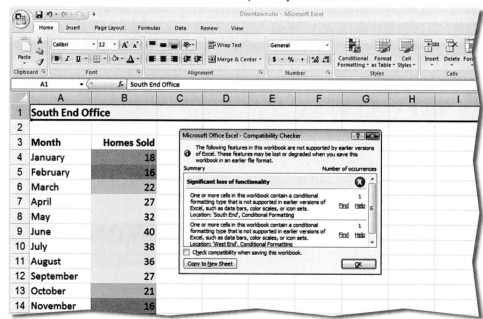

Step-By-Step

1 Start **Excel**. Choose **Office>Open**. The **Open** dialog box opens.

2 Click the **Look in** box drop-down arrow and select the location of your data files. Ask your teacher for the correct location.

3 Click the file **Budget.xlsx**. Click **Open**.

4 Choose **Office>Save As**. In the **File name** box, key: Budget-[your first initial and last name] (for example, *Budget-jking*). Ask your teacher which location to select in the **Save in** box. Click **Save**.

5 Click cell **F2**. Key: 300. Press ENTER.

6 **①CHECK** Your screen should look like Figure 2.1.

7 Key: 650 in cell **F3**. Press ENTER.

8 Key: 250 in cell **F4**. Press ENTER.

9 **①CHECK** Your screen should look like Figure 2.2. Save your file.

➡ *Continue to the next exercise.*

EXERCISE 2-1
Enter Cell Contents

Each cell in a worksheet can contain words, numbers, or both. The **cell content** will depend on the type of worksheet you are making. In this case, you are creating a budget for a business. A **budget** is an estimate of income and expenses over time. After you have entered what you want in a cell, press Enter to move to the cell below.

FIGURE 2.1 Content entered into cell F2

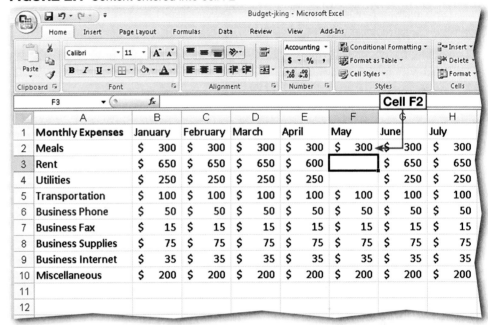

FIGURE 2.2 Cells F2, F3, and F4 with content

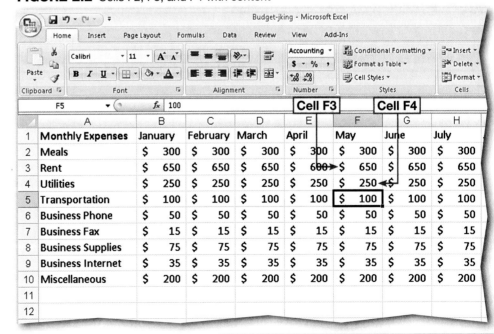

11 Choose **Office** >**New**.

12 Under **Templates**, click **My Templates**.

13 In the **New** dialog box, select the **Homes** template you just created (see Figure 5.11). Click **OK**. A new workbook is created based on the template.

14 Ask your teacher where to save your file. Save as: Bluehills-[your first initial and last name].

15 Click cell **A2**. Key: Blue Hills Office. Press ENTER.

16 Click cell **B5**. Key: 23. Press ENTER. Key: 17. Press ENTER.

17 **CHECK** Your screen should look like Figure 5.12.

18 Save your file.

➡ *Continue to the next exercise.*

Tech Tip

Make each template as complete as possible. Include everything that you think you will need each time you use the template including formulas, formatting, headers, and so on.

EXERCISE 5-5 (Continued)
Create and Edit a Workbook Template

FIGURE 5.11 Templates dialog box

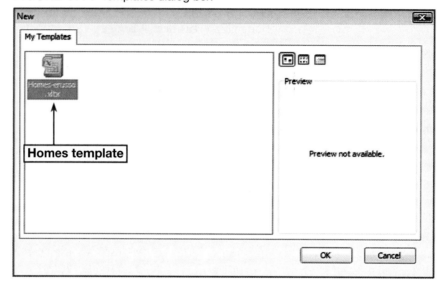

Homes template

FIGURE 5.12 New workbook based on template

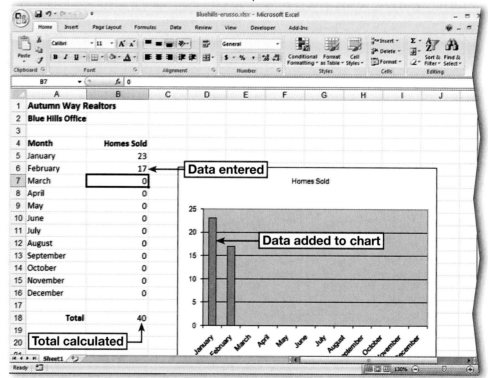

① In your **Budget** file, key the new row labels for cells **A12** through **A15** (see Figure 2.3).

② Click cell **B12**. Choose **Formulas** and click **AutoSum** Σ (see Figure 2.4). Press ENTER.

③ With cell **B13** selected, click the **AutoSum** drop-down arrow. From the drop-down list, choose **Average**.

④ Click cell **B2** and drag the pointer down to cell **B10**. Press ENTER.

⑤ With cell **B14** selected, click the **AutoSum** drop-down arrow and click **Min**.

⑥ Click cell **B2** and drag the pointer down to cell **B10**. Press ENTER.

⑦ With cell **B15** selected, click the **AutoSum** drop-down arrow and click **Max**.

⑧ Click cell **B2** and drag the pointer down to cell **B10**. Press ENTER.

⑨ **✪CHECK** Your screen should look like Figure 2.4. Save your file.

➡ *Continue to the next exercise.*

EXERCISE 2-2
Use AutoSum, AVERAGE, MIN, and MAX

Excel provides built-in formulas called **functions**. The **AutoSum** function is used to add values in rows or columns. The **AVERAGE** function is used to find the numeric average of a list of cells. Use the **MAX** function to *determine*, or identify, the largest number in a group of selected cells. Use the **MIN** function to identify the smallest number.

FIGURE 2.3 Row labels added to worksheet

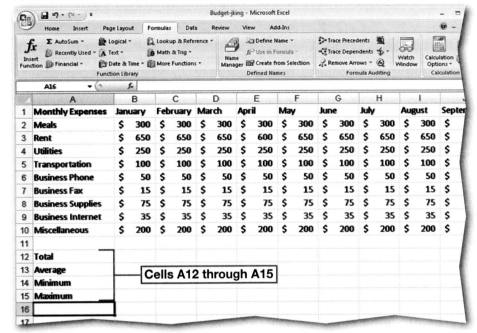

FIGURE 2.4 Function results

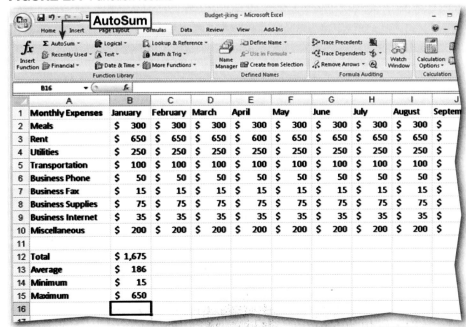

1 Open the data file **Homes.xlsx**.

2 Choose **Office>Save As**. In the **Save As** dialog box, in the **File name** box, key: Homes-[your first initial and last name].

3 Click the **Save as type** drop-down arrow.

4 Choose **Excel Template (*.xltx)**.

5 ⓘ**CHECK** Your dialog box should look like Figure 5.9.

6 Click **Save**. The file is saved as a template.

7 Click cell **B18**. Choose **Home>Editing**, and then click **Sum Σ** twice.

8 ⓘ**CHECK** Your screen should look like Figure 5.10.

9 Select **A4:B4**. Click **Bold**. Deselect the range. Click cell **A1**.

10 Save and close your template.

→ *Continued on the next page.*

You Should Know

Excel comes with common templates such as an expense report and a billing statement.

EXERCISE 5-5
Create and Edit a Workbook Template

If you create many workbooks that are similar to each other, using a template will save time. A **template** is a workbook that is used as the basis for new workbooks. You can use built-in templates, or create your own **user-defined template**. When you create a workbook based on a template, Excel opens a copy of the template, and you fill in the details.

FIGURE 5.9 Save As dialog box

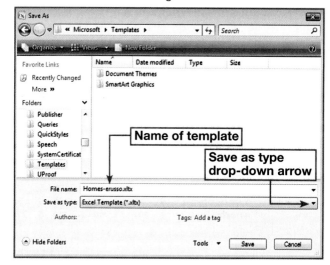

FIGURE 5.10 Formula added

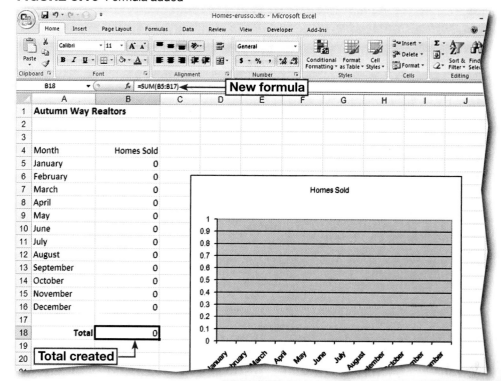

1 In your **Budget** file, double-click cell **E3**.

2 Click to the right of **600**.

3 Press ⟵BACKSPACE twice

4 ⓘCHECK Your screen should look like Figure 2.5.

5 Key: 50.

6 Press ENTER.

7 ⓘCHECK Your screen should look like Figure 2.6.

8 Save your file.

➡ *Continue to the next exercise.*

You Should Know

You can also edit the contents of a cell in the formula bar. Click in the cell you wish to edit. The cell contents will appear in the formula bar, where you can edit them.

Academic Skills

Using a budget can help ensure you are not spending more money than you have. Review the file used in this exercise and identify the costs being tracked. What other costs might a business need to track on a monthly basis?

EXERCISE 2-3
Edit Cell Contents

Sometimes you will find a cell that contains incorrect information. Other times, you may need to enter new or updated data in a cell that already contains information. In either case, you can change, or **edit**, the contents of a cell by double-clicking in that cell.

FIGURE 2.5 Deleted zeros

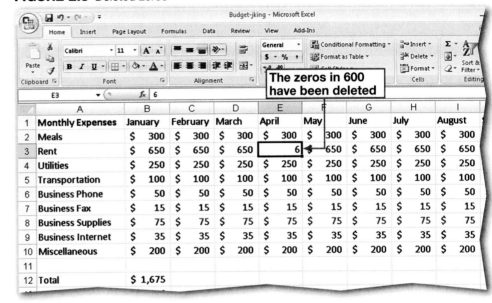

FIGURE 2.6 Edited cell

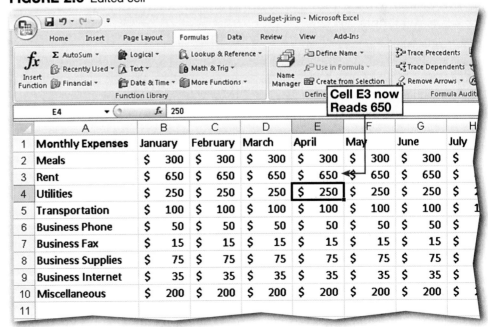

1. In your **Deals** file, choose **Office>Prepare**. Click **Properties** [icon].

2. The **Document Information Panel** opens.

3. **ⓘCHECK** Your screen should look similar to Figure 5.7.

4. In the **Document Information Panel**, click the drop-down arrow next to **Document Properties**. Select **Advanced Properties**.

5. Click the **Contents** tab. Click the tabs **General**, **Statistics**, and **Custom**. Click **Cancel**.

6. Click the **Summary** tab. Double-click the text in the **Author** box and key your name.

7. In the **Subject** box, key: Featured Homes. In the **Keywords** box, key: 6/4/09.

8. **ⓘCHECK** Your dialog box should look similar to Figure 5.8. Click **OK**.

9. Click **Close the Document Information Panel**. Save your file.

→ *Continue to the next exercise.*

EXERCISE 5-4
Add Information to Workbook Properties

You can save useful information as part of a workbook, such as the name of the author, or source, comments about the workbook, worksheets included in the workbook, and the last date the workbook was modified. Each piece of information is called a **property**. In Excel 2007, you can use the **Document Information Panel** to view, add, and edit the document properties easily while you work on the document. This can help you to identify the file inside the Open dialog box and make it easier to find when performing a search.

FIGURE 5.7 Document Information Panel

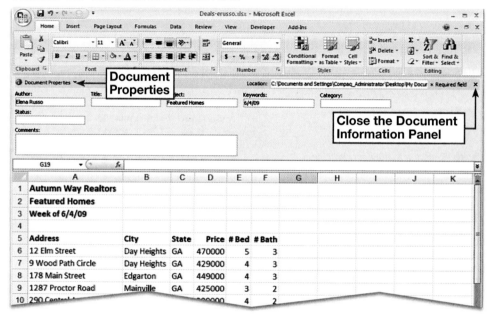

FIGURE 5.8 Properties dialog box

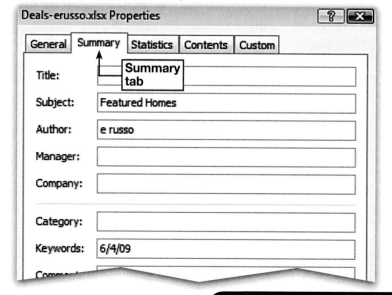

1 In your **Budget** file, click cell **C5**.

2 Press DELETE.

3 **(i)CHECK** Your screen should look like Figure 2.7.

4 Click cell **D5**.

5 Press DELETE.

6 Click cell **E5**.

7 Press DELETE.

8 **(i)CHECK** Your screen should look like Figure 2.8.

9 Save your file.

➡ *Continue to the next exercise.*

> **Microsoft Office 2007**
>
> Pressing DELETE is the same as using the **Clear Contents** button.

EXERCISE 2-4
Clear Cell Contents

When you need to make changes to the contents of a cell, you can edit the cell contents. There will be other times when you will just want to **clear**, or empty, the contents of a cell.

FIGURE 2.7 Clearing cell content

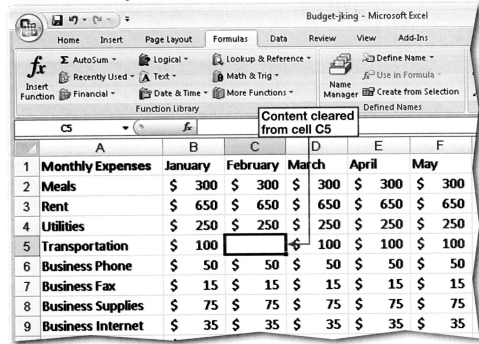

FIGURE 2.8 More cell content deleted

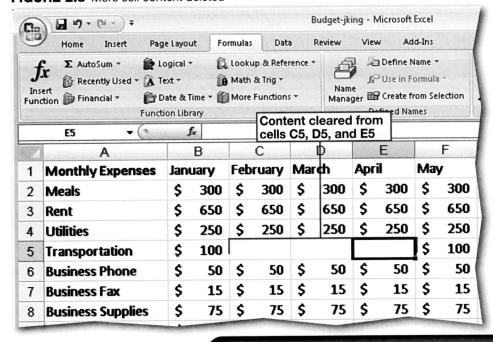

1 In your **Deals** file, click the **Sheet1** tab. Choose **Office** >**Save As**.

2 In the **File name** box, key: Deals-copy-[your first initial and last name].

3 In your **Deals-copy** file, choose **Office** > **Prepare>Inspect Document** .

4 **ⓘCHECK** Your dialog box should look like Figure 5.5.

5 Make sure all boxes in the **Document Inspector** dialog box are checked. Click **Inspect**.

6 **ⓘCHECK** Your screen should look like Figure 5.6.

7 Review the inspection results. Click both **Remove All** buttons.

8 Reinspect the document. Note that all the hidden data and text have been removed.

9 Click **Close**. Save and close your **Deals-copy** file.

➡ *Continue to the next exercise.*

EXERCISE 5-3
Use the Document Inspector

When a document is worked on by many people, it may reveal, or expose, details about your organization or about the workbook that should not be shared publicly. It might also contain comments, revisions, and tracked changes. Before you export, send, or share data with others, you can use the **Document Inspector** to remove hidden data from a worksheet. The Document Inspector reviews documents for hidden data or personal information that is stored in the document or document properties.

FIGURE 5.5 Document Inspector dialog box

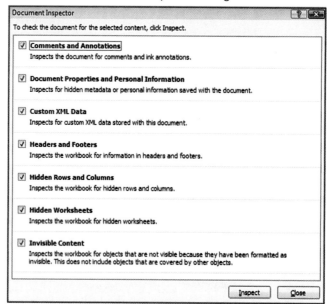

FIGURE 5.6 Document Inspector dialog box with inspection results

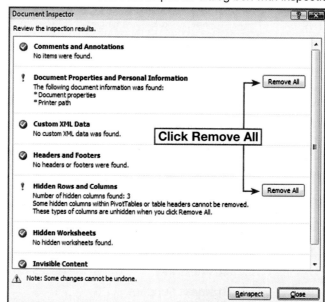

1 In your **Budget** file, choose **Home>Editing>Find & Select**. Click **Replace**.

2 In the **Find and Replace** dialog box, in the **Find what** box, key: Miscellaneous (see Figure 2.9). Press TAB.

3 In the **Replace with** box, key: Insurance.

4 Click **Replace All**.

5 Click **OK** in the message box.

6 In the **Find and Replace** dialog box, click **Close**.

7 ⓘ**CHECK** Your screen should look like Figure 2.10.

8 Save your file.

➥ *Continue to the next exercise.*

You Should Know

Use the **Options** button in the **Find and Replace** dialog box to select whether you want to search within a worksheet or within an entire workbook.

EXERCISE 2-5
Find and Replace Cell Contents

You may sometimes want to find all the cells that contain particular contents and replace the contents with another phrase or number. Although you could do this cell by cell, there is an easier way. The Find and Replace dialog box will automatically find all the cells with particular content and replace it. For instance, you might want to find the word *business* and replace it everywhere with the word *company*.

FIGURE 2.9 Find and Replace dialog box

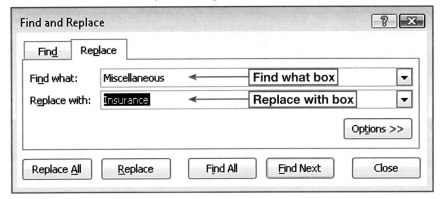

FIGURE 2.10 The replaced text

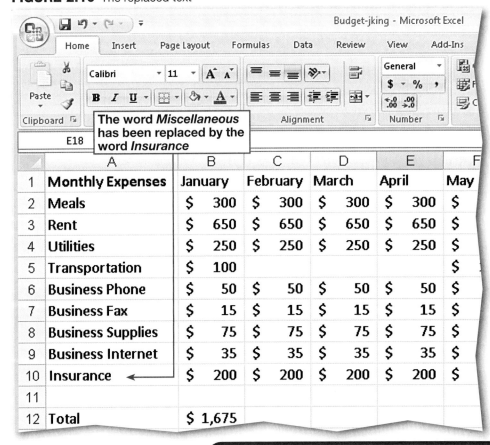

The word *Miscellaneous* has been replaced by the word *Insurance*

	A	B	C	D	E	F
1	**Monthly Expenses**	**January**	**February**	**March**	**April**	**May**
2	Meals	$ 300	$ 300	$ 300	$ 300	$
3	Rent	$ 650	$ 650	$ 650	$ 650	$
4	Utilities	$ 250	$ 250	$ 250	$ 250	$
5	Transportation	$ 100				$
6	Business Phone	$ 50	$ 50	$ 50	$ 50	$
7	Business Fax	$ 15	$ 15	$ 15	$ 15	$
8	Business Supplies	$ 75	$ 75	$ 75	$ 75	$
9	Business Internet	$ 35	$ 35	$ 35	$ 35	$
10	Insurance	$ 200	$ 200	$ 200	$ 200	$
11						
12	Total	$ 1,675				

1 In your **Deals** file, click the **Sheet2** tab.

2 Choose **Data>Get External Data>Existing Connections** 📄.

3 In the **Existing Connections** dialog box, double-click **MSN MoneyCentral Investor Currency Rates** (see Figure 5.3).

4 In the **Import Data** dialog box, make sure **Existing worksheet** is selected.

5 Click **OK**.

6 **ⓘCHECK** Your screen should look similar to Figure 5.4.

7 Save your file.

➤ *Continue to the next exercise.*

Tech Tip

To import data directly from a Web page, choose **Data>Get External Data> From Web** 📄. In the **New Web Query** dialog box, key the Internet address for the Web page, select the data or tables you want to import, and click **Import**.

EXERCISE 5-2
Link to Web Page Data

In addition to importing data from text files, you can also import data from a Web page. To do so, you must create a **Web query**. A Web query opens a Web page and then imports one or more tables of data from the Web page into your workbook. When you use a Web query, you can specify which parts of the Web page you want to import, as well as how much formatting you want to keep. A Web query creates a link to the Web page. This allows you to keep the information as current as possible.

FIGURE 5.3 Existing Connections dialog box

FIGURE 5.4 Data imported from Web page

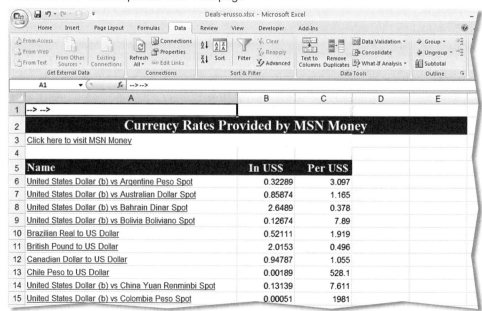

① In your **Budget** file, click cell **A10**.

② Place the pointer over the edge of cell **A10** so that the four-headed arrow pointer ⊹ appears (see Figure 2.11).

③ Click on the edge of cell **A10** and hold the mouse button down.

④ Drag the pointer over cell **A11** and release the mouse button.

⑤ **ⓘCHECK** Your screen should look like Figure 2.12. The content of cell A10 has been moved to A11.

⑥ Save your file.

➥ *Continue to the next exercise.*

Shortcuts

You can move more than one cell at a time. Select all of the cells you want to move. Then grab the edge of the selection and drag the cells to their new location.

EXERCISE 2-6
Move Selected Cells

Sometimes a cell or cells are originally keyed in the wrong place. Instead of deleting the contents of the cells and rekeying them in the correct place, you can simply move the cell or cells to the correct place.

FIGURE 2.11 Pointer turned into the four-headed arrow pointer

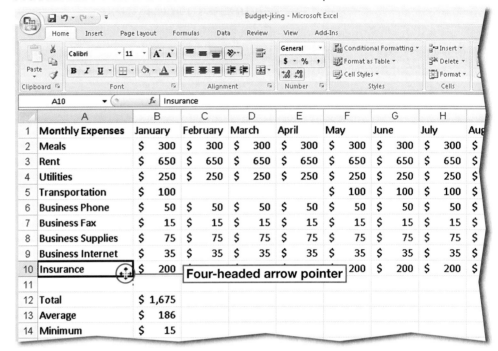

FIGURE 2.12 New cell placement

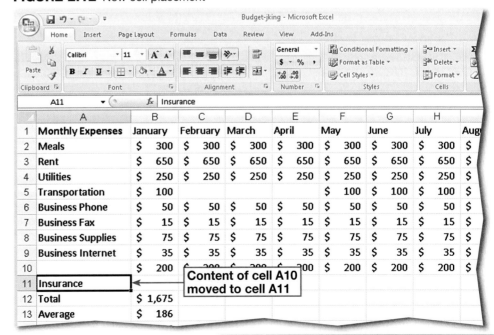

Step-By-Step

1. Start **Excel**.

2. Open the data file **Deals.xlsx**. Save as: Deals-[your first initial and last name]. (For example, *Deals-erusso*.)

3. Click cell **A11**. Choose **Data>Get External Data>From Text**.

4. With your teacher's help, locate the text data file **Specials.txt**. Click **Import**.

5. In the **Text Import Wizard** dialog box, notice that **Delimited** is selected. Click **Next**.

6. Deselect **Tab**. Select **Comma** (see Figure 5.1).

7. Click **Next**. Click **Finish**. Click **OK**.

8. Click the **Select All** button. Choose **Home> Cells>Format** and select **AutoFit Column Width**. Deselect the data.

9. **①CHECK** Your screen should look like Figure 5.2.

10. Save your file.

➡️ *Continue to the next exercise.*

EXERCISE 5-1
Import Data to Excel

Excel can **import** data, or bring it in from other sources and file formats. Importing data is useful because it prevents you from having to rekey it. In this exercise, you will import a text file containing data that is **delimited**, or separated by a comma or other character. Excel uses that character to divide the text into columns.

FIGURE 5.1 Text Import Wizard

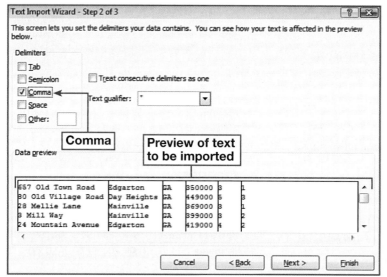

FIGURE 5.2 Worksheet with imported data

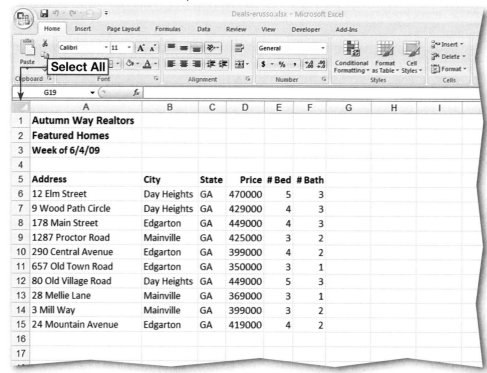

1 In your **Budget** file, click cell **B10**. Click and hold the mouse button down. Drag the pointer to cell **G10**. The range **B10:G10** is now selected.

2 Choose **Home> Clipboard>Cut** ✂.

3 Click cell **B11**.

4 Choose **Home>Clipboard**. Click **Paste** 📋.

5 ⓘ**CHECK** Your screen should look like Figure 2.13.

6 Select cells **H10** through **M10**.

7 Choose **Home> Clipboard>Copy** 📋.

8 Click cell **H11**.

9 Click **Paste** 📋. Press ⎋ to make the moving line disappear.

10 ⓘ**CHECK** Your screen should look like Figure 2.14.

11 Save your file.

➡ *Continue to the next exercise.*

EXERCISE 2-7
Cut, Copy, and Paste Cells

One way to move and copy cells is to use the **Cut**, **Copy**, and **Paste** commands. When you use the Cut command, the cells are removed from their original location and placed on the **Clipboard**. When you use the Copy command, the selected cells are copied, and the copy is placed on the Clipboard. The Paste command then allows you to move cut or copied cells from the Clipboard into your worksheet. Cutting, copying, and pasting cells can help you ensure that your budget is accurate while also saving time.

FIGURE 2.13 Using Cut and Paste

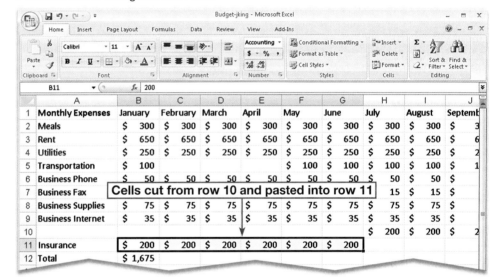

FIGURE 2.14 Using Copy and Paste

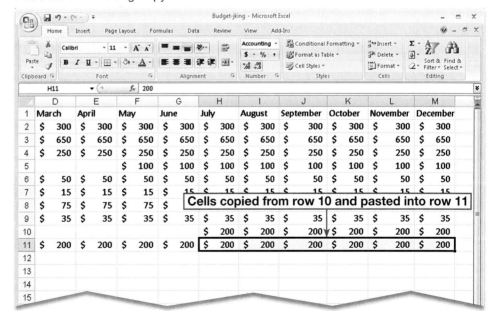

Before You Read

Check for Understanding It is normal to have questions when you read. Having questions means that you are checking your understanding of the material. Good readers realize that a difficult word or concept can make understanding information challenging. When you are involved in the material you are reading, you can fill in the missing knowledge as a way of getting the most out of the text.

Read To Learn

- Incorporate and modify imported data in Excel.
- Combine data from multiple sheets into a summary so that information is easier to access.
- Explore how using Document Properties makes files easy to identify and track.
- Understand how using macros can save time.

Main Idea

Excel offers many advanced tools and features to help you manage, consolidate, and present data.

Vocabulary

Key Terms

Compatibility Checker	macro
delimited	property
Document	summary worksheet
Information Panel	template
Document Inspector	user-defined template
import	Web query
keyboard shortcut	

Academic Vocabulary

These words appear in your reading and on your tests. Make sure you know their meanings.

author
consolidate
perform
reveal

Quick Write Activity

Describe On a separate sheet of paper, describe why a business might benefit from being able to consolidate data stored on different worksheets into one summary sheet. Explain how you think Excel might be useful if a clothing chain needs to track its sales figures for three different regions.

Study Skill

Teach Someone Else Ask a friend or relative what he or she would like to learn about Excel. Then, write down some notes about the topic and give this person a demonstration. Once you can teach Excel to someone else, you will know that you have really mastered it yourself.

Academic Standards

Language Arts
  NCTE 5 Use different writing process elements to communicate effectively.
  NCTE 7 Conduct research and gather, evaluate, and synthesize data to communicate discoveries.

Math
  NCTM (Number and Operations) Understand numbers, ways of representing numbers, relationships among numbers, and number systems.

1. In your **Budget** file, scroll left until you can see column A.

2. Click row heading **10** to select row 10.

3. **ⓘCHECK** Your screen should look like Figure 2.15.

4. Right-click and select **Delete**. Row 10 is deleted, and row 11 becomes row 10.

5. Click column-heading **C** to select column C (see Figure 2.15).

6. Choose **Home>Cells> Delete>Delete Cells** Column C is deleted.

7. **ⓘCHECK** Your screen should look like Figure 2.16. Notice that column D has become column C.

8. Save your file.

Continue to the next exercise.

You Should Know

You can delete all of the contents in a row or column. Select the row or column and press DELETE.

EXERCISE 2-8
Delete Rows and Columns

As you update files, you may often find it necessary to delete an entire row or column. When you delete a row or column, both the contents of the cells and the cells themselves are removed from the worksheet.

FIGURE 2.15 Selecting a row or a column

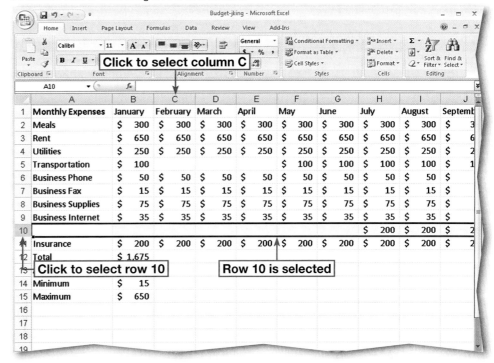

FIGURE 2.16 Deleting rows and columns

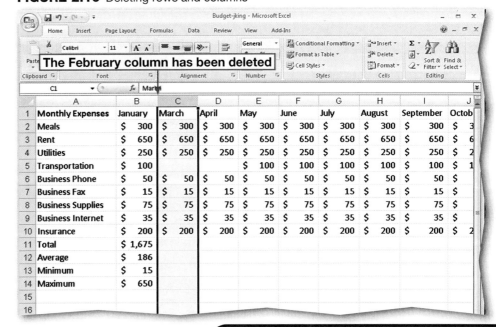

Key Concepts

- Import and export data

- Publish data as a Web page

- Create a template for repeated use

- Consolidate data

- Modify workbook properties

- Save workbooks in a macro-enabled format

- Create and run a macro

Standards

The following standards are covered in this lesson. Refer to pages xix and 314 for a description of the standards listed here.

ISTE Standards Correlation

NETS•S

1c, 1d, 2a, 2d, 3b, 3c, 4c, 6c

Microsoft Office Specialist Correlation

Excel

5.3, 5.4

In this lesson, you will learn skills for managing workbooks. For example, you will import data from files and from Web pages. You will create a template for types of workbooks that you create often, consolidate data by creating formulas across multiple worksheets, and save your workbooks as a PDF. You will also save a workbook in a macro-compatible format and create and run a macro.

21st CENTURY SKILLS

Learn to Adapt Computers have become essential business tools because they enable people to easily change or adapt information from one form to another. Users can also adapt software to fit new challenges and situations that occur at school, at work, or at home. For example, in this lesson, you will learn how to tailor Excel to meet your needs so you can work efficiently. Employers value employees who can adapt to new situations and challenges. They also like workers who can respond successfully to unexpected situations. *Do you believe you adapt well to new situations?*

1 In your **Budget** file, click column heading **C** to select column C, if necessary.

2 Choose **Home>Cells> Insert** and click the **Insert Cells** drop-down arrow. Click **Insert Sheet Columns**.

3 Select cells **B1 through B10**. Drag the selected cells one column to the right. The word *January* appears in cell C1. The rest of the contents are copied.

4 **ⓘCHECK** Your screen should look like Figure 2.17.

5 Click row heading **11** to select row 11. Click the **Insert Cells** drop-down arrow and select **Insert Sheet Rows**.

6 Select row heading **10** and click **Insert**. A new row is added.

7 **ⓘCHECK** Your screen should look like Figure 2.18. Save your file.

Continue to the next exercise.

EXERCISE 2-9
Insert Rows and Columns

You can also insert, or add, new rows and columns between existing rows and columns. The new row or column will be empty when you add it.

FIGURE 2.17 Inserting columns

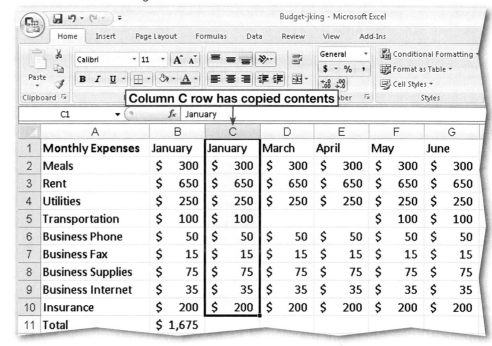

FIGURE 2.18 Inserting rows

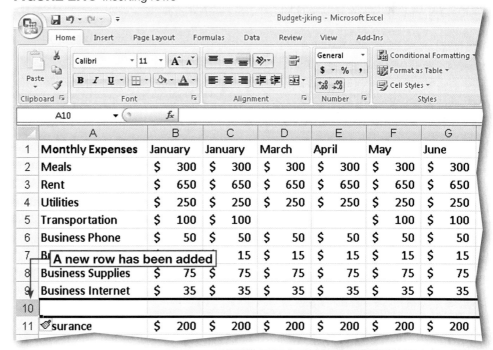

LESSON 4 Challenge Yourself Projects

Before You Begin

Collaborate Sharing information, setting passwords, and tracking changes and comments are important aspects of working collaboratively. These projects teach you how to use Excel's tools to merge workbooks, accept and reject changes, and secure your files.

Reflect Once you complete the projects, open a Word document and answer the following questions:

1. In what ways can you control other people's access to a workbook that you have created?

2. How can you use Track Changes in your day-to-day activities?

3. How can merging workbooks help you manage your time better?

---

9. Protect an Expenses Worksheet

 Language Arts: Set a Password You are in charge of keeping track of the supplies and other expenses for your baseball team. You need to protect your expenses workbook. You need to use a password to protect your file.

- Open the data file **Baseball.xlsx**.
- Set a password to modify the current password: *supplies1*. Use the password *123supplies* to replace the current password.

Save your file as: Baseball-[your first initial and last name]9.

Open a Word document and key a paragraph describing the differences between setting a password to open a file and setting a password to modify a file. Give examples of when it might be best to use each. Describe three rules you should follow when selecting a password.

10. Work Collaboratively

Language Arts: Merge Workbooks One of your teammates has been helping to track purchases made by the baseball team. You sent him a copy of your workbook. Now you need to merge the two workbooks.

- Open your **Baseball-9** workbook.
- Use **Compare and Merge Workbooks** to merge your **Baseball-9** workbook with the data file **Baseball-9-copy**.

Save your merged file as: Baseball-[your first initial and last name]10.

Your teammate wants to learn how to merge a workbook. Open a Word document and list the steps necessary to compare and merge workbooks.

11. Choose Which Changes to Keep

Language Arts: Accept and Reject Changes Now that you have merged the two workbooks, you need to review your teammate's notes.

- Open your **Baseball-10** workbook.
- Turn on **Track Changes**.
- Accept the first three changes that your teammate made.
- Reject the final change.

Open a Word document and key a paragraph that explains what happens when the pointer is rested over a changed cell when **Track Changes** has been applied to a file. What happens when a change is rejected?

Save your file as: Baseball-[your first initial and last name]11.

Lesson 4: Challenge Yourself Projects

Advanced Excel 252

EXERCISE 2-10
Insert and Delete Cells

You can insert or delete a single cell. Be careful—when you insert or delete a cell, the cells around the inserted cell shift, and data may no longer line up with the column or row headings. Usually, you will insert or delete an entire row or column.

1. In your **Budget** file, click cell **B11**.

2. Choose **Home>Cells**. Click the **Insert Cells** drop-down arrow. Select **Insert Cells**.

3. In the **Insert** dialog box, select **Shift cells down**. Click **OK**.

4. (i)**CHECK** Your screen should look like Figure 2.19.

5. With **B11** still selected, right-click and select **Delete**.

6. In the **Delete** dialog box, select **Shift cells up**.

7. Click **OK**.

8. Click row heading **10** to select row 10.

9. Right-click and choose **Delete**. Row 10 is deleted and row 11 moves up to replace it.

10. (i)**CHECK** Your screen should look like Figure 2.20.

11. Save your file.

➡ *Continue to the next exercise.*

FIGURE 2.19 Cell B11 shifted down

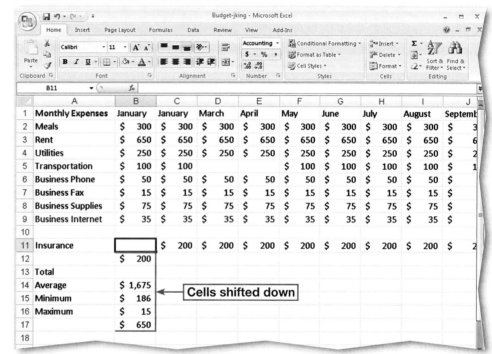

FIGURE 2.20 Row 10 deleted and row 11 taking its place

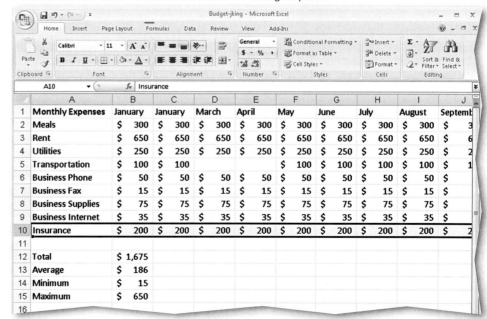

6. Beyond the Classroom Activity

 Language Arts: Track Your Changes You work as the receptionist at a veterinarian's office. When a pet arrives in the office, you key some basic information into a worksheet. Because it is your first week on the job, your boss wants you to use **Track Changes** so he can double-check your work.

Open the data file **Appointments.xlsx**.

- Turn on **Track Changes** so your boss can see your changes.
- Key new information about two pets that arrived in the office today.

Open a Word document and key one or two paragraphs describing how **Track Changes** can be used to protect the integrity of your documents.

Save your file as: Appointments-[your first initial and last name]6.

7. Standards at Work Activity

 Microsoft Office Specialist Correlation
Excel 5.2 *Protect and share workbooks*

Protect Worksheets Protecting a workbook or a worksheet guards against different kinds of changes. Open your **Appointments-6** file from the previous activity.

- Unlock the cells that contain the times for each appointment.
- Change the first appointment to **8:20**.
- Protect the worksheet. Try to make a change to one of the pet's names.

Open a word document and key a paragraph that explains why a business might want to protect cells containing formulas.

Save your file as: Appointments-[your first initial and last name]7.

8. 21st Century Skills Activity

Evaluate Your Progress When you see that you have made progress, you are driven to do more. Test your progress in learning one of the skills in this lesson. For example, to check your understanding of how to set a password to make a document secure, do the following:

- Open the data file **Services.xlsx**. Set a password to open the file.
- Close and reopen the workbook. Key an **incorrect** password.
- Open a Word document and key a paragraph that explains what it means when a password is **case sensitive**. Include examples.

Save your file as: Services-[your first initial and last name]8.

Go Online e-REVIEW
glencoe.com

Go to the **Online Learning Center** to complete the following review activities.

Online Self Check
To test your knowledge of the material, click **Unit 2> Lesson 4** and choose **Self Checks**.

Interactive Review
To review the main points of this lesson, click **Unit 2> Lesson 4** and choose **Interactive Review**.

1. In your **Budget** file, click cell **B1**. Point to the small square that appears on the lower right corner of the cell (see Figure 2.21). The pointer takes the shape of a plus sign ⊞.

2. Click and hold the mouse button. Drag the pointer to the right until it is on cell **C1**. Release the mouse button.

3. Click cell **B12**. Drag the Fill handle to the right until it is in cell **G12**.

4. Click cell **G12**. Drag the Fill handle to the right until it is in cell **M12**.

5. ⓘ**CHECK** Your screen should look like Figure 2.22.

6. Save your file.

➡ *Continue to the next exercise.*

EXERCISE 2-11
Use the Fill Handle

Sometimes you may want to insert the same contents into many different cells. For example, a bill may cost the same amount of money every month. You can use the **Fill handle** to insert repeated content into several cells at once.

FIGURE 2.21 The Fill handle

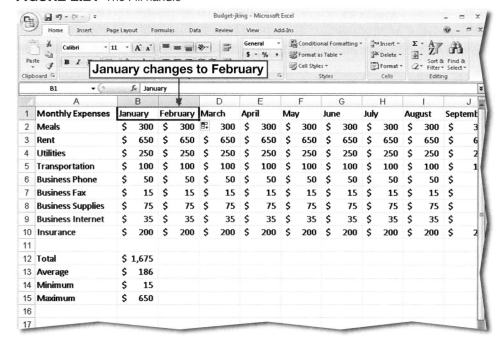

FIGURE 2.22 After using the Fill handle

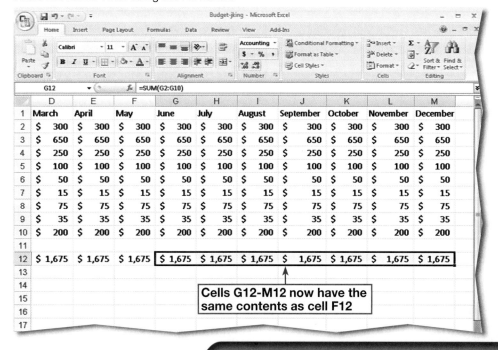

Cells G12-M12 now have the same contents as cell F12

5. Add a Digital Signature and Set a Password to Open a Workbook

Step-By-Step

1 Open your **May-4** file. Save as: May-[your first initial and last name]5.

2 Set a password to open the file. Key: youth09 as the password.

3 Confirm the password.

4 Save and close your file.

5 Reopen your **Museum** file. The **Password** dialog box opens (see Figure 4.37).

6 Key: youth09. Click **OK**.

7 Add a digital signature to the file.

8 **ⓘCHECK** Your screen should look like Figure 4.38.

9 Close your file.

Now that the members of the group have updated their monthly expenses, you decide to create a password to modify the document to prevent further changes. You also attach a digital signature to authenticate the information before forwarding it on to the youth group leader.

FIGURE 4.37 Password dialog box

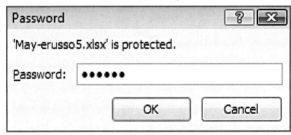

FIGURE 4.38 Digital signature added to file

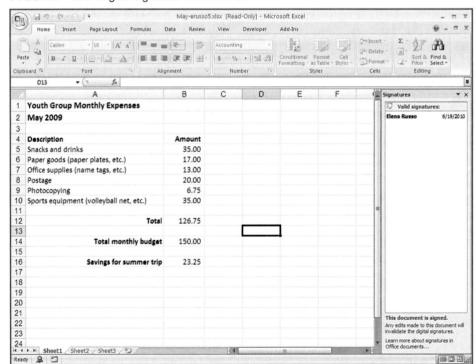

Step-By-Step

1 In your **Budget** file, click cell **C1**. Click **Insert> Links>Insert Hyperlink** .

2 In the **Insert Hyperlink** dialog box, use the **Look in** box to locate and select the data file **Months.xlsx** (see Figure 2.23).

3 Click **OK**. The text in cell C1 turns blue to indicate the presence of a hyperlink.

4 Click cell **C1**, hold, and then release to follow the link. The workbook **Months** opens.

5 Click **Close** to close Months.

6 Right-click cell **C1**. Choose **Edit Hyperlink**. Click **Remove Link**.

7 ⓘ**CHECK** Your screen should look like Figure 2.24. Save and close your file.

Academic Skills

Money management involves both tracking past costs and anticipating future costs. How can identifying these fixed costs help you estimate how much you might spend over a year?

EXERCISE 2-12
Insert and Edit Hyperlinks

A **hyperlink** is a shortcut that connects to a file in another location. If parts of your worksheet are associated with other files, you can insert a hyperlink that will open these files when you click a link in your worksheet. For example, perhaps you track monthly expenses in a separate worksheet and you want to be able to access these expenses from your overall budget file. Adding a hyperlink helps you link related files so that you can easily access them.

FIGURE 2.23 Insert Hyperlink dialog box

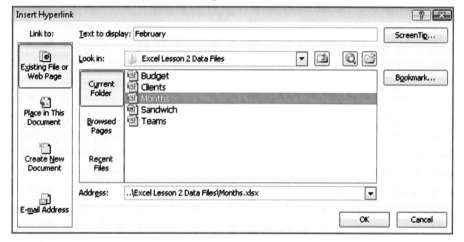

FIGURE 2.24 Workbook with hyperlink removed

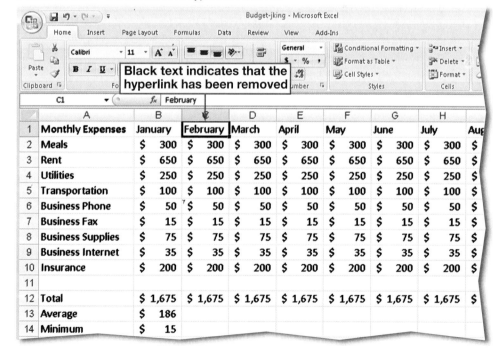

4. Protect Formulas

You have created a worksheet of monthly expenses for your youth group. Members of the group will be updating the amounts. So you decide to protect certain cells to prevent unintentional changes.

Step-By-Step

1. Open the data file **May.xlsx**. Save as: May-[your first initial and last name]4.

2. Select cells **B5:B10**.

3. Choose **Home>Cells> Format**. Under **Protection**, click **Lock Cells** to unlock those cells (see Figure 4.35).

4. Protect the worksheet.

5. Try to change the description of one of the categories. You are not able to because that cell is locked.

6. Try to key a number in cell **B16**. You are not able to because that cell is locked.

7. Change the amount for postage to **20**.

8. **CHECK** Your screen should look like Figure 4.36.

9. Save and close your file.

FIGURE 4.35 Cell Format drop-down menu

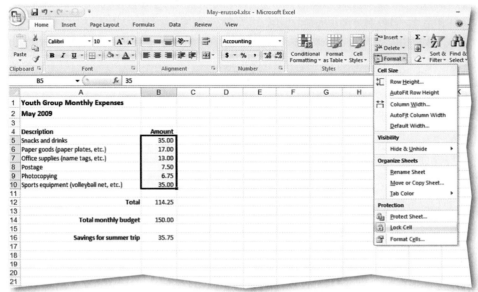

FIGURE 4.36 Change made to protected sheet

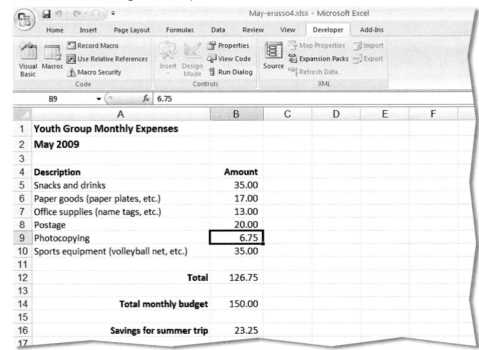

MATH MATTERS

Using Math Formulas

Y ou use math formulas every day without even realizing it. You might calculate how much money it will cost for a movie and snacks. Or, you might use a formula to figure out how much you will earn taking care of your neighbor's house.

The Problem

Your neighbors hire you to take care of their house for three days while they are on a trip. They will pay you $5 to check the mail, $2 each day to get the newspaper, and $7 to water the lawn and plants. You want to figure out how much you will earn.

How Excel Calculates

Excel uses formulas to do calculations like the one described above. Excel can also help you balance your checkbook or figure out how much it will cost to give a party.

Excel calculates formulas the same way you do calculations in your math class. Math follows certain rules to find the correct answer. The *order of precedence* states which part of the formula you calculate first. Some math operations, such as multiplication, take precedence over others. In other words, some operations are done before others. If you key a formula that has an addition symbol ($+$), a subtraction sign ($-$), a multiplication symbol ($*$), and a division ($/$) symbol, Excel will compute the multiplication first, then division, then addition, and then subtraction.

You can use Excel to calculate your earnings in a small business, such as taking care of people's houses while they are on vacation.

SKILLBUILDER

1. **State** If you key a formula that includes addition, subtraction, multiplication, and division, in what order will Excel do the calculations?

2. **Discuss** Explain why the order of precedence is important.

3. **Apply** Solve this problem using the order of precedence. You checked the mail and got the paper each day, but you paid your little sister $4 to water the lawn. How much money will you get to keep? The formula is: $5 + 2 * 3 + 7 - 4$. Multiply 2 times 3 first, then do the other operations from left to right.

---

3. Merge Workbooks

Follow the steps to complete the activity. You must complete Practice It Activity 2 before doing this activity.

FIGURE 4.33 Copy of shared workbook

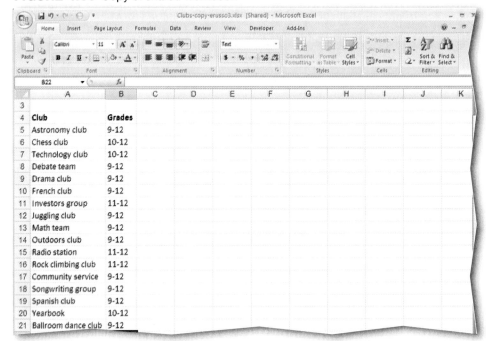

FIGURE 4.34 Merged workbook

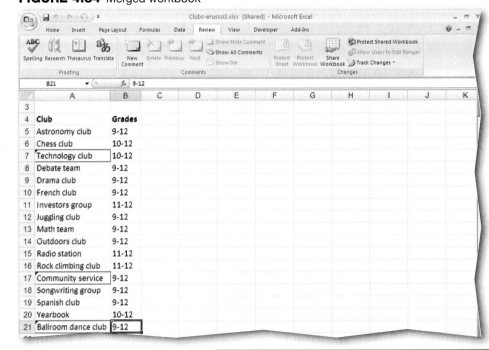

Step-By-Step

1. Open your **Clubs-2** file. Save as: Clubs-[your first initial and last name]3.

2. Choose **Review>Changes>Share Workbook**. Verify that the **Allow changes by more than one user** box is checked. Click **OK**.

3. Start **Excel** again. Open your **Clubs-3** file in the second copy of Excel. Save your **Clubs-3** file as: Clubs-copy-[your first initial and last name]3.

4. In cell **A21**, key: Ballroom dance club. Press TAB. Key: 9-12. Press ENTER.

5. **CHECK** Your screen should look like Figure 4.33. Save and close the file.

6. In your **Clubs-3** file, click **Compare and Merge Workbooks**.

7. Select your **Clubs-copy-3** file. Click **OK**.

8. **CHECK** Your screen should look like Figure 4.34. Save and close your file.

Vocabulary

Key Terms

AutoSum

AVERAGE

budget

cell content

clear

Clipboard

copy

cut

edit

Fill handle

function

hyperlink

MAX

MIN

paste

Academic Vocabulary

determine

insert

Review Vocabulary

Complete the following statements on a separate piece of paper. Choose from the Vocabulary list on the left to complete the statements.

1. The letters and numbers in a cell are called —————————. (p. 29)

2. You can ————————— new rows between existing rows. (p. 37)

3. A(n) ————————— is a shortcut to other files. (p. 40)

4. The ————————— function allows you to add values in rows and columns. (p. 30)

5. A(n) ————————— is a preset formula. (p. 30)

Vocabulary Activity

6. Create a matching game.
  A. Write six of this lesson's vocabulary words on index cards or squares of paper. Write the definitions for the six terms you selected on a different set of index cards or squares of paper.
  B. Place all of the cards face down on your desk and mix them up. Arrange the cards four across and three down.
  C. With your teacher's permission, pair up with a classmate. Take turns turning over two cards at a time. If the two cards are a vocabulary word and its correct definition, keep the cards. If not, put the cards back.
  D. Continue until you have reviewed all of your cards. The person who collects the most pairs at the end of the game wins.

Review Key Concepts

Answer the following questions on a separate piece of paper.

7. Which key should you press to move down one cell in a worksheet? (p. 29)
  A. Backspace   C. Insert
  B. Delete   D. Enter

8. Which group would you use to insert and delete rows and columns? (p. 36)
  A. Page Layout   C. Add-Ins
  B. Cells   D. Editing

9. Which of the following is a function? (p. 30)
  A. MIN   C. AutoSum
  B. AVERAGE   D. All of the above

10. How do you select a cell that you want to edit? (p. 31)
  A. Choose Home>Cells>Format.
  B. Click Copy
  C. Click the cell
  D. Double-click the cell.

2. Accept and Reject Changes

Follow the steps to complete the activity. You must complete Practice It Activity 1 before doing this activity.

Step-By-Step

1 Open your **Clubs-1** file. Save as: Clubs-[your first initial and last name]2.

2 Choose **Review> Changes>Track Changes** . Click **Accept/Reject Changes** .

3 In the **Select Changes to Accept or Reject** dialog box, click **OK**.

4 In the **Accept or Reject Changes** dialog box, click **Accept** (see Figure 4.31). The first change is accepted. The description of **Change 2 of 3** appears.

5 Click **Accept**. The description of **Change 3 of 3** appears.

6 Click **Reject**. The third change is rejected. The original value in cell B20 is restored.

7 **⚫CHECK** Your screen should look like Figure 4.32.

8 Save and close your file.

FIGURE 4.31 Accept or Reject Changes dialog box

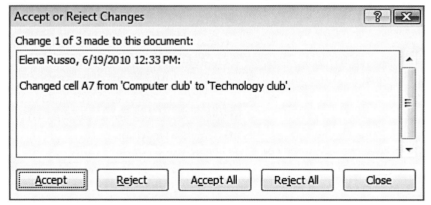

FIGURE 4.32 Worksheet after accepting and rejecting changes

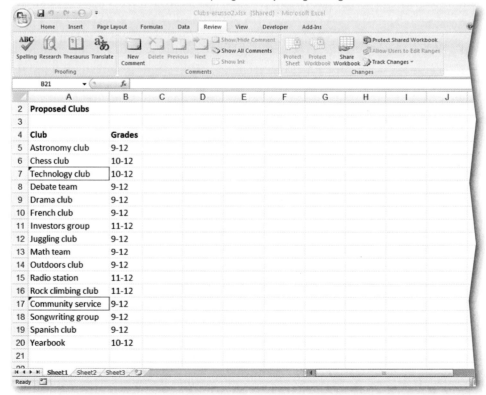

1. Enter, Edit, and Clear Cell Contents

Step-By-Step

Follow the steps to complete the activity.

FIGURE 2.25 List of weeks

1 Open the data file **Clients.xlsx**. Close the task pane, if necessary.

2 Save the file as: Clients-[your first initial and last name]1.

3 Click cell **A6**. Key: Chris. Press `ENTER`.

4 Key: Sam. Press `ENTER`.

5 **CHECK** Your screen should look like Figure 2.25.

6 Double-click cell **B1**. Click between the *k* and *1*. Press the spacebar.

7 Click cell **D5**. Press `BACKSPACE`.

8 **CHECK** Your screen should look like Figure 2.26.

9 Save and close your file.

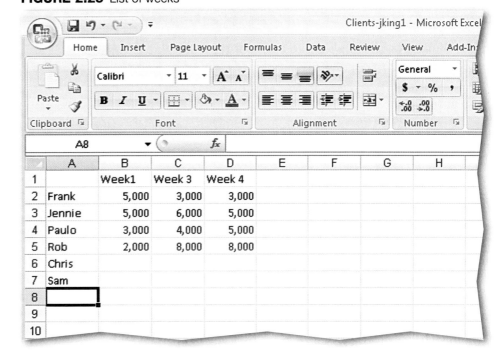

FIGURE 2.26 Editing and clearing contents

LESSON 4 Practice It Activities

1. Share a Workbook and Track Changes

Data File

Follow the steps to complete the activity.

Step-By-Step

1. Open the data file **Clubs.xlsx**. Save as: Clubs-[your first initial and last name]1.
2. Choose **Review>Changes>Track Changes**. Click **Highlight Changes**.
3. Click the **Track changes while editing** check box.
4. **CHECK** Your dialog box should look like Figure 4.29. Click **OK**.
5. A confirmation box opens. Click **OK**. Track Changes is now on.
6. Click cell **A7**. Key: Technology club. Press ENTER.
7. Click cell **A17**. Key: Community service. Press ENTER.
8. Click cell **B20**. Key: 9-12. Press ENTER.
9. **CHECK** Your screen should look like Figure 4.30.
10. Save and close your file.

FIGURE 4.29 Highlight Changes dialog box

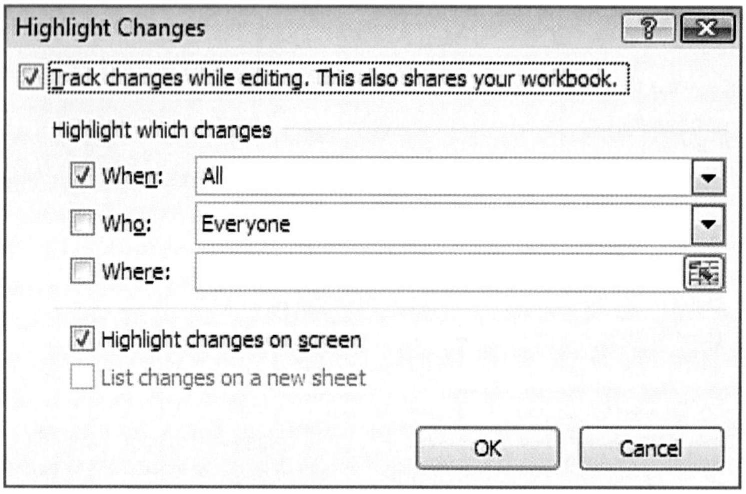

FIGURE 4.30 Tracked changes

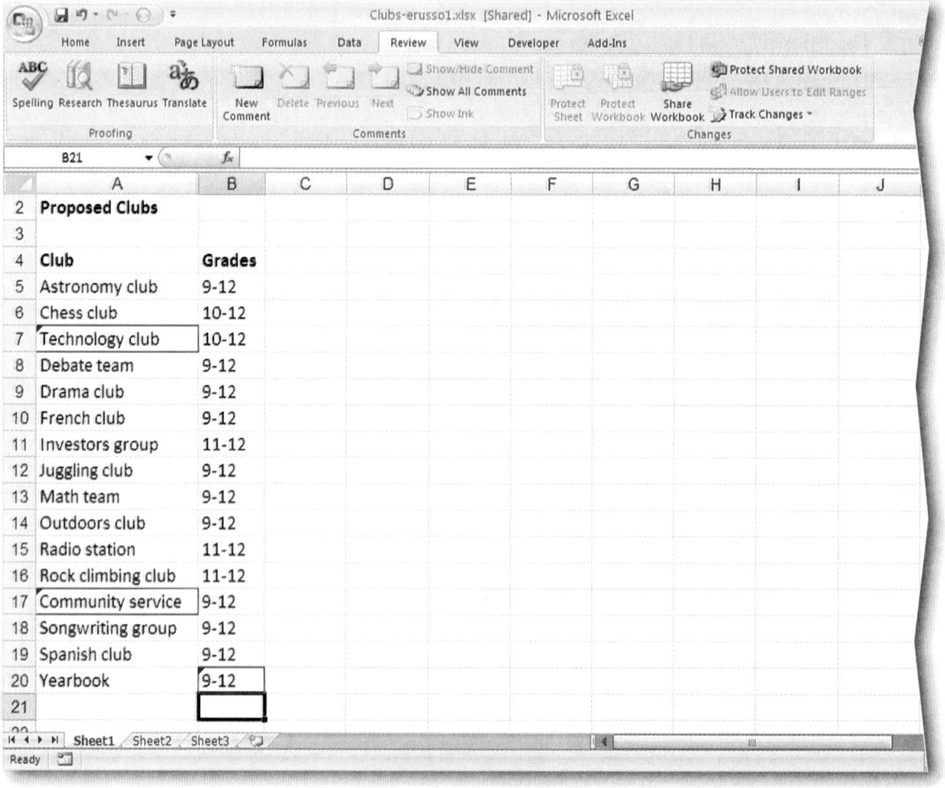

Header

2. Insert and Delete Rows, Columns, and Cells

Follow the steps to complete the activity.

Step-By-Step

1. Open your **Clients-1** file.

2. Save the file as: Clients-[your first initial and last name]2.

3. Click column heading **C**. Choose **Home>Cells**. Click the **Insert Cells** drop-down arrow. Select **Insert Sheet Columns**.

4. **iCHECK** Your screen should look like Figure 2.27.

5. Click cell **C1**. Key: Week 2. Click row heading **5**. Click the **Insert Cells** drop-down arrow. Select **Insert Sheet Rows**. Click cell **A5**. Key: Quentin. Click cell **B5**. Key: 4,000.

6. Point to the lower right corner of cell **B5**. Drag the box to cover cells **B5** through **E5**.

7. Click cell **C5**. Click the **Insert Cells** drop-down arrow. Select **Insert Cells**. Select **Shift cells down**. Click **OK**.

8. **iCHECK** Your screen should look like Figure 2.28.

FIGURE 2.27 Inserting columns

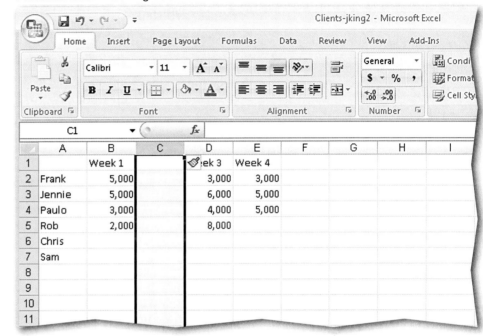

FIGURE 2.28 Inserting rows and cells

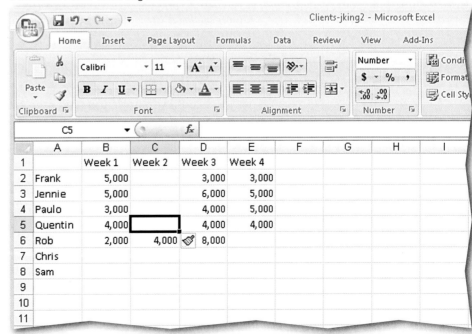

Vocabulary

Key Terms

case sensitive

comment

digital signature

lock

Mark as Final

merge

password

protect

share

Track Changes

Academic Vocabulary

alteration

distribute

reject

source

Review Vocabulary

Complete the following statements on a separate piece of paper. Choose from the Vocabulary list on the left to complete the statements.

1. _____ a worksheet if you do not want people to be able to change it. (p. 230)

2. To show that a workbook comes from a trusted source, you can attach a(n) _____. (p. 243)

3. To allow several people to open and edit a workbook at the same time, _____ the workbook. (p. 234)

4. If a file should only be opened by certain users, create a(n) _____. (p. 232)

5. When you use Track Changes, you can accept or _____ changes made by other users in a shared workbook. (p. 236)

Vocabulary Activity

6. Key a brief report about protecting worksheets and workbooks, setting passwords, and adding a digital signature. For each feature, answer the following questions:
   A. How does this feature help you?
   B. How does this feature protect your worksheet?
   C. In your report, make sure you use and define the vocabulary words *digital signature*, *password*, *source*, and *protect*.

Review Key Facts

Answer the following questions on a separate piece of paper.

7. Which elements can you protect? (pp. 230–231)
   A. A range of cells   C. A workbook
   B. A worksheet   D. All of the above

8. How could you prevent certain users from opening a confidential workbook? (p. 232)
   A. Add a digital signature.   C. Set a password to open.
   B. Protect the worksheet.   D. Enable Track Changes.

9. What would you do to certify yourself as the sender of a file? (p. 243)
   A. Add a digital signature.   C. Set a password to open.
   B. Protect the worksheet.   D. Enable Track Changes.

10. How can you prevent certain users from modifying a file? (p. 233)
    A. Create a digital signature.
    B. Set a password to modify.
    C. Enable worksheet protection.
    D. Enable workbook protection.

3. Use AutoSum, AVERAGE, MIN, and MAX

Follow the steps to complete the activity. You must complete Practice It Activity 2 before doing this activity.

Step-By-Step

1 Open your **Clients-2** file. Save the file as: Clients-[your first initial and last name]3.

2 Select cells **B2** to **B5**. Point to the lower right corner of cell **B5**. Drag to cells **C2** through **C5** (see Figure 2.29).

3 Delete cells **A7** and **A8**. In cell **E6**, key: 5,000. In **A8** through **A11**, key the four cells shown in Figure 2.29.

4 Click cell **B8**. Choose **Formulas>Function Library>AutoSum**. Press ENTER.

5 Click the **AutoSum** drop-down arrow. Choose **Average**. Select cells **B2** to **B6**. Press ENTER.

6 Repeat step 5 but choose **Min**. Select cells **B2** to **B6**. Press ENTER.

7 Repeat step 5 but choose **Max**. Select cells **B2** to **B6**. Press ENTER.

8 **ⓘCHECK** Your screen should look like Figure 2.30. Save and close your file.

FIGURE 2.29 Copy cells

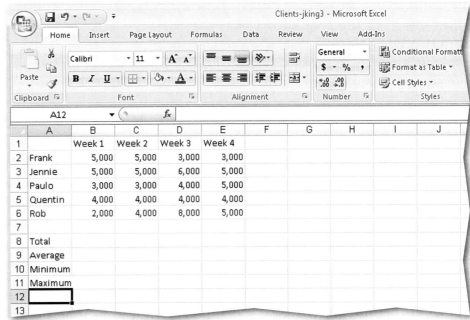

FIGURE 2.30 Function results

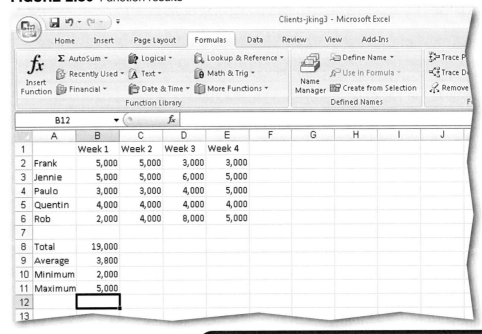

MATH MATTERS

Applying for a Business Loan

Allen has always dreamed of owning a chocolate shop. He has prepared a business plan, which lays out the expenses of the business as well as potential profits. What he does not have, however, are the thousands of dollars needed to set up his shop.

Lending a Hand

This is where a bank or another lending institution comes into the picture. In order to borrow money, Allen must show that his business will be profitable so that he will be able to repay the loan.

Of course, a loan is not free money. Banks charge interest, or a percentage of the total amount of the loan, and add it to the original amount (principal) borrowed. Allen is applying for a $50,000 loan with an interest rate of eight percent. Although there are several factors to consider in calculating how much interest Allen will pay, the basic formula to determine total interest is as follows:

Amount of loan ($50,000) × Interest rate (0.08) = Total interest ($4,000).

(Interest rates can significantly affect the amount of the loan.)

The Bank Loan Application

Banks require a borrower to fill out forms and supply documents such as income tax returns. Banks want information about:

- The credit history of the borrower and the borrower's earnings.
- The business plan.
- The collateral the borrower can use to repay the loan if necessary.

It is important to calculate the interest of a loan to determine the loan's total cost.

SKILLBUILDER

1. **Define** What is a business loan?
2. **Infer** Why do you think banks want to know the credit history of potential borrowers?

3. **Calculate** If Allen takes a business loan of $75,000 at an eight percent interest rate, how much interest will he owe?

LESSON 2 You Try It Activities

Step-By-Step

4. Edit a Worksheet

Data File

You are creating a chart that shows your classmates' favorite sports teams. While proofreading your chart, you notice that there are some errors you need to correct.

1 Open the data file **Teams.xlsx**. Close the task pane if necessary.

2 **CHECK** Your screen should look like Figure 2.31. Save the file as: Teams-[your first initial and last name]4.

3 In cell **A10**, change **Jessic** to **Jessica**.

4 Clear the contents of cell **A11**.

5 Use **Replace** to change every **Jagwars** to **Jaguars**.

6 In cell **D3**, change **RED** to **Red**.

7 Click cell **D2**. Shift the cells in the column down so **D2** becomes cell **D3**.

8 Move the contents of cell **C11** to cell **D2**.

9 Press CTRL + HOME.

10 **CHECK** Your screen should look like Figure 2.32. Save and close your file.

FIGURE 2.31 Favorite teams chart

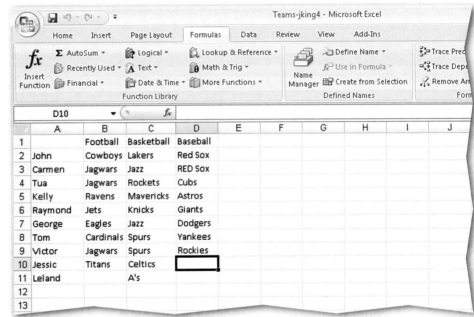

FIGURE 2.32 Favorite teams chart after editing

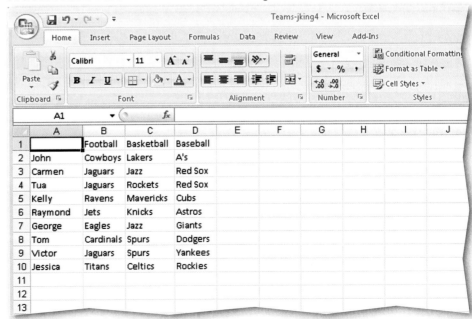

1 Click **Start**. Choose **All Programs>Microsoft Office>Microsoft Office Tools>Digital Certificate for VBA Projects** 📇.

2 In the **Create Digital Certificate** dialog box, in the **Your certificate's name** box, key: [your first name] [your last name] (see Figure 4.27).

3 In the dialog box, click **OK**. click **OK** again.

4 In your **Museum** file, choose **Office** 📇**> Prepare>Add a Digital Signature** 📇. Click **OK**. Click **Sign**. Click **OK**.

5 **ⓘCHECK** Your screen should look like Figure 4.28. Save your file. Exit Excel.

You can attach a **digital signature** to a workbook to identify yourself as the source, or origin, of the workbook. The recipient will know it is from you and that the file has not been tampered with. Think of it as a fingerprint on a document that can be traced back to a specific computer on a particular date with an exact time. Microsoft Office also allows you to protect your documents from unwanted access with a tool called Information Rights Management (IRM).

FIGURE 4.27 Create Digital Certificate dialog box

Tech Tip

While other permissions tools prevent or restrict access from within a network, IRM protects documents wherever they are by storing the permissions information inside the file. The Windows Rights Management Services (RMS) software is built into Windows Vista. You must install RMS Client Service Pack 1 if you are using Windows XP.

FIGURE 4.28 Worksheet after adding digital signature

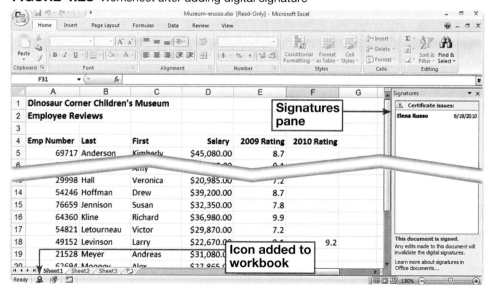

Step-By-Step

1 Create a new workbook. Save the blank workbook as: Sporting-[your first initial and last name]5.

2 In cells **A2** through **A5**, key the four items shown in Figure 2.33.

3 In cells **A7** through **A10**, key the labels shown in Figure 2.33.

4 In cells **B1** through **G1**, key the months **January**, **February**, **March**, **April**, **May**, and **June**.

5 Enter the numbers as shown in Figure 2.33.

6 (i)**CHECK** Your screen should look like Figure 2.33.

7 Use the **AutoSum** functions on the **Formula** tab to determine the **total**, **average**, **minimum**, and **maximum** for each month's sales.

8 (i)**CHECK** Your screen should look like Figure 2.34.

9 Save and close your file.

5. Compute Sales

You are a salesperson at a sporting goods store. Your supervisor has given you the amount of units sold for four items during the months of January through June. The items are baseballs, skis, sleds, and tents. He wants you to create a workbook to analyze the sales.

FIGURE 2.33 Sporting goods sales

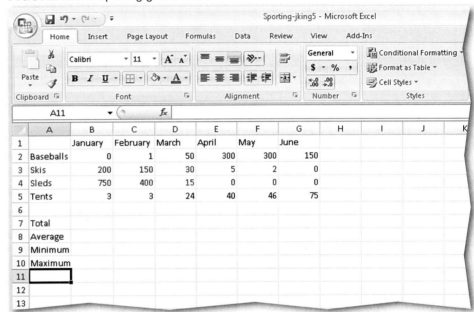

FIGURE 2.34 Function results

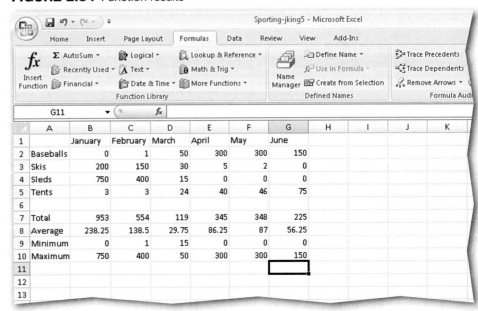

1. In your **Museum** file, choose **Review>Share Workbook**. Deselect the **Allow changes by other users**... check box. Click **OK**. Click **Yes**.

2. Choose **Office** > **Prepare>Mark as Final**. Click **OK**.

3. **CHECK** Your dialog box should look like Figure 4.25.

4. Read the dialog box and click **OK** again.

5. **CHECK** Your screen should look like Figure 4.26. Note the **Mark as Final** icon in the status bar at the bottom of the screen.

6. Select cell **A4**. Press DELETE. You are unable to delete the heading.

7. Click after the heading **Employee Reviews**. Key text after the heading. You are unable to key text into the document.

8. Close your file.

➡ *Continue to the next exercise.*

EXERCISE 4-10
Mark a Document as Final

Before you share a workbook with others, you can use the **Mark as Final** command to make the workbook read-only and prevent any further changes. When the document is marked as final, keying, editing commands, and proofing marks are disabled. This signals that you are sharing a completed version of a document and prevents others from making changes to the document.

FIGURE 4.25 Marking a document as final

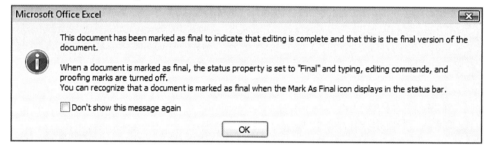

FIGURE 4.26 Document marked as final

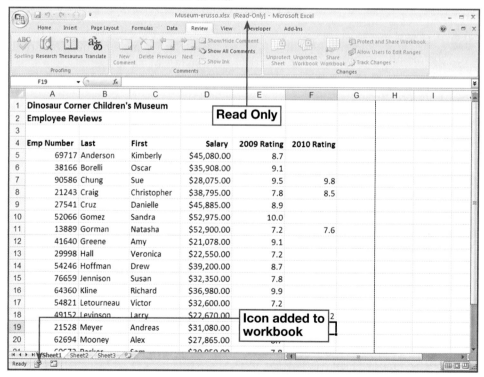

Microsoft Office 2007

Documents marked as final in Office 2007 will not be read-only if they are opened in an earlier version of Office.

6. Beyond the Classroom Activity

Rubric R

 **Math: Identify Income and Expenses** You are applying for a job working in the accounting department of a furniture store. The owner wants to check your spreadsheet skills. Create a new workbook. Then perform the following tasks:

- Label the first column "Sources of Income". In this column, list at least five products sold by the store (such as sofas, chairs, and tables).
- Label the second column "Expenses". In this column, list at least five things that the store must spend money on each month (such as rent, salaries, and gas for the delivery truck).

Save your workbook as: e2rev-[your first initial and last name]6.

7. Standards at Work Activity

 **Microsoft Certified Application Specialist Correlation**
Excel 2.3 *Format Cells and Cell Content*

Use a Hyperlink Create a new workbook and insert a hyperlink to the workbook you created for the owner of the furniture store. To do this:

- Label the first column "Prospective Employers".
- Give the furniture store a name and key the name into cell A2.
- Create a hyperlink to the workbook you saved above in cell A2.
- Key another employer that has a job opening that you are thinking of applying for into cell A3.
- Create a hyperlink to a new workbook that contains at least five things you will need to provide on a personal data form (such as the position you are applying for, education, and employment history).

Save your workbook as: e2rev-[your first initial and last name]7.

8. 21st Century Skills Activity

Rubric R

Create a Budget Identify at least six things that you spend money on each month. You might include food, clothes, movies, and music. Make sure to include all of your major expenses. Then, in a new workbook:

- Key the items you identified into column A. Enter one item per row.
- Enter the amount that you spend on each item into column B.
- Use AutoSum to calculate your total expenses.

Use MAX and MIN to identify items you spend the most and least amount of money on. Include these at the bottom of your worksheet. Save your workbook as: e2rev-[your first initial and last name]8.

Go Online e-REVIEW
glencoe.com

Go to the **Online Learning Center** to complete the following review activities.

Online Self Check
To test your knowledge of the material, click **Unit 1> Lesson 2** and choose **Self Checks**.

Interactive Review
To review the main points of this lesson, click **Unit 1> Lesson 2** and choose **Interactive Review**.

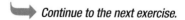

EXERCISE 4-9
Merge Workbooks

Documents are often distributed to coworkers for comment and revision. After sharing a workbook with others, there will be more than one version of the workbook. **Merge**, or combine, the workbook versions to create the final workbook. The workbooks that you combine must have been created from the same shared workbook.

① Close the second copy of Excel running in the current window.

② In your **Museum** file, click **Office** 🔘 and then click **Excel Options**.

③ Click **Customize**. Click the **Choose Commands from** drop-down arrow, and select **All Commands**.

④ Scroll down and select **Compare and Merge Workbooks**. Click **Add**.

⑤ ⓘ**CHECK** Your dialog box should look similar to Figure 4.23. Click **OK**.

⑥ On the **QAT**, click **Compare and Merge Workbooks** 🔘.

⑦ In the **Select Files to Merge Into Current Workbook** dialog box, select your **Museum-copy** file. Click **OK**.

⑧ ⓘ**CHECK** Your screen should look like Figure 4.24. Save your file.

➡ *Continue to the next exercise.*

FIGURE 4.23 Excel Options dialog box

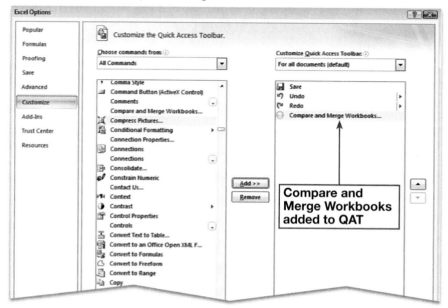

FIGURE 4.24 Merged workbook

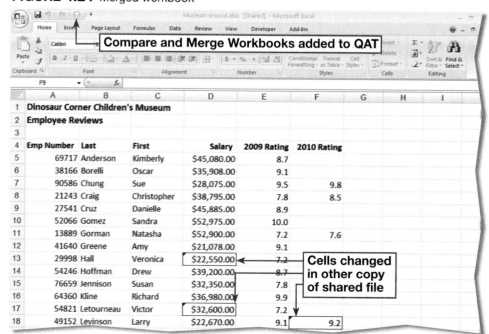

Troubleshooter

When workbooks with tracked changes are merged, all affected cells will be marked. Review your changes carefully.

Before You Begin

Control Inventory Controlling inventory is an essential part of managing a budget. These projects teach you how to use a spreadsheet to create, track, and update an inventory to meet customer business needs.

Reflect Once you complete the projects, open a Word document and key a paragraph that answers the following:

1. What are the benefits of using AVG, MIN, MAX when creating an inventory in Excel?

2. Which sandwich requires the most inventory, which the least?

3. Which is the most and least expensive sandwich to produce?

9. Track Inventory

 Math: Create a Worksheet and Convert Quantities The Tastee Sandwich Shop has hired you to do inventory. Their sandwiches include:

- Roast beef
- Ham
- Chicken
- Turkey
- Veggies

Create a new Excel workbook. Use information in the data file **Sandwich .docx**. In one column, list the types of sandwiches. In a second column, enter the number of ounces of filling in each sandwich. In a third column, show how much of each filling is available. Convert the amount of meat from pounds to ounces (one pound is 16 ounces) and enter the number of ounces in column four. Name each column.

Save as: e2rev-[your first initial and last name]9.

10. Look Ahead

Math: Add Columns and Analyze Data Your boss wants you to track how quickly the items are being sold. Open your **e2rev-9** workbook. Add a column to the workbook named **Number of sandwiches sold per day**. Then, add another column named **Filling needed per week**. Using the information in the data file **Sandwich.docx**, enter into the columns the number or sandwiches sold per day and how much of each type of filling the shop needs for one week.

Save as: e2rev-[your first initial and last name]10.

11. Add Products

Math: Calculate and Analyze Data Two new sandwiches have been added. You need to add these items to your inventory. Open your **e2rev-10** workbook. Then, using the information in the data file **Sandwich.docx**, insert two rows between "Chicken" and "Veggies" on your chart.

- Name the rows for the two new sandwiches. Fill in all the cells in each row. Use the other rows as models.
- Use AutoSum to calculate the total **Number of sandwiches sold per day** and **Filling needed per week** for those columns. Find the AVG, MIN, and MAX in each column.

Identify the type of sandwiches you sell the most and least of in a day. Then identify the filling you use the most and least of per week. Save as: e2rev-[your first initial and last name]11.

1. In your **Museum-copy** file, choose **Insert>Text> Header & Footer** 📄.

2. **ⓘCHECK** Your screen should look like Figure 4.21.

3. Click on the right header text box at the top of your worksheet. Choose **Design>Header & Footer Elements> Current Date** 📅.

4. Click in the main body of the spreadsheet. Choose **Insert>Text>Header & Footer** 📄.

5. Choose **Design>Header & Footer>Footer** 📄. In the drop-down list, select **Page 1, Sheet1** from the list.

6. Click the text **Page 1** in the footer. Place the cursor after **Page &[Page]**. Press the **spacebar**. Key: of. Press the **spacebar**. Select **Header & Footer Elements>Number of Pages** 📄. Deselect the footer.

7. **ⓘCHECK** Your screen should look like Figure 4.22.

8. Choose **View>Workbook Views>Normal** ⬜. Save and close your file.

➡ *Continue to the next exercise.*

EXERCISE 4-8
Add and Modify Headers and Footers

You can use Excel's header and footer options to quickly provide useful information in your worksheets when you are sharing data with others. For example, you can add predefined header and footer information, such as the date and time, or the name of the last person that accessed or edited the file. You can also insert elements such as page numbers and the file name.

FIGURE 4.21 Page Layout View

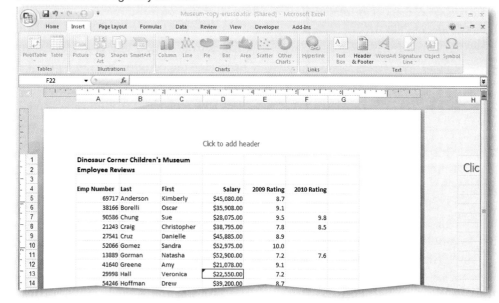

FIGURE 4.22 Modified footer

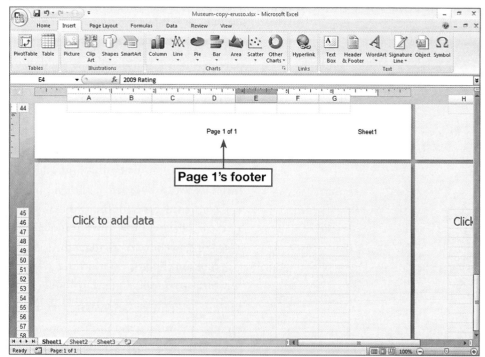

Key Concepts

- Change font, font size, font style, and font color
- Convert text to columns
- Apply cell and table styles
- Modify the size of rows and columns
- Hide and unhide rows, columns, and worksheets
- Change horizontal and vertical alignment
- Insert, move, and modify SmartArt graphics

Standards

The following standards are covered in this lesson. Refer to pages xix and 314 for a description of the standards listed here.

ISTE Standards Correlation

NETS•S

1a, 1c, 2b, 3d, 4c, 5c, 6a, 6b

Microsoft Certified Application Specialist

Excel

1.1, 1.3, 1.5, 2.1, 2.2, 2.3, 2.4, 4.4

In this lesson you will learn to format, or adjust the appearance of, Excel worksheets. You will change the way the font looks and adjust the size of rows and columns. You will also learn to adjust alignment and to insert and size SmartArt graphics.

21st CENTURY SKILLS

Be Flexible Even when you are organized and have a set plan, the unexpected can happen. In order to meet unexpected challenges successfully, you must be flexible. One of the best ways to prepare for the unexpected is to have a backup plan. First, make plans for how you expect things to turn out. Then, come up with an alternate plan in case your original plan does not work out. Your backup plan will help you to be flexible if you need to change plans. For example, if you are taking a car trip, you might want to plan an alternate route to reach your destination. That way, if a road is blocked, you will still get where you need to go.

Can you think of a time when you had to be flexible in order to meet your goals?

Step-By-Step

9. Reopen your **Museum** file. In your **Museum-original** file, choose **Home>Cells> Format** 🔲. Select **Move or Copy Sheet**.

10. In the **Move or Copy** dialog box, click the **To book** drop-down arrow and select **Museum-[your first initial and last name].xlsx** (see Figure 4.19).

11. Under **Before Sheet**, make sure **Sheet1** is selected. Click **OK**. In the warning box that appears, click **OK**.

12. Choose **Home>Cells> Format** 🔲. Select **Move or Copy Sheet**.

13. In the **Move or Copy** dialog box, click the **To book** drop-down arrow and select **(new book)**. Do not click **Create a copy**. Click **OK**.

14. Choose **Office** 🔘>**Save As** 🔲. Save your file as: Original-data-[your first initial and last name]. Close the file.

15. **ⓘCHECK** Your screen should look like Figure 4.20. Save and close the file.

➡ *Continue to the next exercise.*

EXERCISE 4-7 (Continued)
Copy a Worksheet

FIGURE 4.19 Move or Copy dialog box

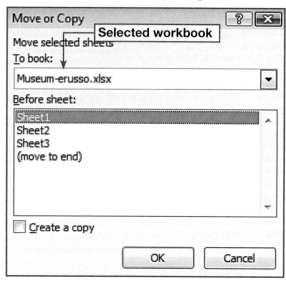

FIGURE 4.20 Original data tab moved from this workbook to new workbook

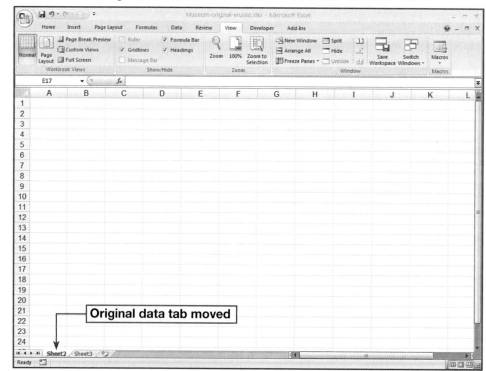

Before You Read

Use Notes When you are reading, keep a notepad handy. Whenever you come upon a section or term you are unfamiliar with, write the word or a question on the paper. After you have finished the lesson, look up the terms or try to answer your questions based on what you have read.

Read To Learn

- Create and modify tables to showcase data.
- Explore ways to format content in order to have an easily understandable worksheet.
- Place and modify graphics in an Excel spreadsheet.

Main Idea

Excel has many ways to format the data and overall look of a spreadsheet.

Vocabulary

Key Terms

background	graphical list
border	horizontal alignment
cell style	SmartArt
delimiter	table style
font	theme
font style	vertical alignment

Academic Vocabulary

These words appear in your reading and on your tests. Make sure you know their meanings.

convey
distinct

Quick Write Activity

Explain On a separate sheet of paper, write a paragraph that explains the kind of formatting you use in your Word documents to organize and present information. How might you use formatting such as **boldface**, *italics*, underlining, fonts, borders, colors, and more in a workbook that contains financial data for an entire year? Try to come up with several different examples.

Study Skills

Take Good Notes Taking good notes and reviewing them frequently reinforces what you learned and helps you prepare for tests.

Academic Standards

English Language Arts
   NCTE 5 Use different writing process elements to communicate effectively.

Math
   NCTM (Number and Operations) Understand numbers, ways of representing numbers, relationships among numbers, and number systems.
   NCTM (Number and Operations) Understand meanings of operations and how they relate to one another.
   NCTM (Algebra) Represent and analyze mathematical situations and structures using algebraic symbols.

1. In your **Museum** file, choose **Office>Save As** [icon]. In the **File name** box, key: Museum-original-[your first initial and last name]. Click **Save**.

2. Choose **Review> Changes>Share Workbook** [icon].

3. Uncheck the **Allow changes...** box. Click **OK**. Click **Yes**.

4. Click **Unprotect Workbook** [icon]. Uncheck the **Protect Structure and Windows** option.

5. Choose **Home>Cells> Format** [icon]. Under **Organize Sheets**, rename **Sheet1** to **Original data**.

6. Click **Format** [icon]. Under **Organize Sheets**, select **Move or Copy Sheet**.

7. In the **Move or Copy** dialog box, click the **Create a copy** check box. Click the **To book** drop-down arrow and select **(new book)** (see Figure 4.17). Click **OK**.

8. (i)**CHECK** Your screen should look like Figure 4.18. Close the workbook. Do not save your change

Continued on the next page.

EXERCISE 4-7
Copy a Worksheet

When sharing workbooks or data with others, you may want to move or copy a worksheet to another workbook so that you can retain the original worksheet data. For example, the accounting department wants to distribute, or give out, a new worksheet that explains how to use a new timesheet software application to all employees in a company. You want to copy the worksheet containing the old timesheet instructions and policy to another workbook in case you need to reference it at a later date.

FIGURE 4.17 Move or Copy dialog box

FIGURE 4.18 Copy of Worksheet

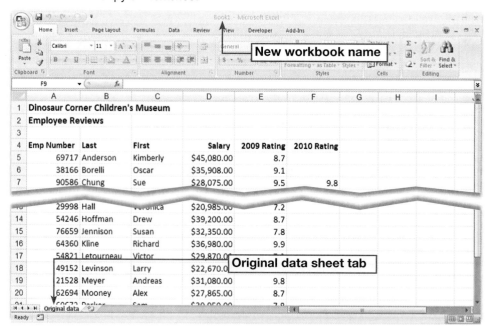

EXERCISE 3-1
Change Font, Font Size, and Style

The **font** is the "look" of the characters. A **font style** is a trait such as **bold**, *italic*, or <u>underline</u> that is applied to a font. Choosing the right fonts helps to make your worksheet more readable. You can either use the Format group or launch the Format Cells dialog box to change a font.

FIGURE 3.1 Font group

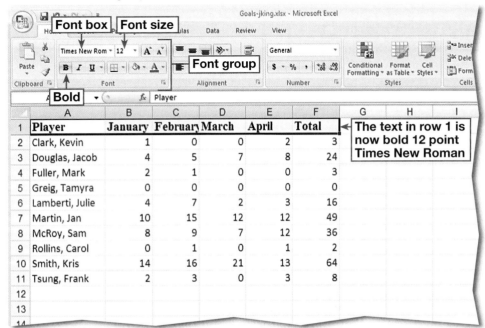

1. Start **Excel**.

2. Open the data file **Goals.xlsx**. Save as: Goals-[your first initial and last name] (for example, *Goals-jking*). Ask your teacher where to save your file.

3. Select **A1:F1**.

4. Choose **Home>Font** and click the **Font** drop-down arrow. Select **Times New Roman**.

5. In the **Font** group, click **Bold** B. In the **Font Size** box, click **12**.

6. **ⓘCHECK** Your screen should look like Figure 3.1.

7. Select **A2:A11**. Click the **Font** drop-down arrow and choose **Times New Roman** (see Figure 3.2).

FIGURE 3.2 Font, font size, and font style changed for selected cells

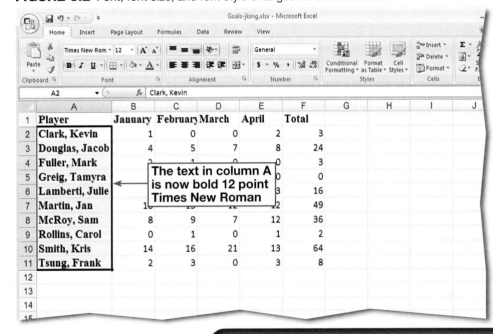

8. Click the **Font Size** drop-down arrow. Choose **12**. Click **Bold** B.

9. **ⓘCHECK** Your screen should look like Figure 3.2. Save your file.

➜ *Continue to the next exercise.*

EXERCISE 4-6 (Continued)
Accept and Reject Changes

10 Click **F13**. Choose **Review>Comments> New Comment** .

11 In the comment box, key: Confirm figure.

12 Click **F18**. Choose **Review>Comments> New Comment** .

13 In the comment box, key: This figure is not accurate.

14 ⓘCHECK Your screen should look like Figure 4.15.

15 Click **F13**. Choose **Review>Comments> Delete Comment** .

16 Click **F18**. Choose **Review>Comments> Edit Comment** .

17 Change your comment to: Reject change.

18 ⓘCHECK Your screen should look like Figure 4.16. Save your file.

➡ *Continue to the next exercise.*

You Should Know

You can also allow specific users to edit cell ranges in a protected worksheet or workbook by choosing **Review>Changes>Allow Users to Edit Ranges** .

FIGURE 4.15 Comment box

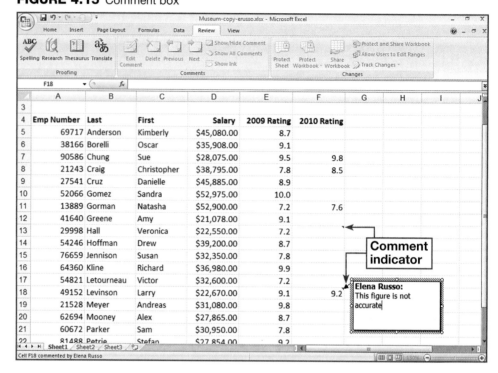

FIGURE 4.16 Cell with comment

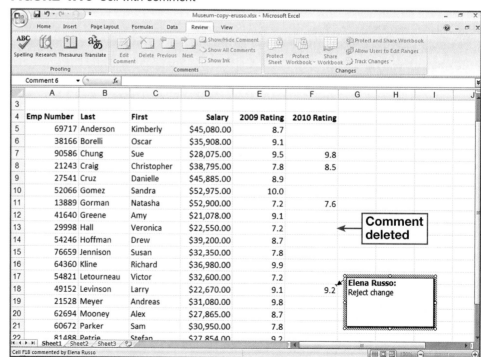

1 In your **Goals** file, select **A1:F1**.

2 Choose **Home>Font**. Click the **Borders** drop-down arrow.

3 Click **Bottom Border** (see Figure 3.3).

4 Select **A2:A11**.

5 Click the **Borders** drop-down arrow.

6 In the drop-down menu, click **Right Border**.

7 Select cell **A11**. Click **Bottom Border**. A bottom border is added to the cell.

8 Click **No Border**. The borders are removed from A11.

9 Click **Right Border**. Now the right border is added back to the cell.

10 ⓘ**CHECK** Your screen should look like Figure 3.4.

Continued on the next page.

Shortcuts

Font, alignment, and other formatting changes only affect the cells that are selected. Remember to select a range, or group of cells, first, and then make the formatting change.

EXERCISE 3-2
Apply Borders and Copy Cell Contents

A **border** is a line along one or more edges of a cell. Borders make worksheet labels easier to find. By applying a border to a cell or groups of cells, you can make information easier and quicker to find. Sometimes you want a border around certain cells and not around others. Excel allows you to copy text without copying the border. You should use the Paste Special dialog box to control which information is pasted into a new cell.

FIGURE 3.3 Bottom border

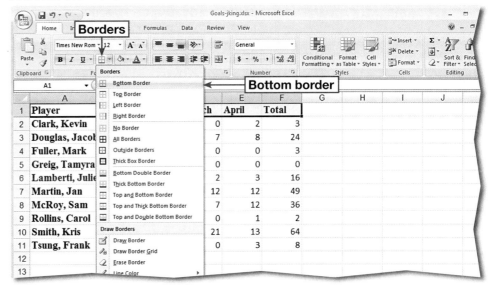

FIGURE 3.4 Cell Borders

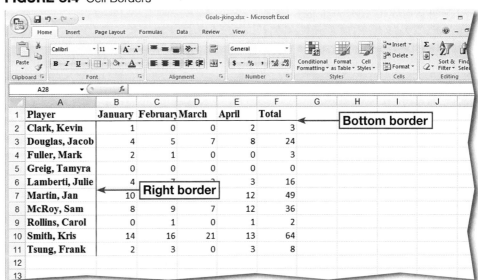

Step-By-Step

1 In your **Museum-copy** file, click **Track Changes** . Click **Accept/Reject Changes** . Click **OK**. The **Select Changes to Accept or Reject** dialog box opens.

2 Click **OK**. The **Accept or Reject Changes** dialog box opens. The description of **Change 1 of 3** appears.

3 ⓘ**CHECK** Your dialog box should look like Figure 4.13.

4 Click **Accept**. The description of **Change 2 of 3** appears.

5 Click **Accept**. The description of **Change 3 of 3** appears.

6 Click **Reject**. The original value in cell **F18** is restored.

7 ⓘ**CHECK** Your screen should look like Figure 4.14.

8 Click **Share Workbook** . Uncheck the **Allow changes by more than one user** box. Click **OK**. Click **Yes**.

9 Choose **Review> Changes>Unprotect Sheet** .

Continued on the next page.

EXERCISE 4-6
Accept and Reject Changes

After the changes are made in a document, you can choose to accept or reject each tracked change. If you accept a change, the cell's content will reflect the update. If you reject, or refuse to accept, a change, the cell's original value will be restored. You can also insert a **comment** to make a suggestion or ask questions about the data. Comments will exhibit a red triangle in the upper left-hand corner of a cell or range of cells. When the pointer is positioned over a changed cell, a window appears containing the reviewer's name, date, and the cell modification or comment.

FIGURE 4.13 Accept or Reject Changes dialog box

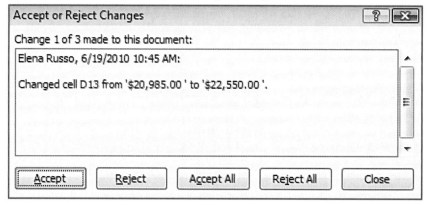

FIGURE 4.14 Accepted and Rejected changes

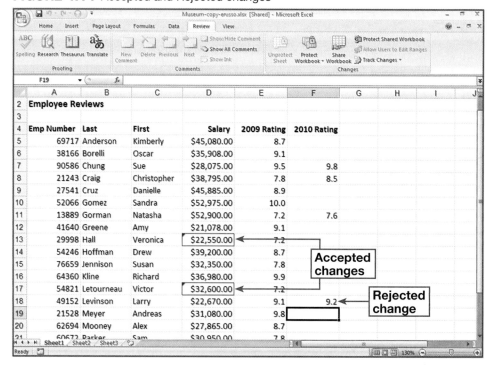

11 With **A11** selected, choose **Home>Clipboard>Copy**.

12 Click cell **A12**. Then click the **Paste** drop-down menu. Choose **Paste Special**.

13 In the **Paste Special** dialog box, click the **All except borders** button (see Figure 3.5). Click **OK**.

14 **ⓘCHECK** Your screen should look like Figure 3.6. Notice that the name **Tsung, Frank**, with the correct font, is copied, but the border is not.

15 Click **Undo** ↩. Click ESC.

16 Save your file.

Continue to the next exercise.

You Should Know

Borders are used to keep different types of information separate. Just as a border separates two countries, a border in an Excel worksheet tells viewers that the information in one column or row is distinct from the information in another column or row.

EXERCISE 3-2 (Continued)
Apply Borders and Copy Cell Contents

FIGURE 3.5 Paste Special dialog box.

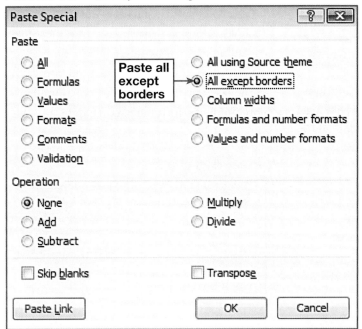

FIGURE 3.6 Cell borders

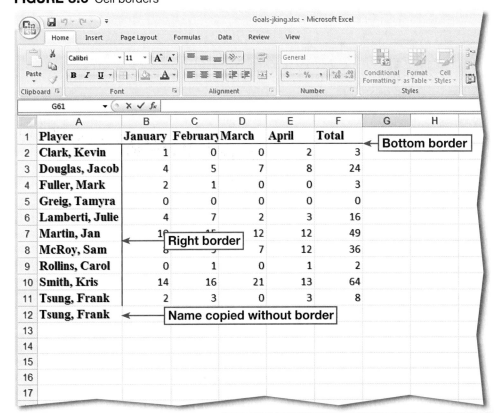

EXERCISE 4-5
Use Track Changes

1. In your **Museum-copy** file, choose **Review> Changes>Track Changes** 📝. Click **Highlight Changes** 📝.

2. In the **Highlight Changes** dialog box, make sure that the **Track changes while editing** box is checked. Uncheck **When**.

3. **ⓘCHECK** Your dialog box should look like Figure 4.11. Click **OK**.

4. A confirmation box opens. Click **OK**.

5. Click cell **D13**. Key: 22550. Press ENTER. Click cell **D17**. Key: 32600. Press ENTER. Click cell **F18**. Key: 9.5. Press ENTER.

6. **ⓘCHECK** Your screen should look like Figure 4.12.

7. Save your file.

➡ *Continue to the next exercise.*

Tech Tip

When using **Track Changes**, you can specify whether or not balloons are shown that contain deletions and comments by choosing **Review> Comments>Show All Comments** 🗔.

Use **Track Changes** to mark edits as you make them. Tracking changes allows other people to review the changes and comments that you have made. Tracking changes in Excel allows you to see the modifications that have been made to a worksheet, including inserted or deleted text, numbers, rows, and columns. Highlighted changes on-screen will exhibit a colored cell border with a small triangle inside the upper-left corner. When the pointer is positioned over a changed cell, a window appears containing the reviewer's name, date, and the cell modification.

FIGURE 4.11 Highlight Changes dialog box

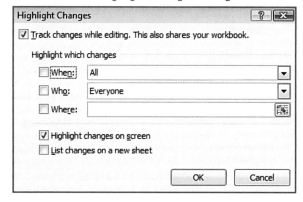

FIGURE 4.12 Tracked changes

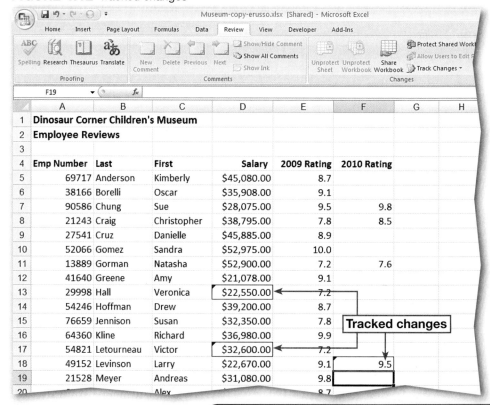

EXERCISE 3-3
Convert Text to Columns

In your **Goals** file, click column heading **B**.

Right-click and select **Insert**. A new column is inserted. Notice that column B has become column C.

Select **A2:A11**. Choose **Data>Data Tools>Text to Columns**. The Convert Text to Columns Wizard opens (see Figure 3.7).

Make sure **Delimited** is selected. Click **Next**.

In the **Convert Text to Columns Wizard** dialog box, under **Delimiters**, click **Comma**. Unclick **Tabs**.

Click **Next**. Click **Finish**. The contents of column A have been separated out into two columns.

ⓘ**CHECK** Your screen should look like Figure 3.8.

Click column heading **B** to select column B. Right-click and select **Delete**.

Save your file.

➡ *Continue to the next exercise.*

Use the Convert Text to Columns Wizard to separate the content of a cell, such as a list of first names and last names, into different columns. Excel makes use of a **delimiter**, or divider, to separate the text. The Convert Text to Columns function saves time by making many changes to a group of data in one step.

FIGURE 3.7 Convert Text to Columns Wizard

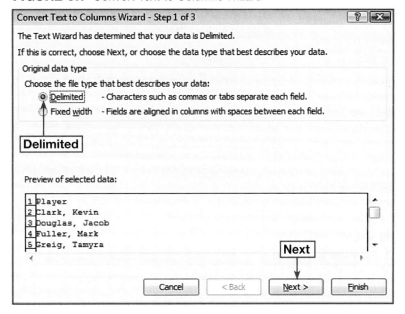

FIGURE 3.8 Players' last names in column A

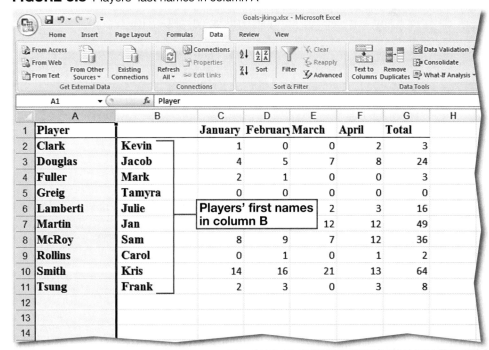

	A	B	C	D	E	F	G	H
1	Player		January	February	March	April	Total	
2	Clark	Kevin	1	0	0	2	3	
3	Douglas	Jacob	4	5	7	8	24	
4	Fuller	Mark	2	1	0	0	3	
5	Greig	Tamyra	0	0	0	0	0	
6	Lamberti	Julie		Players' first names		2	3	16
7	Martin	Jan		in column B		12	12	49
8	McRoy	Sam	8	9	7	12	36	
9	Rollins	Carol	0	1	0	1	2	
10	Smith	Kris	14	16	21	13	64	
11	Tsung	Frank	2	3	0	3	8	
12								
13								
14								

EXERCISE 4-4
Create a Shared Workbook

1. In your **Museum** file, choose **Review> Changes>Share Workbook** . The **Share Workbook** dialog box opens.

2. Check the **Allow changes by more than one user at the same time** box (see Figure 4.9). Click **OK**.

3. In the message that opens, click **OK**.

4. Start **Excel** again. Two copies of Excel are now running.

5. Open your **Museum** file in the second copy of Excel.

6. In the **Password** dialog box, key: mystery7. Click **OK**.

7. Save your **Museum** file as: Museum-copy-[your first initial and last name].

8. **CHECK** Your screen should look like Figure 4.10. Notice that two **Museum** files are now open (the original and the copy) and marked as **Shared**.

9. Save your files.

→ *Continue to the next exercise.*

In an office setting, many users may need to access and edit the same Excel workbook. For instance, a sales team may need to input and update their current sales in a master document. You can **share** the workbook so multiple users can have access to this file at the same time. Each person can add, edit, or delete information in the shared workbook from their own computer.

FIGURE 4.9 Share Workbook dialog box

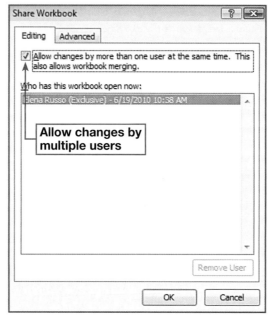

FIGURE 4.10 Shared workbook

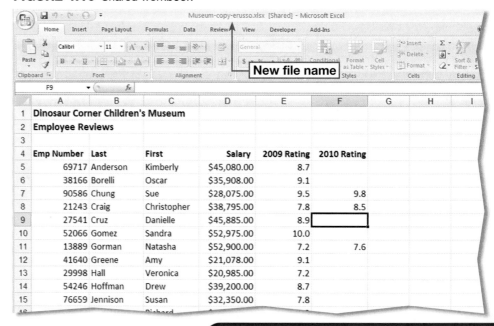

1 In your **Goals** file, select **A1:F11**.

2 Choose **Home>Styles> Format as Table**. Under Light, click **Table Style Light 17**. Click **OK**. Notice that the contextual tab **Table Tools** and **Design** tab are now displayed on the Ribbon.

3 ⓘ**CHECK** Your screen should look like Figure 3.9.

4 With your table still selected, click the **Table Styles** group drop-down arrow in the upper-right corner of your screen (see Figure 3.9).

5 Rest your pointer on each of the Quick Style thumbnails in the Table Styles menu. Note how each style affects your table with the Live Preview (see Figure 3.10).

➡ *Continued on the next page.*

Microsoft Office 2007

When you format a table in Microsoft Office 2007, table headers are added by default. You can change the default names, or you can turn them on or off by choosing **Design> Table Style Options**.

EXERCISE 3-4
Apply Table Styles

A **theme** is a predefined set of colors, fonts, and effects that you can apply to an entire workbook to ensure that the cells have consistent formatting. Microsoft Office Excel 2007 has 16 built-in themes that you can apply or modify to create your own. You can also use the Format as Table command to apply a **table style**, or predefined set of formats, to a range of data. Themes and table styles save time by making formatting changes, such as adding borders and changing font colors, in one step.

FIGURE 3.9 Table Style Light 17 applied to cells

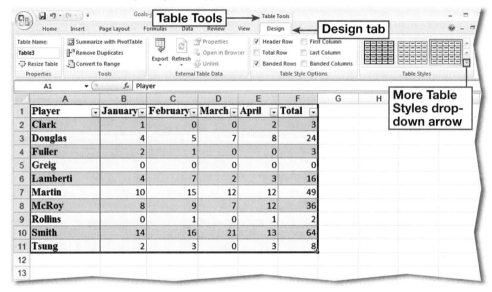

FIGURE 3.10 Table Styles drop-down menu

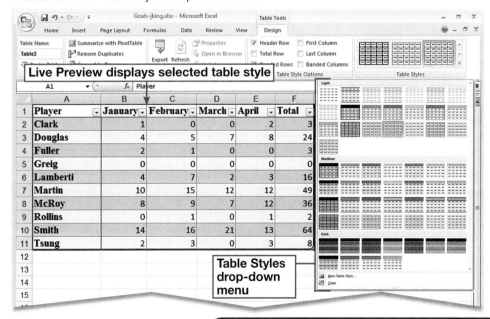

Set a Password to Modify a Workbook

1. In your **Museum** file, choose **Office** >**Save As** .

2. In the **Save As** dialog box, click **Tools**. Click **General Options** (see Figure 4.7).

3. Double-click in the **Password to open** box to select the dots. Press DELETE.

4. In the **Password to modify** box, key: mystery7.

5. Click **OK**. In the **Confirm Password** dialog box, key: mystery7. Click **OK**.

6. Click **Save**, and then click **Yes**. Close the file.

7. Reopen your **Museum** file. The **Password** dialog box opens.

8. Key: mystery7. Click **OK**.

9. Click cell **F8**. Key: 8.5. Press ENTER. You are able to modify the file.

10. **(i)CHECK** Your screen should look like Figure 4.8.

11. Save your file.

➥ *Continue to the next exercise.*

You might want to allow people to view some workbooks without being able to modify them. For example, you might want all employees to be able to open a workbook containing a list of holidays. However, you might not want employees to make an **alteration**, or change, to the list. You can set a password so that others can open, but not modify, the workbook.

FIGURE 4.7 General Options dialog box

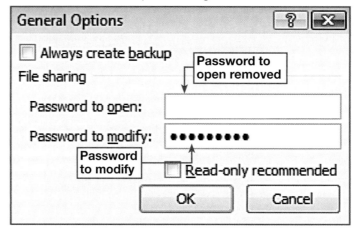

FIGURE 4.8 Modified worksheet

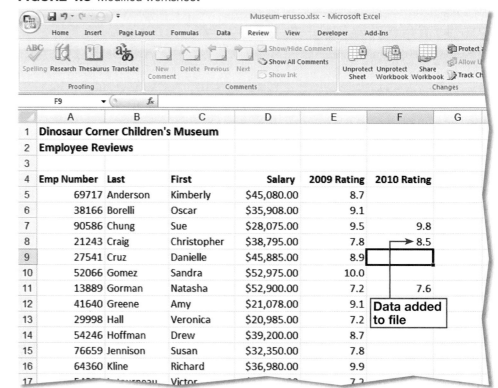

EXERCISE 3-4 (Continued)
Apply Table Styles

6 Click **Table Style Light 19**.

7 With your table still selected, choose **Page Layout>Themes> Themes** (see Figure 3.11). Move your pointer over the built-in themes.

8 Click **Verve**. Notice how the style is updated. Click **Undo**. Click cell **F11**.

9 Under **Table Tools**, click the **Design** tab. In the **Table Styles Options** group, click to add a checkmark next to **Banded Columns**. Note the difference on-screen. Uncheck **Banded Columns**.

10 Uncheck **Header Row**. Note row 1 is now empty. Check **Header Row**.

11 Click to add checkmarks next to **Total Row** and **Last Column**.

12 ⓘ**CHECK** Your screen should look like Figure 3.12. Note that the numbers in the last column are bold and that a Total has been added to Row 12.

13 Save your file.

↪ *Continue to the next exercise.*

FIGURE 3.11 Page Layout Themes

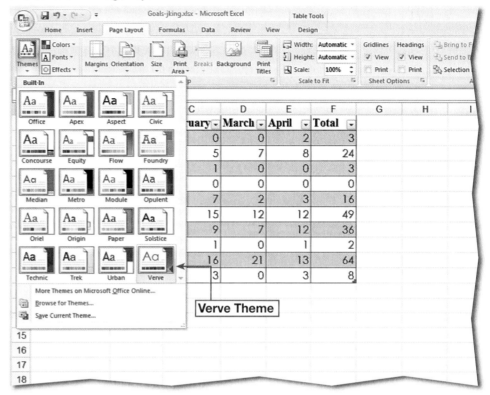

FIGURE 3.12 Format applied to cells

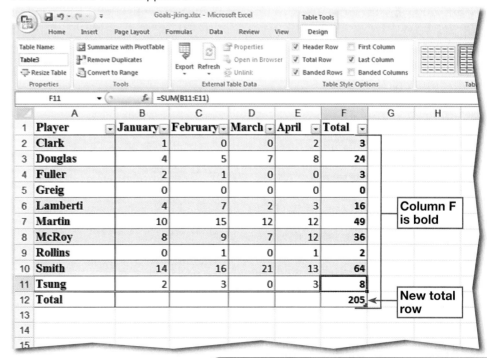

	A	B	C	D	E	F	G	H
1	Player	January	February	March	April	Total		
2	Clark	1	0	0	2	3		
3	Douglas	4	5	7	8	24		
4	Fuller	2	1	0	0	3		
5	Greig	0	0	0	0	0		
6	Lamberti	4	7	2	3	16		
7	Martin	10	15	12	12	49		
8	McRoy	8	9	7	12	36		
9	Rollins	0	1	0	1	2		
10	Smith	14	16	21	13	64		
11	Tsung	2	3	0	3	8		
12	Total					205		

Column F is bold

New total row

1 In your **Museum** file, choose **Office** 📄**>Save As** 💾. In the **Save As** dialog box, click the **Tools** drop-down arrow. Click **General Options**.

2 In the **Password to open** box, key: Magic3.

3 ⓘ**CHECK** Your dialog box should look like Figure 4.5.

4 Click **OK**. The **Confirm Password** dialog box opens. Key: Magic3. Click **OK**. Click **Save**, and then click **Yes**.

5 Save and close the file. Reopen your **Museum** file. The **Password** dialog box opens.

6 Key: Magic3. Click **OK**. The file opens.

7 ⓘ**CHECK** Your screen should look like Figure 4.6. Save your file.

➥ *Continue to the next exercise.*

EXERCISE 4-2
Set a Password to Open a Workbook

Some files are confidential. For example, only the accounting and human resources departments are allowed to see employee salaries in a company. If a workbook contains sensitive material such as salaries or bank statements, you can set a **password** so no user can open the file without the password. Passwords are **case sensitive**, which means that if your password has uppercase, lowercase, or a combination of uppercase and lowercase letters, you must key it the same way every time. Remember, if you forget the password, you will be locked out, too. Record passwords in a secure location.

FIGURE 4.5 General Options dialog box

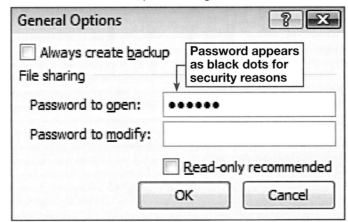

FIGURE 4.6 Reopened document

	A	B	C	D	E	F	G
1	Dinosaur Corner Children's Museum						
2	Employee Reviews						
3							
4	Emp Number	Last	First	Salary	2009 Rating	2010 Rating	
5	69717	Anderson	Kimberly	$45,080.00	8.7		
6	38166	Borelli	Oscar	$35,908.00	9.1		
7	90586	Chung	Sue	$28,075.00	9.5	9.8	
8	21243	Craig	Christopher	$38,795.00	7.8		
9	27541	Cruz	Danielle	$45,885.00	8.9		
10	52066	Gomez	Sandra	$52,975.00	10.0		
11	13889	Gorman	Natasha	$52,900.00	7.2	7.6	
12	41640	Greene	Amy	$21,078.00	9.1		
13	29998	Hall	Veronica	$20,985.00	7.2		
14	54246	Hoffman	Drew	$39,200.00	8.7		
15	76659	Jennison	Susan	$32,350.00	7.8		
16	64360	Kline	Richard	$36,080.00	9.9		

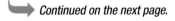

1. In your **Goals** file, select **F12**. Click the **AutoSum** drop-down menu. Choose **More Functions**. In the **Insert Function** dialog box, select **Average** and click **OK**.

2. In the **Function Arguments** dialog box, make sure the range of cells is F2:F11. Click **OK**. The number 20.5 appears as a total.

3. Repeat Step 1 but choose **SUM** from the list. Click **OK**.

4. Repeat Step 2. Click **OK**. The number 205 appears.

5. **ⓘCHECK** Your screen should look like Figure 3.13.

6. Position the pointer over the lower right corner of cell **F12** so that the resize handle appears (see Figure 3.14).

   Continued on the next page.

You Should Know

If you need to add a row or column between existing rows and columns in a table, select the row or column where you want the contents to appear, right-click, and choose **Insert**.

EXERCISE 3-5
Modify Tables to Show New Data

As you create your table, you may decide that you would like Excel to show data in a different way. For example, maybe you would like to see the average number of goals kicked by your team, but later you want to see the total number of goals. You may also discover that you need to include more data in a table. You can either key a value or text in a cell that is directly below or adjacent to the right of the table, or drag the resize handle at the lower-right corner of the table to select rows and columns.

FIGURE 3.13 SUM function

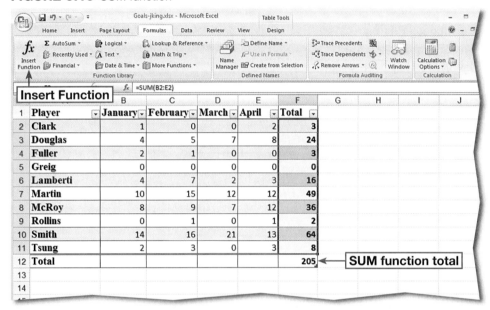

FIGURE 3.14 Resize handle in F12

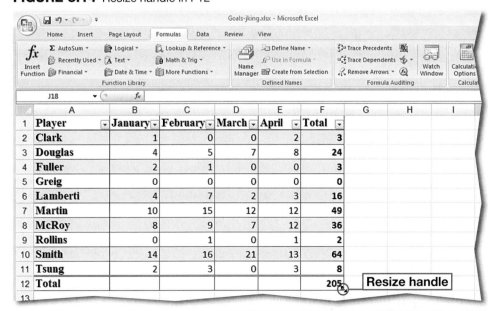

EXERCISE 4-1 (Continued)
Add Protection to Cells, Worksheets, and Workbooks

11. Click cell **A13**. Key: 3. An alert message opens indicating that this cell cannot be modified (see Figure 4.3). Click **OK**.

12. Click cell **F11**. Key: 7.6. Press ENTER. You can modify F11.

13. Choose **Review> Changes>Protect Workbook**. Select **Protect Structure and Windows**. In the dialog box, click **OK**. The workbook is now protected.

14. Click the **Sheet2** tab.

15. Right-click on the **Sheet2** tab. Notice that **Delete** is dimmed. It is not available because the workbook is protected.

16. Click the **Sheet1** tab.

17. **ⓘCHECK** Your screen should look like Figure 4.4. Save your file.

➡ *Continue to the next exercise.*

Troubleshooter
Protect cells containing formulas so users do not inadvertently key values in those cells.

FIGURE 4.3 Alert message

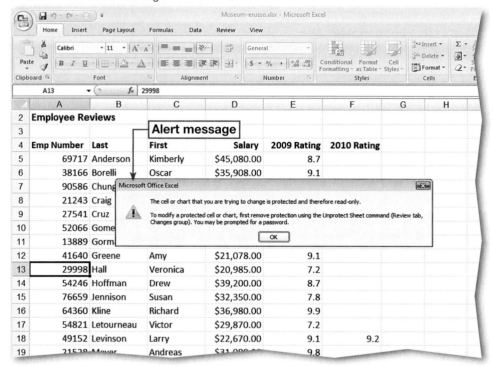

FIGURE 4.4 Protected worksheet

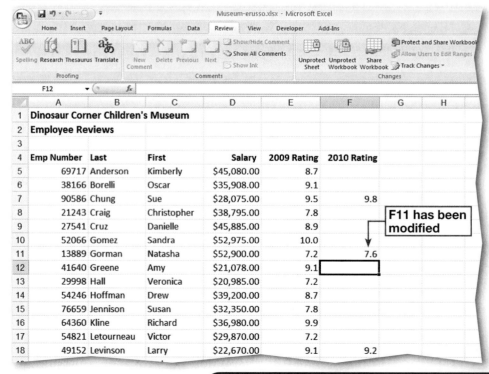

7 Drag the pointer over cell **G12** and release the mouse button. A new column is added to the table.

8 **ⓘCHECK** Your screen should look like Figure 3.15.

9 Click **Undo** 🔄.

10 Click cell **B12**. Choose **Formulas>Function Library>AutoSum** to calculate the total goals for January. Continue until you have the total goals for February, March, and April.

11 Click cell **F13**.

12 **ⓘCHECK** Your screen should look like Figure 3.16.

13 Save your file.

➡ *Continue to the next exercise.*

You Should Know

To delete a table row or column, select the row or column and press DELETE.

EXERCISE 3-5 (Continued)
Modify Tables to Show New Data

FIGURE 3.15 New column added to table

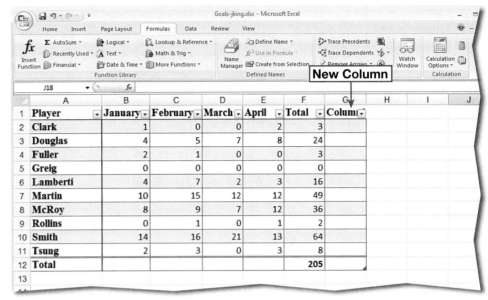

FIGURE 3.16 Total row added

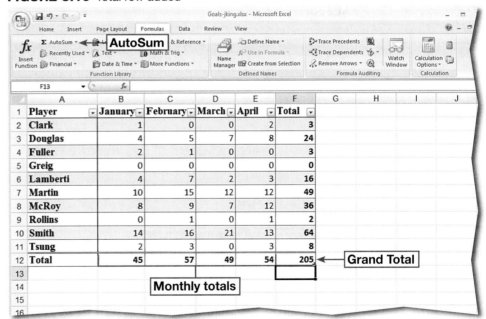

Academic Skills

Investigate how the number 20.5 was arrived at in **Step 2**. The AVERAGE function added (+) all the goals together (205). Then they were divided (/) by the total number of players (10).

1. Start **Excel**.

2. Open the data file **Museum.xlsx**. Save as: Museum-[your first initial and last name]. (For example, *Museum-erusso*.)

3. Select **D5:F24**. Choose **Home>Cells>Format** . Under **Protection**, click **Format Cells** .

4. Click the **Protection** tab. Uncheck the **Locked** box.

5. **ⓘCHECK** Your dialog box should look like Figure 4.1.

6. Click **OK**. Cells **D5:F24** are now unlocked.

7. Deselect the range.

8. Click **Format** . Under **Protection**, click **Protect Sheet** .

9. **ⓘCHECK** Your dialog box should look like Figure 4.2.

10. In the **Protect Sheet** dialog box, click **OK**. The sheet is now protected.

➡ *Continued on the next page.*

EXERCISE 4-1
Add Protection to Cells, Worksheets, and Workbooks

To prevent users from inserting, deleting, and renaming worksheets, **protect** the workbook. When you protect a workbook, you prevent others from making changes to all or part of a workbook or worksheet. Adding protection to a worksheet will **lock** all cells by default. A locked cell cannot be edited or deleted. To allow changes to some cells and not others, unlock the cells that can be changed.

FIGURE 4.1 Custom Lists dialog box

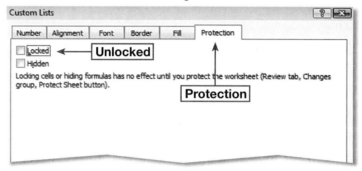

FIGURE 4.2 Protect Sheet dialog box

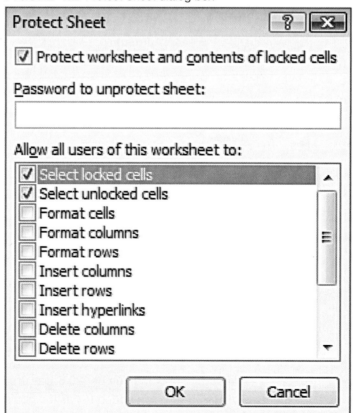

1. In your **Goals** file, select **B12:E12**.

2. Choose **Home>Font**. Click the **Font** group **Dialog Box Launcher**.

3. In the **Format Cells** dialog box, click the **Font** tab.

4. Click the **Color** drop-down arrow. Under **Standard Colors**, choose **Green** (see Figure 3.17). Click **OK**.

5. Click on the lower right corner of cell **E12** and drag it to the right to cell **F12**. In the **Auto Fill Options** drop-down menu, choose **Fill Formatting Only**.

6. Click **F12**. Choose **Home> Font** and click the **Font Color** drop-down arrow. Under **Standard Colors**, choose **Red**.

7. **ⓘCHECK** Your screen should look like Figure 3.18.

8. Save and close your file.

➡ *Continue to the next exercise.*

EXERCISE 3-6
Change Font Color

You can change the font color of text and numbers. You might use different font colors for headings and totals to make them distinct, or separate, from the rest of the worksheet. You can use the Format menu or the Formatting toolbar to change font color. You can also copy a font color from one cell to another without changing any of the data in the cell.

FIGURE 3.17 Font color selected in dialog box

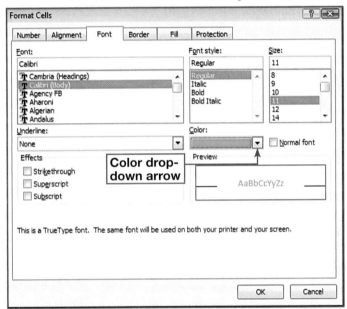

FIGURE 3.18 Font color changed for selected cells

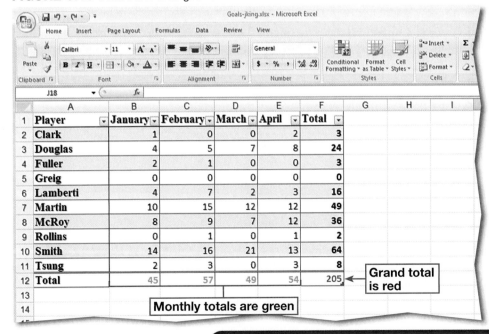

Before You Read

Practice on Your Own Stepping through exercises in a textbook is only the first step in learning a skill. After you have completed an exercise, note the key points you need to remember. Then, close the book and see if you can perform the steps again.

Read To Learn

- Discover the importance of protecting sensitive material in workbooks.
- Consider how to share a workbook so multiple users have access from their own computers.
- Explore how tracking changes in a worksheet improves workflow.
- Understand how to consolidate changes from various reviewers.

Main Idea

Excel has many features that allow you to collaborate with others while ensuring the safety of your data.

Vocabulary

Key Terms

case sensitive	password
comment	protect
digital signature	share
lock	Track Changes
Mark as Final	
merge	

Academic Vocabulary

These words appear in your reading and on your tests. Make sure you know their meanings.

alteration
distribute
reject
source

Quick Write Activity

Describe On a separate sheet of paper, describe why using Excel's features can help you keep your files protected and secure when collaborating with others on worksheets. Explain how you think Excel might help you manage the collaborative project.

Study Skills

Double-Check Your Work Review papers you prepare for school or work to ensure that all questions are answered and relevant. Double-checking your work is a big step toward improving your grades.

Academic Standards

Language Arts
   NCTE 3 Apply strategies to interpret texts.
   NCTE 5 Use different writing process elements to communicate effectively.
Math
   NCTM (Number and Operations) Compute fluently and make reasonable estimates.

Step-By-Step

1 Open the data file **Supplies.xlsx**. Save as: Supplies-[your first initial and last name].

2 Select **B2:B9**.

3 Choose **Home>Styles> Cell Styles**.

4 In the **Cell Styles** list, under **Number Format**, choose **Currency** (see Figure 3.19).

5 Select **C2:C8**.

6 Choose **Home>Styles> Cell Styles**.

7 In the **Cell Styles** list under **Number Format**, click **Percent**.

8 Click **C9**.

9 **①CHECK** Your screen should look like Figure 3.20.

10 Save your file.

→ *Continue to the next exercise.*

Microsoft Office 2007

When you rest your pointer on a cell style thumbnail without clicking, the Microsoft Office 2007 Quick Styles feature allows you to see how the style affects your data.

EXERCISE 3-7
Apply Cell Styles

A **cell style** is a set of formatting traits that has been given a name. When you apply a cell style, you apply all of the formatting traits of that style. Microsoft Office 2007 has several built-in cell styles, called Quick Styles, which allow you to change the look of a group of data (such as currency or percentages) in one quick step.

FIGURE 3.19 Cell Styles

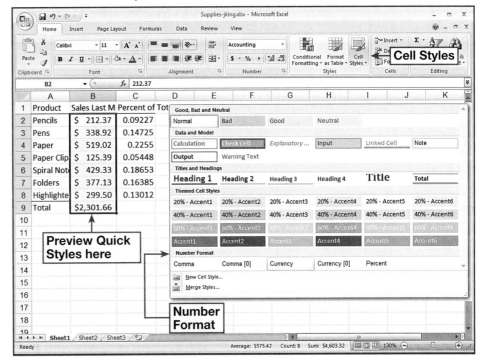

FIGURE 3.20 Percent style applied to selected cells

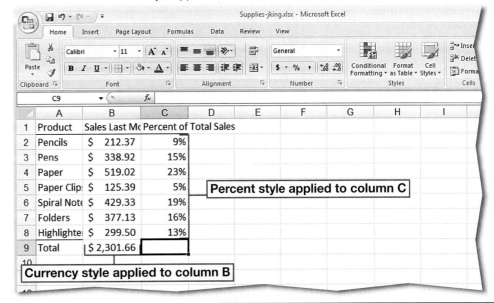

LESSON **4** Advanced Collaboration

In this lesson, you will learn skills to help you work collaboratively with Excel. You will discover how to protect cells and set passwords. You can also insert comments and track changes that have been made to a workbook. Excel offers helpful tools that allow you to share and combine versions of workbooks.

Key Concepts

- Add protection to cells and workbooks
- Set passwords
- Share workbooks
- Track, accept, and reject changes
- Merge workbook versions
- Use digital signatures

Standards

The following standards are covered in this lesson. Refer to pages xix and 314 for a description of the standards listed here.

ISTE Standards Correlation

NETS•S

1c, 2a, 2b, 2c, 6a, 6b

Microsoft Office Specialist Correlation

Excel

1.5, 5.1, 5.2, 5.3, 5.5

21st CENTURY SKILLS

Evaluate Your Progress Drivers look at road signs to measure their progress toward a destination. Your teachers measure your progress in part by keeping track of your grades. Think of a goal that you have. You might want to learn another language. You could evaluate your progress by writing in a notebook once a week. You might write a paragraph explaining what you learned that week, or list ten new words you learned. Evaluating your progress motivates you because it shows you how far you have come. *What is something you do that helps you keep track of your progress?*

1. In your **Supplies** file, click **A1**.

2. In the column heading row, move the pointer to the line between column headings A and B until the pointer becomes a double arrow (see Figure 3.21).

3. Click and drag to the right to make the column wider until you can see all of the text in the cells.

4. Double-click the line between column headings B and C (see Figure 3.21).

5. Click **C1**.

6. Choose **Home>Cells> Format**. Click **Column Width**.

7. In the **Column Width** box, key: 19.

8. Click **OK**.

9. **ⓘCHECK** Your screen should look like Figure 3.22.

10. Save your file.

➡ *Continue to the next exercise.*

EXERCISE 3-8
Change Column Width

Often, the contents of a cell do not fit in the cell. Excel has several methods to change column width. You can drag the line between the column headings, double-click the line between the column headings to AutoFit them, or use the Format menu to adjust column width using a specified value.

FIGURE 3.21 Adjusting column width by dragging

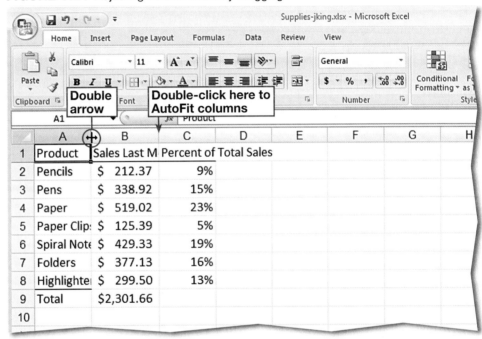

FIGURE 3.22 Resized columns

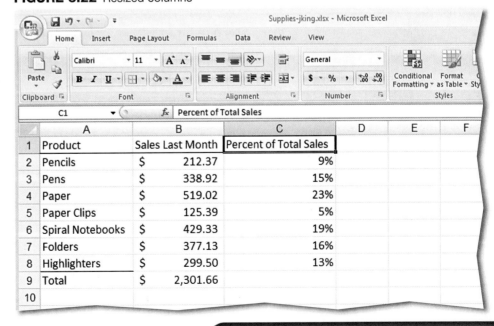

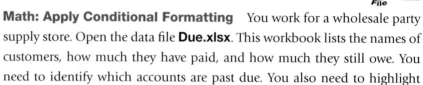

LESSON 3 — Challenge Yourself Projects

Before You Begin

You can use formatting to
make it is easier to complete
tasks and evaluate data.
These projects teach you
how to format data so that
you can identify and
prioritize tasks that are
essential to running a
business.

Reflect Once you complete
the projects, open a Word
document and answer the
following questions:

1. How can conditional formatting help you deter-
mine what tasks need to
be performed?

2. How can a chart help
you prioritize tasks?

9. Identify Accounts

Math: Apply Conditional Formatting   You work for a wholesale party supply store. Open the data file **Due.xlsx**. This workbook lists the names of customers, how much they have paid, and how much they still owe. You need to identify which accounts are past due. You also need to highlight accounts that owe more than $500.

- Apply light red fill with dark red text to accounts that owe more than $500.
- Apply yellow fill with dark yellow text to the past due amounts that are between $250 and $499.

Save your workbook as: Due-[your first initial and last name]9.

10. Format Customer Numbers

Modify Customer Account Numbers   Each customer of the wholesale party supply store has a customer number that begins with *C* (for example, C78162). You need to create a custom format to add *C* to the beginning of each customer number.

- Open your **Due-9** workbook.
- Create a custom format that adds the letter *C* to the beginning of each customer number.

Your boss asks you to add five new customers to the worksheet. Add five new customers. Assign them new customer numbers.

Save your file as: Due-[your first initial and last name]10.xlsx.

11. Customize a Column Chart

Math: Format Parts of a Chart   Your Due workbook contains a chart showing accounts that are past due. You need to finish formatting this chart. Your boss wants you to make changes to the *y* axis and reformat the chart's legend.

- Open your **Due-10** workbook. Click the **Chart** tab.
- Format the *y* axis as currency and add cross minor tick marks.
- Add a border and shadow effect to the legend.
- Label each axis and resize and scale the chart, as necessary.

Save your file as: Due-[your first initial and last name]11.xlsx.

Lesson 3: Challenge Yourself Projects   **Advanced Excel   227**

1. In your **Supplies** file, move the pointer to the line between row headings 1 and 2 (see Figure 3.23).

2. Click and drag down until the line is even with the bottom of row 2.

3. Click **A9**.

4. Choose **Home>Cells> Format**. Click **Row Height**.

5. In the **Row Height** box, key: 25. Click **OK**.

6. Click cell **A9**. Choose **Home>Cells>Format** and then click **AutoFit Row Height**. Now row 9 is just tall enough for the contents in the row.

7. ⓘ**CHECK** Your screen should look like Figure 3.24.

8. Save your file.

➡ *Continue to the next exercise.*

EXERCISE 3-9
Change Row Height

You can change row height to fit the contents of a cell or to call attention to labels or totals. You can change row height by dragging the line between row headings or using the Format menu.

FIGURE 3.23 Adjusting row height by dragging

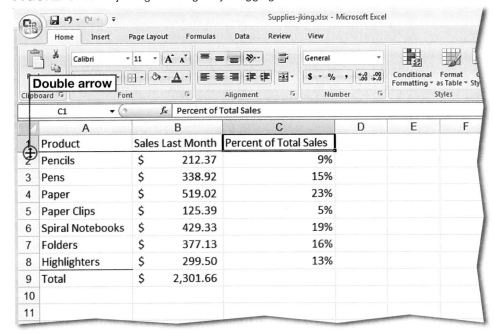

FIGURE 3.24 Row height resized

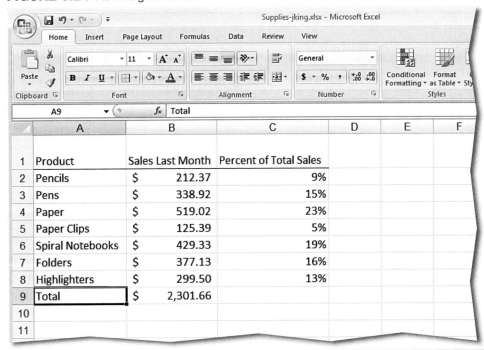

6. Beyond the Classroom Activity

 Language Arts: Use Conditional Formatting You work at a video store. You use Excel to keep track of different kinds of information such as video and DVD rentals, new releases, customer information, and so on.

In a Word document, key a paragraph describing three ways that you could use conditional formatting in your workbooks. For example, you could highlight the most recent new releases or track trends in DVD rentals.

Save your document as: adv-e2rev-[your first initial and last name]6.docx.

7. Standards at Work Activity

Microsoft Certified Application Specialist Correlation
Excel 2.3 *Format cells and cell content*

Create a Custom Format You keep important contact information for your business in an Excel sheet. You need to create a custom format so you can display the telephone numbers correctly.

- Open the data file **Contacts.xlsx**.
- Create a custom format for the telephone numbers column. Use the format ###-###-#### (no parentheses).
- Modify the format to add a **1-** before each phone number.

In the **Contacts.xlsx** file, add five new phone numbers. Check to see that the **1-** appears before each number. If it does not, make changes to the custom format.

Save your file as: Contacts-[your first initial and last name]7.xlsx.

8. 21st Century Skills Activity

Choose the Right Tool It is important to understand how Excel tools work so that you can choose the right one when you have a job to do. For example, there is more than one way that you can demonstrate progress in a particular area. You could choose to format the data or you could use a chart to show the details. Open the data file **Quizzes.xlsx**.

- Use **conditional formatting** to identify each grade that is below 80.
- Use **Blue Data Bars** to represent the value in each cell.
- Insert and format a **chart** that best reflects your progress.

Add five new quiz results to the workbook. Be sure that at least two of them are below 80. Include them in your chart.

Save your file as: Quizzes-[your first initial and last name]8.xlsx.

Go Online e-REVIEW
glencoe.com

Go to the **Online Learning Center** to complete the following review activities.

Online Self Check
To test your knowledge of the material, click **Unit 2> Lesson 3** and choose **Self Checks**.

Interactive Review
To review the main points of the lesson, click **Unit 2> Lesson 3** and choose **Interactive Review**.

EXERCISE 3-10
Hide and Unhide Columns and Rows

To make your worksheet easier to read, you can hide columns or rows. Hiding a column can make it easier to compare data side by side, and hiding a row can help you to focus only on certain data. Unhide columns and rows when you want to see them again.

FIGURE 3.25 Data added to worksheet

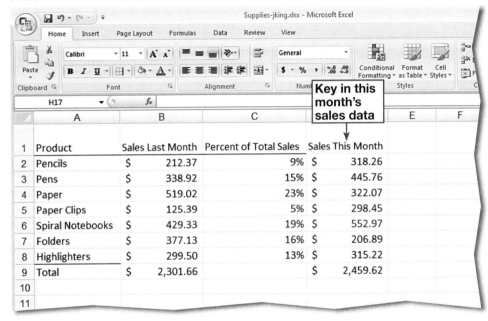

FIGURE 3.26 Column and row hidden

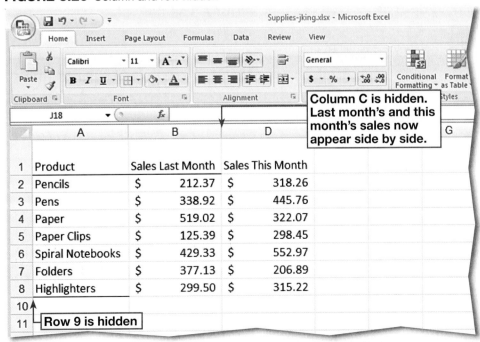

1 In your **Supplies** file, key the data shown in column D of Figure 3.25.

2 Use the **Cell Styles** drop-down menu to apply the **Currency Number Format** to cells D2:D9. AutoFit column D.

3 Click column heading **C** to select column C.

4 Choose **Home>Cells> Format**. Under **Visibility**, choose **Hide & Unhide> Hide Columns**.

5 Click row heading **9** to select the row.

6 Choose **Home>Cells> Format**. Under **Visibility**, choose **Hide & Unhide> Hide Rows**.

7 ⓘ**CHECK** Your screen should look like Figure 3.26.

8 Select column heading **B** through column heading **D**. Choose **Home>Cells> Format>Hide & Unhide**. Click **Unhide Columns**.

9 Select row heading **8** through row heading **10**. Choose **Home>Cells> Format>Hide & Unhide**. Click **Unhide Rows**. Save your file.

➡ *Continue to the next exercise.*

5. Customize a Graphic

Step-By-Step

The drama club at your school is preparing for the upcoming school play. You have volunteered to create a spreadsheet for the play's budget. First, you will modify the club's old graphic so that it will be ready to use.

1. Open the data file **Drama.xlsx**. Save as: Drama-[your first initial and last name]5.

2. Increase the contrast of the graphic.

3. Decrease the brightness of the graphic.

4. Scale the graphic to **50%** of its original size.

5. ⓘ**CHECK** Your screen should look like Figure 3.37. Deselect the graphic.

6. Move the graphic to the upper-left corner of the worksheet.

7. Rotate the graphic so that it is flipped horizontally. Deselect the graphic.

8. ⓘ**CHECK** Your screen should look like Figure 3.38.

9. Save and close your file.

FIGURE 3.37 Graphic resized to 50 percent of its original size

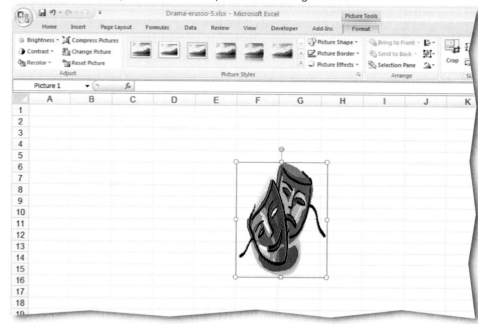

FIGURE 3.38 Resized and rotated graphic

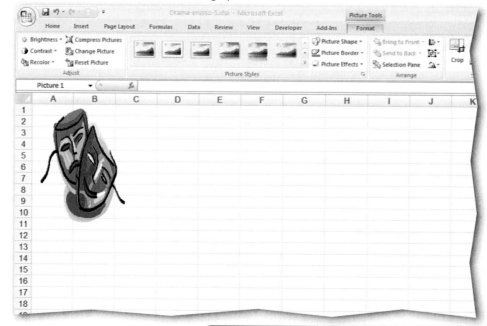

Change Horizontal Alignment

Change the **horizontal alignment** to align the contents of a cell to the left, center, or right. You can use the Format Cells dialog box or the buttons in the Alignment group on the Home tab to change the alignment of a cell's contents.

1 In your **Supplies** file, select **C2:C8**.

2 On the **Home** tab, click the **Alignment** group **Dialog Box Launcher** (see Figure 3.27).

3 In the **Format Cells** dialog box, click the **Alignment** tab.

4 Click the **Horizontal** drop-down arrow. Select **Center**. Click **OK**.

5 **CHECK** Your screen should look like Figure 3.28.

6 Save and close your file.

➔ *Continue to the next exercise.*

FIGURE 3.27 Alignment tab in Format Cells dialog box

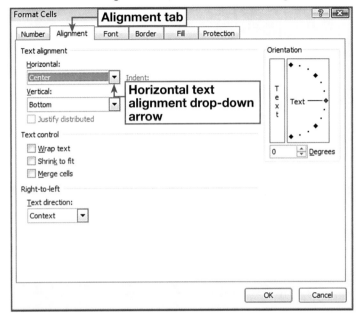

Microsoft Office 2007

When you select text, use the **Left**, **Center**, and **Right** buttons on the Mini **Toolbar** to change alignment more quickly.

FIGURE 3.28 Cells with center alignment

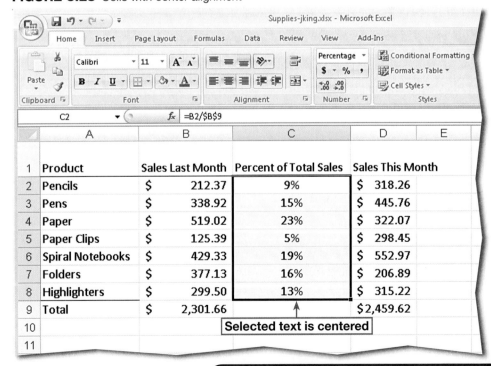

	A	B	C	D	E
1	Product	Sales Last Month	Percent of Total Sales	Sales This Month	
2	Pencils	$ 212.37	9%	$ 318.26	
3	Pens	$ 338.92	15%	$ 445.76	
4	Paper	$ 519.02	23%	$ 322.07	
5	Paper Clips	$ 125.39	5%	$ 298.45	
6	Spiral Notebooks	$ 429.33	19%	$ 552.97	
7	Folders	$ 377.13	16%	$ 206.89	
8	Highlighters	$ 299.50	13%	$ 315.22	
9	Total	$ 2,301.66		$2,459.62	
10			Selected text is centered		
11					

4. Format a Chart

Over the last year, your soccer team has raised money for an end-of-the-year team party. You charted the amount of money raised over the year. Now you want to format the chart to make it easier to read.

Step-By-Step

1 Open the data file **Party.xlsx**. Save as: Party-[your first initial and last name]4.

2 Select **A6:B18**. Choose **Insert>Charts> Column**.

3 Under 3-D Column, select **3-D Clustered Column**.

4 **ⓘCHECK** Your screen should look like Figure 3.35.

5 Format the numbers on the *y* axis to include dollar signs and zero decimal places.

6 Include **cross** minor tick marks on the *x* axis.

7 Change the text alignment on the *x* axis to a **–60°** custom angle.

8 Delete the legend on the right side of the graphic. Add a gradient fill to the chart wall.

9 **ⓘCHECK** Your screen should look like Figure 3.36.

10 Save and close the file.

FIGURE 3.35 Unformatted chart

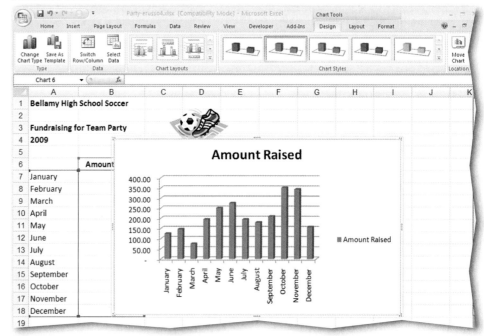

FIGURE 3.36 Formatted chart

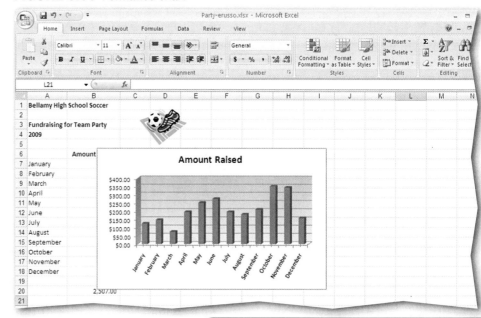

EXERCISE 3-12
Center Across Selection

If you want to center text across a range of cells, use the Center Across Selection feature. For example, you can center a title over a range of cells for extra emphasis. You can also use this feature to emphasize headings.

1. Open the data file **Computers.xlsx**. Save as: Computers-[your first initial and last name].

2. Click **B1**.

3. Key: Monthly Sales.

4. Press ENTER.

5. Select **B1:D1**.

6. On the **Home** tab, click the **Alignment Dialog Box Launcher**.

7. In the **Format Cells** dialog box, click the **Alignment** tab.

8. Click the **Horizontal** drop-down arrow. Select **Center Across Selection** (see Figure 3.29). Click **OK**.

9. ⓘ**CHECK** Your screen should look like Figure 3.30.

10. Save your file.

➥ *Continue to the next exercise.*

FIGURE 3.29 Center Across Selection selected on Alignment tab

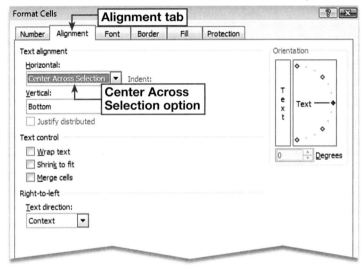

FIGURE 3.30 Center Across Selection applied to selected text

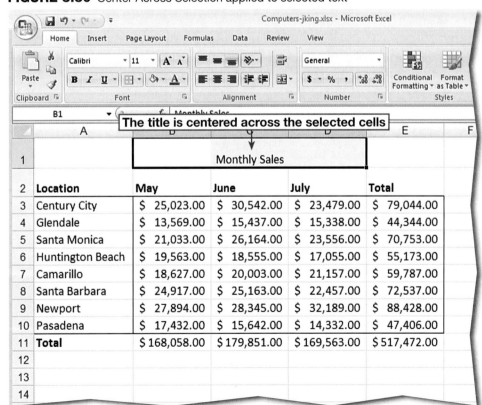

Shortcuts

In Microsoft Office 2007, you can merge and center cell contents by choosing **Home>Alignment> Merge & Center.**

3. Resize and Scale Graphics

Follow the steps to complete the activity. You must complete Practice It Activity 2 before doing this activity.

Step-By-Step

① Open your **Soccer-2** file. Save as: Soccer-[your first initial and last name]3.

② Double-click the graphic. Click the dialog box launcher for the **Size** group. The **Size and Properties** dialog box opens. On the **Size** tab, under **Scale**, double-click the number in the **Height** box. Key 25. Press TAB.

③ ⓘCHECK Your dialog box should look like Figure 3.33. Click **Close**.

④ Click the graphic, point to the lower-right corner sizing handle. Drag the handle to approximately the middle of cell **G14**. Release the mouse button.

⑤ Drag the graphic to cells **B4:B6**. Use the sizing handles to resize the graphic so it fits within **B4:B6**. Deselect the graphic.

⑥ ⓘCHECK Your screen should look like Figure 3.34.

⑦ Save and close your file.

FIGURE 3.33 Size and Properties dialog box

FIGURE 3.34 Resized graphic

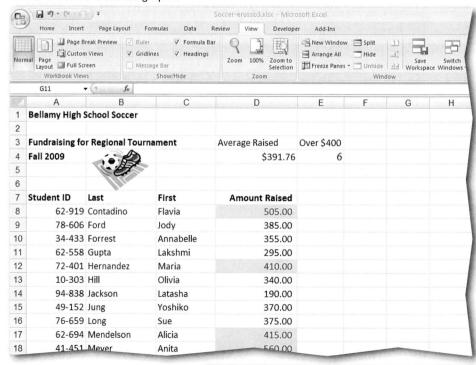

① In your **Computers** file, select **A2:E2**.

② On the **Home** tab, click the **Alignment** group **Dialog Box Launcher**.

③ In the **Format Cells** dialog box, click the **Alignment** tab.

④ Click the **Vertical** drop-down arrow. Select **Top** (see Figure 3.31).

⑤ Click **OK**.

⑥ ⓘ**CHECK** Your screen should look like Figure 3.32.

⑦ Save your file.

➥ *Continue to the next exercise.*

You Should Know

Use the **Top Align**, **Middle Align**, and **Bottom Align** buttons on the **Home** tab to change vertical alignment more quickly.

Shortcuts

You can open the **Format Cells** dialog box by right-clicking a cell or range of cells and choosing **Format Cells** in the shortcut menu.

EXERCISE 3-13
Change Vertical Alignment

You can use the Format Cells dialog box to change the vertical alignment of a cell's contents. **Vertical alignment** refers to how the content is positioned in relation to the top and bottom of the cell. For example, content that is top aligned is placed near the top of a cell.

FIGURE 3.31 Vertical alignment selected

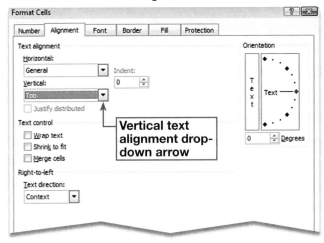

FIGURE 3.32 Cells with top alignment applied

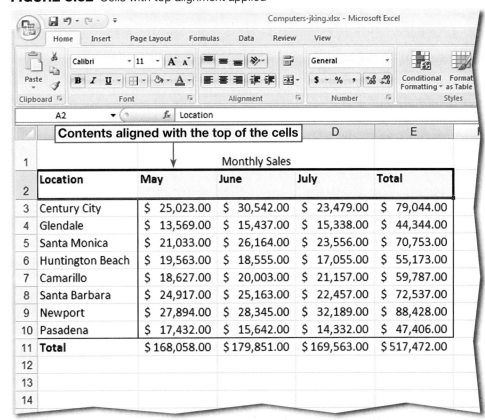

	Location	May	June	July	Total
1			Monthly Sales		
2	Location	May	June	July	Total
3	Century City	$ 25,023.00	$ 30,542.00	$ 23,479.00	$ 79,044.00
4	Glendale	$ 13,569.00	$ 15,437.00	$ 15,338.00	$ 44,344.00
5	Santa Monica	$ 21,033.00	$ 26,164.00	$ 23,556.00	$ 70,753.00
6	Huntington Beach	$ 19,563.00	$ 18,555.00	$ 17,055.00	$ 55,173.00
7	Camarillo	$ 18,627.00	$ 20,003.00	$ 21,157.00	$ 59,787.00
8	Santa Barbara	$ 24,917.00	$ 25,163.00	$ 22,457.00	$ 72,537.00
9	Newport	$ 27,894.00	$ 28,345.00	$ 32,189.00	$ 88,428.00
10	Pasadena	$ 17,432.00	$ 15,642.00	$ 14,332.00	$ 47,406.00
11	**Total**	$ 168,058.00	$ 179,851.00	$ 169,563.00	$ 517,472.00

Contents aligned with the top of the cells

2. Use Conditional Formatting

Follow the steps to complete the activity. You must complete Practice It Activity 1 before doing this activity.

Step-By-Step

1. Open your **Soccer-1** file. Save as: Soccer-[your first initial and last name]2.

2. Select **D8:D27**. Choose **Home>Styles>Conditional Formatting** 📋. Select **Highlight Cell Rules** and click **Greater Than**.

3. In the **Format cells that are GREATER THAN** box, key: 400. Click **OK**.

4. **ⓘCHECK** Your screen should look like Figure 3.31.

5. Press ⌨ALT⌨ + ⌨O⌨ / ⌨D⌨ to open the **Conditional Formatting Rules Manager**.

6. Click **Edit Rule**, and then click **Format**. Click the **Fill** tab and select a light blue color. Click **OK** twice.

7. Click **Apply**. Close the **Conditional Formatting Rules Manager**. Deselect the range.

8. **ⓘCHECK** Your screen should look like Figure 3.32.

9. Save and close your file.

FIGURE 3.31 Conditional formatting

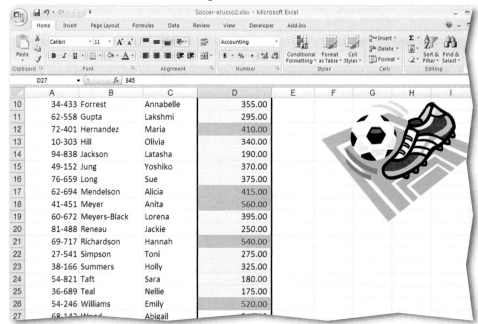

FIGURE 3.32 Formatted Sales Data Chart

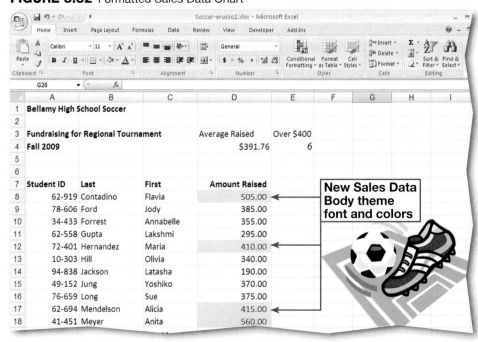

New Sales Data Body theme font and colors

1 In your **Computers** file, click cell **A1**.

2 Choose **View>Show/Hide** and remove the checkmark from the **Gridlines** check-box. Notice that the gridlines are hidden.

3 ⓘ**CHECK** Your screen should look like Figure 3.33.

4 Choose **View>Show/Hide** and check **Gridlines**. The gridlines reappear.

5 Choose **View>Show/Hide** and remove the checkmark from the **Headings** box. Notice that the row and column headings are hidden.

6 Choose **View>Show/Hide**. Click the **Headings** box. The headings reappear.

7 ⓘ**CHECK** Your screen should look like Figure 3.34.

8 Save your file.

➡ *Continue to the next exercise.*

Tech Tip

You can print without grid-lines by choosing **Page Layout>Sheet Options** and deselecting, or clearing, the **Gridlines** check box.

EXERCISE 3-14
Show and Hide Gridlines and Headings

Just as you can hide and unhide rows and columns, you can hide and unhide a worksheet or an entire workbook's gridlines and headings. Viewing a worksheet without gridlines and headings allows you to see what a chart or table will look like when you print it.

FIGURE 3.33 Hidden gridlines

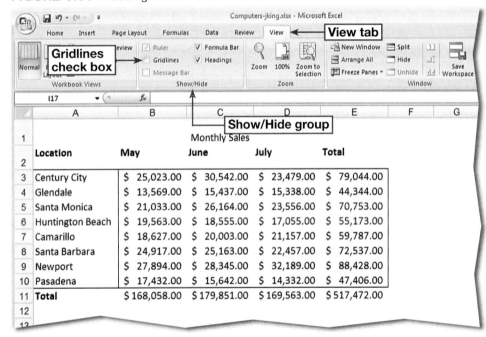

FIGURE 3.34 The gridlines and headings are visible

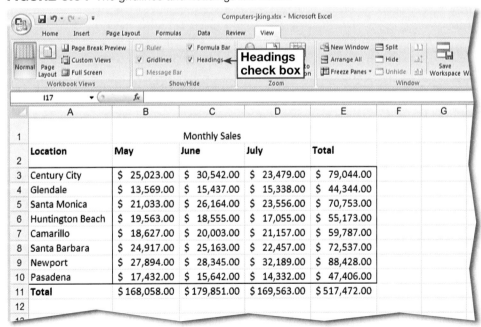

Step-By-Step

1 Open the **Soccer.xlsx** data file. Save as: Soccer-[your first initial and last name]1.

2 Select **A8:A27**.

3 On the **Home** tab, click the dialog box launcher for the **Number** group. The **Format Cells** dialog box opens.

4 In the **Category** list, choose **Custom**. Double-click in the **Type** box. Key: ##-###.

5 Click **OK**. Deselect the range.

6 **CHECK** Your screen should look like Figure 3.29.

7 Click cell **A27**. Press DELETE. Key: 68142. Press ENTER.

8 **CHECK** Your screen should look like Figure 3.30.

9 Save and close your file.

1. Create a Custom Number Format

Follow the steps to complete the activity.

FIGURE 3.29 Numbers formatted using custom format

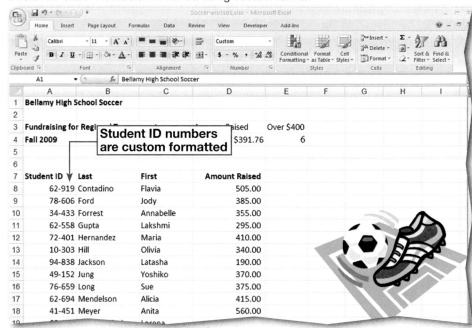

FIGURE 3.30 New number formatted using custom format

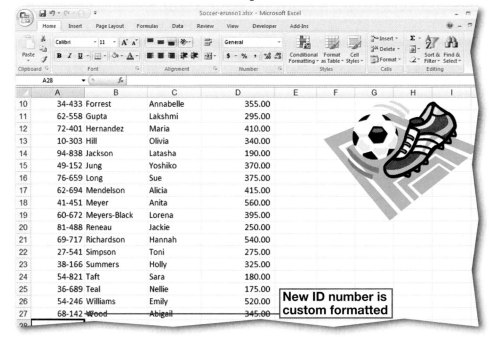

1 In your **Computers** file, choose **Home>Cells> Format**. Under **Organize Sheets**, click **Rename Sheet**. **Sheet1** is highlighted (see Figure 3.35).

2 Key: 1st Quarter Sales.

3 Press ENTER.

4 Repeat Step 1 choosing **Sheet 2**. Key: 2nd Quarter Sales.

5 Click **Insert Worksheet** twice. Rename the two worksheets: 3rd Quarter Sales and 4th Quarter Sales.

6 Click **1st Quarter Sales** tab. Choose **Home> Cells>Format**. Under **Organize Sheets**, select **Tab Color**.

7 Under **Standard Colors**, select **Orange, Accent 6**.

8 Click the tab for **2nd Quarter Sales**.

9 **①CHECK** Your screen should look like Figure 3.36.

10 Save your file.

➡ *Continue to the next exercise.*

EXERCISE 3-15
Rename a Worksheet and Change the Tab Color

You can organize your work by storing information on multiple sheets. For example, if you are compiling quarterly sales reports for your company, you might create four worksheets, one for each quarter. Each worksheet should have a name that is easy to understand. Change the tab color so you can find each sheet quickly.

FIGURE 3.35 Renaming a worksheet

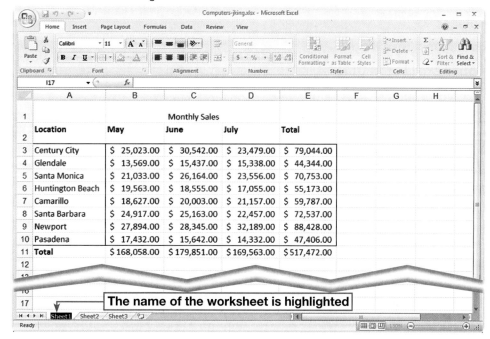

The name of the worksheet is highlighted

FIGURE 3.36 Change tab color

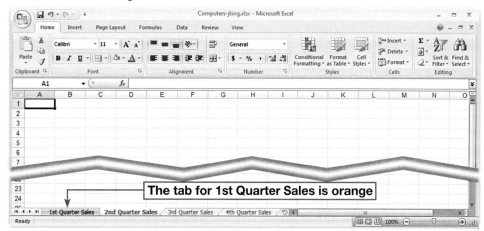

The tab for 1st Quarter Sales is orange

Vocabulary

Key Terms

brightness

color scale

conditional formatting

Conditional Formatting
   Rules Manager

contrast

custom number format

data bar

icon set

legend

rotate

scale

sizing handle

Academic Vocabulary

conflict

trend

utilize

Review Vocabulary

Complete the following statements on a separate piece of paper. Choose from the Vocabulary list on the left to complete the statements.

1. Applying conditional formatting can help you see a(n) —————— in the numbers on a spreadsheet. (p. 207)

2. —————— a graphic to change the size to a certain percent of its original size. (p. 213)

3. —————— applies only to cells that meet certain conditions. (p. 207)

4. The difference between lighter and darker areas of a graphic is called ——————. (p. 207)

5. To turn a graphic clockwise, —————— it. (p. 214)

Vocabulary Activity

6. Use the skills that you learned in this lesson to help you remember the vocabulary. Write the following terms on small pieces of paper: *brightness, contrast, sizing handle,* and *scale*. Then:
   A. In a new workbook, insert a graphic.
   B. Look at the pieces of paper one at a time. Make a change to the graphic related to the term. If you do not remember what the term means, refer to the definitions in this lesson. Make the change to the graphic.

Review Key Concepts

Answer the following questions on a separate piece of paper.

7. Which custom format would display a value of 7987 as 7,987? (p. 206)
   A. 0,000
   B. *,***
   C. #,###
   D. @,@@@

8. The Brightness button is found in which Picture Tools group? (p. 241)
   A. Arrange
   B. Picture Styles
   C. Adjust
   D. Styles

9. What part of a chart gives information about what the different colors and patterns represent? (p. 245)
   A. brightness
   B. legend
   C. contrast
   D. color scale

10. How can you format most parts of a chart? (p. 245)
   A. Choose **Chart Tools>Layout**.
   B. Choose **Format>Chart**.
   C. Click the part of the chart that you want to change.
   D. Double-click the part of the chart that you want to change.

EXERCISE 3-16
Choose a Background

Data File

1 In your **Computers** file, click the **2nd Quarter Sales** tab.

2 Click the **Select All** button in the top left corner of the worksheet, just to the left of column A and just above row 1.

3 Choose **Home>Styles> Cell Styles**. Select **Neutral**.

4 (i)**CHECK** Your screen should look like Figure 3.37.

5 Select the **1st Quarter Sales** tab. Choose **Page Layout> Page Setup>Background**.

6 In the **Sheet Background** dialog box, browse to and select your data file folder.

7 In the **Files of type** box, make sure **All Pictures** is selected. In the data file list, select the file **CompuBold.JPG**.

8 (i)**CHECK** Your screen should look like Figure 3.38.

9 Save your file.

➡ *Continue to the next exercise.*

A **background** is a graphic or color that appears behind the information in your worksheet. Sometimes backgrounds act as watermarks. Logos often appear as watermarks. They are usually translucent, which means you can see through them. A background will only show on the computer screen. It will not appear if you print the document out.

FIGURE 3.37 Worksheet with a background color

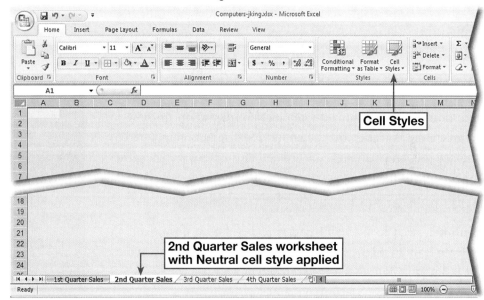

FIGURE 3.38 Background logo inserted in sheet

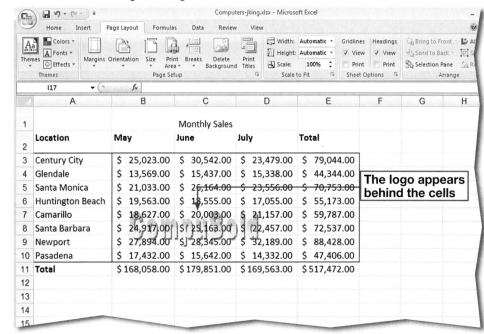

Writing MATTERS

How to Read a Technical Document

You have probably seen booklets explaining how something works or how to operate something, such as a digital camera. Manuals such as these are types of technical documents.

What is a Technical Document?

Technical documents provide step-by-step instruction on how to complete specific tasks. They often include diagrams, numbered or bulleted lists, and headings. The text and illustrations work together to show the reader how to perform the steps being described.

Reading a Technical Document

You often need to read and understand technical documents in order to learn new processes or how to use new equipment. In fact, the lessons in this textbook are written to provide you with technical knowledge. Think of a technical manual that you read recently. Ask yourself the following questions about the manual:

- What was I trying to learn how to do?
- How did the figures or graphics help me understand the process?
- How did the headings or organization of the text add to my understanding?
- Did the manual include step-by-step instructions, or numbered or bulleted lists? How were these helpful?

Knowing how to read technical documents is the first step toward gaining technical knowledge.

Reading technical documents can teach you how to use software applications and other business tools.

SKILLBUILDER

1. **List** What are some of the features of a technical document?
2. **Compare** Think about two sets of instructions you have read recently. Which document was clearer? Why?
3. **Assess** Find and evaluate a technical document. (For example, a page in a manual, the instructions for an appliance you own, etc.) In what ways do you think the document can be improved?

EXERCISE 3-17
Hide and Unhide Worksheets

Just as you can hide and unhide rows and columns, you can hide and unhide entire worksheets. When a worksheet is hidden, it is still available. It is just not visible. Hide worksheets to focus on just one part of your workbook.

1 In your **Computers** file, click the **2nd Quarter Sales** tab. Choose **Home>Cells>Format**. Under **Visibility**, click **Hide & Unhide** and select **Hide Sheet**.

2 Click the **3rd Quarter Sales** tab if it does not automatically become selected.

3 Choose **Home>Cells>Format**. Click **Hide & Unhide** and select **Hide Sheet**. Hide the **4th Quarter Sales** worksheet. The only visible worksheet is **1st Quarter Sales** (see Figure 3.39).

4 Choose **Home>Cells>Format**. Click **Hide & Unhide** and select **Unhide Sheet**.

5 In the **Unhide** dialog box, click **2nd Quarter Sales** (see Figure 3.40). Click **OK**.

6 Repeat Step 5 and click **3rd Quarter Sales**. Click **OK**. Repeat using the **4th Quarter Sales** tab.

7 **CHECK** Your screen should look like Figure 3.40.

8 Save your file.

Continue to the next exercise.

FIGURE 3.39 Hidden sheets

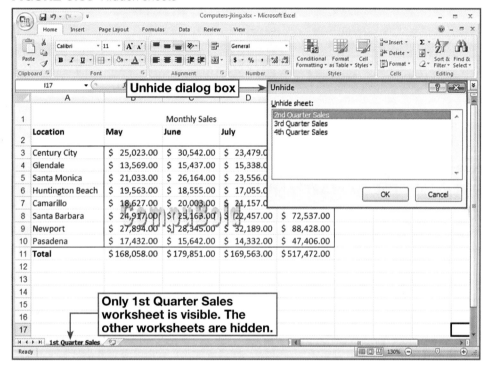

FIGURE 3.40 Unhiding worksheets

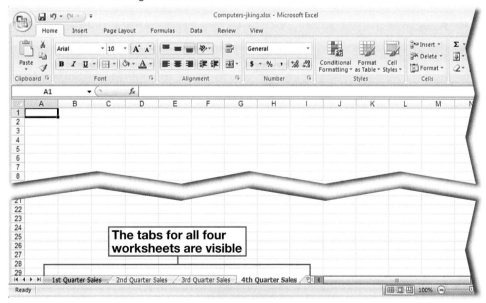

EXERCISE 3-9 (Continued)
Apply Themes to Worksheets

8 Select **Create New Theme Colors**. Under **Theme Colors**, click the **Accent 1** button and change it to **Blue** under standard colors.

9 Click the **Accent 2** button and change it to **Green, Accent 1**. In the **Name** box, key: Sales Data. Click **Save**. Click **Theme Colors** .

10 **⚫CHECK** Your screen should look like Figure 3.27.

11 Choose **Page Layout> Themes** and click **Theme Fonts** . Select **Create New Theme Fonts**.

12 In the **Create New Theme Fonts** dialog box, click the **Body font** drop-down arrow and select **Arial**. In the **Name** box, key: Sales Data. Click **Save**.

13 **⚫CHECK** Your screen should look like Figure 3.28.

14 Click **Themes** . Select **Save Current Theme**.

15 In **File name** box, key: Sales Data. Click **Save**.

16 Click **Themes** . Note that the Sales Data Theme is added to the thumbnails.

17 Save and close your file.

FIGURE 3.27 Chart1 formatted with Sales Data Theme

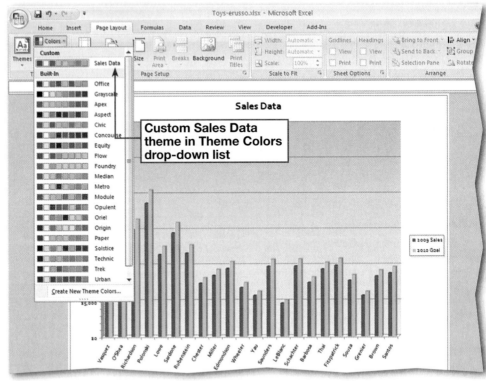

FIGURE 3.28 Formatted Sales Data chart

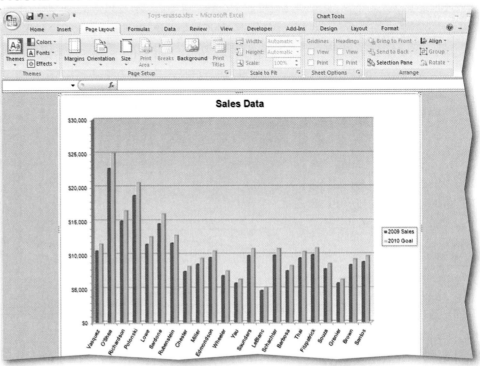

1. In your **Computers** file, click the **1st Quarter Sales** tab.

2. Choose **Insert>SmartArt**.

3. In the **Choose a SmartArt Graphic** dialog box, under **Process**, scroll down and click **Upward Arrow** (see Figure 3.41). Click **OK**.

4. Right-click anywhere on the blue SmartArt arrow. Choose **Add a Shape> Add Shape After**. A new blue dot is added to the graphic.

5. Click the word **Text** at the bottom of the arrow. Key: May. Key: $27,894.

6. Enter the remainder of the sales data into the **Text** pane as shown in Figure 3.42: June $28,345, July $32,189, Newport's Total Sales $88,428.

7. **CHECK** Your screen should look like Figure 3.42.

8. Click the **SmartArt Tools** tab. Then click **Format**.

   Continued on the next page.

In this exercise you will create a SmartArt graphic for a monthly sales report. Excel provides a variety of **SmartArt** shapes, such as a **graphical list** (like a bulleted or numbered list), a process diagram (which shows how information changes in a process), and an organizational chart (which demonstrates an organized arrangement), to visually communicate, or convey, information. Graphics are often used to summarize information and demonstrate the data's significance.

FIGURE 3.41 Choose a SmartArt Graphic dialog box

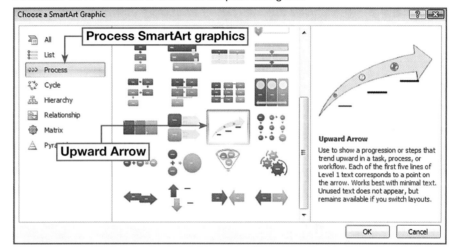

FIGURE 3.42 Newport Sales data added to

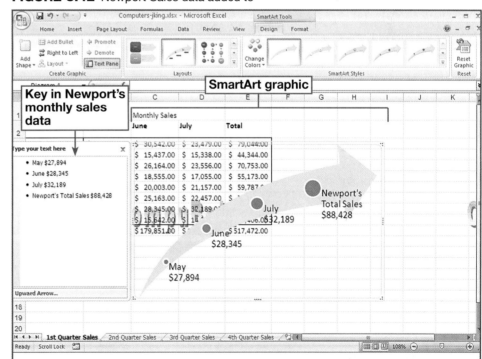

1. In your **Toys** file, double-click the **Sales Data** chart to open the **Chart Tools** contextual tab. Choose **Design>Location>Move Chart**.

2. In the **Move Chart** dialog box, select **New sheet**. Click **OK**. A new sheet tab is created for the sales data chart.

3. With the **Chart1** sheet tab selected, choose **Page Layout>Themes** and click **Themes**. Click the **Metro** theme thumbnail.

4. **⒤CHECK** Your screen should look like Figure 3.25.

5. Click the **Sales Data** sheet tab. Double-click the block arrow graphic. Click the **Shape Fill** drop-down arrow. Click the theme color **Pink, Accent 2**.

6. **⒤CHECK** Your screen should look like Figure 3.26.

7. Click the **Chart1** sheet tab. Choose **Page Layout>Themes** and click **Theme Colors**.

   → *Continued on the next page.*

EXERCISE 3-9
Apply Themes to Worksheets

You can enhance your workbooks by using built-in styles and themes to ensure that cells have consistent formatting and design. A theme allows you to automatically apply several formats such as 3-D effects, colors, boldface, and shading to an entire workbook in one step. Themes also allow you to change the colors, fonts, and effects used in a table, graph, or worksheet to make the entire workbook consistent.

FIGURE 3.25 Themes drop-down list

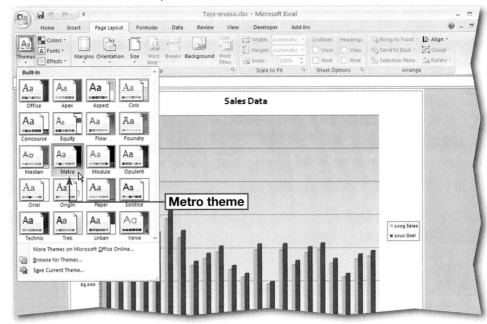

FIGURE 3.26 Metro theme applied to Sales data worksheet

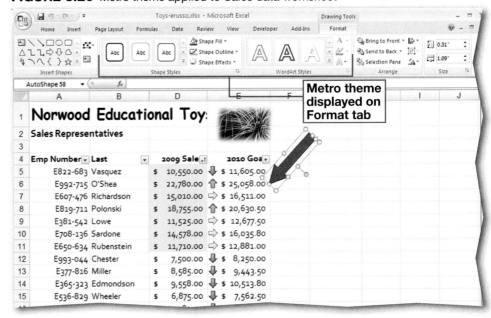

EXERCISE 3-18 (Continued)
Insert, Move, and Size SmartArt Graphics

9 Click the **Shape Effects** button and select **Preset 9** (see Figure 3.43).

10 Click the arrow to select the SmartArt graphic.

11 Position your pointer over the left corner of the graphic until it takes the shape of the four-headed arrow.

12 Click and drag the four-headed arrow down and to the left so it is directly under the Monthly Sales figures in the worksheet.

13 Choose **SmartArt Tools> Design**. Then click **Change Colors** and select **Colored Fill**, **Accent 3**.

14 **ⓘCHECK** Your screen should look like Figure 3.44.

15 Click the arrow to select the SmartArt graphic.

16 Position your pointer over the arrow's lower-right dot (see Figure 3.44) until it becomes a two-headed arrow. Click and drag the dot down and to the right.

17 Resize the arrow until you are satisfied with how it looks. Save your workbook. Close the workbook and exit Excel.

FIGURE 3.43 Shape Effects

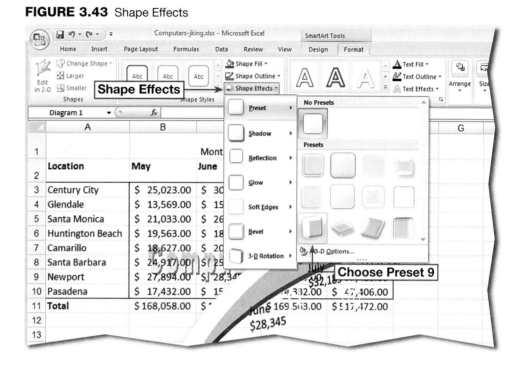

FIGURE 3.44 SmartArt displays Newport's sales figures

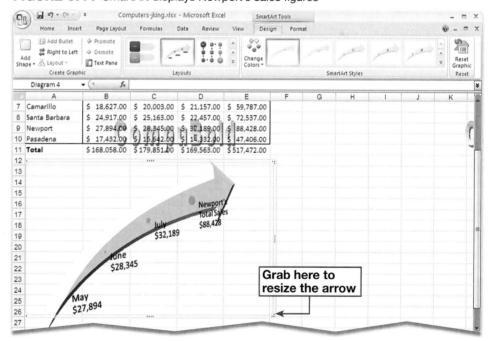

EXERCISE 3-8 (Continued)
Apply Formats to Charts and Diagrams

8 Click **Alignment**. Change the **Custom angle** to **–60°**. Click **Close**.

9 Choose **Layout>Labels> Legend** . Select **None**.

10 Click **Legend** . Select **Show Legend at Right**. Click **Legend** again. Select **More Legend Options.** In the **Format Legend** dialog box, click **Border Color** and select **Solid line**.

11 Click **Shadow**. Choose **Presets>Outer** and select **Offset Diagonal Bottom Right**. Click **Close**. Click a blank part of the chart.

12 ⓘ**CHECK** Your screen should look like Figure 3.23.

13 Select the chart. Choose **Layout>Labels>Chart Title** . Select **Above Chart**. Name the chart **Sales Data**.

14 Choose **Layout> Background>Chart Wall** . Select **More Walls Options**. Click **Fill** and select **Gradient fill**. Click **Close**.

15 ⓘ**CHECK** Your screen should look like Figure 3.24. Save your file.

➥ *Continue to the next exercise.*

FIGURE 3.23 Partially formatted chart

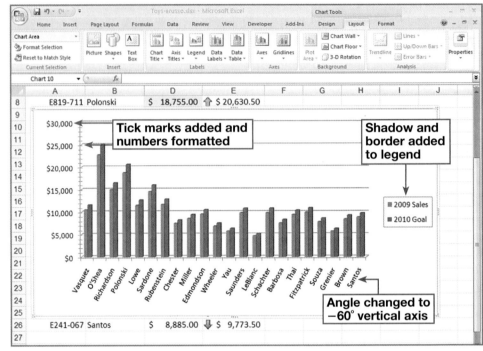

FIGURE 3.24 Formatted chart

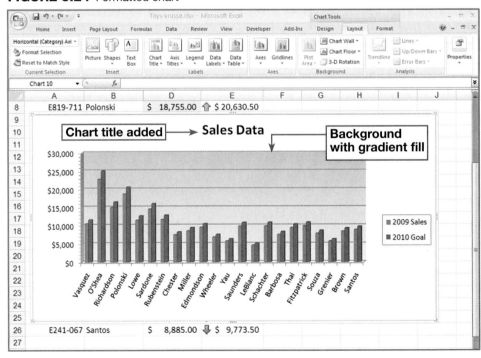

21st Century WORKPLACE

Develop Interview Skills

Rosa sits up straight and calmly describes her past work experience. She wears a brown suit and little makeup. Her hair is tied back in a neat ponytail. She asks about training on the job at the company.

Shayn fidgets and looks at the floor. His shirt is partially untucked. He gives one-word answers to the questions, and he does not have any questions for the interviewer.

Imagine you are the interviewer. Which candidate would probably interest you more? Who would make the better impression?

When you interview for a job, dress in a way that is appropriate. Speaking clearly, making eye contact with the interviewer, and showing that you can think quickly by responding to questions will also help you make a good impression.

MEET THE MANAGER

Rachel Orzoff, a career counselor in Minneapolis, Minnesota, teaches students how to prepare for interviews. She says, "Every interviewer is looking for the answers to three questions: Can you do the job? Will you do the job? And do I want to do the job with you?" Job candidates need to be able to perform the tasks of the position, she says. They also need to be likable, professional, and ready to be part of a team.

Making the right impression at an interview includes dressing appropriately and making eye contact.

SKILLBUILDER

1. **List** Create a list of pointers for a person getting ready for an interview.

2. **Write** Imagine you are interested in a job in the data-entry department of a jewelry manufacturing business. Write three questions you might ask the interviewer about the company, the job, or the work environment.

3. **Prioritize** Write a sentence explaining which of the following you think is most important for a successful interview. Then rank the other four.
   a. wearing conservative clothing
   b. having good manners
   c. asking intelligent questions
   d. making eye contact and smiling
   e. appearing calm and confident

EXERCISE 3-8
Apply Formats to Charts and Diagrams

1. In your **Toys** file, select column **C**. Right-click and select **Hide**. With column C hidden, select **B4:E26**. Choose **Insert>Charts> Column** 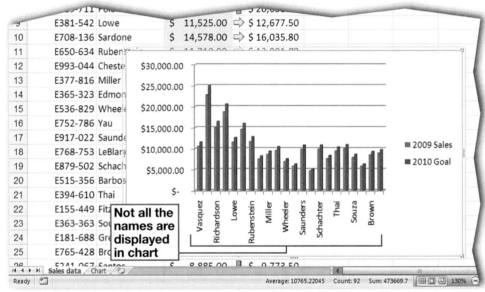. Under **3-D Column**, select **3-D Clustered Column**.

2. ⓘ**CHECK** Your screen should look like Figure 3.21.

3. Click and drag the chart's sizing handles until all 22 names are visible.

4. Choose **Layout>Axes> Axes** . Choose **Primary Vertical Axis>More Primary Vertical Axis Options**. In the **Format Axis** dialog box, change the **Minor tick mark type** to **Cross** (see Figure 3.22).

5. Click **Number** in the **Format Axis** dialog box, click **Percentage**. Click **Currency**. In the **Decimal places** box, key: 0. Click **Close**.

6. ⓘ**CHECK** Your dialog box should look like Figure 3.22.

7. Choose **Layout>Axes> Primary Horizontal Axis** and select **More Primary Vertical Axis Options**.

→ *Continued on the next page.*

Charts and diagrams offer a graphical representation of data that helps you better visualize and analyze it. After you create a chart, there are many different ways it can be formatted and modified. For example, you could change the font size of the chart title, the color and appearance of the background, or you could add shading to the legend. The **legend** is the part of a chart that indicates what each color or pattern represents. To format part of a chart, double-click it. In this exercise, you will create and format a chart that displays the 2009 sales and 2010 sales goals.

FIGURE 3.21 Sales data in 3-D Clustered Column chart

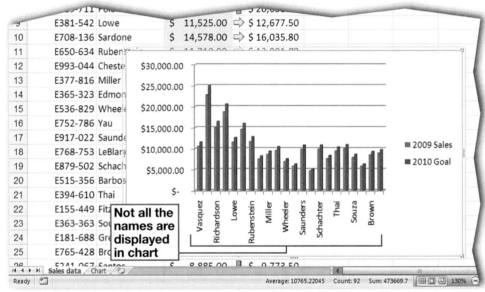

FIGURE 3.22 Format Axis dialog box

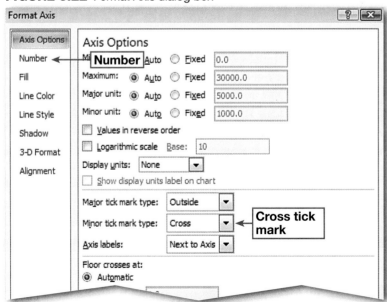

Vocabulary

Key Terms

background

border

cell style

delimiter

font

font style

graphical list

horizontal alignment

SmartArt

table style

theme

vertical alignment

Academic Vocabulary

convey

distinct

Review Vocabulary

Complete the following statements on a separate piece of paper. Choose from the Vocabulary list on the left to complete the statements.

1. A(n) ——————— is a graphic or color that appears behind the information in a worksheet. (p. 70)

2. The side-to-side placement of a cell's contents is called the ———————. (p. 65)

3. A(n) ——————— is a movable, resizable graphic used to visually communicate information. (p. 72)

4. Font colors help to make certain cells ——————— from the rest of the worksheet (p. 60)

5. A(n) ——————— is a line along one or more sides of a cell. (p. 53)

Vocabulary Activity

6. Create a matching quiz based on this lesson's vocabulary words.
   A. Choose six terms from the vocabulary list. On the left side of a piece of paper, write the terms. On the right side, write the definitions—but not in the same order as the terms.
   B. After you have created your quiz, with your teacher's permission, team up with a classmate and exchange quizzes.
   C. Match the vocabulary word to its correct definition with a line. Note any definitions that you did not know and find the correct answer.

Reviewing Key Concepts

Answer the following questions on a separate piece of paper.

7. Which tab would you use to change a workbook's theme? (p. 57)
   A. Data
   B. Home
   C. Page Layout
   D. View

8. What group on the Home tab do you use to change the horizontal alignment of a cell's contents? (p. 65)
   A. Clipboard
   B. Cells
   C. Alignment
   D. Editing

9. Which tab would you use to create a SmartArt graphic? (p. 72)
   A. Review
   B. Add-Ins
   C. Formulas
   D. Insert

10. Which would you use to center your table's heading across columns A, B, and C? (p. 66)
   A. Center Across Selection
   B. Center
   C. Align Right
   D. General

Rotate a Graphic

1 In your **Toys** file, scroll down and double-click the block arrow graphic. The **Drawing Tools** contextual tab should open (see Figure 3.19).

2 Choose **Format>Arrange** group, and click **Rotate**. Select **Rotate Left 90°**. The arrow points up.

3 Move your pointer over the green dot to the left of the arrow. Your pointer becomes a rotate arrow.

4 Click and drag in a circular motion until the block arrow is pointing down and to the left. Deselect the block arrow.

5 Drag the block arrow so that it is pointing to cell **E6**. Deselect the block arrow.

6 ⓘ**CHECK** Your screen should look like Figure 3.20. Save your file.

➡ *Continue to the next exercise.*

Academic Skills

A complete rotation is 360 degrees. If you rotate a graphic 90 degrees counter-clockwise, the top of the image will point to the left side of the page.

Rotate a graphic to turn it clockwise (to the right) or counterclockwise (to the left). You can rotate a graphic 90 degrees or you can use the rotation handle to rotate it as many degrees as you want. You can also flip a graphic horizontally or vertically. You can remove a picture and replace it with a new picture. To keep the size and formatting of the original picture, choose Format>Adjust>Change Picture on the Picture Tools tab.

FIGURE 3.19 Drawing Tools

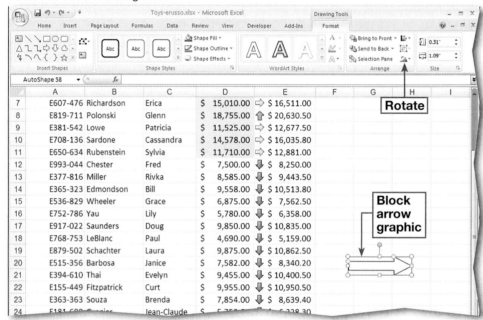

FIGURE 3.20 Rotated block arrow

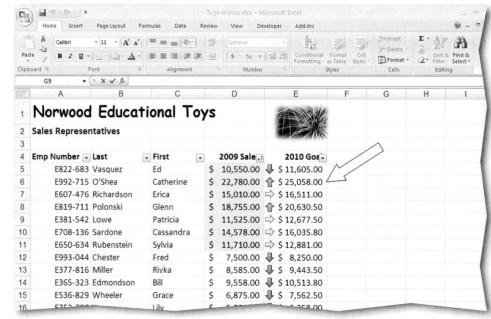

LESSON 3 Practice It Activities

1. Format a Worksheet

Follow the steps to complete the activity.

Step-By-Step

1. Open the data file **Office.xlsx**. Save as: Office-[your first initial and last name]1.

2. Select **A1:E7**. On the **Home** tab, in the **Font** group, choose the font **Bookman Old Style** (see Figure 3.45).

3. Select **A2:A7**. Change the **Font Size** to **12**. Click **Bold** B.

4. From the **Border** drop-down list, choose **Right Border**.

5. Select **B1:E1**. Click **Bold** B.

6. Change the **Font Size** to **12**.

7. On the **Border** drop-down list, choose **Bottom Border**.

8. Double-click the lines between the column heads to increase the width of columns A, B, C, D, and E.

9. **CHECK** Your screen should look like Figure 3.46. Save and close your file.

FIGURE 3.45 Font box in Font group

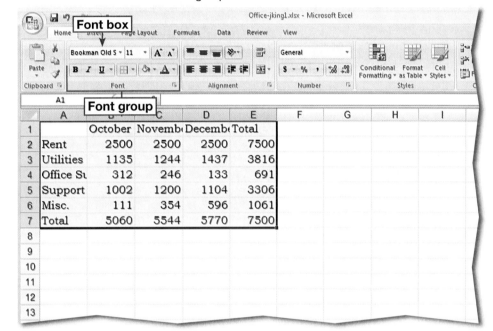

FIGURE 3.46 Modify column width

	A	B	C	D	E
1		October	November	December	Total
2	Rent	2500	2500	2500	7500
3	Utilities	1135	1244	1437	3816
4	Office Supplies	312	246	133	691
5	Support Services	1002	1200	1104	3306
6	Misc.	111	354	596	1061
7	Total	5060	5544	5770	7500

1. In your **Toys** file, double-click the graphic of the fireworks. Select the **Picture Tools>Format> Size** dialog box launcher.

2. In the **Size and Properties** dialog box, under **Scale**, double-click the number in the **Height** box to select it.

3. Key: 25 Press `TAB`.

4. **①CHECK** Your dialog box should look similar to Figure 3.17.

5. Click **Close.** Click and drag the graphic up so it fits in cells **F1:G2**. Resize if necessary. Deselect the graphic.

6. **①CHECK** Your screen should look like Figure 3.18.

7. Save your file.

   Continue to the next exercise.

You Should Know

The numbers in your dialog box under **Size and rotate** may not match those in Figure 3.17. The height and width will depend on how you resized the image in Step 15 of Exercise 3-5.

EXERCISE 3-6
Scale a Graphic

Increase or decrease the **scale** of a graphic if you want to change its size in percentages. For instance, you can make a graphic 10 percent bigger or 15 percent smaller. To change the graphic back to its original size, change the scale to 100 percent.

FIGURE 3.17 Size and Properties dialog box

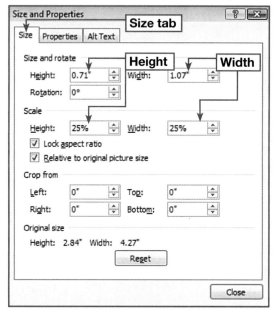

FIGURE 3.18 Resized graphic

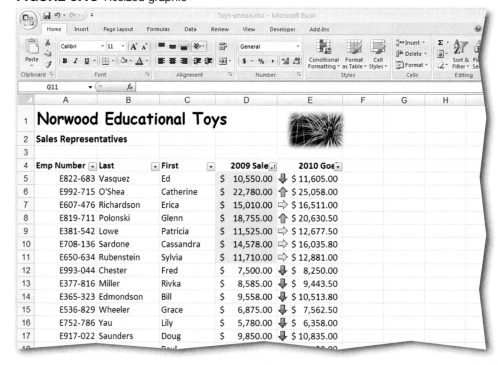

2. Format as a Table and Use Cell Styles

Follow the steps to complete the activity. You must complete Practice It Activity 1 before doing this activity.

Step-By-Step

1. Open your **Office-1** file. Save as: Office-[your first initial and last name]2.

2. Select **A1:E7**. Choose **Home> Styles>Format as a Table**. Select **Table Style Light 9**. Click **OK**.

3. Select **B2:E7**. Choose **Home>Cell Styles> Currency** (see Figure 3.47). If necessary, double-click the lines between column headings to increase the width of columns B, C, D, and E.

4. In cell **A1**, change the column heading to **Monthly Expenses**.

5. Change the **Font Size** to **12**. Adjust the column width, if necessary.

6. **ⓘCHECK** Your screen should look like Figure 3.48.

7. Save and close your file.

FIGURE 3.47 Currency style selected in Cell Style menu

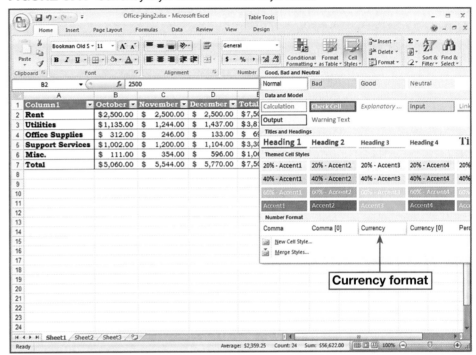

FIGURE 3.48 Column header added to cell A1

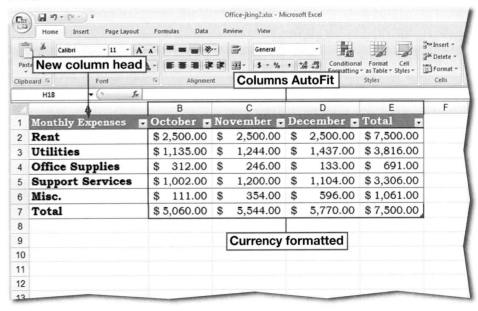

10 In your **Toys** file, click the graphic of the fireworks.

11 Point to the sizing handle in the lower-right corner of the graphic.

12 ⓘ**CHECK** Your screen should look like Figure 3.15.

13 Drag the sizing handle toward the center of the picture. Release the mouse button.

14 Point to the lower-right sizing handle again. Drag the sizing handle into column J.

15 ⓘ**CHECK** Your screen should look similar to Figure 3.16.

16 Save your file.

➤ *Continue to the next exercise.*

Academic Skills

Contrast is the difference between two things. When you change the contrast of an image, for example, you make it easier to see the difference between the light areas and the dark areas because you make the light areas lighter and the darker areas darker.

EXERCISE 3-5 (Continued)
Insert and Modify a Graphic

FIGURE 3.15 Resizing a graphic

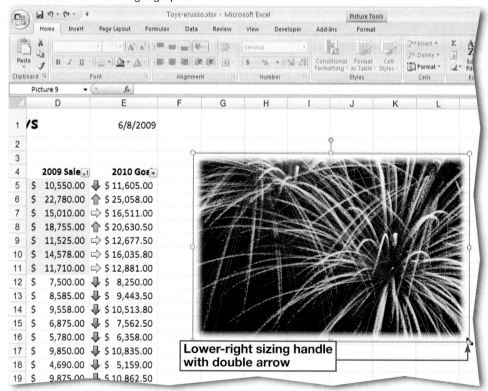

Lower-right sizing handle with double arrow

FIGURE 3.16 Resized graphic

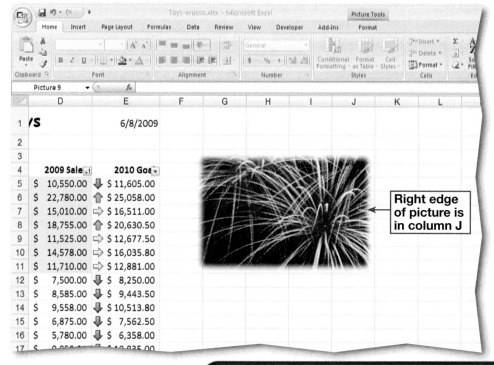

Right edge of picture is in column J

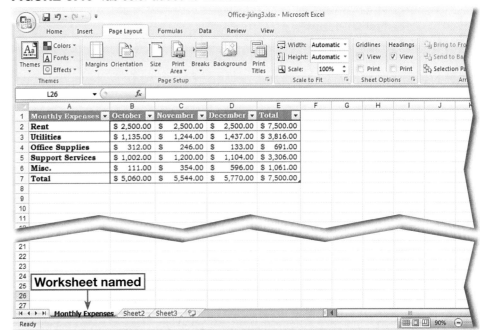

LESSON 3 Practice It Activities

3. Add a Background and Rename a Worksheet

Follow the steps to complete the activity. You must complete Practice It Activity 2 before doing this activity.

Step-By-Step

1. Open your **Office-2** file. Save as: Office-[your first initial and last name]3.

2. Choose **Home>Cells> Format**. Under **Organize Sheets**, click **Rename Sheet**.

3. Key: Monthly Expenses. Press ENTER.

4. Choose **Home>Cells> Format**. Under **Organize Sheets**, click **Tab Color**.

5. Select **Red**.

6. **CHECK** Your screen should look like Figure 3.49.

7. Choose **Page Layout> Page Setup> Background**.

8. Navigate to the folder containing the data file **OfficeInc.JPG**. Select the file. Click **Insert**.

9. **CHECK** Your screen should look like Figure 3.50.

10. Save and close your file.

FIGURE 3.49 Tab color added to worksheet

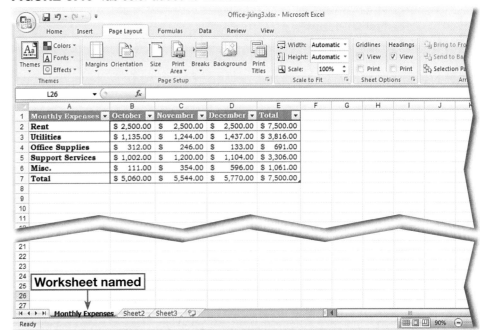

FIGURE 3.50 Office Inc. background added to worksheet

EXERCISE 3-5
Insert and Modify a Graphic

When you select a graphic or illustration, the Picture Tools contextual tab opens. You can use the tools on this tab to insert and modify pictures. You can change the picture's **contrast**, or difference between light and dark. You can also change the **brightness**, or overall lightness or darkness, of a picture. You can resize a graphic by dragging its **sizing handles**. Sizing handles are dots that appear around the edges of the graphic you have selected. Corner sizing handles resize graphics proportionally.

1. In your **Toys** file, scroll to the right to display the entire graphic of the sun.

2. Double-click the graphic. Choose **Insert> Illustrations>Picture**. The **Insert Picture** dialog box opens.

3. Navigate to and select the **fireworks.jpg** data file. Click **Insert**. Click the sun graphic.

4. (**i**)**CHECK** Your screen should look like Figure 3.13. Press `DELETE`.

5. Drag the fireworks picture up to where the sun graphic was located.

6. Double-click the graphic. Choose **Format>Adjust> Brightness**. Select **+20%**.

7. Choose **Format>Adjust> Contrast**. Select **+30%**.

8. Choose **Format>Picture Styles** and click the **More** drop-down arrow. Select **Soft Edge Rectangle**.

9. (**i**)**CHECK** Your screen should look like Figure 3.14.

   Continued on the next page.

FIGURE 3.13 Picture inserted

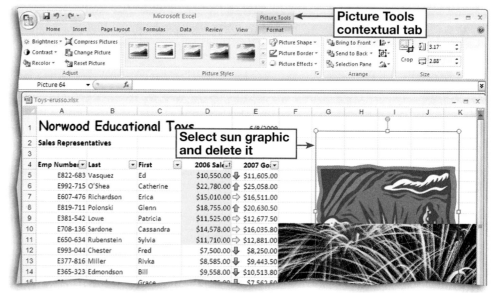

FIGURE 3.14 Graphic after adding Soft Edge Rectangle style

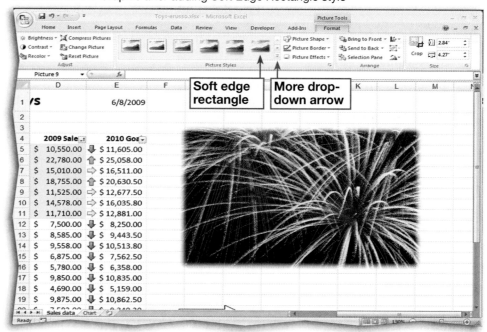

4. Schedule Change

One characteristic of being flexible is the willingness to change the way you do things. Create a schedule that lists the way you typically spend your after-school and evening time. Consider the things you normally do such as chores. Next to that list, key in how you think you might be more efficient during those hours. Remember to proofread for mistakes.

Step-By-Step

1. Open the data file **Planner.xlsx**. Save as: Planner-[your first initial and last name]4.

2. Change the **Font Size** of **A2:C2** to **12**.

3. Bold the text in **A2:C2**. Change the font of **A1** to font size **14** and **Bold**.

4. Adjust the width of column **A**.

5. Change the **Font Color** of row 2 and column A to **blue**. Center the title in **A1** across **A1:C1**.

6. **ⓘCHECK** Your screen should look like Figure 3.51.

7. In column **B**, list how you spend your after-school hours. In column **C**, list how you could spend your time more efficiently.

8. Adjust the width of columns **B** and **C**.

9. **ⓘCHECK** Your screen should look similar to Figure 3.52.

10. Save and close your file.

FIGURE 3.51 Planner with formatting applied

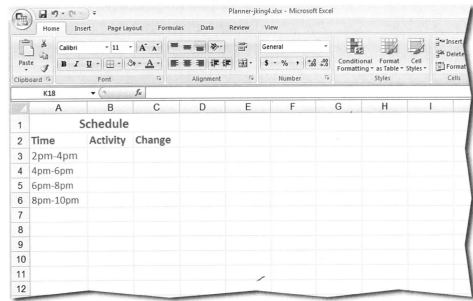

FIGURE 3.52 Completed planner

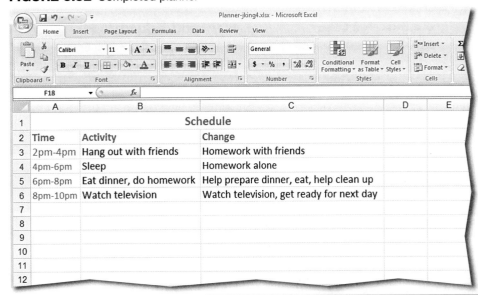

EXERCISE 3-4 (Continued)
Use the Conditional Formatting Rules Manager

9 Click **Conditional Formatting** and select **Manage Rules**.

10 Click **Move Down** . Click **OK**.

11 Click **Conditional Formatting** and select **Manage Rules**. Select the **3 Symbols** rule. Click **Delete Rule** . Click **OK**.

12 Select **A4:E26**. Choose **Home>Editing>Sort & Filter>Filter** .

13 Click the drop-down arrow next to **2010 Goals**. Choose **Filter By Color> Filter By Cell Icon** and select the green up arrow from the list.

14 **ⓘCHECK** Your screen should look like Figure 3.11.

15 Click the **2010 Goal** filter icon and select **Clear Filter from "2010 Goal"**.

16 Click the **2009 Goals** drop-down arrow. Choose **Sort By Color**. Click the yellow rectangle. Deselect the cells.

17 **ⓘCHECK** Your screen should look like Figure 3.12. Save your file.

Continue to the next exercise.

FIGURE 3.11 Sales figures filtered using conditional formatting

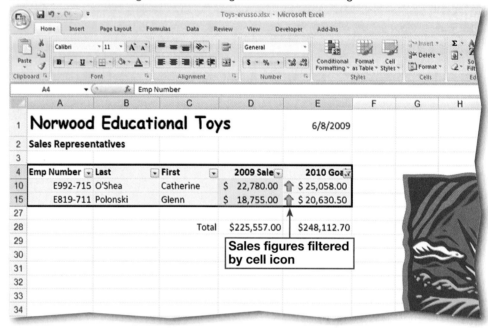

FIGURE 3.12 Sales figures sorted using conditional formatting

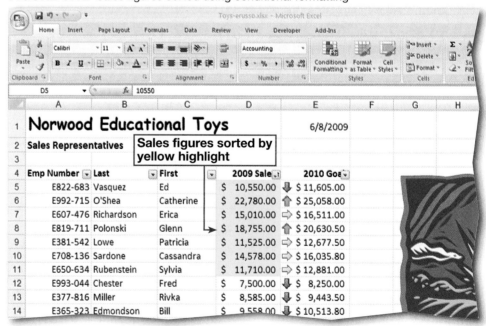

5. Being Prepared

As part of a contest, you and a group of friends must spend a week in the wilderness living out of a backpack. Create a worksheet to list what you should take on your trip.

Step-By-Step

1. Open the data file **Backpacking.xlsx**. Save the file as: Backpacking-[your first initial and last name]5.

2. Add a bottom border for cells **A1:C1**.

3. Select **A1:C1**. Bold and center the cell contents.

4. In each column, list three items you would need for that category. Adjust the width of each column.

5. **ⓘCHECK** Your screen should look similar to Figure 3.53.

6. Rename the worksheet tab Packing and change the tab color to **Green**.

7. Choose Page **Layout>Page Setup> Background**. Locate the data file **Pack.JPG** and insert it.

8. Hide **Sheet2** and **Sheet3**.

9. **ⓘCHECK** Your screen should look similar to Figure 3.54.

10. Save and close your file.

FIGURE 3.53 Backpacking list

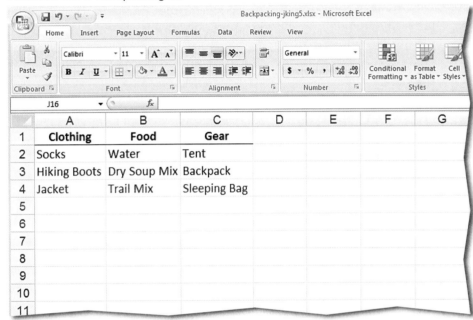

FIGURE 3.54 Formatted backpacking list

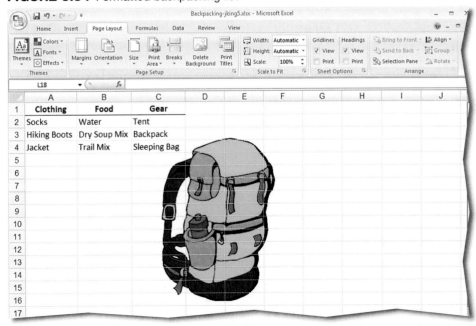

① In your **Toys** file, select **E5:E26**, if necessary. Choose the **Home> Styles>Conditional Formatting** drop-down menu.

② Click **Manage Rules**. In the **Conditional Formatting Rules Manager**, click **New Rule**.

③ In the **New Formatting Rule** dialog box, make sure **Format all cells based on their values** is selected.

④ Click the **Format Style** drop-down arrow. Select **Data Bar**. Click **OK** twice.

⑤ Click **Conditional Formatting** and select **Manage Rules**. Select the **Data Bar** rule in the list. Click **Edit Rule**.

⑥ Click the **Format Style** drop-down arrow and select **Icon Sets**.

⑦ Click the **Icon Style** drop-down arrow and select **3 Symbols (Uncircled)** (see Figure 3.9) Click **OK** twice.

⑧ *ⓘCHECK* Your screen should look like Figure 3.10.

➡ *Continued on the next page.*

EXERCISE 3-4
Use the Conditional Formatting Rules Manager

Use the **Conditional Formatting Rules Manager** to create, edit, delete, and view all conditional formatting rules in a worksheet or workbook. When formatting rules do not conflict, both rules are applied to the range of cells. For example, if one rule formats a cell range with a yellow background and another rule formats the same range with a bold font, both rules are applied. If the rules are in conflict, or are not in agreement, the Conditional Formatting Rules Manager applies the rule that appears higher in the list.

FIGURE 3.9 Conditional Formatting Rules Manager

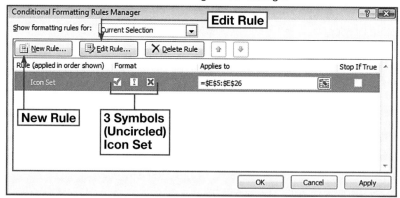

FIGURE 3.10 Sales figures formatted using 3 Symbols

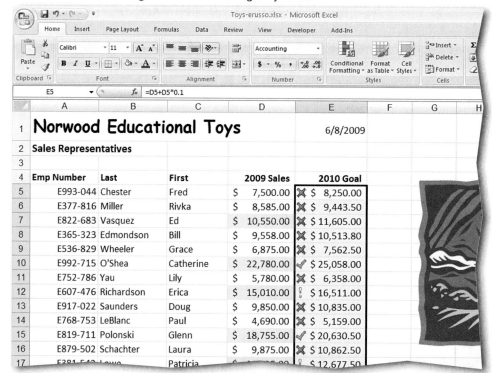

6. Beyond the Classroom Activity

Language Arts: Create a Directory Use Excel to create a directory that includes information about ten of your friends and family members. Use one row for each person. Include a column for each of the following:

- address
- home phone number
- cellular phone number
- e-mail address
- birthday

Use a large font and bold for column labels. AutoFit rows and columns as necessary. Add a new column to include additional information about the people, such as how many children they have, what you bought them for their last birthday, the best time to reach them, and so on.

Save your workbook as: e3rev-[your first initial and last name]6.

7. Standards at Work Activity

Microsoft Certified Application Specialist Correlation
Excel 2.4 *Format Data as a Table*

Format a Table You work for a small company that makes pottery. Your supervisor has asked you to format a worksheet that contains information about specific pottery items that the company makes and has sold in recent months. Your boss wants you to format the worksheet so the information stands out. Open the data file **Pottery.xlsx**. Save as: e3rev-[your first initial and last name]7. Decide which table and cell styles are the most appropriate for the data. Apply the styles. Key a paragraph in cell H6 that identifies why you chose the styles. In your paragraph, list the styles that you selected to format your data.

8. 21st Century Skills Activity

Create a Backup Plan Having a backup plan is a great step towards being flexible. Think of your first choice for a summer job. Open a new workbook. List the job at the top of a column in a worksheet. Underneath the job, list the reasons that you are qualified for the job. In case you do not get this job, list a second job choice in the second column. Include the reasons that you are qualified for your second job choice. The second column is now your backup plan. Modify the format so that your first job choice is in red and bold, and your backup job is in blue and italics. Adjust the column size to fit the content.

Save your workbook as: e3rev-[your first initial and last name]8.

Go Online e-REVIEW
glencoe.com

Go to the **Online Learning Center** to complete the following review activities.

Online Self Check
To test your knowledge of the material, click **Unit 1> Lesson 3** and choose **Self Checks**.

Interactive Review
To review the main points of the lesson, click **Unit 1> Lesson 3** and choose **Interactive Review**.

EXERCISE 3-3 (Continued)
Use Conditional Formatting

8. Click **Conditional Formatting**. Select **Top/Bottom Rules>Top 10 Items**. Click the **with** box drop-down arrow. Select **Green Fill with Dark Green Text**. Click **OK**.

9. Click **Conditional Formatting**. Select **Top/Bottom Rules>Bottom 10 Items**. Click **OK**.

10. Click **Undo** twice. Click **Conditional Formatting** and select **Data Bars**.

11. **CHECK** Your screen should look like Figure 3.7.

12. Click **Conditional Formatting** and select **Color Scales**.

13. Click **Conditional Formatting** and select **Icon Sets**. Click **3 Arrows (Colored)**.

14. **CHECK** Your screen should look like Figure 3.8. Save your file.

→ *Continue to the next exercise.*

Academic Skills

Sorting and filtering by format is helpful for analyzing data. You can see data changes and trends at a glance.

FIGURE 3.7 Data Bars

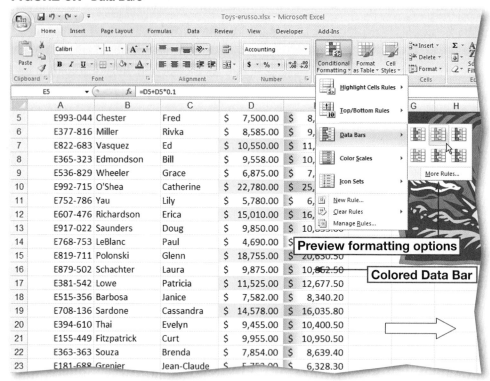

FIGURE 3.8 Sales figures formatted with 3 Arrows (Colored) icon set

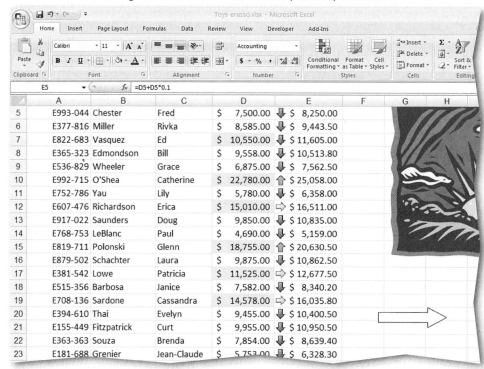

Before You Begin

Format Data Formatting influences how an audience responds to a document. These projects teach you how to format a worksheet so it is easy to read and to understand.

Reflect Once you complete the projects, open a Word document and answer the following:

1. How can formatting be used to draw the reader's attention?

2. How did Excel's Quick Styles feature help you maintain consistency in your worksheets?

9. Create a Sales Worksheet

Math: Create a Worksheet You are the owner of a small business that sells frames. Make a worksheet that shows the monthly sales for each size of frame. Include the following:

- three frame sizes: $8'' \times 10''$, $11'' \times 14''$, and $16'' \times 20''$
- prices for each frame size ($8'' \times 10'' = \$11.95$; $11'' \times 14'' = \$12.95$; $16'' \times 20'' = \$13.95$)
- sales for three months, assuming that smaller frames sell better
- total, average, minimum, and maximum for each month

Create a row for each size and a column for each month. Use AutoSum functions to calculate the total, average, minimum, and maximum for each month. Save as: e3rev-[your first initial and last name]9.

10. Format a Sales Worksheet

Language Arts: Change Font and Use Formats You decide to post your frame sales worksheet (created in Project 9 above) for your employees. Make the following format changes to increase the readibility:

- Make the font size for column and row labels larger.
- Use a different color for each month, and add the title **Quarterly Sales**. Center it across three cells, and apply an appropriate format.

Then, key a paragraph below the table that describes how the format changes add to the readability. Save your workbook as: e3rev-[your first initial and last name]10.

11. Design a Work Schedule

Math: Insert and Format SmartArt You need to create a work schedule for the five employees at your frame shop. Design a worksheet that shows a schedule, in hourly increments, from 9:00 a.m. to 6:00 p.m. for Monday through Saturday. Include a column for each day and a row for each hour increment. For each day, assign two employees to the 9 a.m. to 1 p.m. shift and two employees to the 1 p.m. to 6 p.m. shift. Do your best to evenly distribute the hours among the employees, and avoid having any employee work two shifts in a row. Include the following:

- Below the schedules, add a SmartArt graphic that lists each employee's total hours. (Hint: Choose a SmartArt graphic from the **List** category in the **Choose a SmartArt** graphic dialog box).
- Save your workbook as: e3rev-[your first initial and last name]11.

1. In your **Toys** file, select **D5:D26**. Choose **Home> Styles>Conditional Formatting** 🔲. Choose **Highlight Cells Rules** and select **Greater Than** (see Figure 3.5).

2. In the **Greater Than** dialog box, in the **Format cells that are GREATER THAN** box, key: 10000. Click **OK**.

3. Choose **Conditional Formatting>Manage Rules** 🔲. In the **Conditional Formatting Rules Manager** dialog box, click **Edit Rule**. Click **Format**.

4. In the **Format** dialog box, click the **Color** drop-down arrow and change the **Font** to **Black, Text 1**. Click the **Fill** tab. Choose the yellow **Background Color**.

5. Click **OK**. The dialog box previews the formatting. Click **OK** twice. Deselect the range.

6. ⓘ**CHECK** Your screen should look like Figure 3.6.

7. Select **E5:E26**.

➡ *Continued on the next page.*

EXERCISE 3-3
Use Conditional Formatting

You can apply conditional formatting to a cell range or table to help you analyze data. **Conditional formatting** changes the appearance of a cell or cell range only if it meets certain conditions. The formatting can include changes such as font color, italics, strikethrough, borders, highlighting, or shading to emphasize values. For example, a **data bar** adds a colored bar to cells based on the value of the data. A **color scale** varies colors based on the values in a range. An **icon set** allows you to highlight specific values with preset icons. All these tools make it much easier to see a **trend**, or pattern.

FIGURE 3.5 Conditional Formatting drop-down list

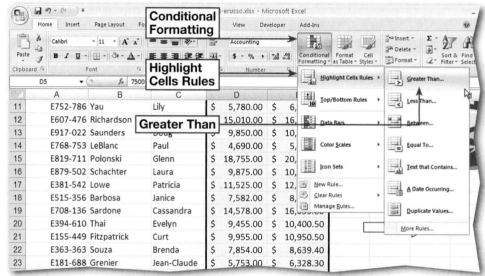

FIGURE 3.6 Sales figures formatted using conditional formatting

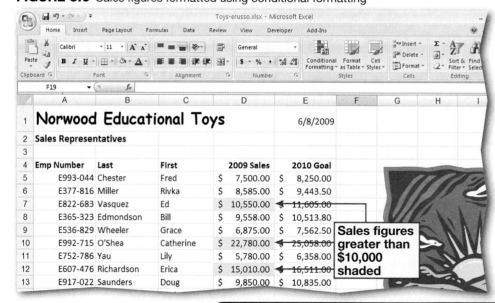

In this lesson, you will use Excel to help you analyze data. You will sort data in ascending and descending order, as well as filter data to see only the information that you need. You will learn to use absolute and relative references to make different calculations, and create charts to visually represent your data.

Key Concepts

- Filter and sort data

- Write, edit, and use formulas

- Use absolute, relative, and mixed references

- Create, modify, and position diagrams

- Create, modify, and position charts

Standards

The following standards are covered in this lesson. Refer to pages xix and 314 for a description of the standards listed here.

ISTE Standards Correlation

NETS•S

1a, 3b, 3c, 3d, 4d, 6b

Microsoft Certified Application Specialist

Excel

2.3, 3.1, 3.2, 3.6, 4.1, 4.2, 4.6

21st CENTURY SKILLS

Improve Self-Management Successful self-management means setting a goal, figuring out what you need to do to meet that goal, and having the discipline to work steadily toward achieving it. For example, imagine that you want to run in a 10-mile race six months from now. What do you need to do now to prepare yourself? Once you determine your needs, use organizational tools such as calendars and Microsoft Excel to check your progress every week. It is easier to stick to a plan if you chart your progress so that you can see that you are getting closer to your goal. *Which of your goals require successful self-management?*

1 In your **Toys** file, select **A6:A26**. Choose **Home> Cells>Format Cells**. In the **Format Cells** dialog box, click the **Number** tab.

2 In the **Category** list, click **Custom**. Scroll to the bottom of the **Type** box. Click **"E"###-###**.

3 (i)**CHECK** Your dialog box should look like Figure 3.3. Click **OK**.

4 Deselect the range. Click cell **A26**. Key: 241067. Press ENTER.

5 Click cell **E1**. Click the **Number Format** drop-down arrow (see Figure 3.4). Select **Short Date**. Key: June 8, 2009.

6 Select **D5:E26**. Click the **Number Format** drop-down arrow. Select **Currency** from the list.

7 Click cell **D28**. Click **Increase Decimal** twice.

8 Select **D28:E28**. Click the **Number Format** drop-down arrow. Select **Currency**.

9 (i)**CHECK** Your screen should look like Figure 3.4. Save your file.

Continue to the next exercise.

EXERCISE 3-2
Apply a Custom Number Format

Once you create a custom format, you can apply it to any cell in the current workbook. You can find your custom format listed in the Format Cells dialog box. Custom formats are saved within the workbook so you can utilize, or use, them repeatedly.

FIGURE 3.3 Format Cells dialog box

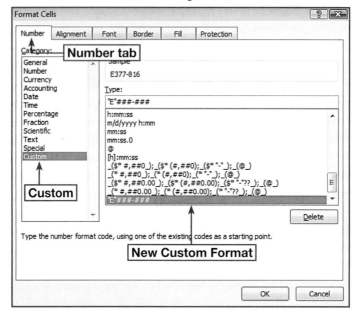

FIGURE 3.4 Number formatted using custom and currency formats

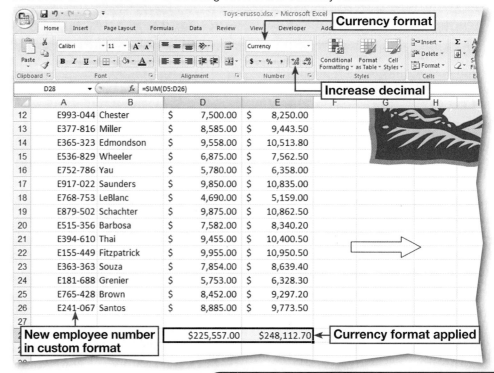

Before You Read

Understanding It is normal to have questions when you read. Write down questions while reading—many of them will be answered as you continue. If they are not, you will have a list ready for your teacher when you finish.

Read To Learn

- Sort and filter columns to target the data you need.
- Create worksheets to calculate loan options.
- Customize how data is calculated using relative and absolute references.
- Make numerical data easier to understand by using charts and diagrams.

Main Idea

Excel is an excellent tool for analyzing, developing, and displaying data.

Vocabulary

Key Terms

absolute reference	filter	operator
chart	function	PMT
condition	IF	range
COUNT	mixed reference	relative reference
COUNTA	NOW	sort

Academic Vocabulary

These words appear in your reading and on your tests. Make sure you know their meanings.

adjust
version

Quick Write Activity

Describe When reading a report, seeing pages of words or figures can hinder the learning process. On a separate sheet of paper, describe why a full page of data and text may be difficult for viewers to understand. Explain how you think a chart or diagram can display information more clearly.

Study Skills

Study with a Friend When you explain something to another person, you are likely to remember that conversation at a later date. If you study with a friend, you are more likely to remember that discussion at test time. Verbalizing a concept lets you know if you really understand it. Discuss and compare a lesson's main ideas with a partner.

Academic Standards

Math

NCTM (Data Analysis and Probability) Select and use appropriate statistical methods to analyze data.

NCTM (Number and Operations) Understand meanings of operations and how they relate to one another.

NCTM (Algebra) Understand patterns, relations, and functions.

NCTM (Algebra) Represent and analyze mathematical situations and structures using algebraic symbols.

NCTM (Algebra) Use mathematical models to represent and understand quantitative relationships.

NCTM (Algebra) Analyze change in various contexts.

Step-By-Step

1 Start **Excel**.

2 Open the data file **Toys.xlsx**. Save as: Toys-[your first initial and last name]. (For example, *Toys-erusso*.)

3 Click cell **A5**. Choose **Home>Number Dialog Box Launcher** [icon].

4 In the **Format Cells** dialog box, select the **Number** tab. In the **Category** list, click **Custom**.

5 Double-click in the **Type** box to select the text. Key: "E"###-###.

6 *i***CHECK** Your dialog box should look like Figure 3.1. Click **OK**.

7 *i***CHECK** Your screen should look like Figure 3.2.

8 Save your file.

↪ *Continue to the next exercise.*

EXERCISE 3-1
Create a Custom Number Format

Using the Format Cells dialog box, you can format data in a variety of number formats, including Accounting, Currency, and Scientific. However, you might need a number format that is not listed in the Format Cells dialog box. For example, you might want all student ID numbers to end with the letter Z. You can create a **custom number format** so that the Z appears automatically.

FIGURE 3.1 Format Cells dialog box

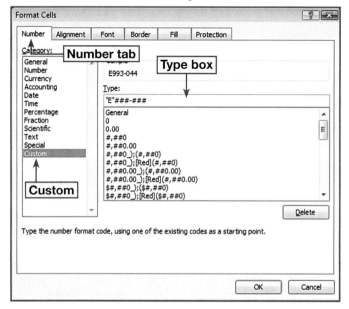

FIGURE 3.2 Number formatted using custom format

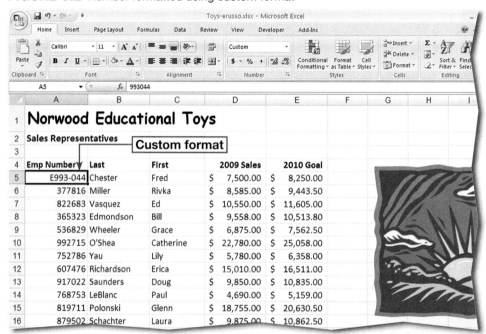

Step-By-Step

1 Start Excel. Open the data file **February Sales.xlsx**. Save as: February Sales-[your first initial and last name] (for example, *February Sales-jking*). Ask your teacher where to save your file.

2 Click cell **A2**. Choose **Data>Sort & Filter> Filter**. Click the drop-down arrow at the top of column A (see Figure 4.1).

3 Click **(Select All)** to remove the check marks next to every name. Then choose **Carmen Estrella**. Click **OK**. Only the products that Carmen sold are shown.

4 Click the column A drop-down arrow again and choose **(Select All)**. Click **OK**. The screen displays all of the employees.

5 Click the column B drop-down arrow. Choose **(Select All)**. Select **Thunderhead Parka**. Click **OK**.

6 *i*CHECK Your screen should look like Figure 4.2.

7 Choose **Data>Sort & Filter>Filter** to turn off the AutoFilter. Save your file.

➥ *Continue to the next exercise.*

EXERCISE 4-1
Use AutoFilter

Some worksheets contain so much information that it is difficult to understand the data. You can **filter** the worksheet, or show only the parts that you need. To use the AutoFilter command, you must first click on a cell in the **range**, or group of cells, that you wish to filter.

FIGURE 4.1 AutoFilter arrows

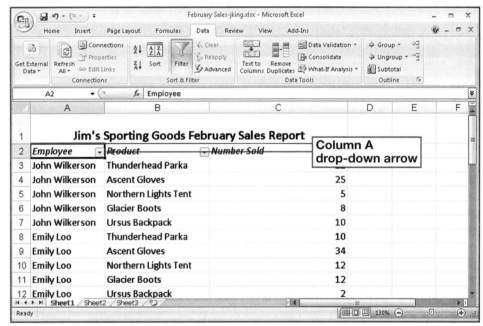

FIGURE 4.2 Thunderhead parkas sold

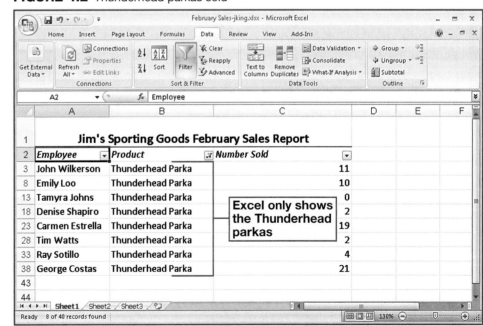

Before You Read

Think of an Example To make learning easier, think of an example of how or when you could use formatting to improve the presentation of complicated data. Thinking of examples of how you can apply skills demonstrates their importance and can help motivate your learning.

Read To Learn

- Evaluate how creating and saving a custom format can meet business needs.
- Consider how to use conditional formatting to make specific data stand out in a worksheet.
- Explore how to arrange and format graphics and charts to express information in your worksheet.
- Apply design concepts to enhance workbooks.

Main Idea

In Excel, you can create custom and conditional formats. You can also use graphics, charts, and themes to give your worksheet a polished look.

Vocabulary

Key Terms

brightness	data bar
color scale	icon set
conditional formatting	legend
Conditional Formatting Rules Manager	rotate
	scale
contrast	sizing handle
custom number format	

Academic Vocabulary

These words appear in your reading and on your tests. Make sure you know their meanings.

conflict
trend
utilize

Quick Write Activity

Describe On a separate sheet of paper, describe interesting graphics and well-designed charts that you have seen in advertisements. What drew you to the advertisement? Did the graphics stand out? How do the graphics support the message of the advertisement? Did the colors in the advertisement work together? Why or why not? Include any other details you can remember.

Study Skills

Look It Up If you hear or read a word that you do not know, look it up in the dictionary or on your computer. Before long, this practice will become a habit. You will be amazed at how many new words you learn.

Academic Standards

English Language Arts
   NCTE 3 Apply strategies to interpret texts.

Math
   NCTM (Number and Operations) Understand meanings and operations and how they relate to one another.
   NCTM (Representation) Create and use representations to organize, record, and communicate mathematical ideas.

Sort Data

1. In your **February Sales** file, click any cell in column **A**.

2. Choose **Data>Sort & Filter>Sort A to Z** ⬇.

3. **ⓘCHECK** Your screen should look like Figure 4.3.

4. Click cell **C2**.

5. In the **Sort & Filter** group, click **Sort Z to A** ⬆.

6. **ⓘCHECK** Your screen should look like Figure 4.4.

7. Save and close your file.

➡ *Continue to the next exercise.*

You Should Know

You do not have to select the cell at the top of a column to use **Sort**. You can click any cell in that column to sort.

Excel can automatically **sort**, or organize, information for you. The Sort A to Z button alphabetizes names from A to Z or lists numbers in increasing order. You can choose Sort Z to A to sort from Z to A or in decreasing numerical order. You can also sort by more than one criteria, such as A to Z and in decreasing numerical order.

FIGURE 4.3 Using Sort to alphabetize

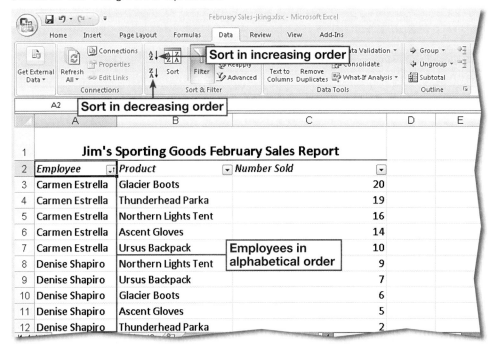

FIGURE 4.4 Using Sort on lists of numbers

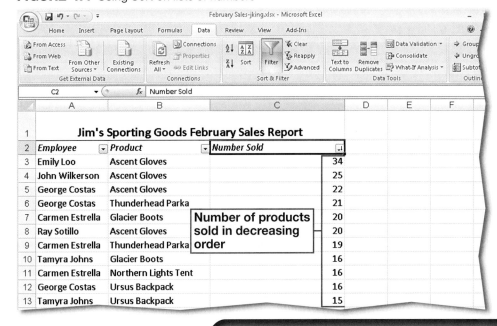

Data in Excel worksheets can have a stronger visual impact if you apply advanced formatting techniques. In this lesson, you will learn sophisticated ways to format data. You will create custom formats and use conditional formatting so that if data has a specified value, it appears a certain way. You will also learn to change the contrast of the pictures in your worksheets, as well as how to scale and rotate graphics. Charts are very important because they make complicated data easier to understand. In this lesson, you will learn to format the axes, the legend, and other parts of a chart.

Key Concepts

● Create custom formats

● Use conditional formatting

● Change the brightness and contrast of a picture

● Resize and rotate a graphic

● Format parts of a chart

Standards

The following standards are covered in this lesson. Refer to pages xix and 314 for a description of the standards listed here.

ISTE Standards Correlation

NETS•S

1a, 1b, 1c, 3d, 4c, 6a, 6b

Microsoft Office Specialist Correlation

2.1, 2.3, 4.1, 4.2, 4.3, 4.4

21st CENTURY SKILLS

Choose the Right Tool When you are faced with a task, often the first step towards completion is to determine which tool is the best for the job. Choosing the right tool initially will save you time and keep you on track. When you are using Excel to show others how data has changed, you may have to choose between formatting content and using graphics to get your message across. *Can you think of a task in your schoolwork for which Excel would be the best tool?*

Step-By-Step

1. Open the data file **Bonus. xlsx**. Save as: Bonus-[your first initial and last name].

2. Click cell **C3**.

3. Key: =B3*.02.

4. ⓘ**CHECK** Your screen should look like Figure 4.5.

5. Press ENTER. The results of the calculation appear in cell C2.

6. Press ↑.

7. ⓘ**CHECK** Your screen should look like Figure 4.6.

8. Save your file.

➡ *Continue to the next exercise.*

Academic **Skills**

Try to analyze how Excel formulas work. Then you can practice writing your own formulas in Excel. Test the formulas to make sure they work.

EXERCISE 4-3
Key a Basic Formula

In Excel, a formula is an equation that performs a calculation, such as a sum or an average. You can tell Excel which numbers to use and what mathematical operation to perform by creating a formula. Every formula begins with an equal sign (=) and includes values or cell references. Depending on the type of calculation you wish to perform, you will need to use an **operator**, or a symbol for mathematical operations, such as * for multiplication, + for addition, − for subtraction, and / for division. In this exercise, you will calculate the two-percent bonus of an employee.

FIGURE 4.5 Entering a formula

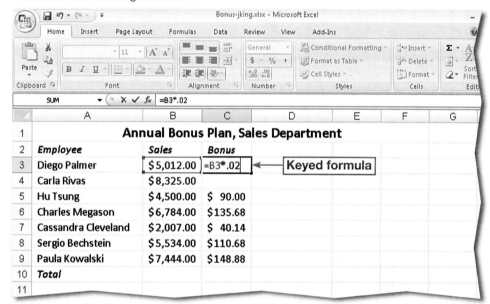

FIGURE 4.6 Formula results

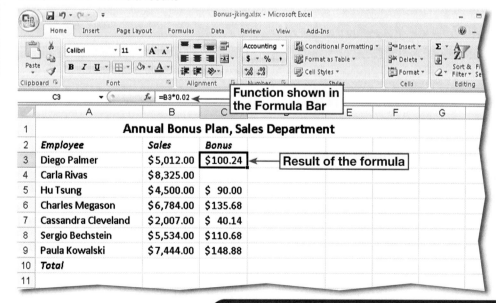

LESSON 2 — Challenge Yourself Projects

Before You Begin

Analyze Data Gathering and organizing data is just the start of creating a useful spreadsheet. You also need to learn how to analyze the data you have gathered. These projects teach you how to quickly and efficiently analyze data.

Reflect Once you complete the projects, open a Word document and answer the following questions:

1. In what ways do you think displaying a formula can help you better coordinate and quickly manage data?

2. How might a business use What-If scenarios in its daily activities?

9. Monitor Price Changes

Rubric R

Math: Display and Print Formulas The school bookstore is considering raising prices and wants to analyze possible changes. To make analyzing the price change easier, you want to see all the worksheet's formulas at once. Display and print the formulas for **Sheet 1** of your **Bookstore-8** file.

Save your file as: Bookstore-[your first initial and last name]9.xlsx.

10. Analyze Scenarios

Rubric R

Math: Use What-If Analysis Now that you know the prices are going to increase next year, you want to buy some items from the school bookstore before the prices go up. You are thinking of buying a school sweatshirt and two T-shirts. Create What-If scenarios to help you analyze your options and make a decision.

- Open your **Bookstore-9** file. Click **Sheet2** tab.
- Add a scenario called **shirts**. Change cells **C9** and **C10** so that you buy two T-shirts and one sweatshirt.
- Add another scenario called **supplies only**. Change cells **C9** and **C10** so that you buy no T-shirts or sweatshirts.
- Display each scenario.

Use the results to decide what you will buy. Key your decision into the Excel sheet and briefly explain your decision.

Save your file as: Bookstore-[your first initial and last name]10.

11. Analyze Price Increase

Rubric R

Math: Use SUMIF Your school principal is concerned that the price increase will be too high. She has asked you to complete an analysis that summarizes the impact of the price increase. In particular, you need to find the total of all the 2010 priced items that will cost less than $3.

- Open your **Bookstore-10** file.
- Click the **Sheet1** tab. Hide the formulas if necessary.
- Click **A18**. Create a formula using the **SUMIF** function.
- Format and label your findings.

Open a Word document and key a paragraph describing whether the price increase is too high based on your analysis of the Excel data.

Save as: Bookstore-[your first initial and last name]11.xlsx.

1 In your **Bonus** file, click cell **C4**.

2 Key: =B3*.05.

3 Press ENTER. This formula calculates the bonus amount for row 3.

4 **(i)CHECK** Your screen should look like Figure 4.7. Notice the exclamation point in the yellow diamond next to cell C4. This symbol is an error message.

5 In the **Formula Bar**, change **B3** to **B4** and change **.05** to **.02**.

6 Press ENTER.

7 **(i)CHECK** Your screen should look like Figure 4.8.

8 Save your file.

➡ *Continue to the next exercise.*

Microsoft Office 2007

The total number of characters that you can enter into one cell in Excel 2007 is 32,767.

EXERCISE 4-4
Edit Formulas

If a formula has been keyed incorrectly, you can edit the formula in the formula bar. You can also edit a formula by double-clicking the cell that contains the formula. When you edit a formula, make sure that it contains the correct numbers and cell references.

FIGURE 4.7 Inconsistent formula identified in worksheet

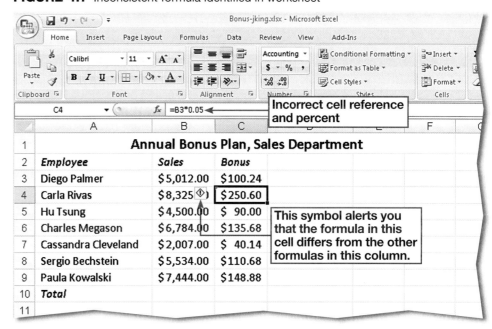

FIGURE 4.8 Edited formula

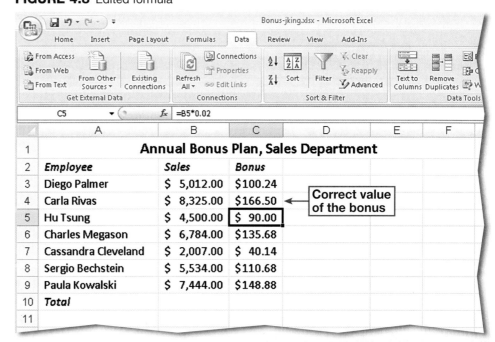

6. Beyond the Classroom Activity

 Math: Create a PivotTable with a PivotChart You want to create a visual to show the members of the soccer team the amount of money that they raised over the year. You decide to create a PivotChart so that the team can see how much they have raised. Open your **Tournament-5** file. In the file:

- Create a PivotTable. Generate a PivotChart from the data in the table.
- Choose a field to represent each student's contribution in the report. For example, **Last name** or **Student ID**.
- Choose a chart type to display the data and label each axis.
- Delete the Legend box and title your chart Fundraising for Regional Tournament Fall 2009. (Scale and resize your chart, as necessary.)

Save your file as: Tournament-[your first initial and last name]6.xlsx.

7. Standards at Work Activity

 Microsoft Certified Application Specialist Correlation
Excel 3.7 *Format or modify text using formulas*

Modify Text Using a Formula Modifying text with a formula is a great way to clarify information that may be difficult to read at first glance. You decide that you want the last names in your worksheet to stand out from the first names and student IDs. Open your **Tournament-6** file. Use a formula to format the names in the **Last** column in **uppercase**.

Save your file as: Tournament-[your first initial and last name]7.xlsx.

8. 21st Century Skills Activity

Use Decision-Making Tools Excel's What-If Analysis tool is helpful for evaluating options to make the most informed decision. You work at the school bookstore. You need to decide how much you want to increase the price of the sweatshirts you will sell next year. Open the **Bookstore. xlsx** data file. On **Sheet 1**, create two new What-If scenarios by changing cell **C14**. One scenario should show what next year's prices will be if the price increases by 4 percent. The second scenario should show what next year's prices will be if the price is increased by 8 percent.

Display each scenario. Use the results to decide how much you will increase the price of sweatshirts. Key your decision into the Excel sheet and briefly explain your decision.

Save your file as: Bookstore-[your first initial and last name]8.xlsx.

Go Online **e-REVIEW**
glencoe.com

Go to the **Online Learning Center** to complete the following review activities.

Online Self Checks
To test your knowledge of the material, click **Unit 2> Lesson 2** and choose **Self Checks**.

Interactive Review
To review the main points of the lesson, click **Unit 2> Lesson 2** and choose **Interactive Review**.

1 In your **Bonus** file, click cell **B10**.

2 On the formula bar, click **Insert Function** f_x.

3 In the **Insert Function** dialog box, under **Select a function**, click **SUM** (see Figure 4.9).

4 Click **OK**. The **Function Arguments** dialog box opens.

5 In the dialog box, check the line labeled **Number1** to make sure it reads **B3:B9**.

6 Click **OK**.

7 **ⓘCHECK** Your screen should look like Figure 4.10.

8 Save your file.

➡ *Continue to the next exercise.*

Academic Skills

In this exercise, you use the **SUM** function to tell Excel to add the numbers in column B. Math problems use an addition sign (+) to indicate when numbers should be added together.

EXERCISE 4-5
Use Functions to Create Formulas

In addition to keying in formulas, you can create a formula by choosing a **function**, or preset formula, from a list. All you have to do is choose the function you want to use and fill in the correct numbers or cell references.

FIGURE 4.9 Insert Function dialog box

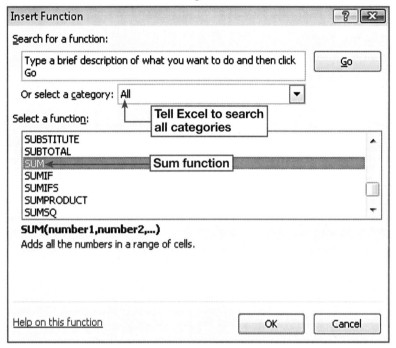

FIGURE 4.10 Numbers added using the SUM function

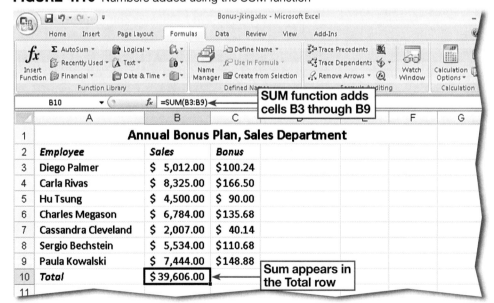

5. Use AVERAGEIF and COUNTIF in a Formula

Step-By-Step

Over the last year, the soccer team has raised money for a regional tournament. You charted the amount of money raised over the year. Now you want to recognize players' fundraising achievements at the next team meeting. First, you must find the average amount per player raised over $200. Then, you must find the number of times the amount raised per player exceeded $400.

1. Open the data file **Tournament.xlsx**. Save as: Tournament-[your first initial and last name]5.

2. Click cell **D4**. Key: =AVERAGEIF(D8:D27, ">200"). Press ENTER.

3. **CHECK** Your screen should look like Figure 2.40.

4. Click cell **D4**. Choose **Home>Number** and click the **Number Format** drop-down arrow. Select **Currency**.

5. Click cell **E4**. Key: =COUNTIF(D8:D27,">400"). Press ENTER.

6. Click cell **D3**. Key: Average Raised.

7. Click cell **E3**. Key: Over $400.

8. **CHECK** Your screen should look like Figure 2.41.

9. Save and close your file.

FIGURE 2.40 Average contribution raised over $200

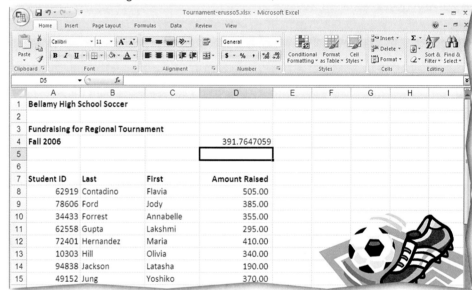

FIGURE 2.41 Count of contributions raised that exceed $400

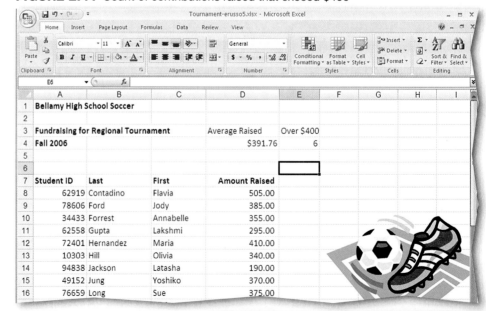

1. In your **Bonus** file, click cell **B10**.

2. Choose **Home> Clipboard>Copy** (see Figure 4.11).

3. Click cell **C10**.

4. Choose **Home> Clipboard>Paste**.

5. ⓘCHECK Your screen should look like Figure 4.12.

6. Save and close your file.

➡ *Continue to the next exercise.*

Tech Tip

To keep the original row number or column letter when you move or copy a formula, use a dollar sign ($) in the cell address, a technique known as **absolute addressing**. For example, if you use $D$3 in a formula, the cell address *will not* change when the formula is copied.

EXERCISE 4-6
Copy and Move Formulas

If you want to put the same kind of formula in one cell that you have already created in another cell, you can use the Copy and Paste commands. Instead of creating another formula, you can copy the first formula into the second cell. Excel will automatically adjust, or modify, the cell references accordingly in the new formula so it calculates correctly.

FIGURE 4.11 Formula in cell B10 copied

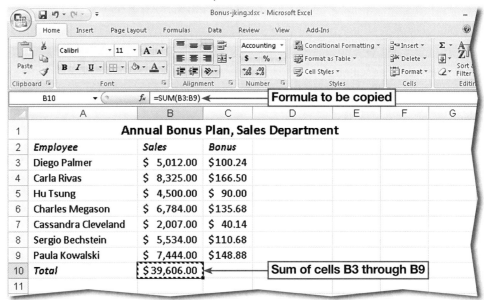

FIGURE 4.12 Formula copied and pasted into cell C10

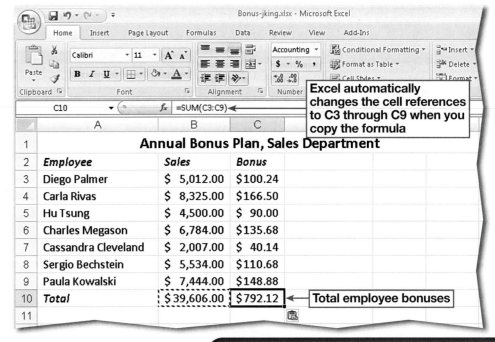

4. Perform a What-If Analysis

You have helped Elena correct the errors in her monthly budget to make it simpler and more efficient. Due to fluctuating gas prices, Elena has now asked you to use a What-If Analysis to compare the results of scenarios in which she plans to spend $40 on fuel for her car and $15 on fuel for her scooter.

Step-By-Step

1. Open your **Budget2-Scenario-3** file. Save as: Budget2-Scenario[your first initial and last name]4.

2. Click cell **B14**. Choose **Data>Data Tools>What-If Analysis** and select **Scenario Manager**.

3. Add a scenario called: gas low. Click **OK**.

4. In the **Scenario Values** box, key: 15. Click **OK**.

5. In the **Scenarios** list, click **gas low**. Click **Show**.

6. (i**CHECK**) Your screen should look like Figure 2.38.

7. In the **Scenarios** list, click **gas high**. Click **Show**.

8. (i**CHECK**) Your screen should look like Figure 2.39.

9. Close the **Scenario Manager**.

10. Save and close your file.

FIGURE 2.38 The scooter scenario

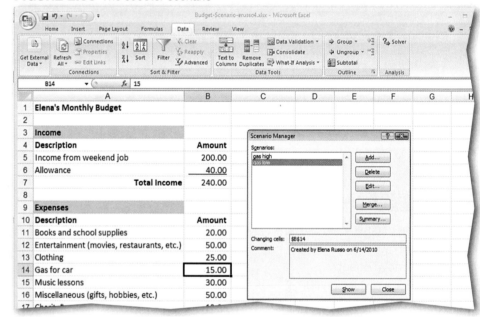

FIGURE 2.39 The car scenario

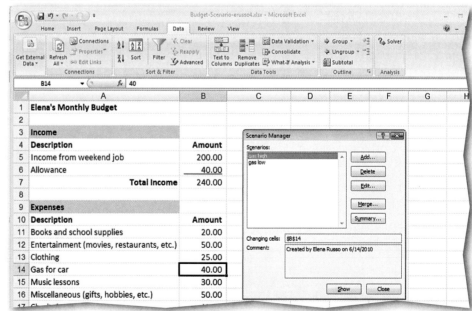

Step-By-Step

1. Open the data file **Books.xlsx**. Save as: Books-[your first initial and last name].

2. Click cell **C13**.

3. Key: =SUM(. Make sure you do not forget the left parenthesis.

4. In the pop-up box that appears, click **number1**.

5. Click cell **C3**. Hold the mouse button down and drag the pointer down to cell **C11**. Release the mouse button.

6. ⓘCHECK Your screen should look like Figure 4.13.

7. Press ENTER.

8. ⓘCHECK Your screen should look like Figure 4.14.

9. Save your file.

➡ *Continue to the next exercise.*

Shortcuts

Entering a range in a formula by dragging can be more accurate than keying in a range because you see exactly which range you are selecting.

EXERCISE 4-7
Enter a Range by Dragging

When you are keying a formula, you do not have to key the range for the formula. Instead, you can enter a range by dragging the pointer over the range you wish to enter.

FIGURE 4.13 Range entered in formula by dragging

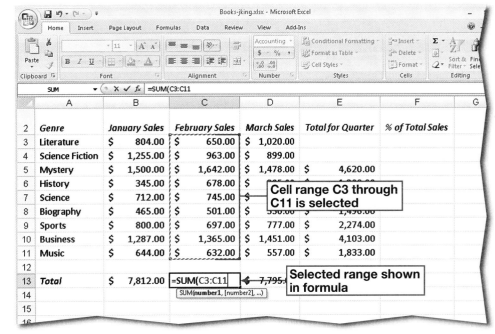

FIGURE 4.14 Total calculated using new formula

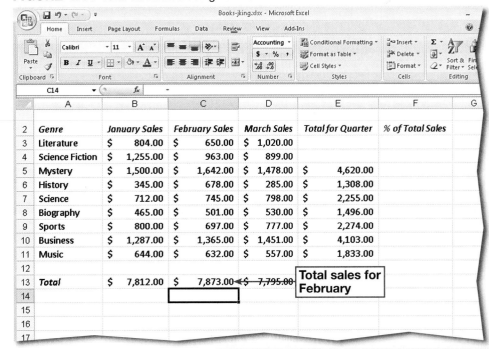

3. Create Scenarios

Follow the steps to complete the activity. You must complete Practice It Activity 2 before doing this activity.

Step-By-Step

1 Open your **Budget2-Names-2** file. Save as: Budget2-Scenario-[your first initial and last name]3.

2 Click cell **B14**. Choose **Data>Data Tools>What-If Analysis** 📝. Click **Scenario Manager**.

3 Click **Add**.

4 In the **Scenario Name** box, key: gas high.

5 *i*CHECK Your dialog box should look like Figure 2.36.

6 Click **OK**. The **Scenario Values** dialog box opens.

7 Key: $40. Click **OK**.

8 *i*CHECK Your dialog box should look like Figure 2.37.

9 Close the **Scenario Manager** dialog box.

10 Save and close your file.

FIGURE 2.36 Add Scenario dialog box

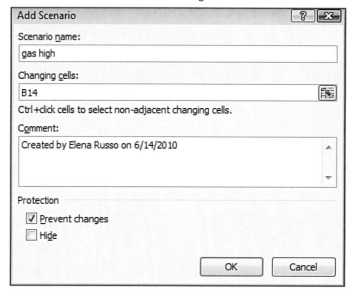

FIGURE 2.37 Scenario Manager dialog box

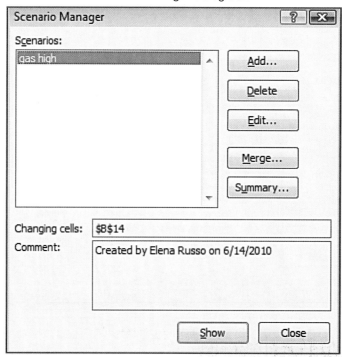

1. In your **Books** file, click cell **E3**.

2. Key: =SUM(B3:D3).

3. **ⓘCHECK** Your screen should look like Figure 4.15.

4. Press **ENTER**. The total quarterly sales for Literature appear in cell **E3**.

5. Click cell **E3**. Choose **Home>Clipboard> Copy** 📋.

6. Click cell **E4**. Choose **Home>Clipboard> Paste** 📋.

7. **ⓘCHECK** Your screen should look like Figure 4.16. Save your file.

➡ *Continue to the next exercise.*

EXERCISE 4-8
Use Relative References

There are two types of cell references for formulas in Excel. The first type, which you have already used, is called a **relative reference**. A relative reference changes when the formula is pasted into a new location. A relative reference is written with the column letter and row number, such as B2.

FIGURE 4.15 Keying a relative reference

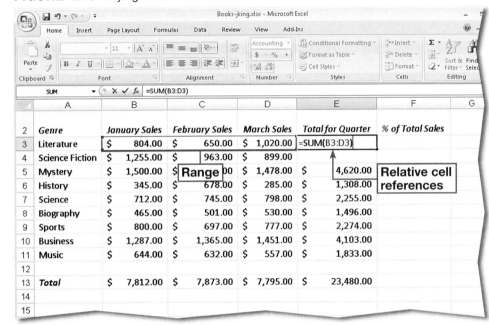

FIGURE 4.16 Pasting a relative reference

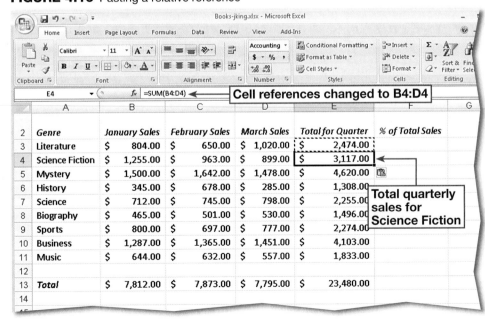

Academic Skills

The word *relative* refers to an object that is dependent on something else. In Step 6, when you copy the formula from cell E3 into cell E4, the formula changes to include the numbers in row 4. The total then changes. This shows how the formula is *relative* to the data in row 4. What would happen if you copied the formula from cell E4 to cell E5?

2. Use a Name and SUMIIF in a Formula

Follow the steps to complete the activity.

Step-By-Step

1. Open the **Budget2.xlsx** data file. Save as: Budget2-Names-[your first initial and last name]2.

2. Click cell **B20**. Key: =Income-Total. Press ENTER. Click cell **B20**.

3. **(i) CHECK** Your screen should look like Figure 2.34.

4. Click cell **B18**. Key: =SUM(Expenses). Press ENTER. Click cell **B18**.

5. Click cell **C18**. Key: Expenses <50. Bold the text you keyed into cell **C18**.

6. Click cell **D18**. Key: =SUMIF(Expenses, "<50.00"). Press ENTER.

7. Click cell **D18**. Click **Increase Decimal** to format the formula results in **D18**.

8. **(i) CHECK** Your screen should look similar to Figure 2.35.

9. Save and close your file.

FIGURE 2.34 Using names in a formula

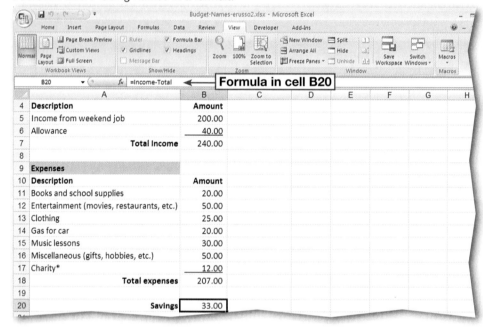
Formula in cell B20

FIGURE 2.35 Formula using names

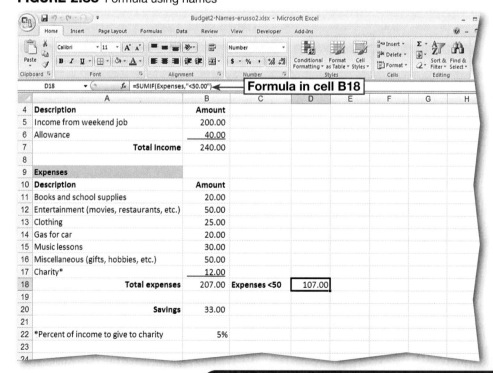
Formula in cell B18

EXERCISE 4-9
Use Absolute References

1 In your **Books** file, click cell **F3**.

2 Key: =E3/$E$13. Press ENTER.

3 ⓘCHECK Your screen should look like Figure 4.17.

4 Click cell **F3**.

5 Click **Copy** 📋.

6 Select cells **F4:F11**.

7 Click **Paste** 📋.

8 ⓘCHECK Your screen should look like Figure 4.18.

9 Save your file.

➡ *Continue to the next exercise.*

Academic Skills

The equation=E3/$E$13 means that the contents of cell E3 should be divided by the total in cell E13 to determine the percentage of Literature sales for the quarter. What would the equation be in order to determine the percentage of Sports sales?

An **absolute reference** is a locked cell that maintains a constant reference when copied to another location. Unlike a relative reference, an absolute reference does not change when you copy the formula to a new location. Use an absolute reference when more than one formula should refer to the same cell. For example, the formulas to calculate the percent of total sales for Literature and Science Fiction will both include the sales total $23,480 in cell E13. To write an absolute reference, place a dollar sign ($) in front of both the column letter and the row number. In this exercise, you will use the absolute reference $E$13.

FIGURE 4.17 Literature sales percentage

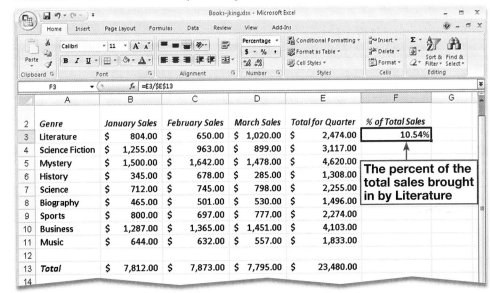

FIGURE 4.18 Absolute reference

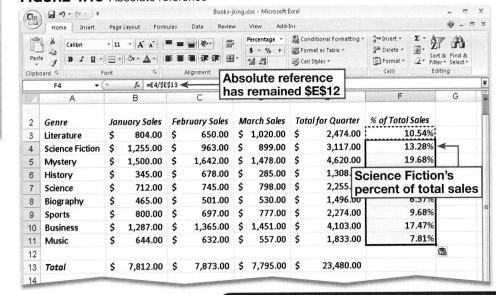

1. Create a PivotTable and a PivotChart

Follow the steps to complete the activity.

Step-By-Step

1. Open the **Jobs2.xlsx** data file. Save as: Jobs2-PivotChart-[your first initial and last name]1.

2. Click any cell in the list. Choose **Insert>Tables> PivotTable**. Click **OK**.

3. In the **PivotTable Field List**, drag **Customer** to the **Row Labels** box.

4. In the **PivotTable Field List**, drag **Job** to the **Drop Column Labels** box. Drag **Amount** to the **Values** box.

5. Choose **Options>Tools> PivotChart** and click **Stacked Column**. Click **OK**.

6. **CHECK** Your screen should look like Figure 2.32.

7. Close the **PivotTable Field List**. Close the **PivotChart Filter Pane**.

8. Click the **Layout** tab under the **PivotChart Tools** to label each axis.

9. **CHECK** Your screen should look like Figure 2.33. Save and close your file.

FIGURE 2.32 Unfinished PivotTable

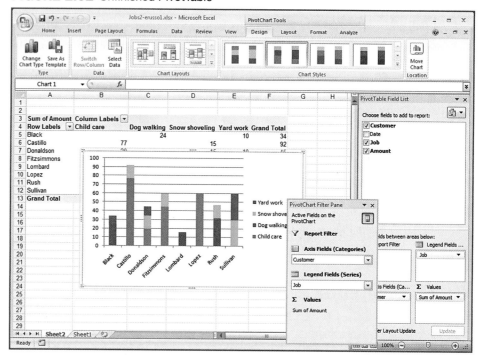

FIGURE 2.33 Finished PivotTable

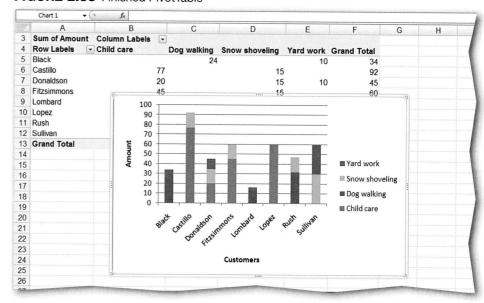

1. In your **Books** file, click cell **F3**. This displays the formula that you keyed into the worksheet in the last exercise. Double-click cell **F3** and change the formula to read =**E3/$E13**.

2. Click outside cell **F3**. Notice that the percentage for Literature sales did not change.

3. Click cell **F3**. Click **Copy**.

4. Select cells **F4:F11**. Click **Paste**.

5. (i)**CHECK** Your screen should look like Figure 4.19.

6. Click cell **F4**. The mixed cell reference **$E13** causes the formula to automatically increment to **$E14** when it is copied to the range **F4:F11**. The formula now contains a reference to a blank cell, or zero, which cannot be a divisor.

7. Click **Undo** twice. Repeat Steps 3 and 4.

8. (i)**CHECK** Your screen should look like Figure 4.20. Save and close your file.

→ *Continue to the next exercise.*

EXERCISE 4-10
Use Mixed References

A **mixed reference** is a cell reference that is part relative and part absolute. This means it has either an absolute column and a relative row, or a relative column and an absolute row. For example, if you place a dollar sign in front of the reference to column A ($A1), when you drag the formula to the right the column reference will not change, because the column reference is absolute. However, if you drag the formula down, the row reference will automatically adjust incrementally, because it is relative. If you copy a formula across rows or down columns, a relative reference automatically adjusts, and an absolute reference does not change.

FIGURE 4.19 #DIV/0! errors in column F

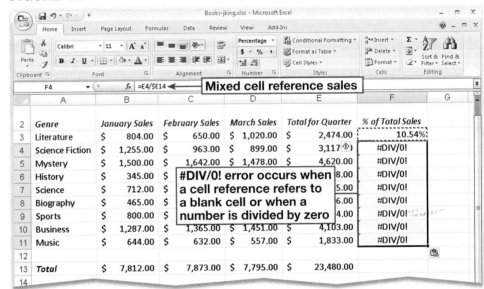

FIGURE 4.20 Literature percent formula

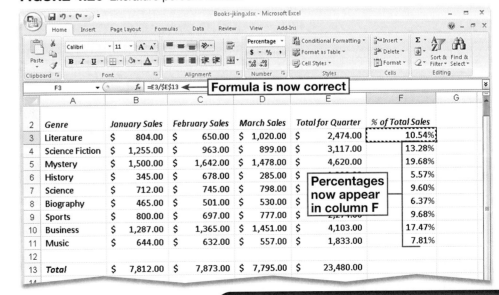

Vocabulary

Key Terms
argument

conditional logic

constraint

criteria

database function

LOWER

PivotChart

PivotTable

PROPER

scenario

SUBSTITUTE

UPPER

What-If Analysis

Academic Vocabulary
generate

locate

Review Vocabulary

Complete the following statements on a separate piece of paper. Choose from the Vocabulary list on the left to complete the statements.

1. The _____ function will change the case of text in a cell or range of cells to capital letters. (p. 180)

2. When you use the Solver, you can set a(n) _____, or limit. (p. 185)

3. To test whether conditions are true or false and make logical comparisons between outcomes, use _____. (p. 190)

4. To test out a possible situation, use the _____ tool. (p. 182)

5. A(n) _____ is a formula that acts only on cells that meet certain criteria. (p. 180)

Vocabulary Activity

6. Make flash cards based on the vocabulary from this lesson.
   A. On the front of the card, write the vocabulary word.
   B. Look at each vocabulary word. On the back of the card, write the definition.
   C. Team up with a classmate and take turns using the flash cards to quiz each other.

Review Key Concepts

Answer the following questions on a separate piece of paper.

7. Which of the following displays and hides the formulas on a worksheet? (p. 191)
   A. CTRL + '
   B. CTRL + `
   C. ALT + ~
   D. ALT + `

8. What is the second argument of the LOOKUP function? (p. 192)
   A. the LOOKUP table
   B. the value in the worksheet you are looking for
   C. the row or column in the LOOKUP table that contains the value
   D. the database

9. How do you perform a What-If Analysis? (p. 182)
   A. create a PivotChart
   B. group and outline data
   C. trace errors
   D. compare scenarios

10. What does the SUMIFS function do? (p. 187)
   A. returns the average of cells in a range that meet criteria
   B. adds all numbers in a range of cells, based on a given criteria
   C. adds values in a range based on multiple conditions
   D. averages cells that meet multiple criteria

Step-By-Step

1. Open the data file **Shoes. xlsx**. Save as: Shoes-[your first initial and last name].

2. Select cells **A3** through **C15**.

3. Choose **Insert>Charts> Column**.

4. In the drop-down menu, under **2-D Column**, select **Clustered Column** (see Figure 4.21).

5. **ⓘCHECK** Your screen should look like Figure 4.22.

6. Save your file.

Continue to the next exercise.

Academic Skills

In this exercise, you created a chart to compare the number of boots and sandals sold within a specific month. Based on this chart, identify which type of shoe sold the most in December. Which shoe sold the most in July? How does the chart help you to identify this information quickly?

EXERCISE 4-11
Create Diagrams and Charts

A **chart** is a graphic that organizes data visually so that you can compare different kinds of data or evaluate how data changes over time. In order to understand the data in a worksheet quickly, you can create bar charts, column charts, line charts, and pie charts. The Charts group allows you to create charts automatically based on the data that you select.

FIGURE 4.21 Column drop-down menu

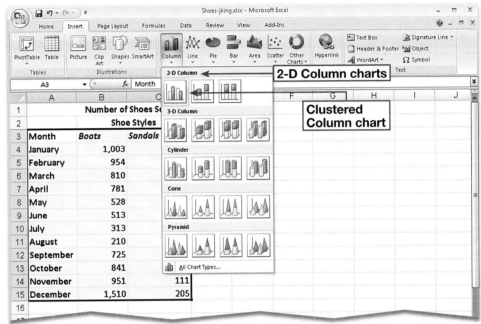

FIGURE 4.22 Completed chart

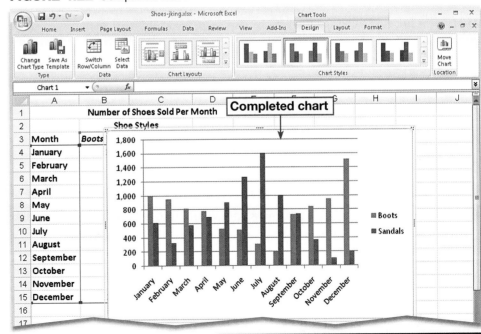

Writing MATTERS

Writing an Itinerary

Mr. Clark's history class is going on a trip to Washington, D.C. What do his students need before they leave? They need an itinerary!

What Is an Itinerary?

An itinerary is a detailed schedule for a trip. It gives information about arrangements for transportation, hotels, meetings, and meals. An itinerary helps you keep track of where you are supposed to be and when. It can also be helpful to others who may want to get in touch with you while you are gone.

Creating an Itinerary

The first step is to plan your trip. Once you have planned your trip, double-check all names, addresses, flight numbers, and so on, for accuracy. Be sure to include phone numbers on your itinerary, in case travel plans change.

Here are some guidelines for formatting an itinerary:

- Use a two-column format.
- Center the heading.
- Use side headings if the itinerary covers more than one day.
- Double-space between entries.

ITINERARY
For Mr. Clark's History Class
April 2-4, 2010

Tuesday, April 2

5:00 a.m.	Meet at Marshall Airport. Get your ticket from Mr. Lewis or Ms. Hernandez.
7:00 a.m.	Depart, Flight 555.
9:15 a.m.	Arrive Washington, D.C. Take Metro to McPherson Square stop to check in at the Plaza Hotel (202) 555-1671.
10:45 a.m.-1:30 p.m.	Meet at Smithsonian stop and divide into groups.

This itinerary includes a detailed schedule of times and places for part of the class trip.

SKILLBUILDER

1. **List** What does an itinerary include?

2. **Explain** Why are itineraries useful documents?

3. **Apply** What are some special kinds of itineraries that travelers might use?

4. **Plan** Find an online tourist site with information about Washington, D.C. Use the formatting suggestions above to create the itinerary for the second day of Mr. Clark's class trip. Include events or destinations that really interest you.

EXERCISE 4-12
Modify and Position Chart Elements

1. If necessary, in your **Shoes** file, click the white area of the chart box to display the **Chart Tools**. Choose **Layout>Labels>Axis Titles** (see Figure 4.23).

2. Choose **Primary Horizontal Axis Title> Title Below Axis**. In the **Horizontal (Category) Axis Title** box, key: Month.

3. Choose **Layout>Labels> Axis Titles**. Choose **Primary Vertical Axis Title>Rotated Title**. In the **Vertical Axis (Value) Title** box, key: Monthly Totals. Choose **Layout> Labels>Chart Title> Above Chart**. In the **Chart Title** text box, key: Sales Comparison for Year 2009.

4. Click the white area of the chart once to display the sizing handles. Drag a bottom corner sizing handle to make the chart bigger yet still keep its scale.

5. Choose **Chart Tools> Format**. In the **Size** group, in the first drop-down list, select **3**. In the second drop-down list, choose **5**.

6. **①CHECK** Your screen should look like Figure 4.24. Save your file.

➡ *Continue to the next exercise.*

There are many ways that you can modify charts to make data easier to read. For example, you can change the size of the chart to highlight sales trends, salary increases, or the decrease of a loan balance as payments are made.

FIGURE 4.23 Labels group on Layout tab

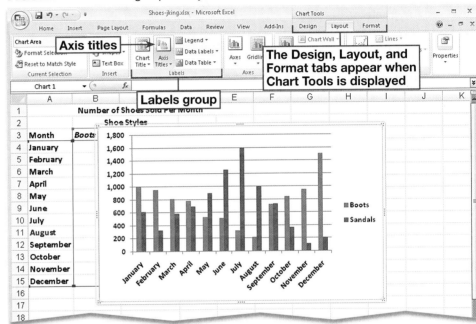

FIGURE 4.24 Sizing and positioning chart

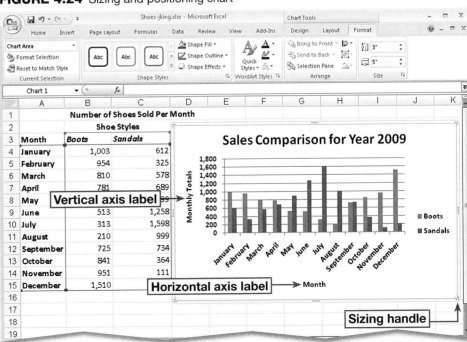

EXERCISE 2-11 (Continued)
Use LOOKUP and Reference Functions

12 Press INSERT. Cell B5 displays **#N/A** because A5 is empty. Click cell **A5**. Key: 99. Cell B5 displays **#N/A** because 99 does not have an exact match in the **lookup_table**.

13 Click cell **A5**. Key: 100.

14 **CHECK** Your screen should look like Figure 2.30.

15 Click cell **A7**. Key: =HLOOKUP("Cost",lookup_table,3,FALSE). Press ENTER.

16 Excel looks up **Cost in row 1** and returns the value from row 3 (13) that is in the same column.

17 Click cell **A7**. Key: =HLOOKUP("Quantity", lookup_table,4,TRUE). Press ENTER.

18 **CHECK** Your screen should look like Figure 2.31.

19 Save and close your file.

You Should Know

Functions that look up values in a list by using an approximate match only work if the values in the first column (column A) or row (row 1) have been sorted in *ascending order*, or from smallest to largest.

FIGURE 2.30 LOOKUP function finds cost per 100 shirts

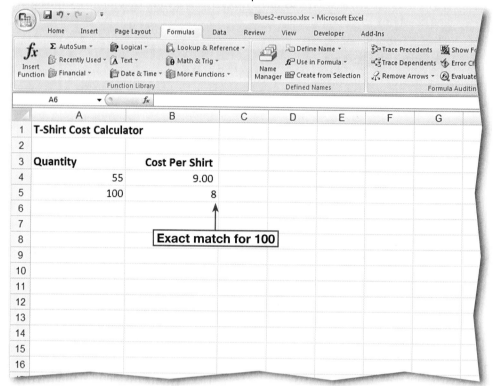

FIGURE 2.31 Using a LOOKUP function

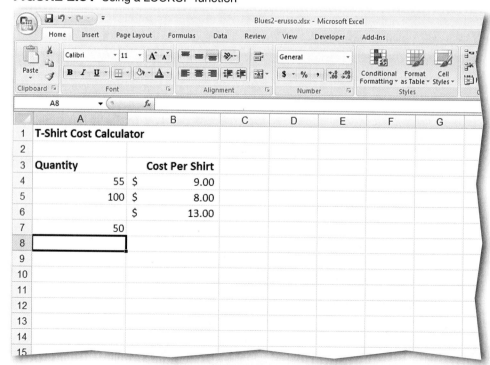

① If necessary, in your **Shoes** file, click in the white area of the chart box to display the **Chart Tools**.

② Choose **Design>Type> Change Chart Type**. The **Change Chart Type** dialog box opens (see Figure 4.25).

③ In the **Change Chart Type** dialog box, under **Line**, choose **Line with Markers**. Click **OK**.

④ Click cell **A3**.

⑤ **ⓘCHECK** Your screen should look like Figure 4.26. Save your file.

➡ *Continue to the next exercise.*

Academic Skills

Consider your data when choosing a chart type. For example, use a *bar chart* to compare items to each other. Use a *pie chart* to show how one item is part of a whole. A *line chart* can help you compare sales over time. In this exercise, how did the amount of boots sold compare with the number of sandals sold during summer? Why do you think that is?

EXERCISE 4-13
Change Chart Type

One way to modify an existing chart is to change the chart type. For example, you can give a clustered column chart a completely different look by changing its chart type to a line, bar, or area chart. Sometimes changing a chart type is the best way to make information easy for viewers to read and understand.

FIGURE 4.25 Change Chart Type dialog box

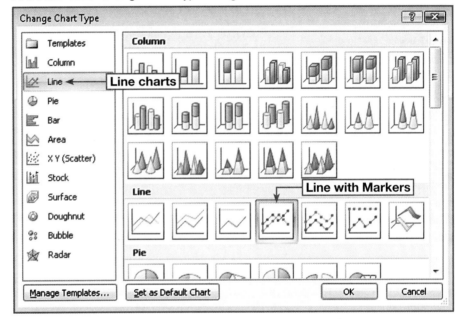

FIGURE 4.26 Chart type changed to Line with Markers

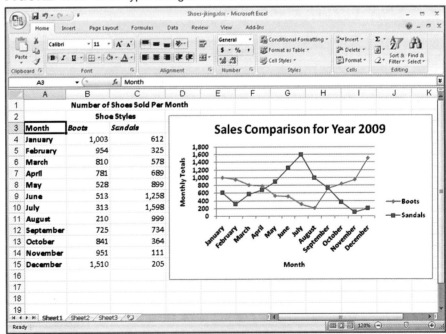

1 In your **Blues2** file, click the **Cost of T-shirts** sheet tab, if necessary.

2 Select **A1:B5**. Choose **Formulas>Defined Names>Define Name**. In the **Names in workbook** box, key: lookup_table. Click **OK**.

3 *CHECK* Your screen should look like Figure 2.28.

4 Click the **T-shirt cost calculator** sheet tab. Click cell **B4**.

5 Key: =VLOOKUP(A4, lookup_table,2,TRUE).

6 Press ENTER. Cell B4 displays **#N/A** because **A4** is empty. Click cell **A4**. Key: 2.

7 Press ENTER. The cost per shirt for two shirts is $15.

8 Click cell **A4**. Key: 55. Press ENTER.

9 *CHECK* Your screen should look like Figure 2.29.

10 If necessary, click the **T-shirt cost calculator** sheet tab.

11 Click cell **B5**. Key: =VLOOKUP(A5, lookup_table,2,FALSE).

Continued on the next page.

EXERCISE 2-11
Use LOOKUP and Reference Functions

LOOKUP functions locate, or find, a value in a table. HLOOKUP looks for a value in the top row. VLOOKUP looks for a value in the left column. When you use LOOKUP functions, you must specify three arguments: the value you are looking for, the LOOKUP table, and the row or column in the LOOKUP table that contains the value. In this exercise, you will use LOOKUP functions to create a price calculator for T-shirts.

FIGURE 2.28 The LOOKUP table

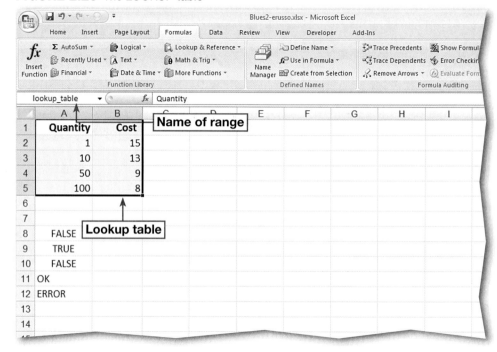

FIGURE 2.29 Using a LOOKUP function

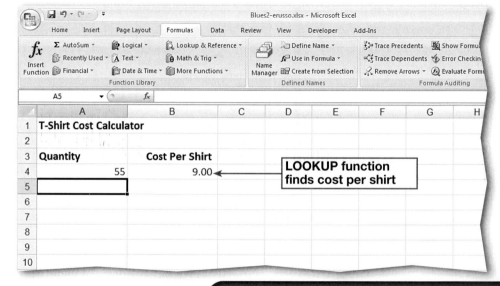

EXERCISE 4-14
Add a Chart to a New Sheet

Sometimes crowding a worksheet with numbers and a chart can be overwhelming. A good strategy is to put the data in one sheet and move the accompanying chart to another sheet in the same workbook. You can move a chart from one sheet to another, or you can add it as an object.

1. If necessary, in your **Shoes** file, click the white area of the chart box to display the **Chart Tools**. Click the **Design** tab.

2. Click the **Move Chart Location** button.

3. In the **Move Chart** dialog box, Choose **New Sheet**.

4. In the text box, key: Shoe Sales (see Figure 4.27).

5. Click **OK**.

6. **CHECK** Your screen should look like Figure 4.28. Notice the chart moves from Sheet1 to a new sheet named **Shoe Sales**.

7. In the **Shoe Sales** sheet, right-click the chart and select **Move Chart**.

8. In the **Move Chart** dialog box, choose **Object In**.

9. Make sure **Sheet1** is selected. Click **OK**. The chart is moved back to Sheet1, and the Shoe Sales sheet is deleted.

10. Save and close your file.

→ *Continue to the next exercise.*

FIGURE 4.27 Move Chart dialog box

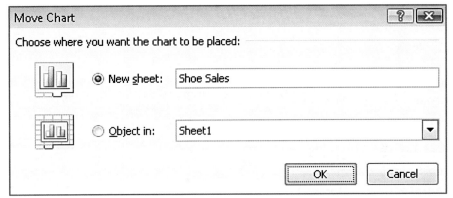

FIGURE 4.28 Chart moved to a new sheet

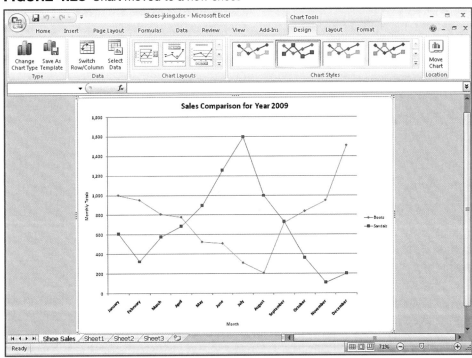

1 In your **Blues2** file, press CTRL + [']. AutoFit column A to show all of the displayed formulas.

2 **CHECK** Your screen should look like Figure 2.26.

3 Choose **Office** >**Print**> **Print**. Ensure that the correct printer name is in the **Name** box. Check that there is a **1** in the **Number of copies** box. Click **OK**.

4 Press CTRL + ['] to hide the formulas. Select **A8:A12**. Choose **Home> Cells>Format** and select **Format Cells**.

5 Click the **Protection** tab. Select **Hidden**. Click **OK**.

6 Click **Format** and select **Protect Sheet**. Select the **Protect worksheet and contents of locked cells** check box. Click **OK**.

7 **CHECK** Your screen should look like Figure 2.27.

8 Click cell **A8**. Click each cell that contains a formula in column **A**. The formulas do not display in the **Formula Bar**. Click **Format**. Click **Unprotect Sheet**. Save your file.

➡ *Continue to the next exercise.*

EXERCISE 2-10
Display and Print Formulas

You may want to view or print all the formulas on a worksheet to check for errors, or you may want to hide formulas for security or privacy. In Excel, you can easily switch between displaying formulas and their values in a worksheet. You can also print the formulas that you have previously created.

FIGURE 2.26 Displayed formulas

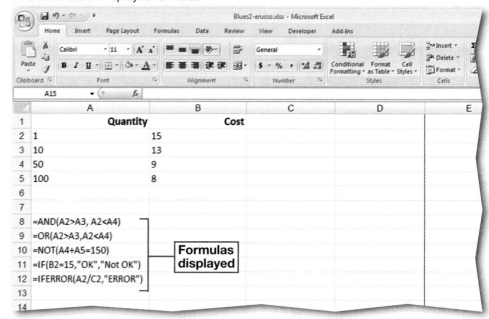

FIGURE 2.27 Hidden formulas

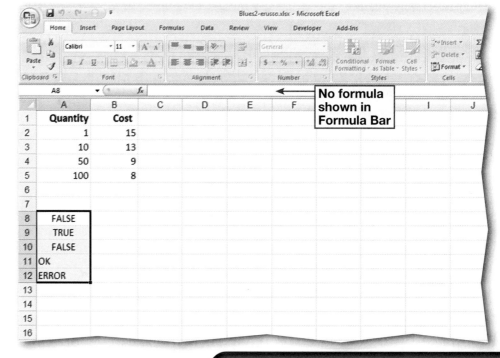

EXERCISE 4-15
Use the COUNT and COUNTA Functions

To find the number of cells in a range that contain numerals, use the **COUNT** function. For example, you can use this function to find the number of expenses, as opposed to the total amount of those expenses. In some places in Excel, such as in the Sum drop-down list, the COUNT function is called Count Numbers. To find the number of cells in a range that contain any kind of data (both numbers and text), use the **COUNTA** function.

1 Open the data file **Expenses.xlsx**. Save as: Expenses-[your first initial and last name].

2 Click cell **C29**. Choose **Home>Editing**. Click the **Sum Σ** drop-down arrow. Click **Count Numbers** (see Figure 4.29).

3 Select cells **C3** through **C27**. Press ENTER. The number of expenses (13) appears in cell **C29**. Because this cell is formatted for dollar values, the number displays as a dollar value.

4 Click cell **C24**. Key: 33.36. Press ENTER. The number of expenses increases to 14.

5 ⓘCHECK Your screen should look like Figure 4.30.

➡ *Continued on the next page.*

Tech Tip

The COUNT (or Count Numbers) function counts all cells in a range that contain numbers, even if the number is 0. If you do not want the COUNT function to count a cell, leave it blank or replace any numbers with text.

FIGURE 4.29 Count Numbers function in Sum list

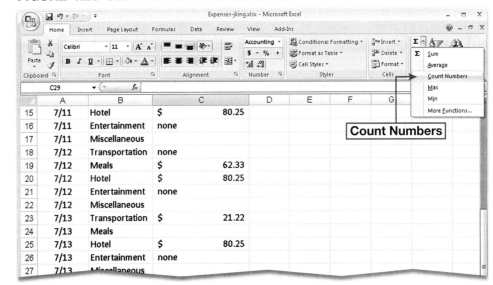

FIGURE 4.30 Expense added to worksheet

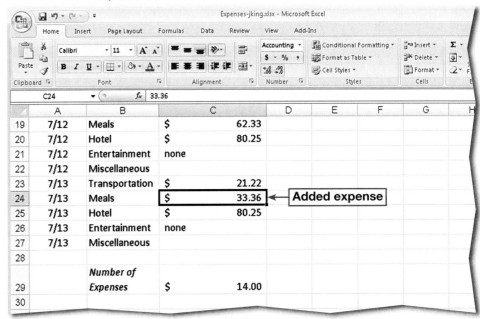

EXERCISE 2-9
Use Conditional Logic in a Formula

Conditional logic tests whether statements are true or false and makes logical comparisons between outcomes. You can use the AND, OR, NOT, and IF functions (described in Table 2.1) to specify what should happen if a cell has one value rather than another. In this exercise, you will test whether conditions are true or false and make logical comparisons about the costs and quantities of T-shirts.

1 In your **Blues2** file, click the **Cost of T-shirts** tab.

2 Click cell **A8**. Key: =AND (A2>A3,A2<A4). Press ENTER. The formula returns a FALSE result because the quantity 1 is not greater than 10 and less than 50.

3 Click cell **A9**. Key: =OR (A2>A3,A2<A4). Press ENTER. The formula returns a TRUE result because although the quantity 1 is not greater than 10, it is less than 50.

4 Click cell **A10**. Key: =NOT (A4+A5=150). Press ENTER. The formula returns a FALSE result because 50 plus 100 equals 150.

5 Click cell **A11**. Key: =IF (B2=15,"OK","Not OK").

6 Press ENTER. The formula returns an OK result because the value in cell B2 equals 15.

7 Click cell **A12**. Key: =IFERROR(A2/C2, "ERROR"). Press ENTER. The formula returns an ERROR result.

8 **(i)CHECK** Your screen should look like Figure 2.25. Save your file.

Continue to the next exercise.

TABLE 2.1 Conditional functions

Function	Meaning
AND	Excel returns a TRUE result if both criteria are met. A FALSE result is returned if one or both of the criteria are not met. (126 is >100 **AND** <150 = TRUE.)
OR	Excel returns a TRUE result if one of the criteria is met. It returns a FALSE result if neither or both of the criteria are met. (126 is >100 **OR** 99 is <150 = TRUE.)
NOT	Excel returns a TRUE result if data *does not* meet specified criteria and a FALSE result if it *does* meet specified criteria. (All data that is **NOT** <1 = TRUE).
IF	Excel determines whether criteria are met. If so, then it returns a specified result. If criteria are not met, it returns a different result. (**IF** a quantity is >100, **THEN** Excel inserts a specified word or symbol into the cell.)

FIGURE 2.25 Formula using IFERROR function

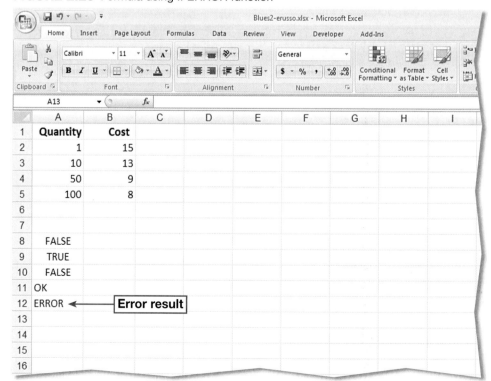

EXERCISE 4-15 (Continued)
Use the COUNT and COUNTA Functions

6 Click cell **C30**. Click the **Sum Σ** drop-down arrow. Choose **More Functions**.

7 Make sure **Or select a category** is set to **All**. Under **Select a function**, choose **COUNTA**. Click **OK**.

8 In the **Value1** box, key: C3:C27. Only 20 of the expense category amounts have been filled out.

9 Click **OK**. A number appears in cell **C30** (see Figure 4.31).

10 Click **Undo**. To complete the expense report, in each empty cell in column C, key: none.

11 **ⓘCHECK** Your screen should look like Figure 4.32. Save and close your file.

Continue to the next exercise.

FIGURE 4.31 Number appears using COUNTA function

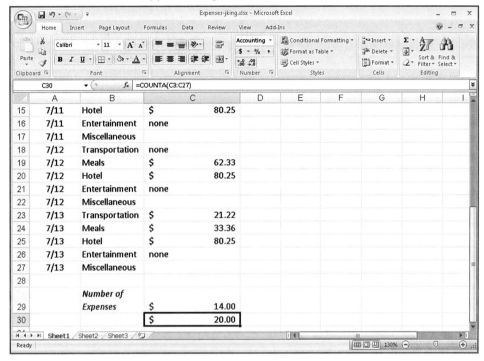

FIGURE 4.32 Final spreadsheet

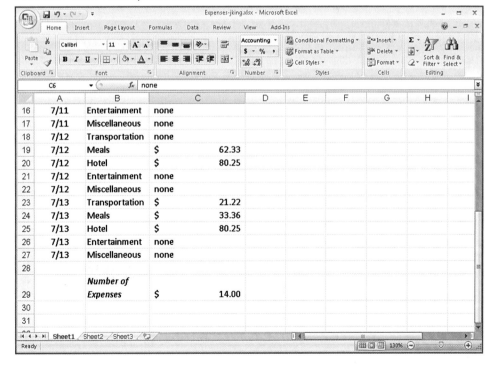

① In your **Blues2** file, click
the **Advertising plan**
sheet tab.

② Click cell **B20**. Key:
=AVERAGEIF(B5:
B13,"<500") .

③ Press ENTER.

④ ⓘCHECK Your screen
should look like Figure 2.23.

⑤ Click cell **A23**. Key:
June>5.0%, July<4.0%.

⑥ Press TAB.

⑦ In **A24**, key: =AVERAGEIFS
(B5:B13,C5:13,">=5.0%",
E5:E13,"<4.0%").

⑧ Press ENTER.

⑨ ⓘCHECK Your screen
should look like Figure 2.24.
Save your file.

→ *Continue to the next exercise.*

Academic Skills

You can figure the average
of a group of numbers by
adding them together and
then dividing the sum by
the total count of numbers.
The AVERAGEIF function
allows you to exclude from
the average any numbers
that do not meet certain
criteria.

EXERCISE 2-8
Use AVERAGEIF and AVERAGEIFS in a Formula

The AVERAGEIF function returns the average of all the cells in a range that meet a given set of criteria. The AVERAGEIFS function averages cells that meet multiple criteria. In this exercise, you will find the average of the advertising methods that cost less than $500. You will then use the AVERAGEIFS function to find the average of the low-budget methods that account for greater than 5% of the total cost spent on advertising in June but less than 4% of the total cost spent on advertising in July.

FIGURE 2.23 Formula using AVERAGEIF

	A	B	C	D	E	F
1	Advertising Plan					
2			Jun-09		Jul-09	
4	METHOD	AMOUNT	PERCENT OF TOTAL	AMOUNT	PERCENT OF TOTAL	PROMOT
5	Business cards	$ 350.00	3.8% $	300.00	3.2%	print/p
6	Newspaper ads	$ 2,000.00	21.6% $	1,500.00	16.2%	
7	Radio ads	$ 2,000.00	21.6% $	1,500.00	16.2%	
8	Web site	$ 1,500.00	16.2% $	1,500.00	16.2%	
9	Mailings	$ 2,000.00	21.6% $	2,000.00	21.6%	print/p
10	Posters	$ 462.50	5.0% $	300.00	3.2%	
11	Bumper stickers	$ 437.50	4.7% $	500.00	5.4%	
12	Pens	$ 200.00	2.2% $	250.00	2.7%	
13	Buttons	$ 300.00	3.2% $	300.00	3.2%	
14						
15	Total	$ 9,250.00	Total $	8,150.00		
16						
17						
18	Low-Budget Methods					
19	Total	$ 1,750.00				
20	Average	$ 350.00				
21						
22	June <5.0%, July >4.0%	437.50				
23						

Average of methods costing less than $500

FIGURE 2.24 Formula using AVERAGEIFS

	A	B	C	D	E	F
4	METHOD	AMOUNT	PERCENT OF TOTAL	AMOUNT	PERCENT OF TOTAL	PROMOT
5	Business cards	$ 350.00	3.8% $	300.00	3.2%	print/p
6	Newspaper ads	$ 2,000.00	21.6% $	1,500.00	16.2%	
7	Radio ads	$ 2,000.00	21.6% $	1,500.00	16.2%	
8	Web site	$ 1,500.00	16.2% $	1,500.00	16.2%	
9	Mailings	$ 2,000.00	21.6% $	2,000.00	21.6%	print/p
10	Posters	$ 462.50	5.0% $	300.00	3.2%	
11	Bumper stickers	$ 437.50	4.7% $	500.00	5.4%	
12	Pens	$ 200.00	2.2% $	250.00	2.7%	
13	Buttons	$ 300.00	3.2% $	300.00	3.2%	
14						
15	Total	$ 9,250.00	Total $	8,150.00		
16						
17						
18	Low-Budget Methods					
19	Total	$ 1,750.00				
20	Average	$ 350.00				
21						
22	June <5.0%, July >4.0%	437.50				
23	June >5.0%, July <4.0%	462.50				
24						
25						

Average costing more than 5% of June but less than 4% of July

EXERCISE 4-16
Use the NOW and PMT Functions

1 Open the data file **Car. xlsx**. Save as: Car-[your first initial and last name].

2 Click cell **B2**. Key: =NOW(). Press ENTER.

3 ⓘ**CHECK** Your screen should look similar to Figure 4.33. Your current date and time should appear in cell **B2**.

4 Click cell **D5**.

5 On the formula bar, click **Insert Function** f_x.

6 In the **Insert Function** dialog box, under **Search for a function**, key: PMT (see Figure 4.34). Click **Go**.

7 Click **OK**. The **Function Arguments** dialog box opens.

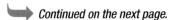 *Continued on the next page.*

The **NOW** function displays the date and time that a worksheet is opened or used. This feature can be useful when a worksheet has been changed many times. The date and time shown on a printout of the worksheet will tell you which **version**, or variation of the original, of the file you are using. The **PMT** function calculates the monthly payment for a loan using the amount of the loan, the interest rate, and the number of payments. Both of these functions are very useful if you want to create and update your own personal budget.

FIGURE 4.33 Date and time added to worksheet

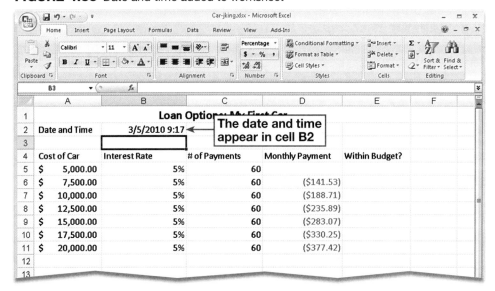

FIGURE 4.34 Insert Function dialog box

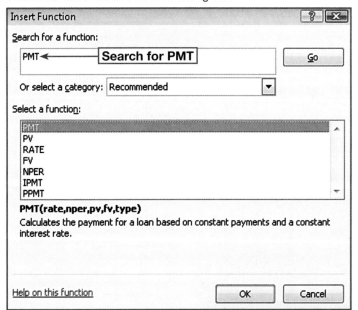

Academic *Skills*

You need to know how much you can afford to spend in order to create an effective budget. Be sure to consider taxes, interest rates, and other expenses. Excel can help you to incorporate these items into your budget.

EXERCISE 2-7
Use COUNTIF and COUNTIFS in a Formula

1 In your **Blues2** file, click the **Merchandise sales** sheet tab.

2 Scroll down and click cell **A58**. Key: CD count.

3 Press TAB. Key: =COUNTIF(C5:C55,"CDs"). Press ENTER.

4 **ⓘCHECK** Your screen should look like Figure 2.21. The number of cells in column **C** that contain CDs appears in cell **B58**.

5 Scroll down and click cell **A59**. Key: CD count >$300.

6 Press TAB. Key: =COUNTIFS(C5: C55,"=CDs",D5: D55,">300"). Press ENTER.

7 **ⓘCHECK** Your screen should look like Figure 2.22. The number of times the sales for CDs exceeded $300 appears in cell **B59**. Save your file.

➥ *Continue to the next exercise.*

You Should Know

Criteria can be in the form of a number, expression, or text that defines which cells will be added. For example, criteria can be expressed as **12**, **"12"**, **>12"**, **"data"**, or **C4**.

The COUNTIF function is a formula that counts the number of cells within a range that meet a given criteria. It is often convenient to use the COUNTIFS function to count the number of cells within a range that meet multiple criteria as well. For example, a business can use the COUNTIFS function to count the number of times its sales personnel exceed a sales quota or sales goal. In this exercise, you will count the number of times CD sales appear in the table and how many times the sales for CDs exceed $300.

FIGURE 2.21 Formula using COUNTIF

	A	B	C	D	E	F	G	H
41	8/2/2009	Nashville	CDs	$ 110.00				
42	8/2/2009	Nashville	T-shirts	$ 225.00				
43	8/2/2009	Nashville	Mugs	$ 24.00				
44	8/1/2009	Nashville	CDs	$ 190.00				
45	8/1/2009	Nashville	T-shirts	$ 325.00				
46	8/1/2009	Nashville	Mugs	$ 32.00				
47	7/14/2009	Atlanta	CDs	$ 110.00				
48	7/14/2009	Atlanta	T-shirts	$ 350.00				
49	7/14/2009	Atlanta	Mugs	$ 64.00				
50	6/27/2009	Baltimore	CDs	$ 310.00				
51	6/27/2009	Baltimore	T-shirts	$ 250.00				
52	6/27/2009	Baltimore	Mugs	$ 40.00				
53	6/26/2009	Baltimore	CDs	$ 250.00				
54	6/26/2009	Baltimore	T-shirts	$ 75.00				
55	6/26/2009	Baltimore	Mugs	$ 64.00				
56								
57								
58	CD count		17 ← **17 cells contain CDs**					
59								
60								

Chart1 | **Merchandise sales** | Advertising plan | T-shirt cost calculator | Cost of T-shirt
Ready | 130%

FIGURE 2.22 Formula using COUNTIFS

	A	B	C	D	E	F	G	H
43	8/2/2009	Nashville	Mugs	$ 24.00				
44	8/1/2009	Nashville	CDs	$ 190.00				
45	8/1/2009	Nashville	T-shirts	$ 325.00				
46	8/1/2009	Nashville	Mugs	$ 32.00				
47	7/14/2009	Atlanta	CDs	$ 110.00				
48	7/14/2009	Atlanta	T-shirts	$ 350.00				
49	7/14/2009	Atlanta	Mugs	$ 64.00				
50	6/27/2009	Baltimore	CDs	$ 310.00				
51	6/27/2009	Baltimore	T-shirts	$ 250.00				
52	6/27/2009	Baltimore	Mugs	$ 40.00				
53	6/26/2009	Baltimore	CDs	$ 250.00				
54	6/26/2009	Baltimore	T-shirts	$ 75.00				
55	6/26/2009	Baltimore	Mugs	$ 64.00				
56								
57								
58	CD count		17					
59	CD count >$300		4 ← **4 CD sales exceeded $300**					
60								
61								
62								

Chart1 | **Merchandise sales** | Advertising plan | T-shirt cost calculator | Cost of T-shirt
Ready | 130%

Step-By-Step

8 In the **Rate** line, key: 0.05/12 (see Figure 4.35).

9 In the **Nper** line, key: 60. Nper is the total number of payments to be made.

10 In the **Pv** line, key: A5. Pv is the amount of the loan. Click **OK**.

11 *i*CHECK Your screen should look like Figure 4.36. Save your file.

➡ *Continue to the next exercise.*

You Should Know

The Function Arguments dialog box will help you calculate your monthly payments if you take out a loan. Rate refers to the interest rate for a loan, presented as a percentage. Nper is the total number of payments for the loan (a five-year loan would have 60 monthly payments). Pv is the present value or amount of the loan.

Academic Skills

The results from the PMT function are red and in parentheses because they represent negative amounts. The numbers represent money that you owe for the car. In finance, the amount owed is usually represented like this.

FIGURE 4.35 Function Arguments dialog box

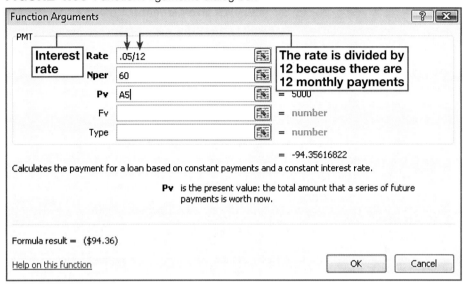

FIGURE 4.36 Payment amounts calculated

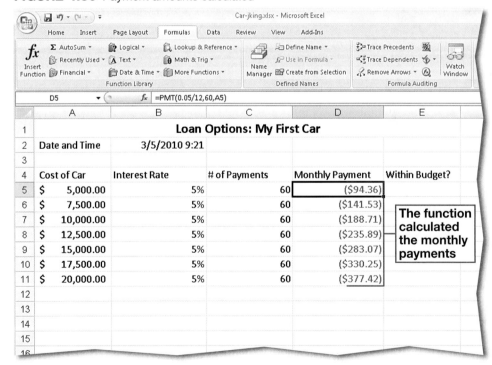

1. In your **Blues2** file, click cell **B19**.

2. Key: =SUMIF(B5:B13,"<500"). Press ENTER.

3. **ⓘCHECK** Your screen should look like Figure 2.19.

4. Select row **D** and insert 2 new sheet columns. Key the headers and the data for the month of **July 2009** into the worksheet, as shown in Figure 2.20.

5. Click cell **A22**. Key: June <5.0%, July >4.0%.

6. Click cell **B23**. Key: =SUMIFS(B5:B13,C5:C13,"<5.0%",E5:E13,">4.0%").

7. Press ENTER.

8. **ⓘCHECK** Your screen should look like Figure 2.20. Save your file.

↪ *Continue to the next exercise.*

Academic Skills

A condition is a description of characteristics. For example, you might describe a person's health by saying that she has a heart condition. In Excel, a condition describes characteristics that must be met in order for a function to work.

EXERCISE 2-6
Use SUMIF and SUMIFS in a Formula

In Excel, the SUMIF, or SUM and IF, function, adds all numbers in a range of cells, based on given criteria. You can also use SUMIFS to add values in a range based on multiple conditions. In this exercise, you will find the sum of the advertising methods that cost less than $500. You will then use the SUMIFS function to find the sum of the low-budget methods that accounted for less than 5% of the total cost spent on advertising in June, but more than 4% of the total cost spent on advertising in July.

FIGURE 2.19 Sum of advertising methods $500 or less

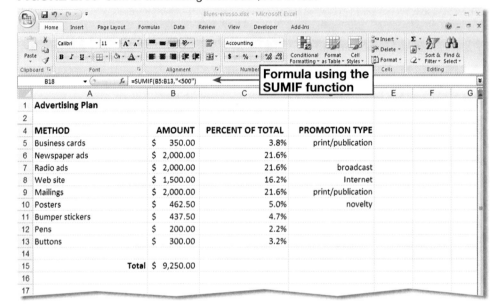

FIGURE 2.20 Methods that cost less than 5% in June but more than 4% in July

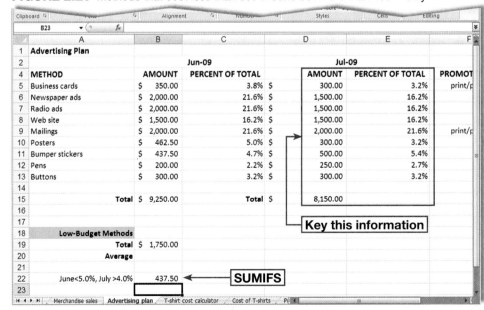

Step-By-Step

1 In your **Car** file, click **E5**.

2 On the formula bar, click **Insert Function** f_x.

3 In the **Insert Function** dialog box, under **Search for a function**, key: IF.

4 **ⓘCHECK** Your dialog box should look like Figure 4.37.

5 Click **Go**.

6 Click **OK**.

Continued on the next page.

You Should Know

Instead of having the IF function display text, you can have it display numbers. For example, you can test to see if you owe more than $500 for a particular bill. If you do, you can have a standard response, such as *$500,* appear.

EXERCISE 4-17
Use the IF Function

The **IF** function allows a worksheet to compare numbers. In this exercise, you will use the IF function to determine whether a monthly car payment is within your budget. To do this, the IF function compares numbers to see if a **condition**, or rule, that you create is true.

For example, you might want to buy a car, under one condition—you cannot spend more than $250 a month. If the condition is true, meaning that the payment will be less than $250, the function displays one result, such as *Yes*. If the condition is false, meaning that the payment will be more than $250, the function displays another result, such as *No*. By using the IF function, Excel will tell you whether the car payment will be within your budget.

The IF function can also be used to make other comparisons. It can be used to compare weights, measurements, or almost any kind of data that can be entered as a number.

FIGURE 4.37 Insert Function dialog box

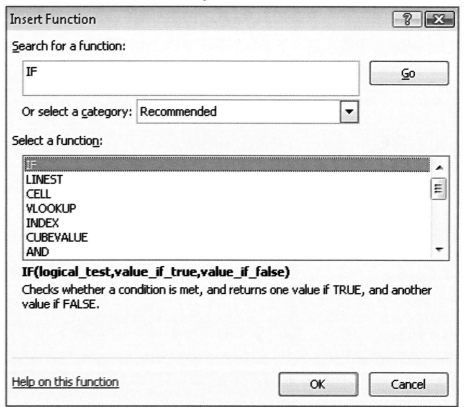

EXERCISE 2-5 (Continued)
Use the Solver Add-In

6 In the **Add Constraint** dialog box, in the **Cell Reference** box, key: total.

7 Click the drop-down arrow in the middle box. Choose **=**.

8 In the **Constraint** box, key: 9250 (see Figure 2.17).

9 In the **Add Constraint** dialog box, click **OK**. The **Solver Parameters** dialog box reopens.

10 Click **Solve**. The **Solver Results** dialog box opens. A message displays that the **Solver** found a solution. Click **OK**.

11 **⚫CHECK** Your screen should look like Figure 2.18.

12 Save your file.

→ *Continue to the next exercise.*

FIGURE 2.17 The Add Constraint dialog box

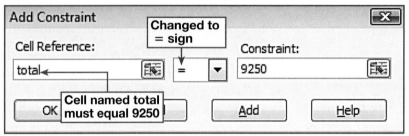

FIGURE 2.18 Solution found

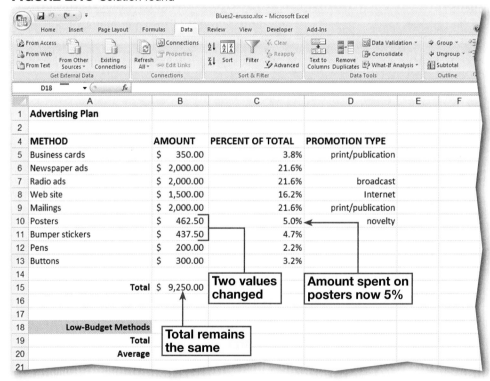

Troubleshooter

If the **Solver** reports no solution, check the criteria that you set. Make sure the situation is logical. For example, if you set the target cell equal to **Max** (largest possible value) without any constraints, there may be no solution. The **Solver** can only find a solution that is a definite value.

Academic Skills

Look at the different methods of advertising that are listed on this spreadsheet. Each of them is designed for a different target audience. Imagine you are in charge of setting the budget. Which methods do you think are most effective? Can you think of any additional advertising methods that you might use?

EXERCISE 4-17 (Continued)
Use the IF Function

7 In the **Function Arguments** dialog box, in the **Logical_test** box, key: D5>=250 (see Figure 4.38).

8 In **Value_if_true** box, key: Yes.

9 In the **Value_if_false** box, key: No. Excel automatically inserts quotation marks in the **Value_if_false** box.

10 ⓘ**CHECK** Your dialog box should look like Figure 4.38. Click **OK**.

11 Click the lower right corner of cell **E5** and drag it down to cell **E11**. Release the mouse button.

12 ⓘ**CHECK** Your screen should look like Figure 4.39. The most expensive car you can afford is $12,500.

13 Save and close your file.

➡ *Continue to the next exercise.*

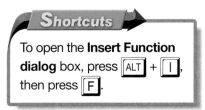

Shortcuts

To open the **Insert Function dialog** box, press ALT + I, then press F.

FIGURE 4.38 Function Arguments for IF

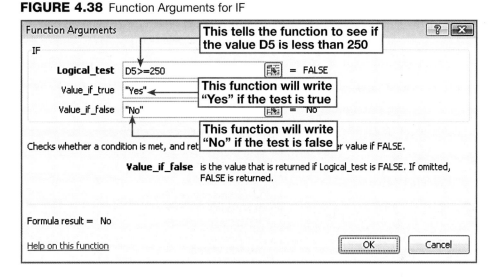

FIGURE 4.39 Budget check

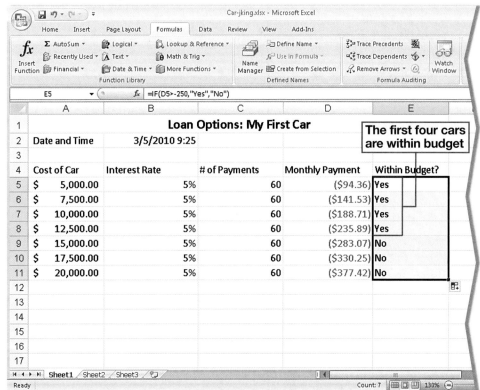

EXERCISE 2-5
Use the Solver Add-In

1. In your **Blues2** file, click the **Advertising plan** tab. Choose **Office** >Excel **Options>Add-Ins**. Select **Excel Add-Ins** and click **Go**. In the **Add-Ins** dialog box, select the **Solver Add-In** (see Figure 2.15).

2. Click **OK**. Choose **Data> Analysis>Solver** .

3. In the **Solver Parameters** dialog box, in the **Set Target Cell** box, key: C10. The dollar signs will be inserted automatically.

4. Click the **Value of** button. In the **Value of** box, key: .05. In the **By Changing Cells** box, key: B10, B11.

5. **CHECK** Your dialog box should look like Figure 2.16. Click **Add**.

Continued on the next page.

Excel includes several extra features, called add-ins, that can be installed as needed. For example, the Solver add-in changes one or more cells to find a solution based on criteria that you set. In this exercise, you will use the Solver to change the values for posters and buttons so five percent of the advertising expenses is spent on posters. You will also set the **constraint**, or limit, that the total cannot exceed.

FIGURE 2.15 The Add-Ins dialog box

FIGURE 2.16 Solver Parameters dialog box

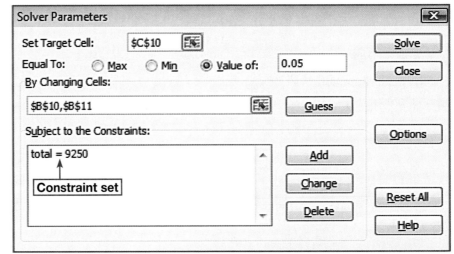

Academic Skills

In Step 5, the value .05 represents 5 percent, or 5%. In order to figure percentages mathematically, you need to express the percentage in its proper decimal form. For example, 50% would be 0.5, while 25% would be 0.25.

MATH MATTERS

Presenting Information Graphically

Your boss is worried that the restaurant he manages is losing sales. He asks you to prepare a report that analyzes the current sales data. You need to decide how you want to present the data so it is easily understandable.

Using Graphics

When you need information about a business's performance, a good place to look is a business report. A business report can be anything from a one-page summary of sales to a 200-page analysis of an entire industry. It may propose a new product or marketing strategy, describe a current development, or track profits over a period of time.

While business reports are good for analyzing and summarizing large amounts of data, there are times when you want to show your data so it is immediately understandable. Using a graphic such as a chart or graph allows you to organize data so it can be evaluated at a glance. For instance, an upward line on a graph shows that sales are increasing, while a downward line will signal that sales are on the decline.

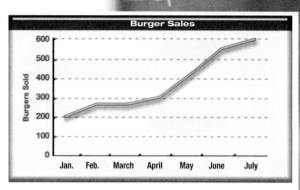

Use graphics to display information visually.

Seeing the Numbers

You decide to create a graph that shows your boss the amount of burger sales over the last seven months. Your graph (shown above right) illustrates how sales have generally increased over the last few months—which is a relief for your boss!

SKILLBUILDER

1. **Describe** What are some of the purposes of a business report?
2. **Evaluate** Why is it sometimes better to present data as a graphic than as numbers or words?

3. **Connect** How can math and writing skills help you to read or write a business report? How might your business report be improved with a basic knowledge of Excel? Explain your answer in a brief paragraph.

EXERCISE 2-4 (Continued)
Use the What-If Analysis Tool to Create Scenarios

16 If necessary, move the **Scenario Manager** dialog box so you can see the data in the worksheet.

17 In the **Scenarios** list, double-click **ads low**. Excel runs the scenario where you have $500 to spend on newspaper ads.

18 ⓘ**CHECK** Your screen should look like Figure 2.13. Notice that your total budget is now $7,750.

FIGURE 2.13 The ads low scenario

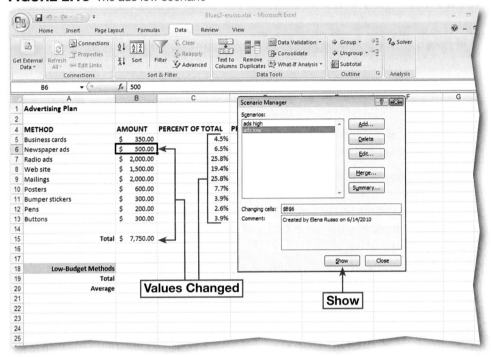

19 In the **Scenarios** list, double-click **ads high**.

20 ⓘ**CHECK** Your screen should look like Figure 2.14. Notice that the **ads high** scenario changes your total budget to $9,250.

21 In the **Scenario Manager** dialog box, click **Close**.

22 Save your file.

➡ *Continue to the next exercise.*

You Should Know

When you change a value that is used in one or more formulas, it affects every cell that uses those formulas. Cell **B6** is part of the **Total** formula. The **Total** formula is in turn part of the formulas used in **Column C**.

FIGURE 2.14 The ads high scenario

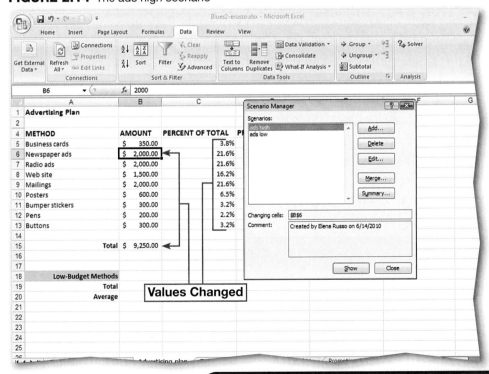

Vocabulary

Key Terms

absolute reference

chart

condition

COUNT

COUNTA

filter

function

IF

mixed reference

NOW

operator

PMT

range

relative reference

sort

Academic Vocabulary

adjust

version

Review Vocabulary

Complete the following statements on a separate piece of paper. Choose from the Vocabulary list on the left to complete the statements.

1. A reference that does not change when the formula is copied to a new location is a(n) _____. (p. 93)

2. A group of cells is called a(n) _____. (p. 85)

3. You can use the _____ function to add the current date and time to a worksheet. (p. 101)

4. The _____ buttons can organize cells in ascending or descending order. (p. 86)

5. You cannot change, or _____ an absolute reference. (p. 90)

Vocabulary Activity

6. Create a quiz to review this lesson's Vocabulary words.
   A. On a separate sheet of paper, write the definitions for this lesson's list of Vocabulary words. Do not write the words themselves.
   B. Exchange quizzes with a partner and then take your partner's quiz. Write the correct Vocabulary word beside each definition.
   C. Note any definitions that you did not know and identify the correct answer.

Review Key Concepts

Answer the following questions on a separate piece of paper.

7. Which of the following tabs contains the Filter command? (p. 85)
   A. File   C. Insert
   B. Edit   D. Data

8. Which of these buttons would you use to create a formula? (p. 89)
   A. Copy   C. Sum
   B. Insert Function   D. Sort Ascending

9. In which of these references will both the column letter and row number change when the formula is copied to a new location? (p. 92)
   A. A1   C. A$1
   B. $A1   D. $A$1

10. Which of these functions calculates the monthly payment on a loan? (p. 101)
   A. SUM   C. PMT
   B. IF   D. COUNTA

10 In your **Blues2** file, click cell **B6**.

11 Choose **Data>Data Tools>What-If Analysis**. Select **Scenario Manager**.

12 In the **Scenario Manager** dialog box, click **Add**.

13 In the **Add Scenario** dialog box, in the **Scenario name** box, key: ads low (see Figure 2.11). Click **OK**.

14 In the **Scenario Values** dialog box, key: 500. Click **OK**.

15 ⓘCHECK Your dialog box should look like Figure 2.12. Under **Scenarios**, notice that the scenario **ads low** has been added to the **Scenarios** list.

➡ *Continued on the next page.*

Troubleshooter

When you create a scenario, your original worksheet is not saved. If you want to restore the worksheet after showing a scenario, you must create a scenario that uses the original values.

EXERCISE 2-4 (Continued)
Use the What-If Analysis Tool to Create Scenarios

FIGURE 2.11 Add Scenario dialog box

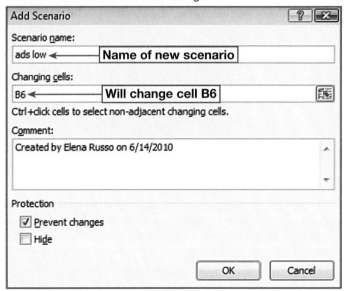

FIGURE 2.12 Scenarios listed in the Scenario Manager dialog box

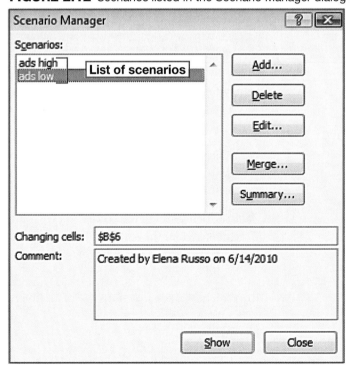

1. Create, Copy, and Paste Formulas

Data File

Follow the steps to complete the activity.

Step-By-Step

1. Open the data file **Commission.xlsx**. Save as: Commission-[your first initial and last name]1.

2. Click cell **E3**.

3. Key: =SUM(B3:D3).

4. **CHECK** Your screen should look like Figure 4.40.

5. Press ENTER. Press the up arrow. Cell **E3** should be selected.

6. Click **Copy**.

7. Select cells **E3** through **E8**.

8. Click **Paste**.

9. **CHECK** Your screen should look like Figure 4.41.

10. Save and close your file.

FIGURE 4.40 Creating a formula

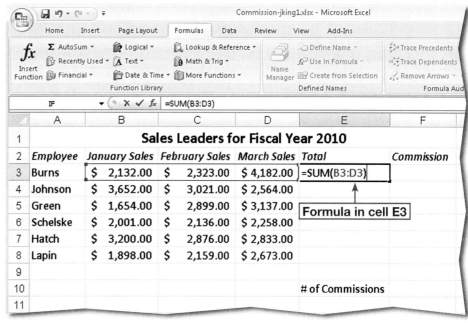

FIGURE 4.41 Pasted formula

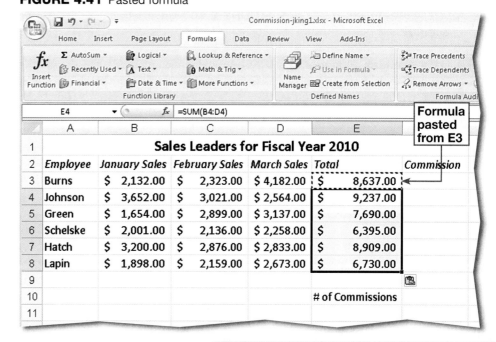

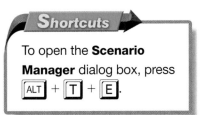

In your **Blues2** file, click the **Advertising plan** sheet tab. Click cell **B6**.

① In your **Blues2** file, click the **Advertising plan** sheet tab. Click cell **B6**.

② Choose **Data>Data Tools>What-If Analysis**. Select **Scenario Manager**.

③ In the **Scenario Manager** dialog box, click **Add**.

④ In the **Add Scenario** dialog box, in the **Scenario name** box, key: ads high (see Figure 2.9).

⑤ Click **OK**. The **Scenario Values** dialog box opens.

⑥ If necessary, key: 2000. Click **OK**.

⑦ The **Scenario Manager** dialog box reopens. The scenario **ads high** has been added to the **Scenarios** list.

⑧ In the **Scenario Manager** dialog box, click **Close**.

⑨ ⓘ**CHECK** Your screen should look like Figure 2.10.

➡ *Continued on the next page.*

Shortcuts

To open the **Scenario Manager** dialog box, press [ALT] + [T] + [E].

EXERCISE 2-4
Use the What-If Analysis Tool to Create Scenarios

You can perform a **What-If Analysis** to test possible outcomes. Excel allows you to create What-If scenarios for each possible situation so that you can compare the scenarios and make a decision. A **scenario** is a version of your data that you save and name. What-If scenarios are useful if some values in your worksheet cannot change but others can. For example, if you have a budget that contains nine advertising options, you can change the values of each option without changing the budget total. In this exercise, you will create two scenarios in which you set your upper and lower spending limits on newspaper ads.

FIGURE 2.9 Add Scenario dialog box

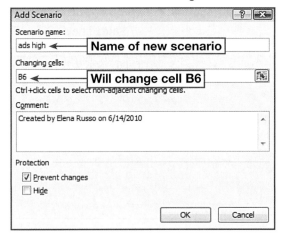

FIGURE 2.10 Worksheet with original values

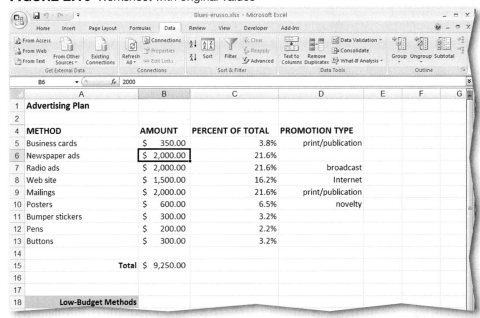

2. Create a Formula and Use the Count Numbers Function

Follow the steps to complete the activity. You must complete Practice It Activity 1 before doing this activity.

Step-By-Step

1 Open your **Commission-1** file. Save as: Commission-[your first initial and last name]2.

2 In cell **F3**, key: =E3*.06. Press ENTER.

3 Press the up arrow. Click **Copy** 📋.

4 Select cells **F4** through **F8**. Click **Paste** 📋.

5 ⓘ**CHECK** Your screen should look like Figure 4.42.

6 Select cell **F10**. Click the **Sum** drop-down arrow. Click **Count Numbers**.

7 Select cells **F3:F8**. Press ENTER. With cell **F10** selected, choose **Home> Accounting**. Click the **$** drop-down arrow and select **More Accounting Formats**.

8 In the **Format Cells** dialog box, choose **General**. Click **OK**.

9 ⓘ**CHECK** Your screen should look like Figure 4.43.

10 Save and close your file.

FIGURE 4.42 Calculating 6% commission

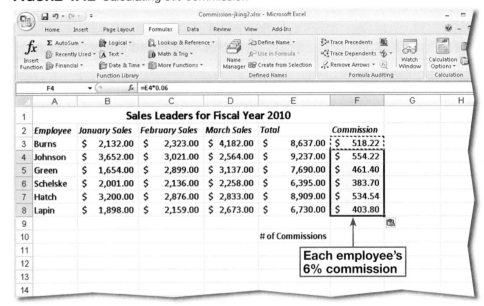

FIGURE 4.43 Commission count

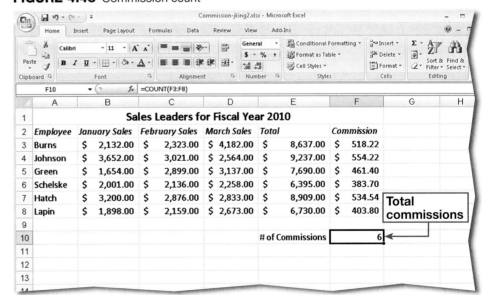

2 Click cell **D2**. Key: =SUBSTITUTE(C2:C13, "ADV-", "").

3 Press ENTER.

4 **ⓘCHECK** Your screen should look like Figure 2.7. Note that *ADV-* has been removed from the business cards promotion code.

5 Click cell **D2**. Drag the fill handle down to **D13**.

6 **ⓘCHECK** Your screen should look like Figure 2.8. The remaining promotion codes are filled in without *ADV-*.

7 Save your file.

➡ *Continue to the next exercise.*

Microsoft Office 2007

To **AutoFit**, or change the column width to fit the contents of a cell, double-click the boundary between two column headings. To quickly AutoFit all columns in a worksheet, click **Select All** ⬜ and then double-click any boundary between two column headings.

EXERCISE 2-3
Modify Text Content Using Formulas

You can use formulas to change the content of your worksheets. For instance, the **SUBSTITUTE** function allows you to substitute one word for another quickly. As the data in your worksheet continues to change, this function can be very helpful.

FIGURE 2.7 Formula using the SUBSTITUTE function

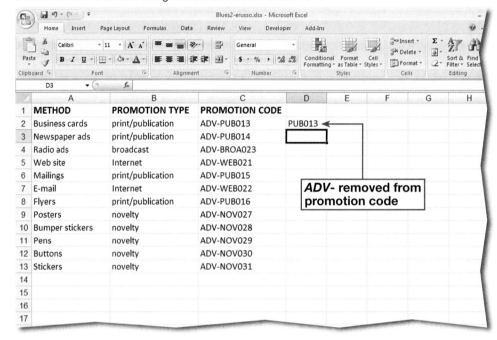

ADV- removed from promotion code

FIGURE 2.8 *ADV-* removed from promotion codes

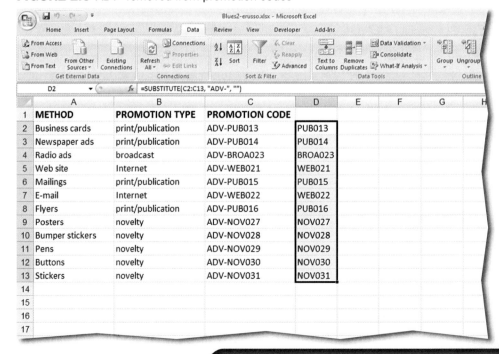

3. Create, Modify, and Position a Chart

Step-By-Step

Follow the steps to complete the activity. You must complete Practice It Activity 2 before doing this activity.

1 Open your **Commission-2** file. Save as: Commission-[your first initial and last name]3.

2 Select the range **A2:B8**. Choose **Insert>Charts> Column**. Under **2-D Column**, choose **Clustered Column** (see Figure 4.44).

3 With the chart still selected, choose **Layout>Labels> Axis Titles.** Select **Primary Horizontal Axis Title>Title Below Axis**. In the **Horizontal (Category) Axis Title** box, key: Employees. Press ENTER.

4 Choose **Axis Titles> Primary Vertical Axis Title>Rotated Title**. In the **Vertical (Value) Axis Title** box, key: Sales (Dollars). Press ENTER.

5 Use the sizing handles to make the chart bigger. Position the chart below the data in your worksheet.

6 *i***CHECK** Your screen should look like Figure 4.45. Save and close your file.

FIGURE 4.44 Column drop-down menu

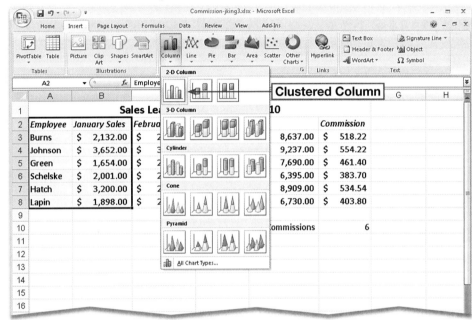

FIGURE 4.45 Completed chart

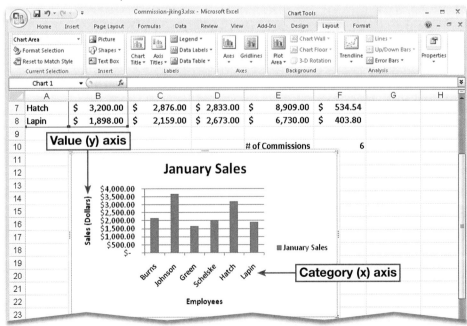

Modify Text Formatting Using Formulas

1. In your **Blues2** file, click the **Advertising plan** sheet tab. Select row **4**. Choose **Home>Cells> Insert Cells** to add a row in the advertising plan.

2. Click cell **A4**. Key: =LOWER(A3). Press ENTER.

3. **CHECK** Your screen should look like Figure 2.5.

4. Click **A4** and drag the fill handle to **D4**. The new row of headings is in lowercase.

5. Click cell **A4**. Key: =PROPER(A3). Press ENTER. Select cell **A4** and drag the fill handle to **C4**.

6. Click **A4** and change the formula to: =UPPER(A3). Press ENTER.

7. Copy the formula to cells **B4:D4**. Select row **3**. Right-click and select **Hide**.

8. **CHECK** Your screen should look like Figure 2.6. Save your file.

→ *Continue to the next exercise.*

You can use database functions to analyze and modify data. A **database function** is a formula that acts on only those items that meet certain **criteria** or conditions. Each of those items is called an **argument**. To make analyzing data easier, you may want to convert the text from uppercase to lowercase or to proper case to improve the worksheet's readability. To modify text with a formula, you can use the **UPPER** function to make the text uppercase, the **LOWER** function to change text to lowercase, or the **PROPER** function to make only the first letter uppercase.

FIGURE 2.5 Text modified using formula

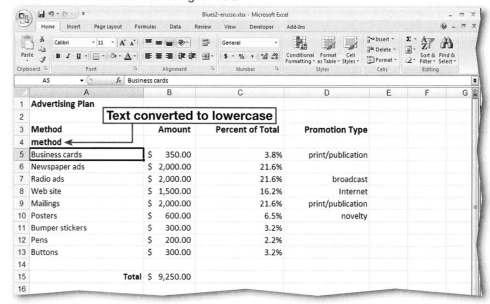

FIGURE 2.6 Text modified to uppercase using formula

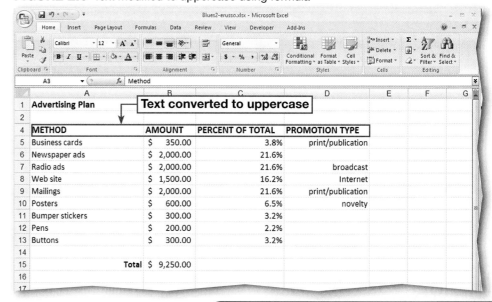

Academic Skills

Proper case refers to the capitalization of a name. Your name, and the name of the town or city where you live, are proper nouns.

4. Make a Study Schedule

Think about how much time you have after school each day to study. Be realistic about how much time you schedule for yourself. For instance, you probably need to schedule less study time on days when you have after-school activities. You can use Excel to track your study time.

Step-By-Step

1 Open the data file **Homework.xlsx**. Save as: Homework-[your first initial and last name]4.

2 In cells **B2:F2**, enter the amount of time (in hours) you want to study each day for Week 1.

3 In cells **B3:F3**, enter the amount of time (in hours) you want to study each day for Week 2.

4 In cell **G2**, write a formula to find the total study time for Week 1 (see Figure 4.46).

5 Copy the formula from cell **G2** and paste it into cell **G3**.

6 In cell **H1**, key: Average.

7 Use **SUM** to put the average number of hours per day you want to study in Week 1 in cell H2, and the **AVG** for Week 2 in cell H3.

8 ⓘCHECK Your screen should look similar to Figure 4.47.

9 Save and close your file.

FIGURE 4.46 Homework total

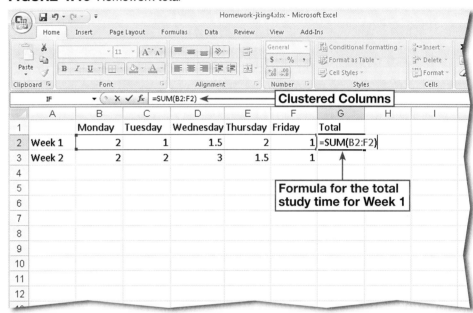

FIGURE 4.47 Average hours per day

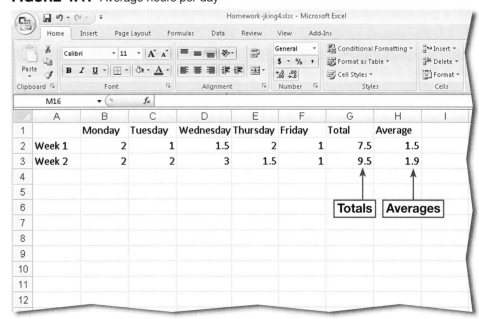

Step-By-Step

EXERCISE 2-1 (Continued)
Create PivotTable with PivotChart Reports

9 In the **PivotTable Field List**, drag **Sales** to the **Values** box.

10 ℹ️**CHECK** Your screen should look like Figure 2.3.

11 Choose **Options>Tools> PivotChart** 📊. In the **Insert Chart** dialog box, under **Column**, select **Stacked Column**. Click **OK**.

12 Close the **PivotTable Field List**. Close the **PivotChart Filter Pane**.

13 On the **Ribbon**, click the **Layout** tab under **PivotChart Tools**. Choose **Labels>Axis Titles>Primary Horizontal Axis Label> Title Below Axis**. Key: Location.

14 Choose **Labels>Axis Titles>Primary Vertical Access Label>Rotated Title**. Key: Sum of Sales.

15 ℹ️**CHECK** Your screen should look like Figure 2.4.

16 Click the **Sheet1** sheet tab and rename the sheet **Chart1**.

17 Save your file.

➡️ *Continue to the next exercise.*

FIGURE 2.3 Finished PivotTable

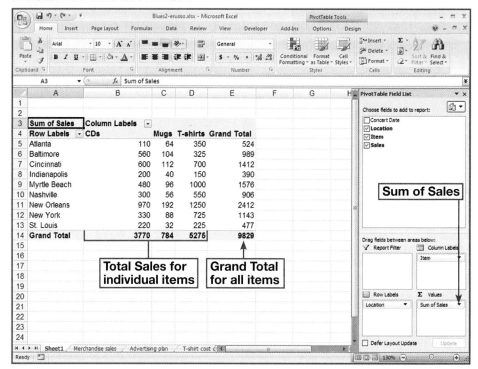

FIGURE 2.4 PivotChart

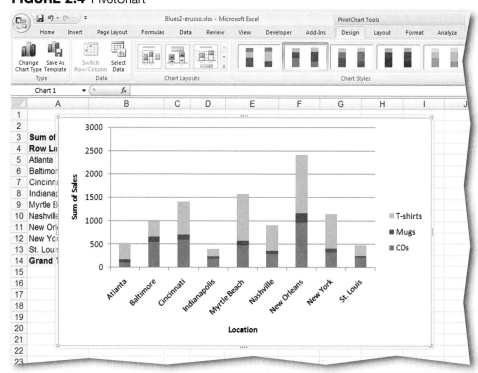

5. Make a Study Chart

Step-By-Step

You want to compare how many hours you will study each day in Week 1 and in Week 2. The best way to do this is to create a bar graph for each week. You must complete You Try It Activity 4 before starting this activity.

1 Open your **Homework-4** file. Save as: Homework-[your first initial and last name]5.

2 Select the range **A1:F3**.

3 Use the **Chart Tools** to create a clustered column graph that shows how many hours you will study each day of Week 1 and Week 2.

4 Title the chart **Homework Schedule**. Name the horizontal axis **Day** and name the vertical axis **Time (Hours)** (see Figure 4.48).

5 Position the chart below the schedule. Adjust the size of the chart so that it is readable.

6 *CHECK* Your screen should look similar to Figure 4.49.

7 Save and close your file.

FIGURE 4.48 Chart with axis information

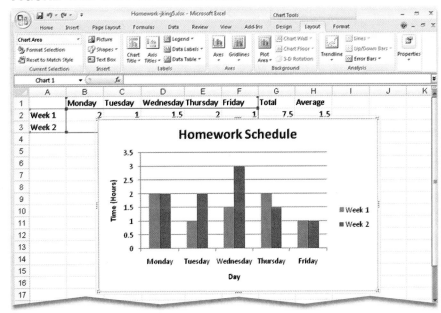

FIGURE 4.49 Completed chart

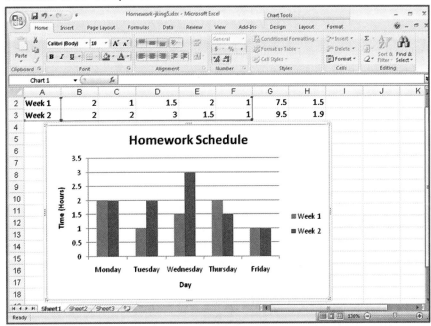

Step-By-Step

1 Open the data file **Blues2.xlsx**. Save your file as: Blues2-[your first initial and last name]. (For example, *Blues2-erusso*.) Click the **Merchandise sales** sheet tab.

2 Select cells **A4:D73**. Choose **Data>Outline> Subtotal** ⊞. In the **Subtotals** dialog box, click **Remove All**.

3 Select any cell in the list, such as cell **C6**.

4 Choose **Insert>Tables** and click the **Insert PivotTable** ⊞ drop-down arrow. Select **PivotTable**.

5 ⓘ**CHECK** Your dialog box should look like Figure 2.1 Click **OK**.

6 The PivotTable is created in a new worksheet. In the **PivotTable Field List**, click and drag **Location** to the box labeled **Row Labels** (under **Drag fields between areas below:**).

7 In the **PivotTable Field List**, drag **Item** to the **Column Labels** box.

8 ⓘ**CHECK** Your screen should look like Figure 2.2.

➡ *Continued on the next page.*

EXERCISE 2-1
Create PivotTable with PivotChart Reports

A **PivotTable** is a sophisticated tool that creates a concise report summarizing large amounts of data based on ranges you select. The data in a PivotTable can then generate, or create, a **PivotChart**. In this exercise, you will create a PivotTable and a PivotChart to show the total amount of each item sold at each location.

FIGURE 2.1 Create PivotTable dialog box

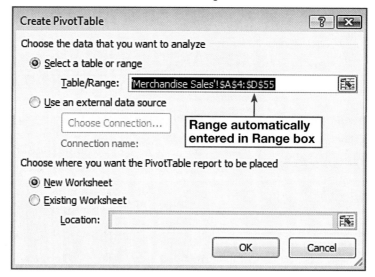

FIGURE 2.2 Unfinished PivotTable

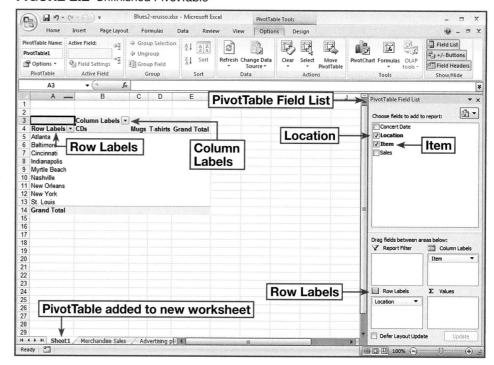

Lesson 2: Exercise 2-1

Advanced Excel 178

6. Beyond the Classroom Activity

 Math: Create an Income Sheet Each week you earn money doing the following chores for your neighbors:

- For sweeping one neighbor's sidewalk and porch, you earn $5.00.
- For mowing another neighbor's lawn, you earn $20.00.
- For cleaning another neighbor's windows, you earn $15.00.

Create a worksheet that has columns for three chores and rows for four weeks. For each week, show the amount you earn for each chore and use the **SUM** function to show how much you earned that week.

Save your worksheet as: e4rev-[your first initial and last name]6.

7. Standards at Work Activity

 Microsoft Certified Application Specialist Correlation
Excel 4.1 *Create and Format Charts*

Create a Column Chart Your supervisor has asked you to create a clustered column chart comparing January and February sales in your **Books** file.

Open the latest version of your **Books** file. Save it as: e4rev-[your first initial and last name]7. Select cells **A1:C10**. Use the **Chart Tools** to create a **Clustered Column** chart. Enlarge the chart and position it so that it does not cover the data in your worksheet.

8. 21st Century Skills Activity

Design an Academic Calendar One way to manage your time well is to create a calendar to schedule your schoolwork. Imagine that you have a five-page English paper due in two weeks. Use Excel to create a schedule for working on your English paper. Your schedule should include the following steps:

A. Research C. Edit the draft
B. Write a draft D. Write a final draft

Remember that you have five pages to write. Make sure you schedule all ten weekdays in the two weeks you have to finish the paper. Give yourself at least three days to research and at least one day to complete each of the remaining stages of the writing process.

Save your worksheet as: e4rev-[your first initial and last name]8.

Go Online e-REVIEW
glencoe.com

Go to the **Online Learning Center** to complete the following review activities.

Online Self Check
To test your knowledge of the material, click **Unit 1> Lesson 4** and choose **Self Checks**.

Interactive Review
To review the main points of the lesson, click **Unit 1> Lesson 4** and choose **Interactive Review.**

Before You Read

Vocabulary Knowing the definition of a word does not always help you understand its full meaning. To gain a more complete understanding of the meaning, use a Vocabulary Journal. Divide a piece of paper into four columns. Label the first column *Vocabulary*. Label the other columns: *What is it?*, *What else is it like?*, and *What are some examples?*. List each vocabulary word and answer the questions as you read.

Read To Learn

- Learn to create and customize reports and charts of data with PivotTables and PivotCharts.
- Evaluate which decision to make using data analysis tools.
- Consider how LOOKUP functions can be used to automate tasks in Excel.

Main Idea

Excel has many tools and features to help you analyze the huge amount of data that businesses work with today.

Vocabulary

Key Terms

argument	PivotTable
conditional logic	PROPER
constraint	scenario
criteria	SUBSTITUTE
database function	UPPER
LOWER	What-If Analysis
PivotChart	

Academic Vocabulary

These words appear in your reading and on your tests. Make sure you know their meanings.

generate
locate

Quick Write Activity

Describe On a separate sheet of paper, describe why analysis can lead you to make better decisions. Think about a time when you had to change or rearrange data to answer questions. Perhaps you had to look at the data from different angles. Explain how you think Excel might have helped you analyze your data to make the best decision.

Study Skill

Use a Whiteboard Put up a whiteboard where you do your homework. If you have an unfinished assignment or project, jot a reminder on the board. Erase each reminder when you complete the task. These reminders will be visible until you complete each assigment or project.

Academic Standards

Language Arts
  NCTE 3 Apply strategies to interpret texts.

Math
  NCTM (Number and Operations) Understand numbers, ways of representing numbers, relationships among numbers, and number systems.
  NCTM (Number and Operations) Understand meanings and operations and how they relate to one another.
  NCTM (Connections) Understand meanings and operations and how they relate to one another.

LESSON 4 — Challenge Yourself Projects

Before You Begin

Self-Management Use self-management skills to direct your activities and achieve your goals. These projects show you how to use an Excel workbook as an organizational tool to help set and meet your goals.

Reflect Once you complete the projects, open a Word document and answer the following:

1. Describe the factors you considered when designing the schedule.

2. How can you use an Excel schedule to improve your self-management skills?

9. Create a Workout Schedule

 Math: Design a Spreadsheet If you are ever self-employed, you will benefit from knowing how to create a workbook. For this project, imagine that you work as a trainer in a gym. Your job is to create a workout schedule for your clients. Each client's schedule must show the following:

- day of the week
- the type of exercise (aerobics, weights, or running)
- the time of day

Design a spreadsheet with a column for each day of the week. Include a row for each type of exercise and the time of day. Create a one-week schedule for a client who wants to work out four days a week, three hours each day. Include all three types of exercise.

Save your worksheet as: e4rev-[your first initial and last name]9.

10. Set Hourly Rates

 Math: Create Formulas As a personal trainer, you need to set an hourly rate for each type of exercise. Create a sample training schedule for four days a week, two hours each day. The schedule should include each type of exercise (aerobics, weights, or running).

Use formulas to calculate:

- cost for each exercise session
- cost for each day
- total cost for the week

Save your worksheet as: e4rev-[your first initial and last name]10.

11. Plan a Discount Program

 Math: Use Functions As a personal trainer, you decide to offer a discount program for your clients. Create a sample schedule that includes:

- five days of exercise a week
- each day's workout schedule
- cost for each day

You decide to give clients a 10 percent discount for each day that costs more than $20. Write a formula that will calculate which days receive a discount (Hint: use the **IF** function).

Save your worksheet as: e4rev-[your first initial and last name]11.

The analytical tools in Excel allow you to summarize data and test how various options affect data. Using PivotTables, conditional logic, scenarios, and What-If Analysis, you can make predictions and solve complex problems. This lesson also covers modifying text formatting and text content with formulas, using the Solver tool, and creating database functions—all of which will enable you to effectively analyze your data.

Key Concepts

- Use a PivotTable and PivotChart

- Modify text formatting and text content using formulas

- Perform What-If Analysis

- Use conditional logic in a formula

- Display and print formulas

- Use LOOKUP and Reference functions

21st CENTURY S K I L L S

Consider the Consequences Making decisions can be a hard task. Consider the following scenario: A video game you really want has just gone on sale. You have enough money to buy it because you have been saving up to buy a portable music player. If you buy the video game now, you will have to wait another month before you can afford to buy the portable music player. Are you willing to wait for the portable music player in order to buy the video game? Analyzing your choices will help you make the best decision. *What is an example of a difficult decision that you made recently?*

Standards

The following standards are covered in this lesson. Refer to pages xix and 314 for a description of the standards listed here.

ISTE Standards Correlation

NETS•S

1a, 1c, 3d, 4a, 4b, 4c, 4d, 6a

Microsoft Certified Application Specialist

Excel

3.4, 3.5, 3.6, 3.7, 3.8

You have learned how to format cells and create formulas. In this lesson, you will learn how to manage workbooks. You will insert, delete, split, and rearrange worksheets. Learning how to split and arrange workbooks will help you manage your work environment. You will also set up a workbook for printing by setting the print area and changing Page Setup options.

Key Concepts

- Use a template

- Organize worksheets

- Split, freeze, hide, and arrange workbooks

- Save and preview worksheets as Web pages

- Set up pages for printing

- Rename folders and convert files to different formats

Standards

The following standards are covered in this lesson. Refer to pages xix and 314 for a description of the standards listed here.

ISTE Standards Correlation

NETS•S

1a, 1c, 1d, 2b, 2d, 3d, 4a, 4b, 4c, 5a, 5c, 6a, 6b, 6d

Microsoft Certified Application Specialist

Excel

1.4 1.5, 5.4, 5.5

21st CENTURY SKILLS

Be Honest Honesty is more than just telling the truth. It is also about speaking up in support of your values and opinions. It can also be a trait of a hard-working employee. Honesty is essential for building trust, whether it be with friends or co-workers. If you have a reputation for being an honest person, people will trust you. Trust is an important part of any business or personal relationship. *How has honesty played a role in your week so far?*

Before You Begin

Make Sense of Data In school, at work, and even at home, organization makes life easier. These projects teach you how to use Excel's tools to sort, filter, and validate data in a concise and logical format.

Reflect Once you complete the projects, open a Word document and answer the following questions:

1. In what ways do you think data validation can help you better organize and quickly manage data?

2. Think about something that you had to organize in your life. What strategies did you use to complete the task?

3. What are some other ways you can use Excel to organize data logically?

9. Organize a Donations Workbook

 Math: Convert a Table to a Range of Data   You are on the fundraising committee at your local zoo. You need to create a sorted list for your donations data. Open the **Zoo.xlsx** data file. In the file:

- Create a table.
- Sort the donations in ascending order.
- Convert the table to a range of data.

Save your file as: Zoo-[your first initial and last name]9.xlsx.

10. Monitor Donation Totals

 Math: Use Advanced Filters   The fundraising committee is considering setting a minimum donation of $30. Before they make a decision, they would like to know who contributed less than $30 to the zoo. Open your **Zoo-9** file.

- Sort the donations by last name.
- Use **advanced filters** to identify all the donations that are less than $30.
- Make sure you leave a blank row between the criteria range and the data range.

Save your file as: Zoo-[your first initial and last name]10.xlsx.

11. Analyze Donations Data

 Math: Use Data Validation   The fundraising committee has decided to set the minimum donation at $30. You need to apply data validation to require the amount for each donation to be $30 or more.

- Open your **Zoo-10** file. If necessary, turn off the filter from the previous activity.
- Use **Data Validation** to control the amount of data entered into cells in your table.
- Change all of the donations that are less than $30 to $30.
- In your file, identify:

  A. The number of donations you changed.

  B. The total amount the donations increased after the minimum donation was changed to $30.

Save your file as: Zoo-[your first initial and last name]11.xlsx.

Before You Read

Use Diagrams to Help Understanding As you are reading through this lesson, write down the main idea. Write down any facts, explanations, or examples you find in the exercise. Start at the main idea and draw arrows to the information that directly supports it. Then draw arrows from these examples to any information that supports them.

Read To Learn

- Learn different ways to create and display your Excel files.
- Use templates to improve the usefulness of your worksheets.
- Explore how to use printing options to adjust the margins, create headers and footers, or print specific parts of a page.
- Consider how to convert your Excel files easily into functioning Web pages.
- Insert, delete, and arrange worksheets as needed to keep track of your hours while on the job.

Main Idea

Excel is an excellent tool that provides multiple ways to view data.

Vocabulary

Key Terms

footer	margin	portrait
freeze	page break	print area
header	page	split
landscape	orientation	template

Academic Vocabulary

These words appear in your reading and on your tests. Make sure you know their meanings.

arrange
common
convert
locate

Quick Write Activity

Describe Think about all the individuals in your class. When you turn in completed Excel worksheet assignments, your teacher needs to know whose work belongs to whom. On a separate sheet of paper, list the information you would place on your worksheet so that the teacher can tell your paper apart from your classmates' papers.

Study Skills

Discover How You Learn Some people learn best by seeing diagrams and charts. Others learn best by listening. Know what learning style works best for you and in which situation.

Academic Standards

English Language Arts

NCTE 12 Use language to accomplish individual purposes.

Math

NCTM (Number and Operations) Compute fluently and make reasonable estimates.

NCTM (Algebra) Represent and analyze mathematical situations and structures using algebraic symbols.

NCTM (Representation) Create and use representations to organize, record, and communicate mathematical ideas.

6. Beyond the Classroom Activity

Math: Validate Data   You have volunteered to sell refreshments at your high school football games. Open the data file **Refreshments.xlsx**, which lists items that you sell and their prices. In the file:

- Use data validation criteria so that each price is a whole number.
- Circle invalid data.
- Round invalid data to the nearest dollar.

Save your file as: Refreshments-[your first initial and last name]6.xlsx.

7. Standards at Work Activity

Microsoft Certified Application Specialist Correlation
Excel 3.1   *Reference data in formulas*

Select and Name a Range of Cells   You are in charge of selling souvenirs at the high school football games. Locate and open the data file **Merchandise.xlsx**. Use the Name Manager to name cells or cell ranges for the following cell(s):

- B3:B14
- C3:C14
- C18
- C19

Save your file as: Merchandise-[your first initial and last name]7.xlsx. Open a Word document and key a paragraph about why working with names makes it easier to understand the purpose of data in a worksheet.

8. 21st Century Skills Activity

Identify and Correct Errors   You can learn by correcting your mistakes. Although Excel comes with many error-checking functions, you should verify the accuracy of the data yourself. Always proofread your worksheets. You need to specify which columns should be checked for duplicate information in the football souvenir's list. Open your **Merchandise-7** file. In the file:

- Review the worksheet and delete any duplicate data.
- Use the **Remove Duplicates** data tool to check your work. Enter and label the number of duplicate values in cell **F3**.
- Delete the remaining duplicate rows from the souvenir list.

Click cell **F4** and key a paragraph describing how you can incorporate Excel tools and proofreading skills to prevent errors in your data. Reflect on how correcting your errors helped you learn from your mistakes. Save as: Merchandise-[your first initial and last name]8.xlsx.

Go Online   e-REVIEW

glencoe.com

Go to the **Online Learning Center** to complete the following review activities.

Online Self Checks
To test your knowledge of the material, click **Unit 2> Lesson 1** and choose **Self Checks**.

Interactive Review
To review the main points of the lesson, click **Unit 2> Lesson 1** and choose **Interactive Review**.

1. Start **Excel**.

2. Choose **Office>New**.

3. In the **New Workbook** dialog box, under **Templates**, click **Installed Templates** (see Figure 5.1).

4. Scroll down and select the **Time Card** template. Click **Create**.

5. Save the file as: TimeCard-[your first initial and last name] (for example, *TimeCard-jking*).

6. **(i)CHECK** Your screen should look like Figure 5.2.

7. Save your file.

→ *Continue to the next exercise.*

Tech Tip

If you are connected to the Internet, you can find many Excel templates at Microsoft Templates Online. In the **New Workbook** dialog box, under **Microsoft Office Online**, click a specific template category. Choose a template and, with your teacher's permission, click **Download**.

EXERCISE 5-1
Create a Workbook from a Template

You can use a **template** to create workbooks that complete specific tasks. Once you choose your template, you can fill in the details. Excel comes with common, or most frequently used, templates, such as invoices, time cards, and personal budgets that contain useful formulas and preset formatting.

FIGURE 5.1 New Workbook dialog box

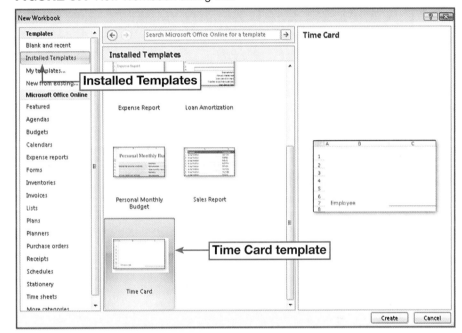

FIGURE 5.2 Time Card template

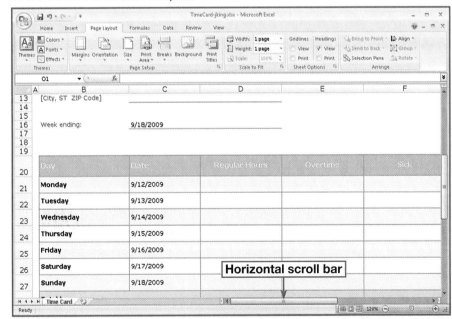

5. Name a Cell Range

Now that you have helped Elena correct the errors in her monthly budget, she wants the budget to be simpler and more efficient. She has asked you to use the Name Manager to create names for some of the data in the workbook to prevent errors when keying in data.

Step-By-Step

1. Open your **Budget-4** file. Save as: Budget-[your first initial and last name]5.

2. Select **A9:B17**. Choose **Formulas>Defined Names>Define Name**.

3. In the **New Name** dialog box, in the **Name** box, key: Expenses (if necessary).

4. ⓘ**CHECK** Your dialog box should look like Figure 1.37. Click **OK**.

5. Click cell **B18**. Click **Define Name**.

6. In the **New Name** dialog box, key: Total. Click **OK**.

7. Click **B7**. Click **Define Name**.

8. In the **New Name** dialog box, key: Income. Click **OK**.

9. ⓘ**CHECK** Your screen should look similar to Figure 1.38.

10. Save and close your file.

FIGURE 1.37 New Name dialog box

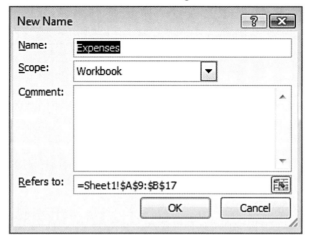

FIGURE 1.38 Cell B7 with name defined

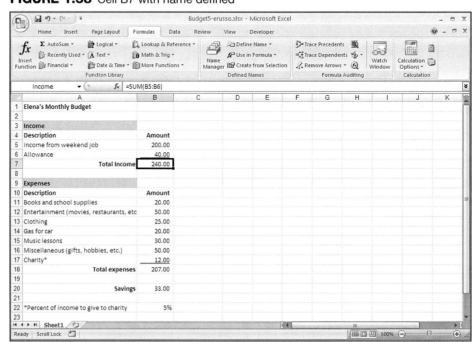

① In your **TimeCard** file, click the cell for **Monday's Regular Hours**.

② Key: 6. Press ENTER .

③ In the **Tuesday** row, key: 6.5.

④ Fill in the rest of the regular hours and overtime hours according to Figure 5.3.

⑤ In cell **D29**, key: 8. In cell **E29**, key: 12.

⑥ Scroll to the bottom right of the spreadsheet.

⑦ ⓘCHECK Your screen should look like Figure 5.4.

⑧ Save your file.

➥ *Continue to the next exercise.*

EXERCISE 5-2
Enter Data into a Template

The Time Card template is designed to automatically total your hours for you and calculate your weekly gross, or pretax, pay. All you have to do is enter your hours and the wage per hour.

FIGURE 5.3 Entering data

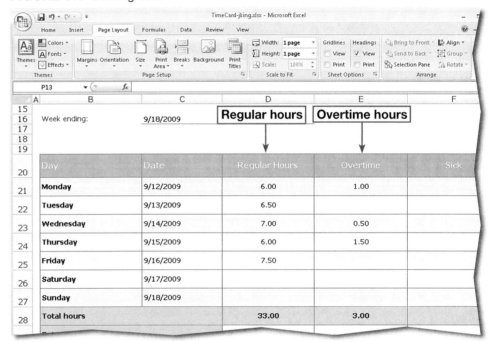

FIGURE 5.4 Totals

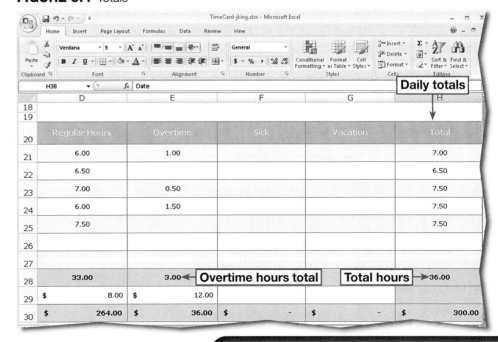

Shortcuts

You can use TAB to move across the spreadsheet. When you finish a row, use the Scroll key or mouse to move down to the next row.

Academic Skills

Click cell **D30** and look at the formula being used. The formula multiplies cell **D28** (hours being worked) by cell **D29** (the pay rate). Now scroll to cell **H30**. How does this formula work?

4. Evaluate Formulas

Elena has created a monthly budget. She knows that there are errors in her worksheet and she has asked for you to help her fix them. Use the Evaluate Formula tool to help her correct the errors.

Step-By-Step

1. Open your **Budget-3** file. Save as: Budget-[your first initial and last name]4.

2. Choose **Formulas> Formula Auditing> Evaluate Formula** 🔍.

3. (**i CHECK**) Your dialog box should look like Figure 1.35.

4. In the **Evaluate Formula** dialog box, click **Evaluate** (see Figure 1.35). The evaluation reads **B7*A22**.

5. Click **Evaluate**. The evaluation now reads **240*A22**.

6. Click **Evaluate**.

7. In the **Evaluate Formula** dialog box, click **Close**.

8. To fix the formula, double-click in cell **B17** and change **A22** to **B22**. Press ENTER.

9. Fix the formula in **B20**.

10. (**i CHECK**) Your screen should look like Figure 1.36.

11. Save and close your file.

FIGURE 1.35 Evaluate Formula dialog box

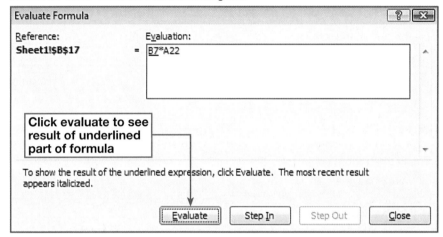

FIGURE 1.36 Corrected formulas

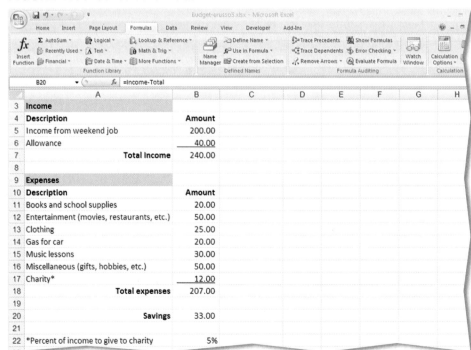

EXERCISE 5-3
Insert and Delete Worksheets

1 In your **TimeCard** file, click **Home>Cells>Insert> Insert Worksheet** . A blank worksheet appears after the **Time Card** worksheet (see Figure 5.5).

2 Click **Insert Worksheet** again. There are now three worksheets in the workbook.

3 Click the **Sheet1** tab.

4 Right-click and select **Delete**. Click the **Time Card** tab.

5 **CHECK** Your screen should look like Figure 5.6.

6 Save your file.

→ *Continue to the next exercise.*

If you need more worksheets in a workbook, you can insert a new worksheet. If a workbook has more worksheets than you need, you can delete a worksheet. You might want your workbook to have four worksheets if you want to submit all your weekly time cards for the month of April, for example.

FIGURE 5.5 New worksheet added to workbook

FIGURE 5.6 Worksheet deleted

3. Circle Invalid Data and Use Data Validation

Follow the steps to complete the activity.

Step-By-Step

1. Open the data file **Budget.xlsx**. Save as Budget-[your first initial and last name]3.

2. Use **Circle Invalid Data** to find the expenses that are too high.

3. **①CHECK** Your screen should look like Figure 1.33.

4. Click **B12**. Choose **Data> Data Tools>Data Validation**.

5. In the **Data Validation** dialog box, click **OK**.

6. Repeat steps 4 and 5 for **B16** and **B17**.

7. Click **B12**. Key: 50 and click ENTER.

8. Press ENTER. The red circle around cell **B12** disappears, indicating that the data are now valid.

9. Click cell **B16**. Key: 50. Press ENTER.

10. **①CHECK** Your screen should now look like Figure 1.34.

11. Save and close your file.

FIGURE 1.33 Invalid data circled

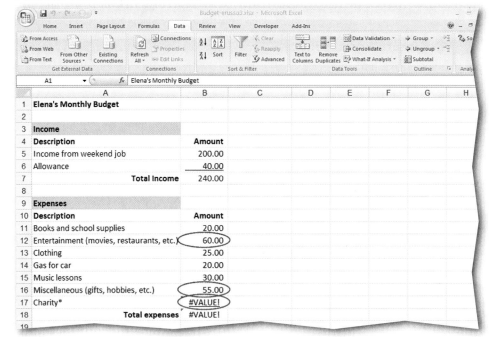

FIGURE 1.34 Worksheet after expense data is corrected

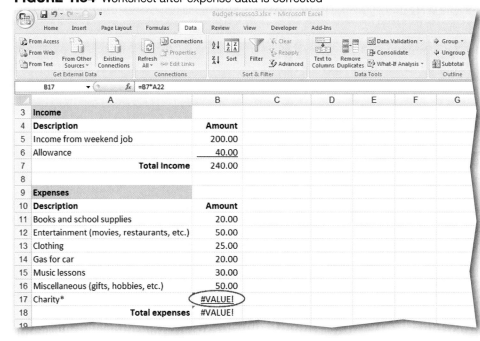

① In your **TimeCard** file, click the **Sheet2** tab.

② Choose **Home>Cells> Format**.

③ Under **Organize Sheets**, select **Move or Copy Sheet**. The **Move or Copy** dialog box opens (see Figure 5.7).

④ Under **Before sheet**, click **Time Card**.

⑤ Click **OK**.

⑥ **ⓘCHECK** Your screen should look like Figure 5.8.

⑦ Save and close your file.

➡ *Continue to the next exercise.*

Shortcuts

To rearrange worksheets faster, drag a sheet tab left or right to its new position.

Tech Tip

You can also move or copy a worksheet between workbooks by right-clicking the **Sheet** tab, selecting **Move or Copy**, and choosing the workbook from the **To book** list.

EXERCISE 5-4
Rearrange Worksheets

You can change the order of worksheets in a workbook. Excel allows you to arrange, or order, worksheets in the way that is most logical to you.

FIGURE 5.7 Move or Copy dialog box

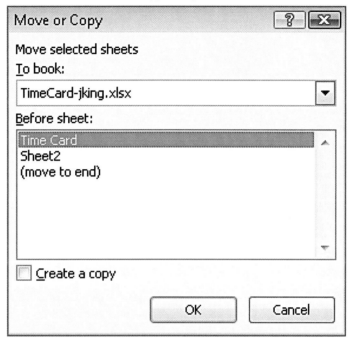

FIGURE 5.8 Repositioned worksheet

Sheet2 moved before Time Card worksheet

2. Create Subtotals and Group and Outline Data

Follow the steps to complete the activity. You must complete Practice It Activity 1 before doing this activity.

Step-By-Step

1. Open your **Jobs-1** file. Save as: Jobs-[your first initial and last name]2.

2. Click any cell in the list. Choose **Insert>Tables> Table**. Click **OK**.

3. In the **Tools** group, click **Convert to Range**. Click **Yes**.

4. Click any cell in the **Job** column. Choose **Home> Editing>Sort & Filter**. Click **Sort A to Z**.

5. Click any cell in the list. Choose **Data>Outline> Subtotal**. From the **At each change in** drop-down list, choose **Job**. Click **OK**.

6. **iCHECK** Your screen should look like Figure 1.31.

7. Click the **Outline** symbol for level **1**. Click the **Outline** symbol for level **2**. Click **Show Detail** to the left of row **25**.

8. **iCHECK** Your screen should look like Figure 1.32.

9. Save and close your file.

FIGURE 1.31 Subtotals for each type of job

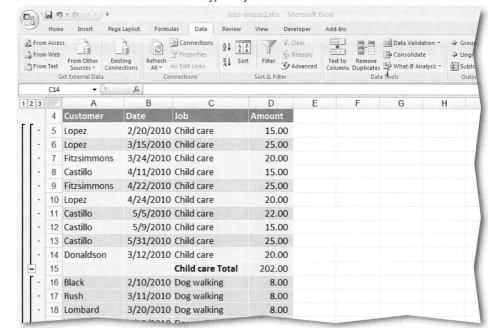

FIGURE 1.32 Detail shown for dog walking

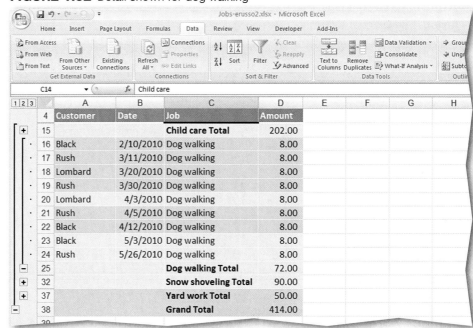

EXERCISE 5-5
Split, Freeze, and Unfreeze Workbooks

1. Open the data file **Insurance.xlsx**. Save as: Insurance-[your first initial and last name].

2. Click the **Year-to-Date Sales** worksheet tab. If necessary, scroll up and click cell **A11**.

3. Choose **View>Windows> Freeze Panes**. Choose **Freeze Panes**. Scroll down to row **64**. Only the bottom window scrolls down (see Figure 5.9).

4. Click **Freeze Panes** and select **Unfreeze Panes**.

5. Choose **Window>Split**.

6. Use the upper vertical scroll bar to scroll down to row **27**. Use the lower vertical scroll bar to scroll down to row **45**.

7. **⬤CHECK** Your screen should look like Figure 5.10.

8. Click **Split**. Save your file.

↪ *Continue to the next exercise.*

Tech Tip

If your window is split into two panes, double-click any part of the split bar that divides the panes to restore the window.

If you move far enough down or to the right in a worksheet, you will no longer see the row and column headings. Excel allows you to **freeze** headings to keep them in place while you move around. If you need to look at two parts of a worksheet that are too far apart to view at the same time, you can **split** the window. Splitting the window divides it into two panes that you can scroll independently.

FIGURE 5.9 Freeze a workbook

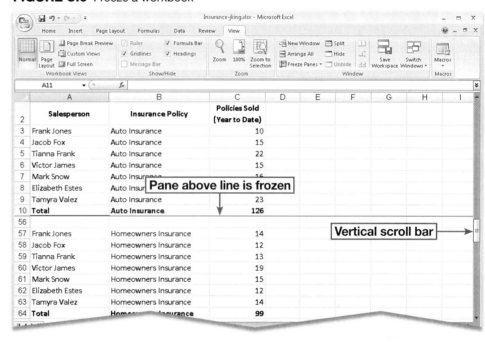

FIGURE 5.10 Split a workbook

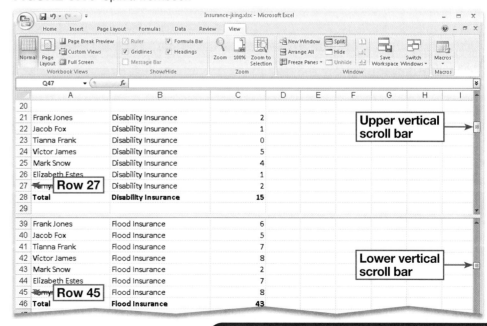

1. Create a List and Use Advanced Filters

Follow the steps to complete the activity.

Step-By-Step

1 Open the data file **Jobs.xlsx**. Save as: Jobs-[your first initial and last name]1.

2 Click any cell in the list of data. Choose **Data>Sort & Filter>Filter** . In the dialog box, click **OK**.

3 Click the drop-down arrow to the right of **Date**. Choose **Sort Oldest to Newest**. The list is sorted in ascending order by date.

4 In cell **C2**, key: Child care. In cell **D2**, key: >20.

5 **CHECK** Your screen should look like Figure 1.29.

6 Click any cell in the list. Choose **Data>Sort & Filter>Advanced** .

7 In the **Criteria Range** box, key: A1:D2. Click **OK**.

8 **CHECK** Your screen should look like Figure 1.30.

9 Click **Clear** in the **Sort & Filter** group to turn off the filter.

10 Save and close your file.

FIGURE 1.29 Criteria range above list

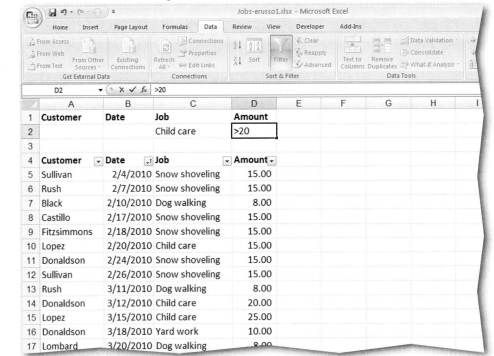

FIGURE 1.30 Filtered list

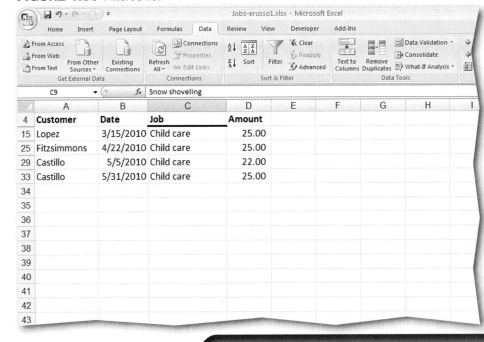

EXERCISE 5-6
Hide, Unhide, and Arrange Workbooks

You can arrange several workbooks to organize them on the screen. You can also hide a workbook from view without closing it.

1 With your **Insurance** file still open, open the data files **Pricing.xlsx** and **Guidelines.xlsx**. Be sure to open the files in order so **Guidelines** is the active file.

2 In the **Guidelines** file, choose **View>Window> Hide** (see Figure 5.11). This will hide **Guidelines**.

3 Choose **View>Window> Arrange All**. In the **Arrange Windows** box, click **Horizontal**. Click **OK**.

4 *CHECK* Your screen should look like Figure 5.12.

5 Choose **View>Window> Unhide**. Select **Guidelines**. Click **OK**.

6 Close **Guidelines** and **Pricing**. Do not save your changes.

7 Click **Maximize** in the **Insurance** window.

8 Save your file.

Continue to the next exercise.

FIGURE 5.11 Window group

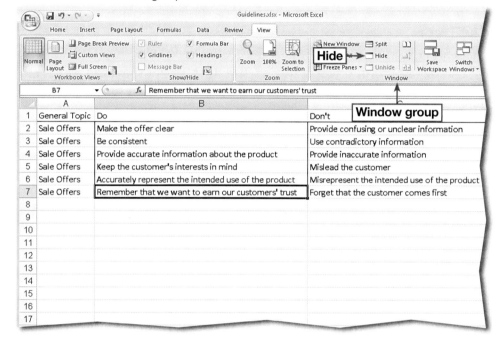

FIGURE 5.12 Windows arranged horizontally

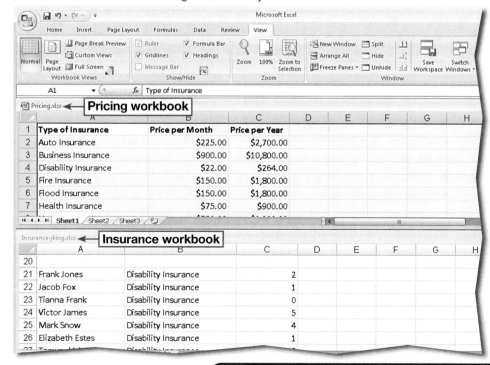

Tech Tip

You can delete a worksheet quickly by right-clicking on the sheet's tab and selecting **Delete**.

Vocabulary

Key Terms

advanced filter

criteria

data validation

duplicate value

Evaluate Formula

name

Name Manager

subset

subtotal

Academic Vocabulary

convert

error

interpret

sum

Review Vocabulary

Complete the following statements on a separate piece of paper. Choose from the Vocabulary list on the left to complete the statements.

1. If you create a table from a list of items, you can ——————— the table back to a normal range of data. (p. 153)

2. When you use an advanced filter, only those items in a range of cells or table that meet certain ——————— will be displayed. (p. 155)

3. A(n) ——————— can be used in a formula in the same way as a conventional cell reference. (p. 163)

4. To control the type of data entered into cells, apply ———————. (p. 158)

5. A(n) ——————— is when all values in a row are an exact match of all the values in another row. (p. 161)

Vocabulary Activity

6. Make flash cards based on the vocabulary terms from this lesson.
   A. On the front of the card, write the vocabulary word.
   B. Look at each vocabulary word. On the back of the card, write the definition.
   C. Team up with a classmate and take turns using the flash cards to quiz each other.

Review Key Concepts

Answer the following questions on a separate piece of paper.

7. When you use an advanced filter, what happens to data that does not meet the criteria you set? (p. 155)
   A. It is displayed dimly.
   B. It is temporarily hidden.
   C. It is deleted.
   D. Its value is changed.

8. What is the total of a group of items within a larger set of items? (p. 156)
   A. subtotal
   B. grand total
   C. AutoSum
   D. total

9. Which of the following tools identifies inaccurate data? (p. 160)
   A. data validation
   B. Group and Outline Data
   C. Circle Invalid Data
   D. Evaluate Formula

10. What does Evaluate Formula do? (p. 162)
    A. points to possible sources of an error
    B. displays tracer arrows
    C. steps through a calculation
    D. displays an explanation of an error

1 In your **Insurance** file, choose **Office>Save As**. The **Save As** dialog box opens.

2 In the **Save as type** box, select **Web page**. Next to **Save**, click **Selection: Sheet**.

3 In the **File** name box, change the file name to Sales Numbers.

4 (CHECK) Your dialog box should look like Figure 5.13. Click **Publish**.

5 In the **Publish as Web Page** dialog box, click **Publish**.

6 Choose **Office>Open**. Select **Sales Numbers .html**.

7 (CHECK) Your screen should look like Figure 5.14.

8 Close the Web browser.

9 Save your file.

↳ *Continue to the next exercise.*

You Should Know

The extension for a Web page is .htm or .html. You do not have to key this extension in the **File** name box as long as **Web Page** is selected in the **Save as type** box.

EXERCISE 5-7
Save and Publish Worksheets as Web Pages

You can save a worksheet, or an entire workbook, as a Web page. This will convert, or change, the information into a format that can be viewed on the Web. When you open an Excel file that has been saved as a Web page, the file opens in a Web browser, not in Excel. Saving an Excel document to a Web format means that people can view it even if they do not have Excel. They just need access to a Web browser. You can use Web Page Preview to see what your worksheet will look like on the Web.

FIGURE 5.13 Save As dialog box

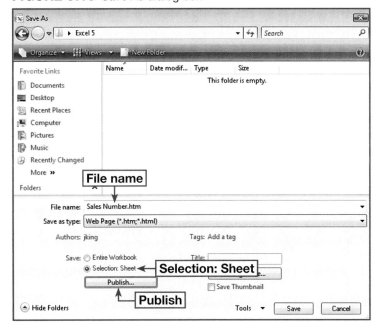

FIGURE 5.14 Sales numbers Web page

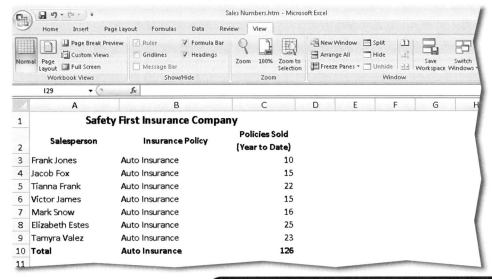

Making Complex Choices

At home, at school, and at work, making tough choices is a part of everyday life. For example, Sarah's teacher is encouraging her to take an advanced math course next fall. Taking the course will mean a lot of extra homework. Sarah already has an after-school job, and she plans to try out for the school play next fall.

When Sarah asks for advice, her parents say taking the math course might help her get into college. Her friends are worried that Sarah will not try out for the play. Sarah weighs the pros and cons and follows some simple problem-solving and decision-making steps she learned at school. Finally, Sarah decides to take the course and cut back her hours at work.

MEET THE MANAGER

Making complex choices is an important part of running a business. Leo Landry, manager of Children's Book Shop in Brookline, Massachusetts, says his employees often have to make difficult decisions about books. They sometimes decide not to carry a popular book they think is low quality, even though they risk losing sales. Other times they try something else. For example, the staff once decided to stock just two copies of a best-selling book that they did not think was very well-written. "We knew people were going to ask for it. Instead of sending customers elsewhere, we gave them a chance to decide about the book here. Most of them looked at it and just handed it back."

Deciding among favorite activities is a choice most of us make every day.

SKILLBUILDER

1. Identify What factors does Sarah have to consider when she makes her decision?

2. Describe What is one decision that has been made at Children's Book Shop?

3. Apply When have you had to make a complex choice? Describe what factors you considered when making your decision. Would you make the same decision if you had it to do again?

1. In your **Insurance** file, choose **Office>Print> Print Preview**. The **Print Preview** screen opens (see Figure 5.15).

2. Click **Next Page** to view the second page that will be printed.

3. Click **Previous Page** .

4. Click **Zoom** .

5. **CHECK** Your screen should look like Figure 5.16.

6. Click **Close Print Preview**.

7. Save your file.

Continue to the next exercise.

You Should Know

In **Print Preview**, your pointer becomes a magnifying glass. Clicking on the document will automatically zoom.

Microsoft Office 2007

You can customize Excel and place the Print Preview feature onto the Quick Access Toolbar (QAT) in order to quickly preview a worksheet.

EXERCISE 5-8
Use Print Preview Features

You can use Print Preview to see what a worksheet will look like before you print it. This preview helps you decide whether your printout will be readable and balanced, and whether all the data will fit on a single page.

FIGURE 5.15 Print Preview screen

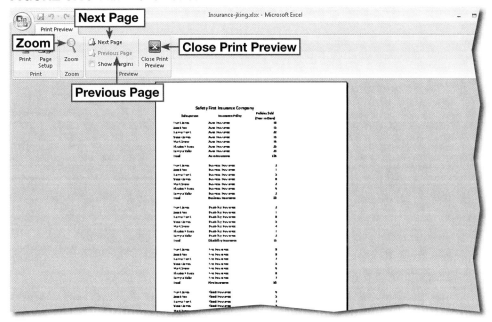

FIGURE 5.16 Zoom used in Print Preview view

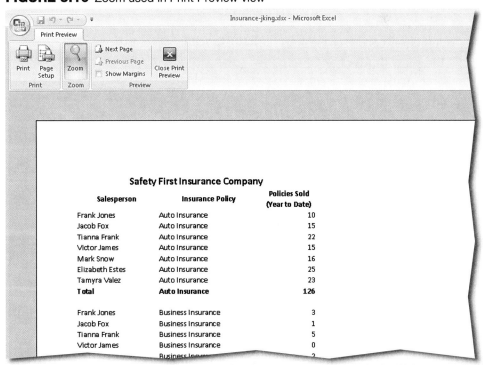

	Safety First Insurance Company		
Salesperson	**Insurance Policy**	**Policies Sold** (Year to Date)
Frank Jones	Auto Insurance	10
Jacob Fox	Auto Insurance	15
Tianna Frank	Auto Insurance	22
Victor James	Auto Insurance	15
Mark Snow	Auto Insurance	16
Elizabeth Estes	Auto Insurance	25
Tamyra Valez	Auto Insurance	23
Total	**Auto Insurance**	**126**
Frank Jones	Business Insurance	3
Jacob Fox	Business Insurance	1
Tianna Frank	Business Insurance	5
Victor James	Business Insurance	0
	Business Insurance	2

1. In your **Blues** file, select cells **A1:D1**.

2. Choose **Home> Alignment>Merge & Center**.

3. **CHECK** Your screen should look like Figure 1.27.

4. Choose **Home> Alignment** and click the **Merge & Center** drop-down arrow. Select **Unmerge Cells**. Cells A1:D1 are now unmerged.

5. Choose **Home> Alignment** and click the **Merge & Center** drop-down arrow. Select **Merge Cells**. The cells are once again merged but not centered.

6. Choose **Home> Alignment** and click the **Merge & Center** drop-down arrow. Select **Unmerge Cells**. Cells A1: D1 are again unmerged.

7. **CHECK** Your screen should look like Figure 1.28.

8. Save your workbook.

9. Exit Excel.

EXERCISE 1-12
Merge and Split Cells in a Range

In some cases, you may need to merge cells together in order to make your workbook look better. When cells are merged, two or more cells are combined and the information inside the cells is either centered in that area or left aligned. If you decide that you no longer want cells to be merged, you can split the merged cells back into their normal sizes.

FIGURE 1.27 Merged and centered cells

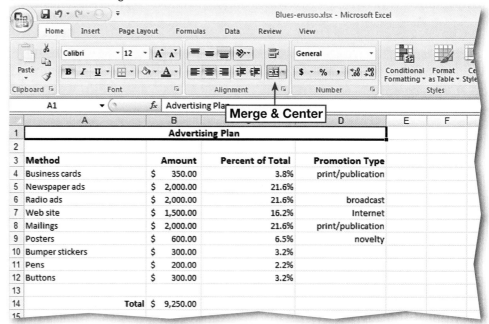

FIGURE 1.28 Split cells

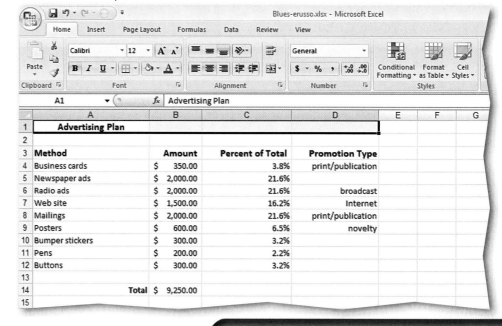

1 In your **Insurance** file, select the **Page Layout** tab. Click the **Page Setup Dialog Box Launcher**.

2 In the **Page Setup** dialog box, click the **Page** tab. Under **Orientation**, click **Landscape** (see Figure 5.17).

3 In the dialog box, click **Print Preview**. If necessary, click **Zoom**.

4 *i*CHECK Your screen should look like Figure 5.18.

5 Click **Page Setup** 📄.

6 In the **Page Setup** dialog box, click **Portrait**. Click **OK**. Your preview should now be in **Portrait** view.

7 Click **Close Print Preview**. Your worksheet should now be in **Normal** view.

8 Save your file.

➡ *Continue to the next exercise.*

Shortcuts

To confirm that the worksheet is in **Normal** view, click the **View** tab. **Normal View** should be selected in the **Workbook Views** group.

EXERCISE 5-9
Change Page Orientation

Use Page Setup to change paper size and **page orientation**. The default page orientation is **portrait**, or vertical. For a horizontal layout, change the orientation to **landscape**, or horizontal. Landscape orientation can be very helpful if your worksheets contain a lot of data in columns.

FIGURE 5.17 Page Setup dialog box

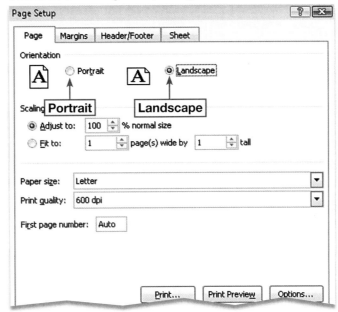

FIGURE 5.18 Worksheet viewed in Landscape orientation

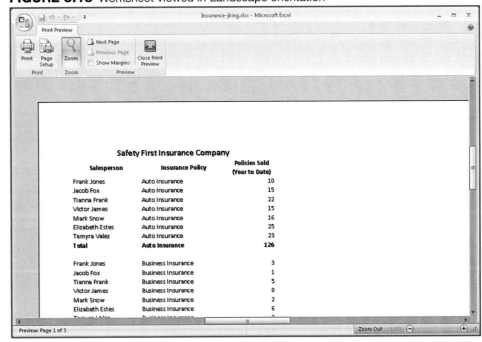

EXERCISE 1-11
Modify and Delete a Named Cell Range

1. In the **Advertising plan** sheet, choose **Formulas> Defined Names>Name Manager**.

2. In the **Name Manager** dialog box, select **data**. Click **Edit**. In the **Edit Name** dialog box, click the **Data Range** button (see Figure 1.25).

3. Select **A3:B12**. Press ENTER.

4. **CHECK** Your screen should look like Figure 1.25. Click **OK**.

5. Close the **Name Manager** dialog box. Select cells **A3:B12**.

6. Click **C3:C12**. Click **Name Manager**. In the **Name Manager** dialog box, click **New**.

7. In the **Name** box, key: Percentage. Click **OK**. Click **Close**.

8. **CHECK** Your screen should look like Figure 1.26.

9. Click **Name Manager**. Select **Percentage** and click **Delete**. Click **OK**.

10. Close the **Name Manager**. Save and close your file.

➡ *Continue to the next exercise.*

If you need to change the name of a cell or a range of cells, you can use the **Name Manager** to modify or delete the defined names used in a workbook. For example, you may want to locate and edit customer names with errors, confirm the value or cell reference of a name, or add a new name to a database.

FIGURE 1.25 Amount column added to data range

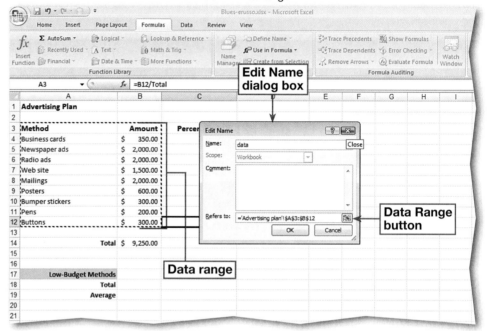

FIGURE 1.26 Percentage Name in Name box

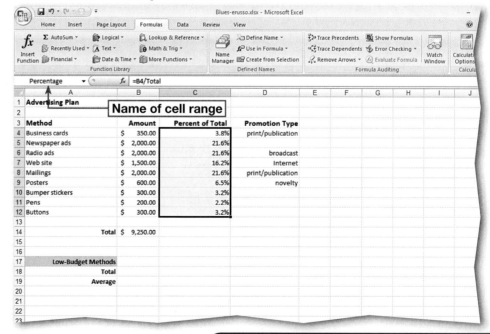

EXERCISE 5-10
Set the Print Area

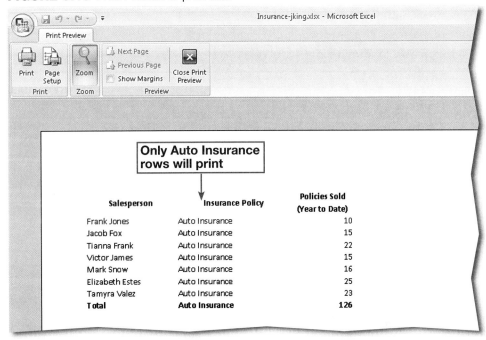

By default, when you choose Print, the entire worksheet prints. If you want to print only a selection of the worksheet, such as a range of cells, set the **print area**. The next time you open the worksheet in Excel, the print area settings you created will be in place. To print the entire worksheet, clear the print area.

1 In your **Insurance** file, select **A2:C10**.

2 Choose **Page Layout> Page Setup>Print Area** and select **Set Print Area**.

3 Choose **Office>Print> Print Preview**. If necessary, click **Zoom**. Notice that only the area that you selected as the print area will print (see Figure 5.19).

4 Click **Close Print Preview**.

5 Click cell **A2**.

6 ⓘCHECK Your screen should look like Figure 5.20.

7 Choose **Page Layout> Page Setup>Print Area** and select **Clear Print Area**.

8 Save your file.

➙ *Continue to the next exercise.*

FIGURE 5.19 Print Preview of print area

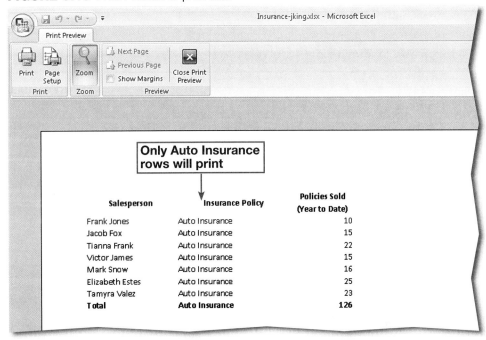

FIGURE 5.20 Print area selected in worksheet

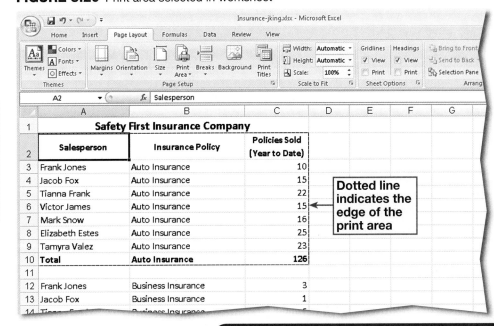

Troubleshooter

Once a print area has been set, it remains the same until you clear or change it, even after you save and close a file.

EXERCISE 1-10
Use a Name in a Formula

1. In your **Blues** file, click the **Advertising plan** sheet tab. Click cell **C4**.

2. Key: =B4/Total (see Figure 1.23).

3. Press ENTER. The percent of the total advertising expenses for **Business cards** reappears.

4. Click cell **C4**. Drag the fill handle down to copy the formula to cells **C5:C12**. Click cell **C10**.

5. ⓘCHECK Your screen should look like Figure 1.24.

6. Click cell **C12**. Look in the formula bar. The formula is **B12/Total**.

7. Click cell **C6**. Look in the formula bar. The formula is **B6/Total**.

8. Save your file.

↳ *Continue to the next exercise.*

You Should Know

Names adjust automatically as you insert and delete rows and columns. For example, suppose the name *July* refers to H5:H24. If you delete three rows from the middle of the range, *July* would then refer to H5:H21.

It is often convenient to use a name in a formula. For example, the name *January* is easier to remember than B4:B67—and less likely to be miskeyed! Choose meaningful names so formulas will be easy to read and interpret, or understand, when you analyze data.

FIGURE 1.23 Formula using a name

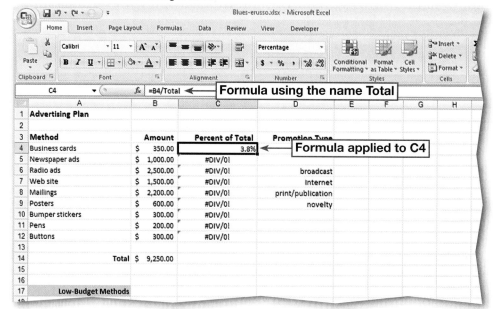

FIGURE 1.24 Corrected formulas

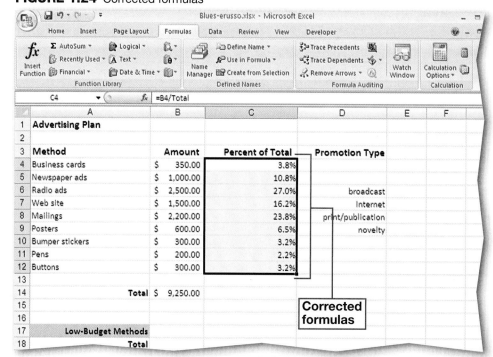

EXERCISE 5-11
Create Headers and Footers

1. In your **Insurance** file, click the **Page Setup Dialog Box Launcher**.

2. In the **Page Setup** dialog box, click the **Header/Footer** tab. Click the **Header** drop-down arrow. Select your **Insurance** file (see Figure 5.21).

3. Click the **Footer** drop-down arrow. Select **Page 1**.

4. **ⓘCHECK** Your dialog box should look like Figure 5.21. Click **OK**.

5. Choose **Office>Print> Print Preview**. If necessary, click **Zoom** to zoom out.

6. **ⓘCHECK** Your screen should look like Figure 5.22.

7. Click **Close Print Preview**.

8. Save your file.

➡ *Continue to the next exercise.*

A **header** is text that appears at the top of the printed page. A **footer** is text that appears at the bottom of the printed page. The header and footer often contain the file name, sheet name, page number, current date, or name of the author.

FIGURE 5.21 Page Setup dialog box

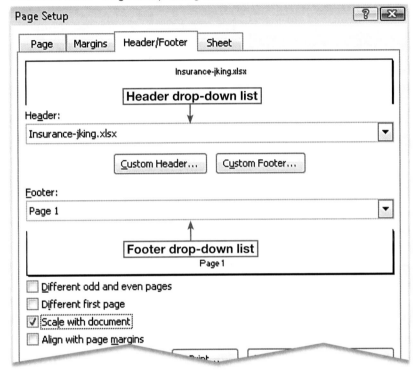

FIGURE 5.22 Header and footer

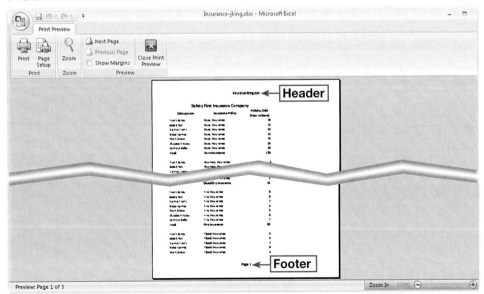

> **Microsoft Office 2007**
>
> Use Excel's **Header & Footer Tools** contextual tab to add built-in header and footer elements, such as the page number, number of pages, current date or time, file name, or file path.

Step-By-Step

1 In the **Advertising plan** worksheet of your **Blues** file, select **A3:A12**.

2 Choose **Formulas> Defined Names> Define Name** 📇.

3 In the **New Name** dialog box, in the **Name** box, delete **Method** and key: data.

4 ⓘCHECK Your dialog box should look like Figure 1.21.

5 Click **OK**. The selected range is now named **data**.

6 Click cell **B14**. Click **Define Name** 📇.

7 The word *Total* should appear in the **Name** box. Click **OK**. The cell is now named *Total*.

8 ⓘCHECK Your screen should look like Figure 1.22. Save your file.

➡ *Continue to the next exercise.*

Academic Skills

If a formula does not work, reword the formula in mathematical terms on a sheet of paper. Then try to solve the problem and find the source of your error. **Use Evaluate Formula** to check your work.

EXERCISE 1-9
Name a Cell Range

If you need to refer to a certain cell or range of cells often, give it a **name**. You can then refer to the cell or range by the name instead of by the cell reference.

FIGURE 1.21 New Name dialog box

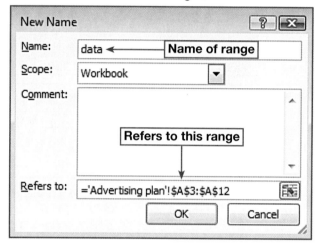

FIGURE 1.22 Named cell

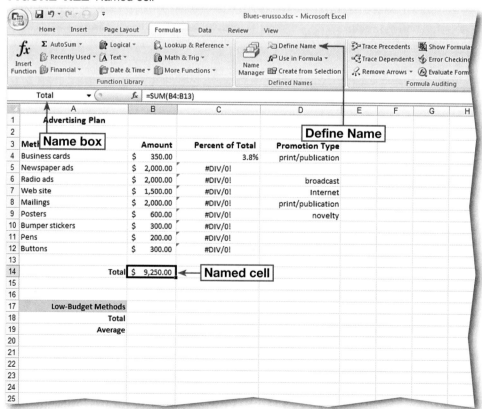

EXERCISE 5-12
Preview and Modify Page Breaks

A **page break** is the place where one printed page ends and the next begins. You can move a page break to control which information prints on each page. You can also insert page breaks to force a page to break at a certain point.

FIGURE 5.23 Page Break Preview

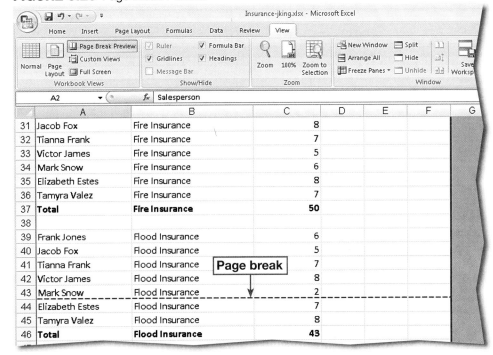

FIGURE 5.24 Modified page break

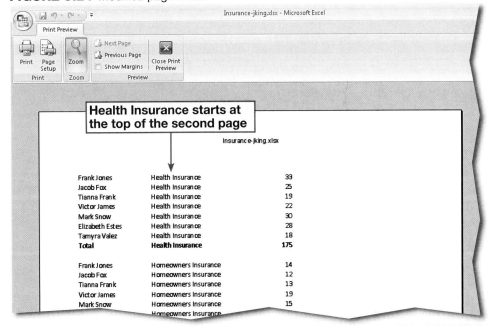

1. In your **Insurance** file, choose **View>Workbook Views>Page Break Preview**. Click **OK**.

2. Click on the blue vertical line and drag it between columns **D** and **E**. Click on the blue vertical line and drag it between **F** and **G** (see Figure 5.23).

3. Scroll down until you see the dotted blue horizontal line between rows **43** and **44** (see Figure 5.23).

4. Point to the horizontal page break. Drag it down between rows **46** and **47**.

5. Choose **Workbook Views>Normal**.

6. Choose **Office>Print>Print Preview**. Click **Zoom**.

7. Click **Next Page**.

8. **CHECK** Your screen should look like Figure 5.24.

9. Click **Close Print Preview**.

10. Save your file.

Continue to the next exercise.

Step-By-Step

1. In your **Blues** file, in the **Advertising plan** worksheet, click cell **C4**. Key: =B4/B14. Press ENTER.

2. Click cell **C4**. Choose **Home>Number** and click the **Percent Style** %.

3. Click **Increase Decimal**.

4. In your **Blues** file, click cell **C4** and drag the fill handle down to copy the formula to **C5:C12**.

5. Click cell **C5**. Choose **Formulas>Formula Auditing>Evaluate Formula**.

6. **CHECK** Your dialog box should look like Figure 1.19.

7. In the **Evaluate Formula** dialog box, click **Evaluate** twice.

8. Click **Evaluate** again. The evaluation now reads **#DIV/0!**. Click **Close**.

9. **CHECK** Your screen should look like Figure 1.20.

10. Save your file.

➡ *Continue to the next exercise.*

EXERCISE 1-8
Use the Evaluate Formula Feature

Evaluate Formula is the most complete error-checking tool available in Excel. You can use the Evaluate Formula tool to see how Excel attempted to calculate the formula. The Evaluate Formula tool will show you what part of the formula is not working. Then you can make changes so that the calculation function will work properly.

FIGURE 1.19 Evaluate Formula dialog box

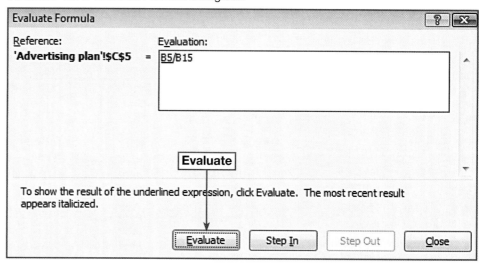

FIGURE 1.20 Percent Style and Increase Decimal buttons

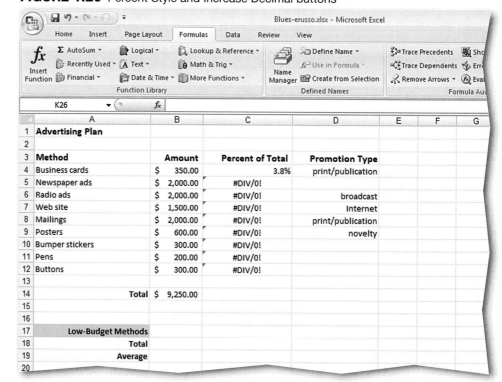

1. In your **Insurance** file, select **A3:C91**.

2. Change the **Font Size** to **12**.

3. Choose **Office>Print> Print Preview**.

4. Click **Next Page**.

5. **CHECK** Your screen should look like Figure 5.25.

6. Click **Close Print Preview**.

7. Choose **Page Layout** and then click the **Page Setup Dialog Box Launcher**.

8. In the **Page Setup** dialog box, click the **Margins** tab.

9. In the **Top** and **Bottom** boxes, click the down arrow until the boxes read **0.75** (see Figure 5.26).

10. Click **Print Preview**.

Continued on the next page.

Academic Skills

In Step 9, 0.75 represents that the top and bottom margins are 3/4 of an inch from the top and bottom of the page. What does the number 0.5 represent in the Footer box?

EXERCISE 5-13
Setup Options for Printing

If your worksheet does not fit on a single printed page and you would like it to, you can decrease the **margin**, the amount of space between the text and edge of the page. Use the Page Setup group or Page Setup dialog box to change a worksheet's margins. You can also use the Options button in the Page Setup dialog box to select other printing options. For example, you can choose to have certain rows or columns repeat on every page.

FIGURE 5.25 Split data in Print Preview

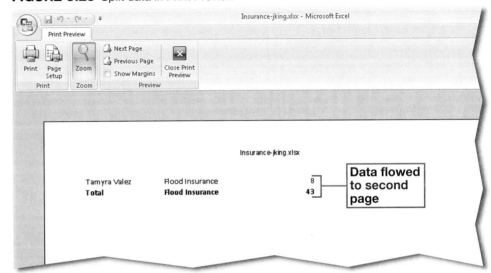

FIGURE 5.26 Page Setup dialog box

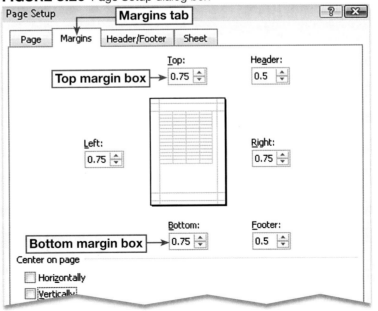

Step-By-Step

1 In your **Blues** file, in the **Advertising plan** worksheet, select cells **A4:B14**.

2 Choose **Data>Data Tools>Remove Duplicates** .

3 In the **Remove Duplicates** dialog box, click **Select All** to delete the duplicate values in the **Method** and **Amount** columns.

4 **ⓘCHECK** Your dialog box should look like Figure 1.17. Click **OK**.

5 A warning message indicates how many duplicate values were removed and how many unique values remain. Click **OK**.

6 **ⓘCHECK** Your screen should look like Figure 1.18. Note the duplicate values for Bumper stickers are no longer listed in the Advertising Plan.

7 Select rows **14** and **15**. Choose **Home>Cells** and click the drop-down arrow for **Delete Cells** . Select **Delete Sheet Rows**.

8 Save your file.

➡ *Continue to the next exercise.*

EXERCISE 1-7
Remove Duplicate Values

You may want to delete duplicate values from a sheet. A **duplicate value** occurs when all values in a row are an exact match of all the values in another row. Using the Remove Duplicates filter allows you to specify which columns should be checked for duplicate information. In this exercise, you will remove the duplicate advertising methods that appear in the Advertising Plan.

FIGURE 1.17 Remove Duplicates dialog box

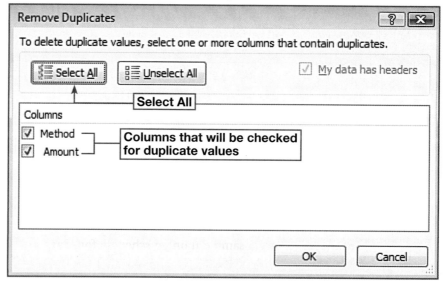

FIGURE 1.18 Duplicate values removed from Advertising Plan

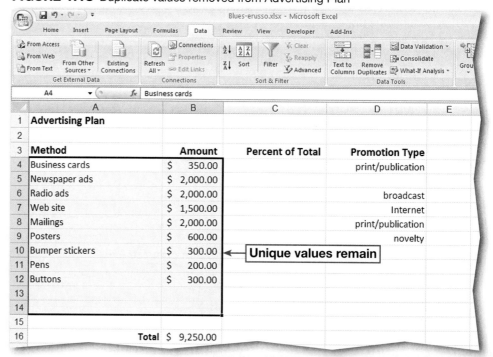

EXERCISE 5-13 (Continued)
Setup Options for Printing

11 Use the vertical scroll bar to scroll to the bottom of the first page.

12 **⏺CHECK** Your screen should look like Figure 5.27.

13 Click **Next Page** 🔲. Scroll to the top of the page. The column headings are not on the second page.

14 Click **Close Print Preview**. Click the **Page Setup Dialog Box Launcher**. Click the **Sheet** tab.

15 Under **Print titles**, in the **Rows to repeat at top** pane, key: A2:C2. Click **OK**.

16 Choose **Office>Print> Print Preview**. Click **Next Page**.

17 **⏺CHECK** Your screen should look similar to Figure 5.28.

18 Click **Close Print Preview**.

19 Save your file.

➡ *Continue to the next exercise.*

Microsoft Office 2007

You can also specify custom page margins by choosing **Page Layout> Page Setup>Margins** and selecting **Custom Margins**.

FIGURE 5.27 New bottom margin

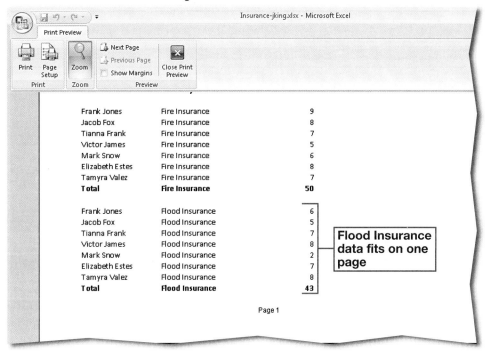

FIGURE 5.28 Repeated row

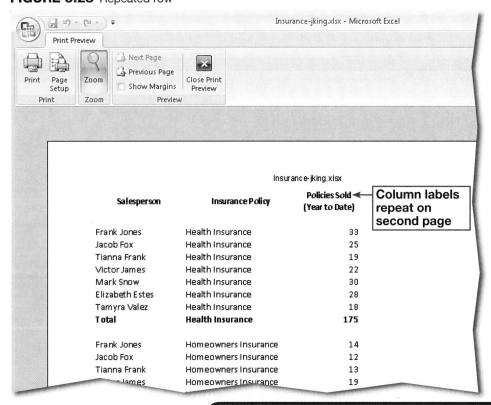

① In your **Blues** file, in the **Advertising plan** worksheet, choose **Data>Data Tools** and click the **Data Validation** drop-down arrow.

② Select **Circle Invalid Data**.

③ ⓘ**CHECK** Your screen should look like Figure 1.15.

④ Click cell **B6**. Key: 2000.

⑤ Press ENTER. The red circle around cell **B6** disappears, indicating that the data are now valid.

⑥ Click cell **B8**. Key: 2000. Press ENTER.

⑦ ⓘ**CHECK** Your screen should look like Figure 1.16.

⑧ Save your file.

→ *Continue to the next exercise.*

Troubleshooter

The **Circle Invalid Data** feature circles any cells that do not meet their data validation criteria, including values that were keyed, copied, or filled in the cells, or calculated by formulas.

EXERCISE 1-6
Circle Invalid Data

Data validation is designed to prevent a user from keying invalid data into a cell. It does not prevent an *error*, or mistake, when you enter data in a cell by copying or filling. If you apply data validation after keying data into a worksheet, you can use the Circle Invalid Data tool to highlight data that do not meet the criteria. This tool puts a red circle around any data that is not allowed so that you can easily find and correct problems.

FIGURE 1.15 Invalid data circled

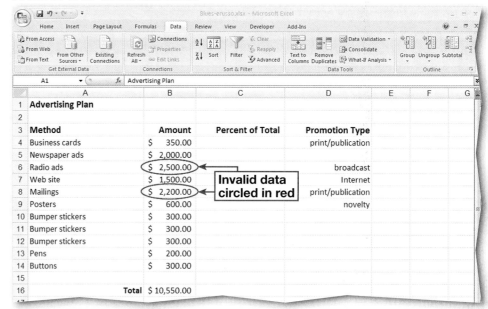

FIGURE 1.16 Worksheet after data corrected

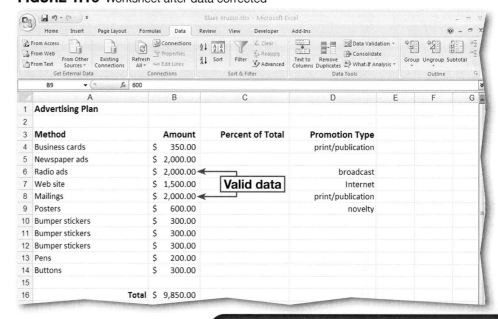

1. In your **Insurance** file, select **A12:C19**.

2. Choose **Office>Print**.

3. In the **Print** dialog box, under **Print what**, click **Selection** (see Figure 5.29).

4. Click **Preview**.

5. **ⓘCHECK** Your screen should look like Figure 5.30.

6. With your teacher's permission, click **Print** in the **Print Preview** screen to print the selection.

7. Click **Close Print Preview**.

8. Save your file.

→ *Continue to the next exercise.*

Troubleshooter

It is not enough to select a range of cells before you print. Remember to choose **Selection** in the **Print** dialog box.

EXERCISE 5-14
Print a Selection

If you always want to print a certain range, make it the print area. The next time you open the file, you will not have to change the print area, because Excel will remember your settings. If you want to print a range just once, you should print it as a selection.

FIGURE 5.29 Print dialog box

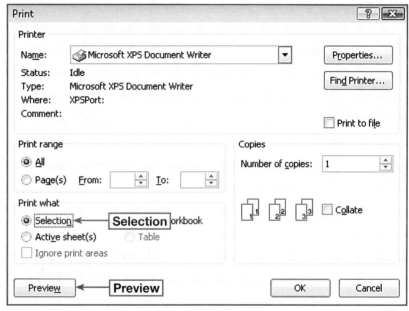

FIGURE 5.30 Print Selection in Print Preview

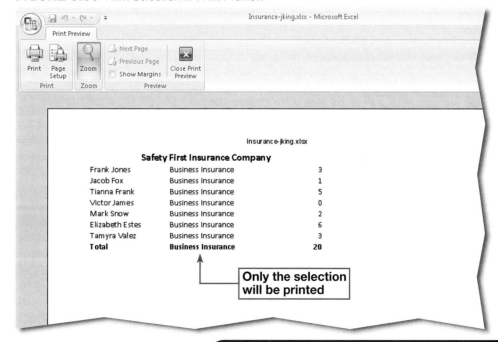

Step-By-Step

9 Select cells **D4:D14** and choose **Data>Data Tools> Data Validation**.

10 In the **Data Validation** dialog box, click the **Allow** drop-down arrow. Choose **List**.

11 Click the icon on the right side of the **Source** box (see Figure 1.13). Select **D6:D9**. Press ENTER.

12 ⓘ**CHECK** Your dialog box should look like Figure 1.13. Click **OK**.

13 Click the drop-down arrow to the right of cell **D4**.

14 ⓘ**CHECK** Your screen should look like Figure 1.14.

15 Select **print/publication** from the list.

16 Save your file.

➡ *Continue to the next exercise.*

You Should Know

To specify whether a cell can be left blank, select or clear the **Ignore blank** check box in the **Data Validation** dialog box.

EXERCISE 1-5 (Continued)
Apply Data Validation Criteria

FIGURE 1.13 Data Validation dialog box

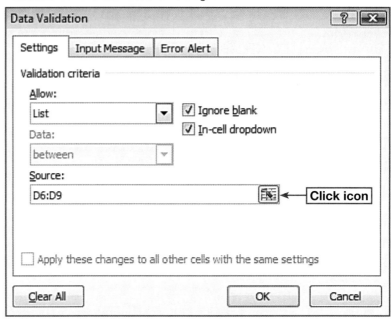

FIGURE 1.14 Drop-down list added to Promotion Type column

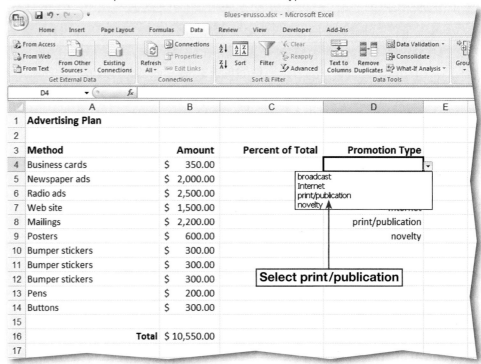

EXERCISE 5-15
Print a Workbook

1. In your **Insurance** file, scroll up and click cell **A1** so the range is no longer selected.

2. Choose **Office>Print**.

3. In the **Print** dialog box, under **Print what**, click **Active sheet(s)** (see Figure 5.31).

4. With your teacher's permission, click **OK** to print the worksheet.

5. Choose **Office>Print**.

6. In the **Print** dialog box, under **Print what**, click **Entire workbook**.

7. With your teacher's permission, click **OK** to print the workbook.

8. ⓘ**CHECK** Your screen should look like Figure 5.32.

9. Save your file.

➡ *Continue to the next exercise.*

Microsoft Office 2007

If a workbook has a defined print area, Excel will only print the area. Check **Ignore print areas** in the **Print** dialog box if you do not want to print a defined print area.

By default, when you choose Print, the current worksheet prints. You can also choose to print the entire workbook.

FIGURE 5.31 Print dialog box

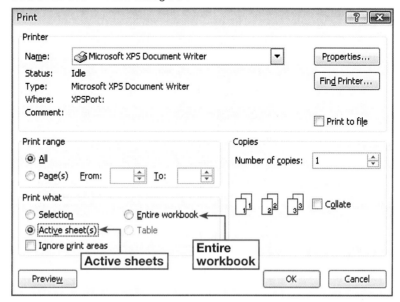

FIGURE 5.32 Workbook

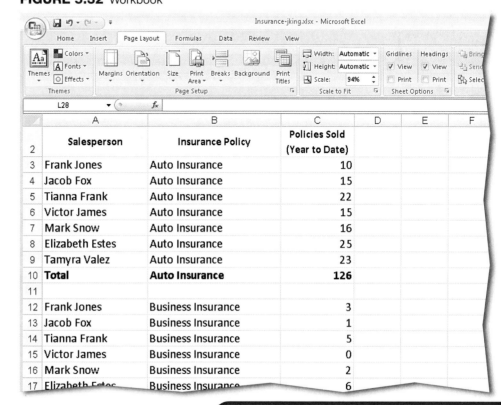

	A	B	C	D	E	F
2	**Salesperson**	**Insurance Policy**	**Policies Sold (Year to Date)**			
3	Frank Jones	Auto Insurance	10			
4	Jacob Fox	Auto Insurance	15			
5	Tianna Frank	Auto Insurance	22			
6	Victor James	Auto Insurance	15			
7	Mark Snow	Auto Insurance	16			
8	Elizabeth Estes	Auto Insurance	25			
9	Tamyra Valez	Auto Insurance	23			
10	**Total**	**Auto Insurance**	**126**			
11						
12	Frank Jones	Business Insurance	3			
13	Jacob Fox	Business Insurance	1			
14	Tianna Frank	Business Insurance	5			
15	Victor James	Business Insurance	0			
16	Mark Snow	Business Insurance	2			
17	Elizabeth Estes	Business Insurance	6			

EXERCISE 1-5
Apply Data Validation Criteria

An Excel worksheet is an ideal place to store the huge amount of data that businesses require today. If the data has typos and mistakes, the filters and reports will not function properly. To control the type of data entered into cells, apply **data validation** criteria. Data validation is the process of ensuring that data is correct based on specific criteria. In this exercise, you will apply data validation to require the amount for each advertising method to be $2,000 or less. You will then add a drop-down list from a range of cells to limit the data that can be entered into a column.

1. In your **Blues** file, click the **Advertising plan** sheet tab.

2. Select **B4:B14**. Choose **Data>Data Tools>Data Validation**.

3. In the **Data Validation** dialog box, click the **Allow** drop-down arrow. Choose **Decimal**.

4. From the **Data** drop-down list, choose **less than or equal to**. In the **Maximum** box, key: 2000.

5. **CHECK** Your dialog box should look like Figure 1.11. Click **OK**.

6. Click cell **B5**. Key: 3000. Press ENTER. An error alert appears.

7. Click **Retry**. Key: 2000. Press ENTER.

8. **CHECK** Your screen should look like Figure 1.12.

Continued on the next page.

You Should Know

Data validation is designed to prevent invalid data entries only when users key data directly into a cell. It does not prevent incorrect data from being copied or filled into a cell.

FIGURE 1.11 Data Validation dialog box

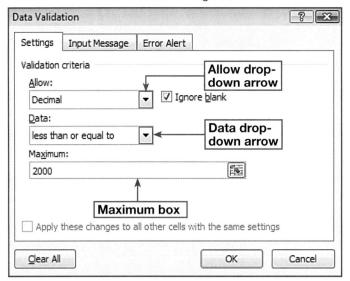

FIGURE 1.12 Valid data entered in cell B5

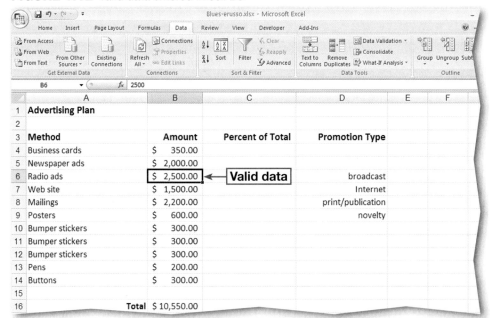

1 In your **Insurance** file, choose **Office>Save As**. Ask your teacher which location to choose in the **Save in** box.

2 Click **New Folder** 🗁. Key: Insurance. Press ENTER (see Figure 5.33).

3 Click the back arrow to get to the previous screen.

4 Click **Organize**. Click **Rename**.

5 Key: Insurance Sales. Press ENTER. If necessary, click **OK** in the warning box.

6 ⓘ**CHECK** Your dialog box should look like Figure 5.34.

7 Click **Open**. Click **Save**. Your **Insurance** file is now saved in the **Insurance Sales** folder.

➡ *Continue to the next exercise.*

Shortcuts

You can also rename a folder by right-clicking the folder and choosing **Rename**.

EXERCISE 5-16
Rename Folders

You can create and rename folders in the Save As dialog box. Make your folder names as descriptive as possible so you can locate, or find, your files quickly and easily.

FIGURE 5.33 Save As dialog box

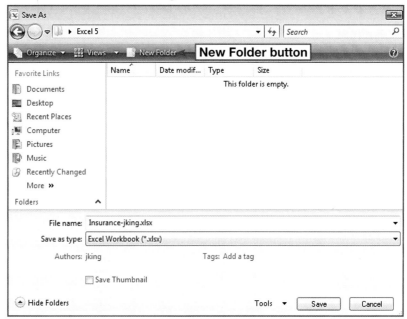

FIGURE 5.34 Insurance Sales folder in Save As dialog box

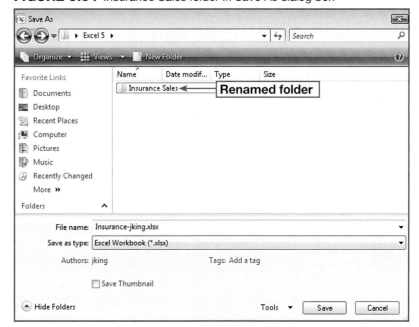

1 In your **Blues** file, in the **Merchandise** worksheet, scroll so that row 4 is the first visible row in the worksheet pane.

2 Notice the **Outline symbols** for the three outline levels (see Figure 1.9).

3 Click the **Outline symbol** 1 for level **1**. Only the Grand Total displays.

4 Click the **Outline symbol** 2 for level **2**. The subtotal for each concert date and the Grand Total display.

5 Click **Show Detail** to the left of row **24**.

6 **①CHECK** Your screen should look like Figure 1.10.

7 Click **Hide Detail** to the left of row **24**.

8 Click the **Outline symbol** 3 for level **3** to return to the original view.

9 Save your file.

➡ *Continue to the next exercise.*

Tech Tip

You can use two commands to show or hide details. Choose **Data>Outline> Ungroup** to remove the **Outline symbols**.

EXERCISE 1-4
Group and Outline Data

Grouping and outlining data allows you to show and hide details in a long list of data. When you create subtotals, grouping and outlining is turned on automatically.

FIGURE 1.9 Outline symbols

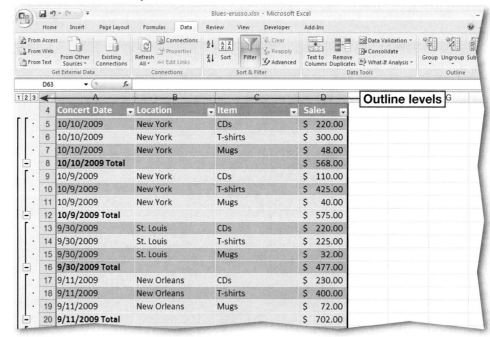

FIGURE 1.10 Detail shown for one concert

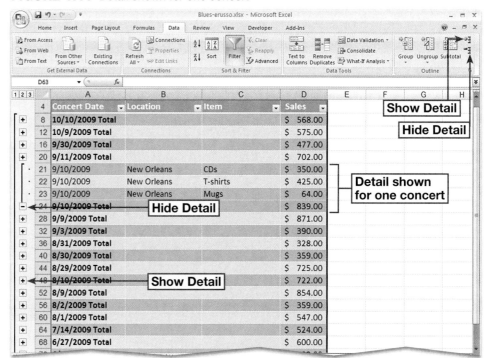

1. In your **Insurance** file, choose **Office>Save As**.

2. In the **Save as type** box, click the **drop-down arrow** (see Figure 5.35).

3. Choose **Formatted Text (Space delimited) (*.prn)**. Click **Save**.

4. A box opens explaining that only the active sheet will be saved. Click **OK**.

5. Another box opens explaining that some features will be lost in the new format. Click **Yes**.

6. (CHECK) Your screen should look like Figure 5.36. Save and close your file. Exit **Excel**.

You Should Know

Whenever you save a file in another file format, some of its formatting may not be supported and may be lost. Microsoft will let you know in a warning that some data and content may not open correctly if saved to a different format.

EXERCISE 5-17
Convert Files to Different Formats

You might need to save a workbook in a different format so it can be used by another application. For example, you can save a worksheet as formatted text so it is easier to work with in Microsoft Word.

FIGURE 5.35 Save as type

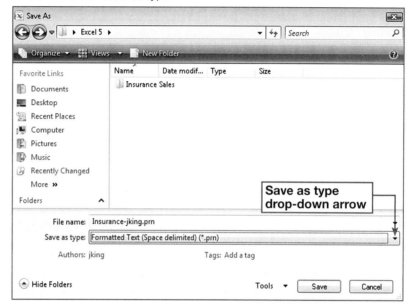

FIGURE 5.36 Workbook saved in .prn format

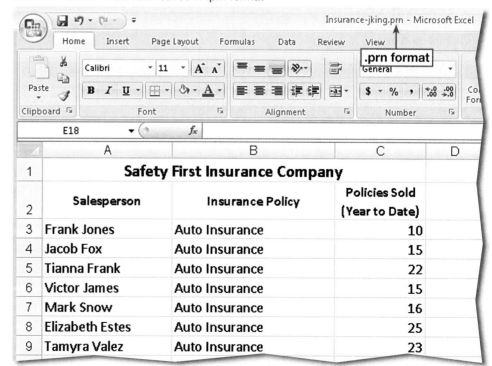

EXERCISE 1-3
Create Subtotals

1. In your **Blues** file, in the **Merchandise** worksheet, select **A4:D55**.

2. Choose **Data>Sort & Filter>Filter** .

3. Click the **Concert Date** drop-down arrow and deselect the **Select All** check box. Click the **August** check box. Click **OK**.

4. Click cell **C13**. Choose **Data>Outline>Subtotal** .

5. In the **Subtotal** dialog box, in the **At each change in** box, make sure that **Concert Date** is selected (see Figure 1.7).

6. In the **Use function** box, select **Average**. Click **OK**.

7. Click **Subtotal** . In the **Use function** box, select **Count**. Click **OK**.

8. Click **Subtotal** . In the **Use function** box, select **Sum**. Click **OK**.

9. Clear the **Filter** from the **Concert Date** column. With **A4:D52** selected, click **Subtotal** .

10. ⓘCHECK Your screen should look like Figure 1.8. Save your file.

Continue to the next exercise.

A **subtotal** is the total, or sum, of a group of items within a larger set of items. To create subtotals in a worksheet, make sure the list is sorted so that similar items are grouped together. Excel will then automatically create the subtotals for you. In this exercise, you will find the subtotal for the sales for each concert in the Blues file.

FIGURE 1.7 Subtotal dialog box

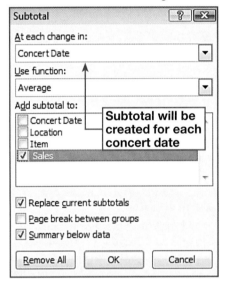

FIGURE 1.8 Subtotals added to list

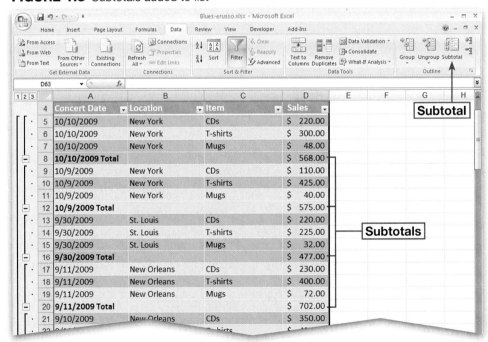

MATH MATTERS

Balance an Account

It is important to keep track of your financial accounts. Always know how much money goes into your account—and how much you spend! If you do not keep track, you may not have enough money in your account to pay for your transactions. You can use Excel to record your money flow, and to calculate how much money you have left in your account.

Using Excel Workbooks

Look at the Excel workbook below. It has columns for the date, check numbers, types of transaction, and amounts added or withdrawn from your account. To get the balance, use this calculation:

= <cell with the beginning balance> − <cell showing withdrawal or payment> + <cell showing deposits>

In the workbook below, you would click F3, and key: "=F2−E3+D3." Then, click on the little black square in the lower right corner of F3, and drag the box down along the F column to calculate the new balance.

Use Excel to balance your accounts.

SKILLBUILDER

1. **List** List some of the benefits of balancing an account in Excel. Include reasons for both personal and business use.

2. **Predict** What are some of the effects of not balancing an account? What might happen if records are not kept accurately? Give an example.

3. **Math** Imagine you have an account with $200. You wrote a check today for $25. Your credit card bill for $247.98 is due in two weeks. You will receive your paycheck for your part-time job ($150) in one week. When should you pay your bill? How much will you have left in your account after paying the bill?

EXERCISE 1-2
Use Advanced Filters

1. In your **Blues** file, in your **Merchandise** worksheet, select **A1:A3**. Choose **Home>Cells** and click the **Insert Cells** drop-down arrow. Select **Insert Sheet Rows**. Three rows are inserted above the list.

2. Select **A4:D4**. Click **Copy**. Click cell **A1**. Press [ENTER] to paste the column heads in row 1.

3. In cell **B2**, key: Cincinnati. In cell **C2**, key: CDs. Click any cell to deselect cell C2.

4. (i)**CHECK** Your screen should look like Figure 1.5.

5. Choose **Data>Sort & Filter>Advanced**.

6. In the dialog box, in the **Criteria range** box, key: A1:D2. Click **OK**.

7. (i)**CHECK** Your screen should look like Figure 1.6.

8. Click **Filter** twice to turn off the filter. Save your file.

→ *Continue to the next exercise.*

You Should Know

When you change criteria, the most recent criteria range will not be deleted. You can use the advanced filter more than once.

AutoFilter allows you to filter data based on simple, preset **criteria**, or conditions. When you use an **advanced filter**, however, you can specify more criteria, and only those items in a range of cells or table that meet the criteria will be displayed. The criteria range contains the conditions that the data must meet in order to be displayed. The range of cells contains the list of data items. There must be a blank row between the criteria range and the data range.

FIGURE 1.5 Criteria range above the list range

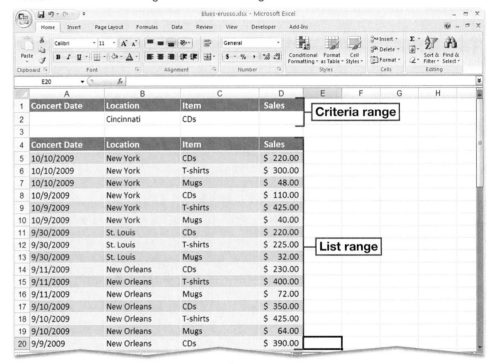

FIGURE 1.6 Filtered list

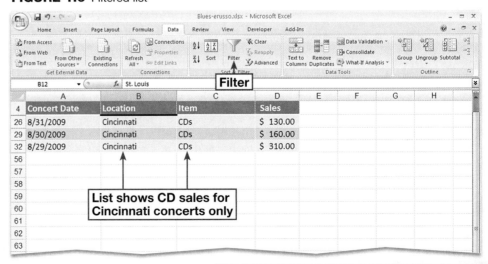

Vocabulary

Key Terms

footer

freeze

header

landscape

margin

page break

page orientation

portrait

print area

split

template

Academic Vocabulary

arrange

common

convert

locate

Review Vocabulary

Complete the following statements on a separate piece of paper. Choose from the Vocabulary list on the left to complete the statements.

1. Text that appears at the bottom of the printed page is the _____. (p. 126)

2. In _____ orientation, the printed worksheet is wider than it is tall. (p. 124)

3. One printed page ends and the next begins at a(n) _____. (p. 127)

4. When saving a file, you need to _____ the properly named file in the correct folder in order to find it again quickly. (p. 132)

5. You can use a(n) _____ as the basis for other workbooks. (p. 116)

Vocabulary Activity

6. Create a guessing game using five of the vocabulary words.
   A. Pick five vocabulary words, but do not reveal the terms you have chosen.
   B. With your teacher's permission, form groups of five students each.
   C. Each student will take a turn trying to help the other students guess a vocabulary word by drawing a picture on a sheet of paper. Each student will have one minute to draw. If a student guesses correctly, the student who drew the picture wins one point, and the student who guessed correctly draws the next picture.

Review Key Concepts

Answer the following questions on a separate piece of paper.

7. Excel's printing options allow you to _____. (p. 128)
   A. adjust margins   C. print specific parts of a page
   B. create headers and footers   D. all of the above

8. Which of the following allows you to view your worksheet as a Web page? (p. 122)
   A. Web Page Preview   C. Publish as a Web Page
   B. Save As   D. Print Preview

9. Which of these commands would you use to display two workbooks on your computer screen at once? (p. 121)
   A. Arrange All   C. Hide
   B. Freeze Panes   D. Split

10. Which group on the Home tab allows you to insert and delete a worksheet? (p. 118)
    A. Styles   C. Editing
    B. Cells   D. Format

EXERCISE 1-1 (Continued)
Create and Modify List Ranges

10. In the **Custom AutoFilter** dialog box, click the first drop-down arrow and select **is less than**. Click the second drop-down arrow and select **$425.00**. Select **And**.

11. Click the first drop-down arrow in the second row and select **is greater than** (see Figure 1.3). In the right box, key: 200. Click **OK**.

12. Click the **Location** filter icon. Select **Clear Filter From "Location"**.

13. Click the **Sales** filter icon. Select **Clear Filter From "Sales"**.

14. Click the **Sales** drop-down arrow. Select **Number Filters>Above Average**.

15. Click the **Sales** filter icon. Select **Clear Filter From "Sales"**.

16. With your table still selected, choose **Table Tools>Design>Tools> Convert to Range**. Click **Yes**.

17. **CHECK** Your screen should look like Figure 1.4. Save your file.

↪ *Continue to the next exercise.*

FIGURE 1.3 Custom AutoFilter dialog box

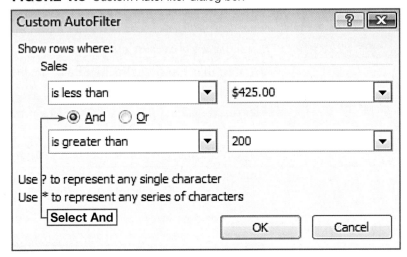

FIGURE 1.4 Table converted back to normal range of data

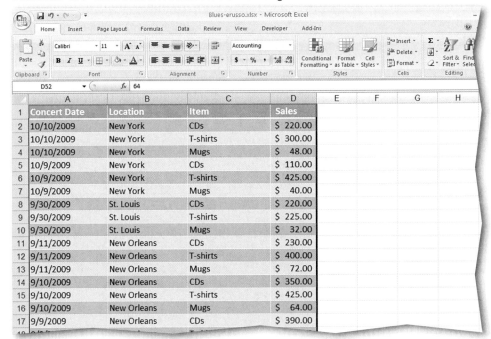

Tech Tip

After you create a table, the **Table Tools** contextual tab appears and the **Design** tab is displayed on the Ribbon. You can use the tools on the **Design** tab to customize or edit your table.

1. Publish a Web Page and Insert and Freeze a Worksheet

Data File

Follow the steps to complete the activity.

Step-By-Step

1. Open the data file **Costs .xlsx**. Save as: Costs-[your first initial and last name]1.

2. Choose **Office>Save As**. In the **Save as type** dialog box, select **Web Page** and then click **Publish** twice.

3. In the **Excel** version of the file, choose **Insert Worksheet**. Right-click the **Sheet1** tab and select **Move or Copy**.

4. In the **Before sheet** box, click **(2009)**. Click **OK**.

5. **iCHECK** Your screen should look like Figure 5.37.

6. Click the **2010** tab.

7. Click cell **E1**. Choose **View>Window>Freeze Panes** and select **Freeze Panes**. Scroll to the right side of the sheet.

8. **iCHECK** Your screen should look like Figure 5.38.

9. Choose **View>Window> Freeze Panes** and select **Unfreeze Panes**.

10. Save and close your file.

FIGURE 5.37 Inserted worksheet

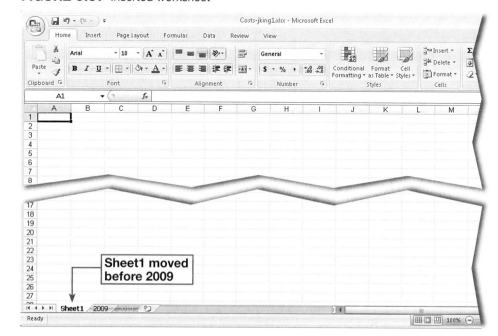

Sheet1 moved before 2009

FIGURE 5.38 Worksheet with frozen pane

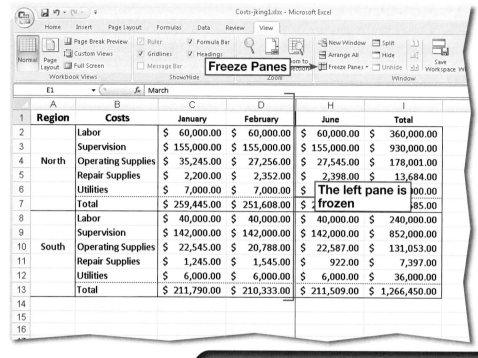

Freeze Panes

The left pane is frozen

EXERCISE 1-1
Create and Modify List Ranges

1. Choose **Start>Programs> Microsoft Office®> Microsoft Office Excel 2007**.

2. Open the data file **Blues.xlsx**. Save as: Blues-[your first initial and last name]. (For example, *Blues-erusso*.)

3. Select the **Merchandise Sales** tab. Click cell **B6**. Choose **Insert>Tables> Table**. In the **Create Table** dialog box, select cells **A1:D52**. Click **OK**.

4. **CHECK** Your screen should look like Figure 1.1.

5. Select cells **A1:D52**. Click the **Concert Date** drop-down arrow. Choose **Sort Newest to Oldest**.

6. Scroll to the top of your worksheet.

7. **CHECK** Your screen should look like Figure 1.2.

8. Click the **Location** drop-down arrow. Click the **Select All** check box. Click the **New York** check box. Click **OK**.

9. Click the **Sales** drop-down arrow. Choose **Number Filters>Custom Filter**.

Continued on the next page.

In Microsoft Excel 2007, you can use a table to manage and organize related data. You can select a range, or sequence, of cells that you want to make into a table. Since many tables have a huge amount of data in them, you can use the AutoFilter tool to find and work with a smaller amount, or **subset**, of data. In this exercise, you will create a table and use the AutoFilter to sort and filter information in the table. You will then **convert**, or change, the table back to a normal range of data.

FIGURE 1.1 Table created from range

FIGURE 1.2 List sorted by concert date

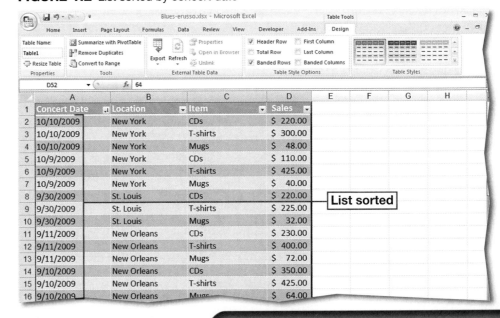

2. Change Page Orientation and Add a Header and Footer

Follow the steps to complete the activity. You must complete Practice It Activity 1 before doing this activity.

Step-By-Step

1 Open your **Costs-1** file. Save as: Costs-[your first initial and last name]2.

2 On the **Page Layout** tab, click the **Page Setup Dialog Box Launcher**. In the **Page Setup** dialog box, click the **Page** tab.

3 Under **Orientation**, click **Landscape**.

4 In the **Page Setup** dialog box, click the **Header/ Footer** tab.

5 In the **Header** drop-down list, choose **Page 1 of ?** (see Figure 5.39).

6 In the **Footer** drop-down list, choose **Costs-[your first initial and last name]2**.

7 Click **Print Preview**. If necessary, click **Zoom**.

8 **(i)CHECK** Your screen should look like Figure 5.40.

9 Click **Close Print Preview**. Save and close your file.

FIGURE 5.39 Page Setup dialog box

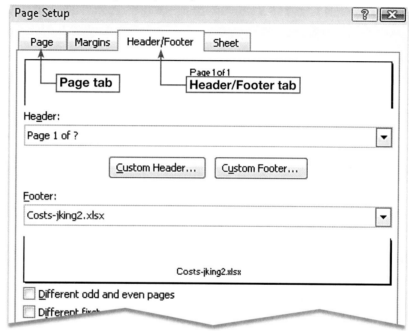

FIGURE 5.40 Header and footer

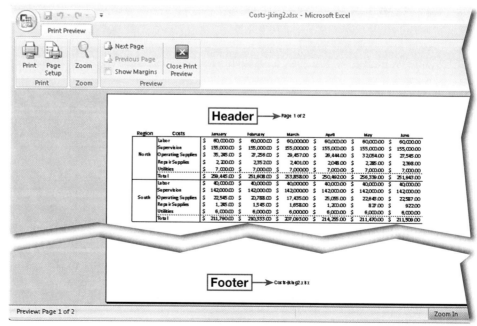

Before You Read

Prior Knowledge The more you know about a subject, or can put it in context, the more you understand. Look over the Key Concepts at the beginning of the lesson. Then, write down what you already know about each objective and what you want to find out by reading the lesson. As you read, find examples for both categories.

Read To Learn

- Use list ranges to manage and organize related data.
- Explore how Excel filters allow you to show or hide specific records.
- Consider how to group your data and create subtotals per group.
- Learn how to use data validation to control how the user keys in records to help prevent errors.

Main Idea

Excel has many advanced tools and features to improve the way you manage, access, and organize data.

Vocabulary

Key Terms

advanced filter   name
criteria   Name Manager
data validation   subset
duplicate value   subtotal
Evaluate Formula

Academic Vocabulary

These words appear in your reading and on your tests. Make sure you know their meanings.

convert
error
interpret
sum

Quick Write Activity

Describe On a separate sheet of paper, describe why Excel is an ideal place to store a huge amount of data. Create a list of the different types of information that a business may need to save.

Study Skills

Review Your Notes You can improve your recall at exam time if you look over your notes the same day you take them. Make sure they are clear and add any information that you forgot to add in class.

Academic Standards

Language Arts
    NCTE 5 Employ a wide range of strategies while writing to communicate effectively with different audiences.

Math
    NCTM (Number and Operations) Understand numbers, ways of representing numbers, relationships among numbers, and number systems.
    NCTM (Number and Operations) Understand meanings of operations and how they relate to one another.

3. Set Print Area and Print a Workbook

Step-By-Step

1. Open your **Costs-2** file. Save as: Costs-[your first initial and last name]3.

2. Click the **2009** tab. Select **A1:D13**.

3. On the **Page Layout** tab, choose **Page Setup>Print Area>Set Print Area**.

4. Click the **2010** tab. Select **A1:D13**.

5. Choose **Page Setup> Print Area>Set Print Area**.

6. Choose **Office>Print> Print Preview**. Click **Zoom**.

7. **CHECK** Your screen should look like Figure 5.41.

8. Click **Print**. In the **Print what** area, click **Entire Workbook**.

9. With your teacher's permission, click **Print** to print the workbook.

10. **CHECK** Your screen should look like Figure 5.42. Save and close your workbook.

Follow the steps to complete the activity. You must complete Practice It Activity 2 before doing this activity.

FIGURE 5.41 Print area in Print Preview

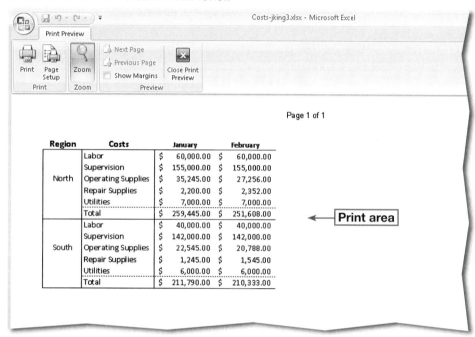

FIGURE 5.42 Print area selected

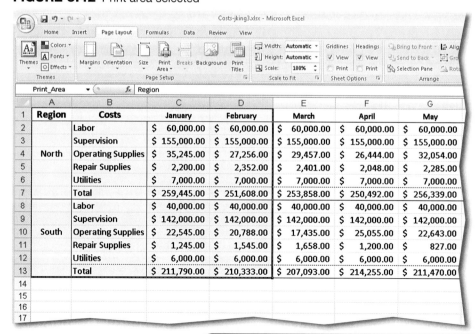

An Excel worksheet is laid out like a huge grid with 18,278 columns and 1,048,576 rows. This makes it an ideal place to store the huge amount of data that businesses require today. Knowing how to organize this data is just as important as gathering the information. In this lesson, you will learn how to use Excel's advanced tools and features to help manage data. You will also learn to group and outline data, name a cell range, and use a name in a formula.

Key Concepts

- Create and modify list ranges
- Create advanced filters
- Create subtotals and grand totals
- Group and outline data
- Apply data validation
- Circle invalid data
- Remove duplicate values
- Name a cell range

21st CENTURY SKILLS

Learn by Doing If you want to learn to dance, you can read or listen to instructions, but unless you try doing it yourself, you will never really know how. The same is true about learning Excel. Watching your teacher demonstrate new concepts or reading about them will give you a general idea of how to use Excel. However, the best way to understand the program thoroughly is to use the features to check your work. You may make mistakes, but with practice you can perfect your skills! *Name a skill that you recently learned well by practicing.*

Standards

The following standards are covered in this lesson. Refer to pages xix and 314 for a description of the standards listed here.

ISTE Standards Correlation

NETS•S

1c, 3d, 4a, 4c, 4d, 6a

Microsoft Certified Application Specialist

Excel

1.2, 2.3, 3.1, 3.3, 4.5, 4.6

4. Create an Expense Statement

You are going on a five-day business trip, and your employer has agreed to reimburse you for all of your expenses. You need to keep track of what you spend in order to get paid back, so you decide to use the Expense Statement template in Excel.

Step-By-Step

1 In **Excel**, open the **New Workbook** dialog box (see Figure 5.43). Click **Installed Templates**.

2 Choose **Expense Report**. Click **Create**. Save as: Expenses-[your first initial and last name]4.

3 On the **Expense Report**, after **Name**, key: your first and last name.

4 Scroll to the right. Under **Pay Period**, by **From**, key: 6/10/2009. By **To**, key: 6/14/2009.

5 Scroll to the left. In the first row under **Date**, key: 6/10/2009. Under **Hotel**, key: 75. Click **Scroll Right**.

6 Add four rows to the table. In those rows, fill in the hotel, transportation, fuel, meals, phone, and entertainment expenses as shown in Figure 5.44.

7 **CHECK** Your screen should look like Figure 5.44.

8 Save and close your file.

FIGURE 5.43 Templates dialog box

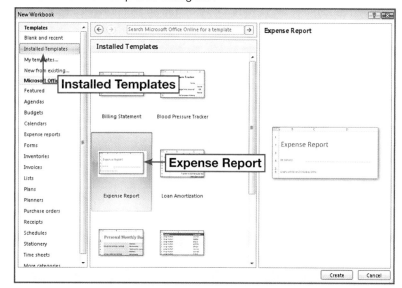

FIGURE 5.44 Expense statement

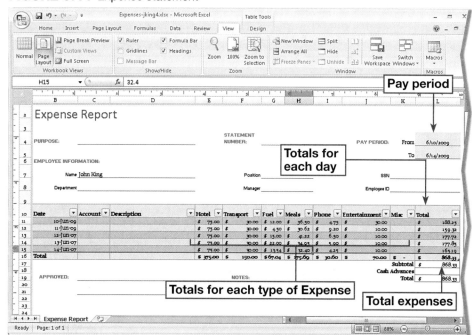

UNIT 2 Careers and Technology

Career ✓ Checklist

To use Excel as an effective decision-making tool in the workplace, remember to:

✓ Combine, interpret, and summarize data from more than one source.

✓ Use formatting options to highlight key information.

✓ Perform complicated calculations.

✓ Use math skills and tools to validate and correct data.

✓ Compare alternative data and evaluate alternatives.

✓ Use your interpersonal skills to explain your recommendations to others.

How Can You Use Excel to Make Decisions in the Workplace?

For many businesses, Excel is used to analyze and interpret data. Based on this analysis, important decisions can be made. For example, the banking industry requires employees at every level to analyze data and to make decisions accordingly. Employees may use Excel to decide whether to take on a new customer, accept a loan application, or invest in a particular stock.

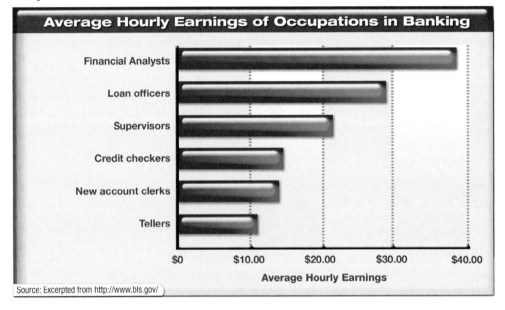

Average Hourly Earnings of Occupations in Banking

Source: Excerpted from http://www.bls.gov/

Using Excel At Work

Every bank employee will probably use Excel at some point in his or her career. A teller may use Excel to track customer transactions. Supervisors can use Excel to create internal budgets and to track payroll. Loan officers and financial analysts will use Excel's advanced tools to calculate loan rates and to evaluate potential financial investments. The more familiar an employee is with Excel's advanced data analysis tools, the more complicated his or her responsibilities and decisions are likely to be.

 READING CHECK

1 **Evaluate** Choose one of the banking careers in the chart above. List three ways that you think Excel skills might help you prepare for that occupation.

2 **Math** Calculate the annual full-time salary for a new account clerk. Assume that the pay is based on a 40-hour work week for 52 weeks per year.

3 **Explain** Why do you think a financial analyst makes more than a teller?

5. Create a Grades Log

You have already created a log of your grades for your business class. You decide to add a worksheet for your science class.

Step-By-Step

1. Open the data file **Subjects.xlsx**. Save as: Subjects-[your first initial and last name]5.

2. Insert one new worksheet. Rename the new worksheet **Science**.

3. Copy the column and row labels in the **Business** worksheet.

4. Click the **Science** tab. Paste the column and row labels into your **Science** worksheet (see Figure 5.45).

5. Fill in your science grades (see Figure 5.46).

6. Change the page orientation to **Landscape**.

7. ⓘ**CHECK** Your screen should look like Figure 5.46.

8. With your teacher's permission, print the entire workbook.

9. Save and close your file.

FIGURE 5.45 Science worksheet

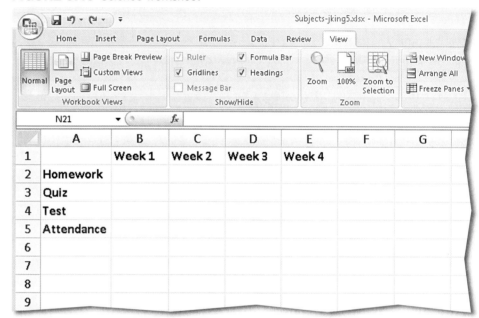

FIGURE 5.46 Science grades

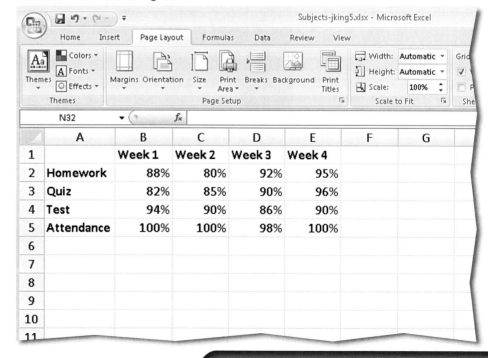

UNIT 2

Advanced Excel 2007: Business Finances

Unit Objectives:

After completing this Unit, you will understand:

LESSON 1
Advanced Data Organization

LESSON 2
Advanced Data Analysis

LESSON 3
Advanced Data Formatting

LESSON 4
Advanced Collaboration

LESSON 5
Advanced Data Management

Why It Matters

A business owner needs to record, summarize, and analyze financial data. Otherwise, he or she cannot know whether orders are being filled, inventory is being stocked, or profits are being made. A spreadsheet application like Excel will enable you to take control of business data. Knowing how to use Excel to control business data will help you get a job in business or start a business of your own. *What would you like to learn to do with Excel?*

 **Go Online**   **REAL WORLD CONNECTION**

glencoe.com

Go to the **Online Learning Center** and select your book. Click **Advanced Excel** to learn more about how different organizations use spreadsheet applications in the real world.

6. Beyond the Classroom Activity

 Math: Calculate Your Hours You just finished your first week at your summer job. Your boss asks you to hand in a time sheet. You decide to use an Excel template so that your total hours are calculated automatically.

Open the Excel **Time Card** template. Enter your first and last name. Key the first *full* week in July for the pay period. Open the data file **Hours.docx**. Enter the hours from the data file into the time card template. With your teacher's permission, print your worksheet.

Save as: e5rev-[your first initial and last name]6.

7. Standards at Work Activity

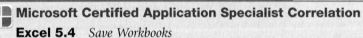
Microsoft Certified Application Specialist Correlation
Excel 5.4 *Save Workbooks*

Publish a Worksheet as a Web Page Your boss has asked you to put the company's sales figures on the company's Web site. You decide to preview the sales figures as a Web page beforehand to see if you need to make any changes to make the data more readable.

- Open the data file **Web.xlsx**.
- Publish the worksheet as a Web page.

With your teacher's permission, print the worksheet.

Save as: Web-[your first initial and last name]7.

8. 21st Century Skills Activity

Be Honest with Customers You work as a sales associate in a store that sells footwear for hiking and other outdoor activities. Create a workbook that includes everything your sales associates should tell customers before they make a purchase. List information about three of your products.

- Include a column for each product.
- Include a row for sizes available, cost, how long the product should last, recommended use, and the return policy.
- Change the page orientation to landscape.
- Change the top, bottom, left, and right margins to 1 inch.
- With your teacher's permission, print the worksheet.

Save your file as: e5rev-[your first initial and last name]8.

Go Online **e-REVIEW**
glencoe.com

Go to the **Online Learning Center** to complete the following review activities.

Online Self Check
To test your knowledge of the material, click **Unit 1> Lesson 5** and choose **Self Checks**.

Interactive Review
To review the main points of the lesson, click **Unit 1> Lesson 5** and choose **Interactive Review**.

Part 4: Create a Chart

Rubric
R

Goal You want to be able to see who your best customers are quickly. You decide to sort your worksheet and create a chart.

Create In the worksheet you created in **Portfolio Project 3**, select a cell in the **Customer Total** column.

- Sort the column in descending order so that your best customers are at the top of the worksheet.
- Select cells **A1** to **E11**. Create a column chart that shows how much each customer spent on each service. Include the title **Customer Totals** in the chart.
- Identify the highest amount spent and the lowest amount spent.
- Drag the column chart below your data and adjust the size so that it is readable.

Self Assess Use the Have You...? checklist to review your worksheet. Make sure your worksheet fulfills all the requirements listed in the previous section.

Carefully proofread your worksheet and make corrections. Pay special attention to the chart as you proofread. Follow your teacher's instructions for naming the file and saving it to your Portfolio Folder.

Have You...?

☑	Sorted the totals for each service
☑	Created a column chart that shows the totals for each service
☑	Added a title to the chart
☑	Added vertical and horizontal axis labels
☑	Positioned the chart below the data
☑	Adjusted the chart's size so that it is readable

 **Go Online**

BEYOND THE BOOK

glencoe.com

Go to the Online Learning Center to learn additional skills and review what you have already learned.

Microsoft Excel
Extend your knowledge of Excel by visiting the Online Learning Center for more MCAS-based exercises. Select **Advanced Excel>Lessons**.

Windows Vista
Select **Windows Vista>Lessons** to explore Microsoft's operating system fully.

Microsoft Outlook
Want to learn all about Outlook and how to e-mail communication and scheduling? Select **Microsoft Outlook>Lessons** for all you need to know.

Additional Projects
Complete additional projects in the following areas:

- **Real-World Business Projects** reinforce Microsoft Office by focusing on real-world business applications.
- **Presentation and Publishing Projects** Use your Office skills to create exciting PowerPoint presentations and desktop publishing activities.
- **Academic Projects** Integrate academic skills while enriching your understanding of Microsoft Office.

More Online Resources
Access additional Web sites and online information relating to key topics covered in Glencoe's *iCheck Series*. Select **Resources Links**.

Before You Begin

Taking Inventory Everyone needs to organize and analyze data to decide how to spend time and money effectively. Whether you are analyzing how you spend your time, or cataloging your CD collection, you need to make sure you use your resources properly.

Reflect Once you complete the projects, open a Word document and answer the following:

1. How can Excel help you manage time effectively?

2. How can Excel help you budget effectively?

9. Keep Track of Your Time

 Math: Calculate Your Weekly Activities A balance of activities and a mix of work and play are important. Create a worksheet that shows how you spent your time last month. Make a column for each week. Insert the following rows:

- Hours at school
- Hours at extracurricular activities
- Hours with family/friends
- Hours at work

Fill in the hours for each week. Add up the hours for each row. Create a pie chart based on your totals showing the percentages of how much time you spend each week completing the tasks in the bulleted list. Save your file as: e5rev-[your first initial and last name]9.

10. Organize Your Music Collection

 Math: Run a MIN and MAX Formula Create a worksheet to keep track of your music collection. Include a column for each of your five favorite artists. Label the following rows:

- Type of music
- CDs I own
- Favorite song

Fill in the spreadsheet. Highlight the column of the artist that has the highest number of CDs in your collection. Create a MIN and MAX formula to see the minimum and maximum numbers of the types of CDs you own. Select the highlighted column. Set this column as the print area. With your teacher's permission, print this column. Save your file as: e5rev-[your first initial and last name]10.

11. Keep Track of Travel Expenses

Math: Calculate Expenses You won a plane ticket to anywhere in the United States plus $500 spending money. Use the **Expense Report** template to calculate your budget for each day. Include expenses for the following:

- Lodging
- Meals
- Transportation
- Entertainment

Your trip can last from five to seven days, depending on how you budget your money. Make sure your total expenses do not go over $500. When finished, look over your report. How did you have to divide your money to stay within your budget? Which expenses cost the most? Which cost the least? How did you decide to estimate your costs? Save your file as: e5rev-[your first initial and last name]11.

UNIT 1 Portfolio Project

Goal You and your business partners want to keep track of the types of work that you do so that you can see how much money each type of work is bringing in. You decide to use Excel to create a worksheet.

Create In a new worksheet, create a column for each of the following data:

- Customer Name
- Lawn Maintenance
- Leaf Raking
- Planting
- Fertilizing
- Customer Total

Use the data in the **Lawns.docx** data file to fill in your worksheet. Apply **Currency** style to the numbers you enter. In the **Customer Total** column, calculate the total for each customer.

- At the bottom of your worksheet, add a row labeled **Total per Service**. Adjust column width as necessary. Find the sum of the column for lawn maintenance, leaf raking, planting, and fertilizing.
- Use borders, shading, and bolding to make your worksheet clear and readable.

Self Assess Use the Have You...? checklist to review your customer worksheet. Make sure your worksheet follows all of the guidelines set out in the previous section.

Carefully proofread your worksheet and make any necessary corrections. Pay special attention to the formulas as you proofread. Follow your teacher's instructions for naming the file and saving it to your Portfolio Folder.

When finished, proceed to Part 4.

Have You...?

- ☑ Labeled each column and row correctly
- ☑ Entered the data from the **Lawns.docx** data file
- ☑ Adjusted column width as necessary
- ☑ Calculated the total per service and the total overall revenue
- ☑ Used borders, shading, and bolding to make your worksheet more readable

In this activity, you will use your math skills to create formulas.

Rubric

Calculate Percentages

The used car lot that you work for is developing a bonus plan for its sales team. Your boss has given you each employee's total sales for last month. He wants you to calculate how much a 5%, 10%, and 15% bonus will be for each employee. Then he will decide what percent to give each salesperson. You decide to create a workbook that calculates the percentages for you.

1. Create a new Excel workbook. (p. 8)

2. In cell **A1**, key: Employee Names. Key 10 names (last name, first initial) in cells **A2** through **A11**.

3. In cells **B1** through **E1**, key the following column labels: **Total Sales, 5% Sales Bonus, 10% Sales Bonus, 15% Sales Bonus**. Adjust the width of each column so that cell contents fit. (p. 62)

4. In cells **B2** through **B11**, key each employee's total sales. Use numbers between 15,000 and 30,000. Apply the **Currency** style to the numbers in column B. (p. 61)

5. Click cell **C2**. Key a formula that calculates 5% of the first employee's total sales. (p. 87)

6. Copy that formula to cells **C3** to **C11**.

7. Click cell **D2**. Key a formula that calculates 10% of the first employee's total sales. (p. 87)

8. Copy that formula to cells **D3** to **D11**.

9. Click cell **E2**. Key a formula that calculates 15% of the first employee's total sales. (p. 87)

10. Copy that formula to cells **E3** to **E11**.

You can use Excel to calculate how much money you may make on a sale or how much money it will cost to buy a new car.

UNIT 1 — Portfolio Project

Rubric R

Goal At the end of the first week, your new business is doing well. Now you need to figure out how many total hours you, Taylor, Sharon, and Mark worked and how much each of you earned for the week.

Create Follow the steps below to make the calculations:

- Open the worksheet that you created in **Portfolio Project 1**.
- In this worksheet, calculate the total number of hours that each person worked.
- Place this figure in the **Total Hours** column. Then write a formula to find how much each person made your first week. The hourly rate is $8.50.
- Finally, calculate the total payroll for that week by adding the **Paycheck** column. Apply the **Currency** style to the **Paycheck** column.

Self Assess Use the Have You...? checklist to review your worksheet. Make sure your worksheet reflects all of the items noted in the checklist.

Carefully proofread your worksheet and make the necessary corrections. Follow your teacher's instructions for naming the file and saving it to your Portfolio Folder.

When finished, proceed to Part 3.

Have You...?

- ☑ Calculated the total hours each person worked
- ☑ Created a formula to find how much each person earned
- ☑ Calculated the total payroll for the week
- ☑ Placed the formulas in the correct cells
- ☑ Applied Currency style to the Paycheck column

Using Online Resources Responsibly

The Internet provides an enormous amount of free information. You can use the Internet to do research, stay informed about world events, or check the weather. Ethical Internet use involves using the information you obtain responsibly, honestly, and in a way that is not harmful to others.

Avoiding Plagiarism

Sometimes it is tempting to present information that you find on the Internet as your own. Plagiarism is using another person's ideas as your own, and is unethical and dishonest. Always cite, or state, the source of your information. When you use information from the Internet, include the Web address to show where you found it. This also helps the reader evaluate the validity of your sources.

Evaluating Internet Sources

How trustworthy is information on the Internet? Facts presented in reference books and textbooks are checked and double-checked for accuracy. But facts on the Internet may not have been checked. Some information on the Internet may even be intentionally misleading. Here are some things you can do to make sure that you are using reliable information:

1. Use reputable and well-known sources. Government sites and many university sites are reliable sources of information.

2. Make sure that the source you are using has cited other sources. Do the other sources appear trustworthy?

3. Back up the research that you do on the Internet with more than one source—online or print.

CASE STUDY

Samantha and Jay are researching a group project about public transportation. Samantha finds information on the Internet that supports the main idea of the project. The information comes from a source unfamiliar to most people. Because few people are aware of their source, Jay proposes that they use the information without citing the source. Samantha is not sure whether this is a good idea.

YOU DECIDE

1. **State** Name one thing that Jay and Samantha could do to make sure the information that they found on the Internet is reliable.

2. **Justify** Write a short paragraph that describes what you think Samantha should do.

APPLICATION ACTIVITY

3. **Create Guidelines** Create an Excel worksheet that lists ethical guidelines for using books, periodicals, and online resources. Ask permission to post the list in your classroom, the computer lab, or library.

Organize Your Landscape Business

You and three friends have decided to start a landscaping business. You want to use Excel to create all of your business records.

Part 1: Create a Payroll Record

Goal Your first task is to create a worksheet to track how many hours you work.

Create Create a worksheet.

- In cells **A2** through **A5**, list your name along with the names **Taylor**, **Sharon**, and **Mark** (your business partners).

- Start in cell **B1** and use seven columns to list the days of the week. Label the column to the right of the weekday columns **Total Hours**.

- Label the column next to the **Total Hours** column **Paycheck**.

- Adjust the column width as necessary. Bold the heads of the columns. Place a border on the right edge of cells **A2** through **A5** and a bottom border on cells **B1** through **J1**.

- Use the information from the data file **Hours.docx** to fill in the payroll record.

Self Assess Use the Have You...? checklist to review your worksheet. With your teacher's permission, print your worksheet and proofread it carefully. Make any necessary corrections. Follow your teacher's instructions for naming the file and saving it to your Portfolio Folder.

When finished, proceed to Part 2.

Have You...?

- ☑ Correctly labeled the rows
- ☑ Correctly labeled the columns
- ☑ Bolded the column heads
- ☑ Added borders to the row and column heads
- ☑ Entered the data correctly